Established in 1603, the army was initially composed almost entirely of English officers and soldiers for the first 30 years of its existence. The army's strength waxed and waned in accordance with the English government's assessment of the security situation in Ireland. However, during the governorship of Thomas Wentworth, it was seen as a possible instrument for enforcing royal rule in all three of the Stuart kingdoms.

By 1640, the army was approximately 8,000 strong and was geared up for a campaign against Charles I's rebellious Scottish subjects. However, it never left Ireland as the Scots had defeated the king by the time the army was ready to leave. It was then reduced to a third of its previous strength and went on to lose almost a quarter of its infantry in surprise attacks during the first few hours of the Catholic uprising in late October 1641. Nevertheless, the remainder were able to hold onto the principal ports until reinforcements arrived from England and Scotland in the following spring.

During the first three decades of the army and the 18 months prior to the uprising, the standing army was under-resourced. A struggle existed between the English government and the government in Dublin as to who should be responsible for maintaining the military. As a result, officers and soldiers received very little pay and the defences of even the most important garrisons fell into disrepair. Another consequence was the supply of recruits from England via impressment ended in 1625 and it is scarcely surprising that Irish soldiers (many of whom were Catholics) were used by commanders to fill up the ranks in their units.

These factors contributed to explaining the disasters that occurred on the night of 23 October 1641. So also did the deployment of troops and companies in scant numbers to all parts of Ireland; a sensible deployment for an occupying army to settle minor unrest during peacetime, but disastrous when faced with a major rebellion that came out of the blue.

Finally, it is possible that English Protestant soldiers stationed for years in the same place fostered closer links with the Catholic population through marriage or economic necessity, as they had recourse to their civilian skills as labourers and craftsmen in order to make ends meet, and this created divided loyalties in 1641.

Living cheek-by-jowl may also help explain a surprising lack of tales of gratuitous acts of violence by army personnel against civilians. Absence of evidence is not, of course, evidence of absence, but criticism of this kind of behaviour does not appear in the lists of grievances sent by the leaders of the Catholic Irish to Kings James and Charles. Instead, they largely focused on the behaviour of an army of occupation under control. Grievances included those such as collecting fines levied by the law courts and unpaid taxes along with requisitioning food while marching from one garrison to another and then failing to initiate the process to pay farmers or shopkeepers.

Professor Wanklyn studied the English Civil War at the University of Manchester. He then joined the staff of what later became the University of Wolverhampton where he completed his doctorate on allegiance in Cheshire and Shropshire in 1642 and taught courses on Early Modern England and Regional History. He also served for ten years as head of History, laid the foundations for the flourishing War Studies department, and supervised the widely used Port Book database of trade on the River Severn 1576-1765. On retiring in 2002 he returned to his first love, and since then has written six books on the British Wars, most notably *Decisive Battles of English Civil War* (2006), *Reconstructing the New Model Army* (2015, 2016) and *Parliament's Generals* (2019), and several articles in leading historical journals.

The Army of Occupation in Ireland 1603-42

Defending the Protestant Hegemony

Malcolm Wanklyn

'This is the Century of the Soldier', Fulvio Testi, Poet, 1641

Helion & Company Limited

Helion & Company Limited
Unit 8 Amherst Business Centre
Budbrooke Road
Warwick
CV34 5WE
England
Tel. 01926 499 619
Email: info@helion.co.uk
Website: www.helion.co.uk
Twitter: @helionbooks
Visit our blog at blog.helion.co.uk

Published by Helion & Company 2022
Designed and typeset by Mary Woolley (www.battlefield-design.co.uk)
Cover designed by Paul Hewitt, Battlefield Design (www.battlefield-design.co.uk)

Text © Malcolm Wanklyn 2022
Front cover artwork by Seán Ó Brógáin © Helion & Company 2022
Maps by George Anderson © Helion & Company 2022

Every reasonable effort has been made to trace copyright holders and to obtain their permission for the use of copyright material. The author and publisher apologise for any errors or omissions in this work and would be grateful if notified of any corrections that should be incorporated in future reprints or editions of this book.

ISBN 978-1-915070-36-4

British Library Cataloguing-in-Publication Data.
A catalogue record for this book is available from the British Library.

All rights reserved. No part of this publication may be reproduced, stored in a retrieval system, or transmitted, in any form, or by any means, electronic, mechanical, photocopying, recording or otherwise, without the express written consent of Helion & Company Limited.

For details of other military history titles published by Helion & Company Limited contact the above address, or visit our website: http://www.helion.co.uk.

We always welcome receiving book proposals from prospective authors.

Contents

Dedication	v
Preface	vi
Acknowledgements	viii
Abbreviations	ix

Part I: The First Thirty Years — 12
1. The End of the Nine Years' War — 13
2. Slimming Down — 22
3. The Perils of Peace 1609–1615 — 30
4. The Perils of Peace 1616–1623 — 40
5. European Entanglements — 54
6. The Duke of Buckingham's Wars 1625–1628 — 65
7. Lord Wilmot as Army Commander 1629–1632 — 79

Part II: The New Commander-in-Chief — 90
8. Army Reform under Lord Wentworth: Preparing the Way — 91
9. Army Reform under Lord Wentworth: Implementation — 103
10. The Coming of War — 119
11. Planning a New War — 133
12. The New Army and the Old Army — 145

Part III: Passing into Oblivion
13. The Demise of the New Army — 159
14. Disbandment and its Consequences — 170
15. The Patriotic Uprising — 181
16. The Dismemberment of the Standing Army — 194
17. Death and Rebirth — 206

Appendices:
I	The Strength of the Standing Army 1601–1641	209
II	Standing Army Units 1606 to 1608	211
III	Standing Army Units 1608 to 1623	215
IV	Standing Army Units 1624–1641	221
V	Regiments in the New Army	234
VI	The Fate of Old Army Units Post October 1641	240

Bibliography 247
Index 251

Dedication

To my wife, who is Irish by descent, and to the many Irish people I have been honoured to know as friends and acquaintances during my long life in particular Fr. Tom Rock R.I.P.

Preface

The purpose of this book is to fill a gap in the military history of the British Isles, but one that is scarcely surprising. A monograph focusing exclusively on the army the English government stationed in Ireland between the end of the Nine Years' War in 1603 and the start of the Catholic insurgency in 1641 is a topic of minimal interest to *aficionados* of military history. It fought no battles, undertook no lengthy sieges, and never came together as a body to campaign against either an internal or an external enemy. To make matters worse it had nothing to make it attractive to researchers. The surviving documentation at the level of the troop or the company is sparse and frequently no more than anecdotal. Moreover, the army's reputation was in tatters when it passed from the scene. To contemporary writers it was an object of scorn and suspicion in various degrees of intensity. To the Dublin government dominated by English newcomers it was expensive but untrustworthy and potentially mutinous in time of crisis; to Protestant settlers a broken reed; and to the Catholic insurgents little more than a joke. Later writers whatever their ethnic or confessional background took them at their word with only Thomas Carte making the occasional favourable comment in his biography of James Butler, First Duke of Ormond, but only when it served to enhance the reputation of the army's last commander-in-chief. It is not therefore surprising that a book, which in other respects is a comprehensive study of the military history of Ireland from the earliest times until almost the present day, passed it by with scarcely a glance.[1]

The standing army does, however, deserve an appraisal which is more even-handed and less narrowly focused than that provided by contemporary and near-contemporary writers. First, it was the first attempt by the rulers of the British Isles to establish and resource an army in time of peace capable of serving as a deterrent and, if that failed, as the first line of defence against invasion and serious internal unrest. To contemporaries it clearly failed, but none took on board the English government's low-level expectations of what a standing army would be capable of achieving in an emergency given the limited amount of cash first it and then the Irish government could spare to resource it.

---

1   T. Bartlett and K. Jeffrey, *A Military History of Ireland* (Cambridge: University Press, 1997).

Second, the standing army was being taken increasingly seriously by movers and shakers in all three countries ruled by the Stuarts kings as the century progressed. For some it was seen as a major threat to the liberty of the subject and not just in Ireland; for others it was a fire brigade which could be called in to maintain order anywhere in the British Isles where it was under threat. Such sentiments came to the surface for the first time in the 1630s, but it is worth mentioning that on 10 separate occasions between 1615 and 1688 there were plans for troops from the army to land in England and/or Scotland, and that on six of those occasions that is just what they did.

Finally, the standing army is unique amongst the instruments of coercion available to the governments of early modern Britain because of the metamorphosis it underwent during its short life. At the start its soldiers were intended to be exclusively English as befitted an army of occupation in a hostile land, but although lip-service continued to be paid to this for the next 40 years, the reality was different. In the crisis of 1641 twenty percent of the horse and foot were Irish, and this goes some way towards explaining how it performed.

It has been exhilarating to work on a topic in early modern history through which there is not already a very well-trodden path, but this incursion into largely unknown territory falls some way short of what I had in mind at the start. Luckily the coronavirus epidemic and the restrictions on travel which followed came nearly at the end of my research programme in England, but it has forced me to be more reliant on calendars than had been my intention. I also had to abandon any hope of working on archives in Ireland, though the only document I regret not having seen was Sir Francis Willoughby's doubtless self-serving account of how he personally saved Dublin from capture on the first day of the 1641 uprising.

I would therefore advise the reader to see this book as something more than a pioneering study but by no means the last word. My hope is that those who read it will be interested, provoked or even enraged into undertaking further research in two areas that circumstances have made it impossible for me to investigate in depth: the repressive regime's use of the army to consolidate and enforce its rule, and the extent to which this ability was undermined by the assimilation of its ordinary soldiers and the non-commissioned officers into the communities in which they lived and often worked but were also required to police.

Acknowledgements

My thanks go to the University of Wolverhampton for help in meeting the costs of archival research, and to Charles Singleton for his support at all times. I would also like to express my gratitude to colleagues who have kept in touch with me in my declining years, most particularly Professors Richard Cust, Peter Gaunt, Ronald Hutton, and John Morrill. A kind word often goes a long way.

Abbreviations

APC Acts of the Privy Council
CSPD Calendar of State Papers Domestic
CSPI Calendar of State Papers Ireland
C. Carew Mss Calendar of the Carew Manuscripts
HMC Historical Manuscripts Commission
JHC Journal of the House of Commons
JHL Journal of the House of Lords
ODNB Oxford Dictionary of National Biography

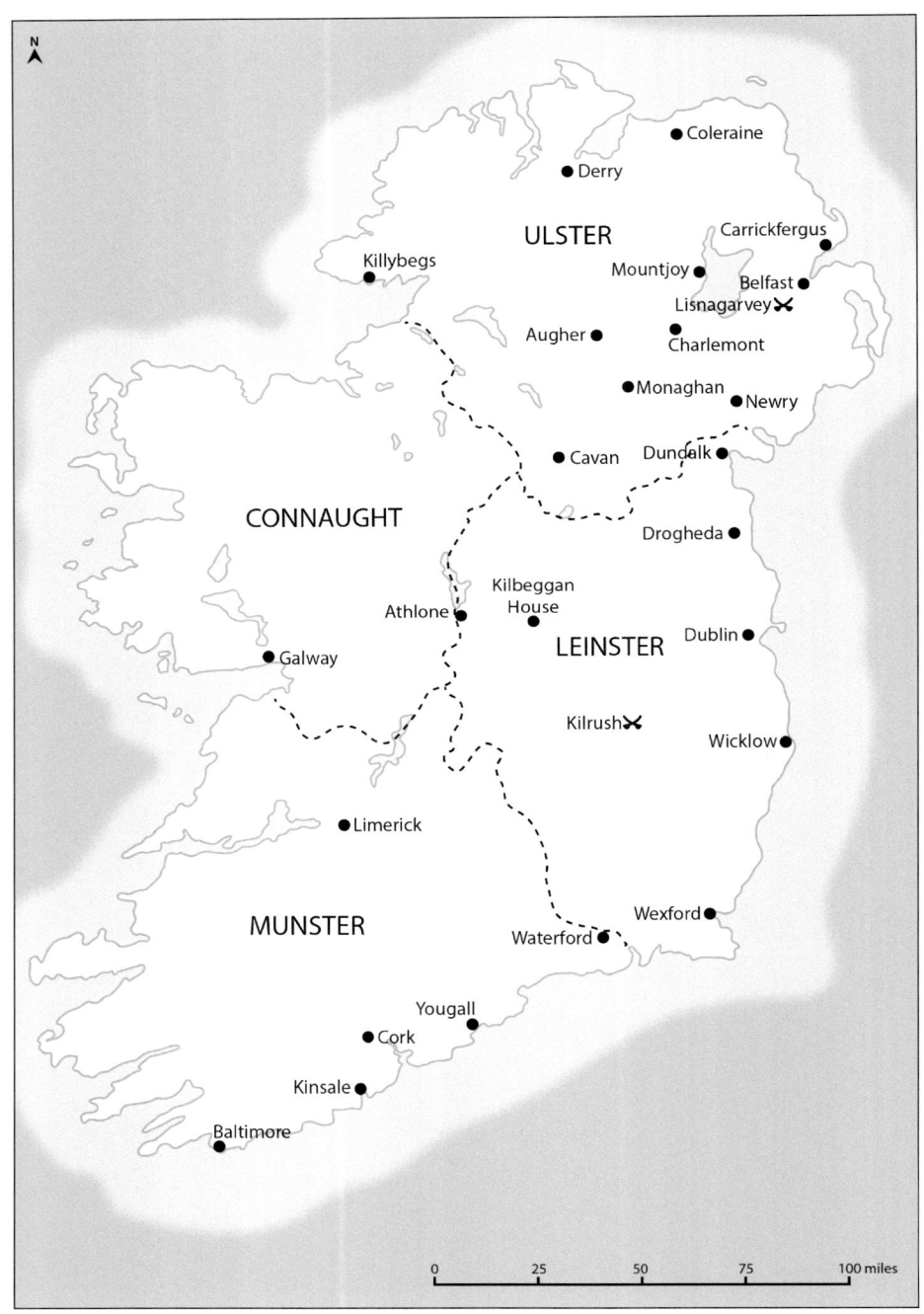

Ireland in the Early Seventeenth Century

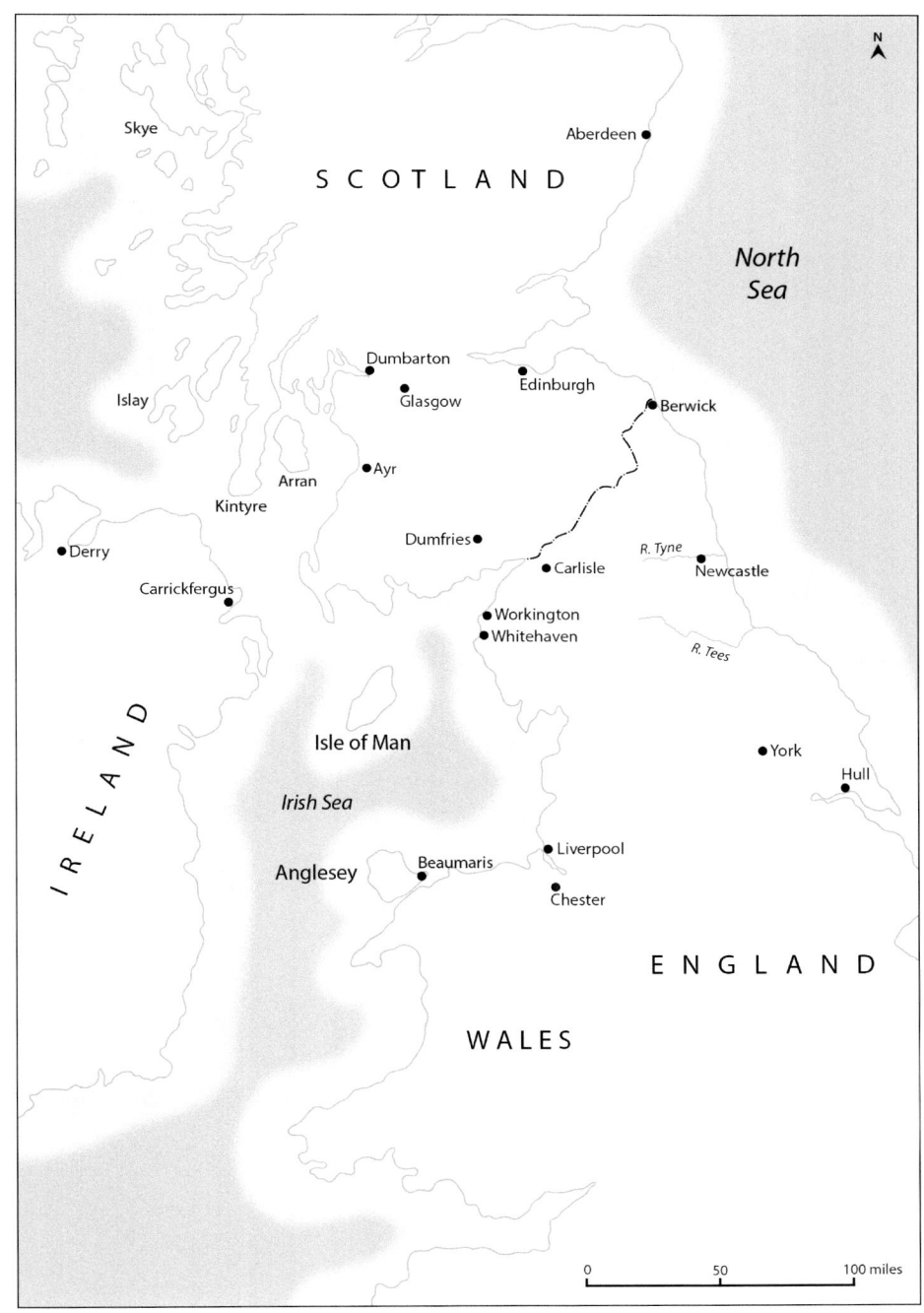

Ireland in the Bishops' Wars

Part I

The First Thirty Years

1

The End of the Nine Years' War

The last uprising of Elizabeth's reign, now commonly described as the Nine Years' War, represented by far the most dangerous and prolonged threat to English rule over Ireland since the campaigns of Edward Bruce in the early fourteenth century. Two leaders of the native Irish nobility, Hugh O'Neill Earl of Tyrone and Hugh Roe, chieftain of the O'Donnells and 'king' of Tyrconnell, the principal landowners in west and central Ulster, had humiliated the English in battle at the Yellow Ford in 1598, and then in the following year run rings around the largest force the Queen had sent across the Irish Sea, thus ruining the military reputation and the political clout of its commander, Robert Devereux, 2nd Earl of Essex. This success persuaded Philip III, the young King of Spain, whose country had been at war with the English since 1585, to support the insurgents by sending a small expeditionary force to the far southwest of Ireland.[1]

On 22 September 1601 infantry and cavalry several thousand strong under the command of Don Juan del Aguila disembarked at Kinsale and Baltimore. The English and Irish governments knew that an expedition was being prepared fully two months earlier, though initially it was thought that King Philip's intention was to reinforce his army fighting the Dutch. By the end of August intelligence indicated that Ireland was a more likely destination, but nothing was certain, and it was not until the day after the Spanish troops landed that the English fleet commanded by Sir Richard Leveson received orders to intercept the enemy. It took another three weeks for the ships to be ready to leave Plymouth, and Leveson's only achievement prior to the decisive encounter on land between Lord Mountjoy, Essex's successor, and the Irish insurgents on 24 December was to destroy six ships which had made landfall at Castle Haven to the west of Kinsale, but only after the troops they were carrying were safely ashore.

---

1   R.B. Wernham, *The Return of the Armadas 1595–1603* (Oxford: University Press, 1994), pp.377–88; P. Lenihan, *Consolidating Conquest: Ireland 1603–1727* (London: Pearson Longmans, 2008), p.15; S. Doran, *Elizabeth I and Her Circle* (Oxford: University Press, 2015), p.183.

The English admiral, did, however, institute a blockade of the havens under Spanish control, and this helped to bring a speedy end to Aguila's stay in Ireland.[2]

The fact that Mountjoy was able to turn the tables on the Queen's enemies owed as much to their mistakes as to his military and diplomatic skills. However, he was quick off the mark. As soon as he heard of Spain's naval preparations, he set about assembling an army in the Dublin area which by the early autumn may have been 8,000 strong, but he did not know where the enemy would land. Ulster seemed Aguila's most likely destination as that was where Tyrone and his principal supporters' estates were situated. He had therefore stationed a sizeable force at Loch Foyle under Sir Henry Docwra's command, though Mountjoy withdrew some of it when he learned that the Spaniards had landed elsewhere. He also demanded very substantial reinforcements from England.[3]

The army composed of English and Irish loyalist troops marching from Dublin via Kilkenny and Clonmel arrived at Cork on 27 September where they were joined by contingents from Ulster, Leinster and Connaught. Then, having, ordered heavy artillery and munitions to be shipped there, Mountjoy prepared to lay siege to Kinsale (which Aguila had chosen as his base). Although it would be impossible to seal the town off completely, Mountjoy's superiority in cavalry meant that the Spaniards would find it impossible to secure food and fodder locally, whilst their being supplied by sea would come to an end once the English navy arrived on the scene. He also set about constructing parallel trenches inching ever closer to the enemy the object being to establish gun platforms close enough to create breaches in the defences. At that point an experienced commanders like Aguila would surely suggest bringing the siege to an end by negotiation thus preventing the slaughter of soldiers and civilians that usually followed a town being captured by storm.[4]

Aguila's only hope of saving his reputation and possibly destroying the enemy army was for the Ulster lords to march south as quickly as possible with as many troops as they could muster. By late November O'Donnell and his troops were within striking distance of Kinsale, having evaded the forces Mountjoy had sent to intercept them, but it was almost a month before he and Tyrone met, the latter having made a more leisurely march towards Kinsale probably in the hope of attracting support on the way. They duly set up camp three miles to the west of the town where they were joined by

---

2 Calendar of State Papers Ireland (CSPI) 1601–03, pp.1–37 *passim*, 49, 81, 83; Calendar of State Papers Domestic (CSPD) 1601–03, pp.46, 53, 72, 78–79, 80, 86; Historical Manuscript Commission (HMC), Marquis of Salisbury Mss, 11, pp.489, 526. The figure of 4,000 foot was given by a Spanish captive in January 1602: *Calendar of the Carew Manuscripts* (C. Carew Mss), J.S. Brewer and W. Bullen (eds), 6 vols (London: Longmans, 1867–73) iv, pp.122, 126, 129, 139–40.
3 CSPD 1601–03, pp.78–80, 86, 100, 102, 104–05; CSPI 1601–03, pp.49, 71, 138; 179–80; C. Carew Mss, iv, pp.140, 142, 145. Mountjoy had 8,000 men under his command at Cork in early October: CSPD 1601–03, p.105.
4 CSPD 1601–03, pp.104–05, 114, 153–56, 209–11.

several companies of Spanish troops from Castle Haven. As Mountjoy showed no signs of abandoning the siege despite the wintry conditions and the growing strength of his adversaries, Aguila put pressure on Tyrone to agree to a combined attack on the siegeworks.[5]

For the night of 23/24 December following instructions from the Spanish commander Tyrone ordered a night march to a position on elevated ground to the north of Kinsale which would best allow for a co-ordinated attack on the enemy. Mountjoy, however, had been warned in advance by an informer, and during the night he moved three regiments of foot and a large force of cavalry commanded by Sir Henry Power into a position at right angles to Tyrone's line of march, whilst he and the rest of the army remained in reserve closer to the siegeworks to deter Aguila from making a sortie in support of the Irish. However, what really upset the applecart for Tyrone and the Spaniards was that co-ordinated attacks were notoriously difficult to carry out successfully even in daylight if the forces involved were not in constant visual contact with one another.

On Aguila's advice Tyrone drew up his infantry in three brigades for the route march – the vanguard comprising O'Donnell's men and the Spanish companies from Castle Haven; the centre or battle consisting of his own Ulstermen; and a rearguard made up of contingents from the other provinces. Of these the largest was the battle which the Earl commanded in person. As for the cavalry he positioned them on his army's left flank as it advanced despite the fact that any enemy attack would come from the opposite direction. Moreover, if a map drawn by somebody who was present but many years after the event is to be believed, they were in single file, not organised in troops or squadrons. All I can suggest is that he dared not regard them as sufficiently disciplined or trained in early seventeenth-century battlefield tactics to be allowed to face English horse, and that they were best kept well away from the fighting until victory had been won, whereupon they would be unleashed to inflict maximum damage on the fleeing enemy.

By dawn the vanguard was only just approaching its intended destination as it had lost its way during the night. The battle in the meantime had reached an area of open ground in sight of Mountjoy's vanguard commanded by Power. Tyrone saw the danger and ordered a battalion to move to the right to defend a ford or fords that lay between his brigade and the enemy whilst he seems to have been either positioning other troops immediately to hand for a textbook encounter in open ground or organising a retreat into the boggy ground to the north of the line of march. But whatever his intention the enemy quickly took advantage of the confusion caused by the redeployment. Power brushed aside Tyrone's flank guard and, having informed Mountjoy about the disorder to his front, received orders to attack the enemy at once

---

5   C. Carew Mss iv, pp.165–66, 186, 189–91, 203; Fynes Moryson, *Itinerary*, 3 vols (London: John Beale, 1617) ii, pp.174–75; George Carew, Earl of Totnes, and Sir Thomas Stafford, *Pacata Hibernia*, 3 vols (London, 1633 reprinted in Dublin 1810) ii, p.406.

with all the troops at his disposal. The English and Irish loyalist horse caused mayhem amongst the disorganised enemy infantry whilst Tyrone's cavalry, unable to intervene because their infantry were in the way, decided that discretion was the better part of valour and left the field.

According to Irish accounts and Fynes Moryson O'Donnell ordered the vanguard to march to the support of the battle, but the Spaniards with him were too slow and were killed in large numbers when Mountjoy attacked with his reserves. Other sources, however, claimed the Irish fled into the bog behind their position leaving their allies in the lurch, which seems to have been confirmed by the fact that there were few Irish dead left on the ground but large numbers of discarded weapons. The rearguard, on the other hand, were too far behind the battle to come to its aid and retreated without sustaining any losses, as the English mounted troops were in poor condition after weeks in the field and too exhausted to pursue them. Tyrone was therefore able to re-form part of his army in the vicinity of Kinsale on the following day, but its morale had plummeted, and given the circumstances he thought it best not to wait around but to lead the survivors back north as fast as possible.[6]

Anguila's troops in Kinsale had played no part in the engagement. The noise produced by the fighting between Tyrone's brigade and Power's forces was thought to be insufficiently loud to signalise anything more serious than a skirmish, and that is not surprising as most of the carnage was caused by the silent sword once Tyrone's flank guard had been driven back. Aguila does, however, seem to have seen Mountjoy's move towards the position that Tyrone's vanguard was supposed to have occupied at first light and interpreted it as a sign that the English army was in trouble. It also coincided with an upsurge in noise from the battlefield, but before he could get his own troops moving in the direction of the fighting he saw Mountjoy's soldiers on O'Donnell's intended objective waving captured Spanish banners, which probably meant that the recent uproar had been produced by enemy guns fired in celebration of victory and that it would be foolish for him not to order an advance. The next day Mountjoy resumed his siege operations, but in less than a fortnight an agreement had been made for the Spanish troops in Kinsale and the other harbours in County Cork to return home by sea taking their arms, their ammunition, and their war chest with them. All the English commanders demanded in return was that they did not involve themselves in any hostile acts before they reached Spain, and that they paid for the provisions they needed for the voyage.[7]

The fiasco at Kinsale did not bring the war to an end. O'Donnell had left for Spain, but Tyrone was still on the loose. The fighting therefore continued but it was grindingly expensive. The financial burden of keeping so large an army in Ireland, as well as

---

6   CSPI 1601–03, pp.28, 38–6 for English accounts based on intelligence and the claims of deserters. Some evidence from the Irish side is cited in Richard Bagwell, *Ireland under the Tudors*, 3 vols (London: Longmans 1888) iii, pp.409–10.

7   C. Carew Mss iv, pp.195–200; HMC, Marquis of Salisbury Mss 12, pp.38–39.

regiments in the Netherlands supporting the Dutch in their fight for independence from Spain, was too great for the English government to bear for any length of time, and the Irish economy was in no position to make a contribution with much of the country devastated by English troops and Irish loyalists intent on damaging Tyrone and his supporters' ability to wage war. It is not therefore surprising that when the Queen's enemies reverted to the type of guerrilla operations that had characterised the first few years of the Nine Years' War, Elizabeth through her ministers put pressure on Mountjoy to reduce the number of troops under his command. He obeyed, and as a result troops receiving pay fell to under 18,000 by October 1602 and to 13,700 three months later.[8] But in terms of the imbalance between revenue received by the English exchequer and expenditure on the war in Ireland it was nowhere enough to make a substantial difference.

The simplest solution was to capture or kill Tyrone, but the Earl won the game of hide and seek again and again and nobody was willing to betray him. By the autumn of 1602 Mountjoy had reached the conclusion that the war was likely to continue indefinitely. The only way of bringing hostilities to an end was therefore to accept Tyrone's surrender on his own terms, which were a royal pardon and the restoration of his ancestral lands.

In a letter written to the Queen couched in the language of a courtier rather than that of a victorious general Mountjoy put his case in favour of acceptance and Elizabeth's chief minister Robert Cecil backed him insofar as he dared without angering the Queen by his temerity. Elizabeth typically took several months to reach a decision and then only in March 1603 when she was on her deathbed. Such an act looks like the logical last statement in her 44-year long mission statement that that her subjects' wellbeing took precedence over her personal ambitions including inflicting condign punishment on rebellious subjects.[9] Her legacy to her subjects would be peace in Ireland and a reduction in the heavy taxes, which she had demanded and they had granted through Parliament to pay for the cost of defending English rule there. However, this gracious act as she left the stage for the last time may have been forced from her by her ministers when she no longer had the mental strength to resist. It is surely suspicious that anyone as determined and resolute as Elizabeth should have departed from her pronouncement on the subject only four weeks before her death when she was still in full possession of her faculties that she might be prepared to save Tyrone's life but not to restore his estates.[10]

---

8   CSPI 1601–03, pp.512, 526, 534, 546, 550.
9   For Mountjoy's letter to the Queen see CSPI 1601–03, pp.512, 514–15. For more on England's financial problems and granting pardon as a way of ending hostilities favoured by Cecil, see C. Carew Mss, iv, pp.375–76, and 'The letters of Sir Robert Cecil to Sir William Carew', J. MacLean (ed.), (London: *Camden Society* 88, 1864), pp.147, 154–55.
10   Doran, *Elizabeth I and her Circle*, pp.295–96, 356.

Once the Queen was dead Robert Cecil and his political allies smoothed the way for King James VI of Scotland to become King James I of England and Ireland. Given the grumblings of his officers that Tyrone had escaped scot free, Mountjoy was concerned that he would be blamed for putting undue pressure on the Queen in her dying days, but he was soon reassured. James had no intention of reversing Elizabeth's decision. After Tyrone had travelled to England in company with the Lord Deputy and pledged his loyalty to the King in person on bended knee, a royal decree was issued that no man should abuse him. Soon afterwards letters from the Privy Council to the mayors of Bristol and Barnstable informed them that Tyrone was returning to Ireland and that he now enjoyed royal favour. Mountjoy's rewards were to be made a member of the English Privy Council and lord lieutenant in Ireland as opposed to lord deputy with the title of Earl of Devonshire.[11]

However, during the last days of Elizabeth's reign and the first few days of James's Mountjoy had other concerns that were not so easily laid to rest. Tyrone was back in the fold, but security remained an issue, though hopefully only in the short term. Guerrilla warfare persisted in parts of the country such as County Kerry which owed allegiance to other chieftains; England was still at war with Spain; and intelligence reports indicated that King Philip was keen to send another expedition to Ireland to free his fellow Catholics from English rule. Mountjoy had also long been worried about how those parts of the country that resented English rule but distrusted Tyrone and his followers would react to Queen Elizabeth's successor. Moreover, a reform of the Irish currency was taking place concurrently which reduced the precious metal content of the higher denominations and thus altered the exchange rate between the English pounds and the Irish harp. This was unsettling for everybody who bought and sold but most particularly for people who were owed money like the officers and soldiers who had fought against Tyrone.[12]

Beyond these were longer term concerns such as how the victors could ensure that the first half of the seventeenth century was not punctuated by major uprisings like the last half of the sixteenth. Mountjoy favoured a policy of mild reconciliation. The spread of fervent Roman Catholicism should be contained by taking every possible measure to prevent missionaries from the Continent arriving in the country and causing trouble by raising hopes of foreign intervention in the island's affairs. On the other hand it would be politic to turn a blind eye to the celebration of the mass provided it was not ostentatious. He also noted that previous uprisings had been led by members of the Irish aristocracy. The King should therefore make sure to distribute rewards and honours evenly between the three vertical divisions of what it would perhaps be a little premature to describe as the Irish upper class – the clan chiefs of

11   C. Carew Mss vi, pp.1–2; CSPD 1603–10, pp.14, 23; Acts of the Privy Council (APC) 32, pp.495, 502.
12   CSPI 1601–03, pp.524–25, 559, 569; *ibid.* 1603–06, p.26; APC 32, pp.389–90; C. Carew Mss iv, pp.429–31, 434–35.

Irish descent, the Old English nobility (who had settled in the country during the time of the Plantagenets and Kings Henry VII and Henry VIII), and the New English, who had arrived there since the Reformation rather than favouring one group to the detriment of the others as had often been the case in the past.[13]

This was a personal view which was not shared by many of his officers, whose first sight of Ireland had been from the decks of an English ship carrying their regiments to fight Tyrone many of whom were the younger sons of English landed families keen to become landowners in their own right in the country they had helped to conquer. Then there were the civilian members of Mountjoy's government most of whose roots in the country went back no more than a couple of generations and who were even more seriously on the make. As New English they could only benefit at the expense of the Irish landed elite or the Old English noble families, who had different surnames but were very similar in dress, behaviour and speech to the Irish. Moreover, both were committed Roman Catholics whilst the soldiers and the bureaucrats and legal official were firm Protestants.

The Lord Lieutenant and the New English, however, were united in their conviction that it would be foolish to reduce or dilute the peacetime army in Ireland to such an extent that it might be overwhelmed by a Catholic uprising. To that end it was agreed that that it must be made up entirely of English officers and English rank and file. The Irish loyalist formations that had fought in the Nine Years' War were therefore disbanded before the 1606 establishment came into force apart from two units commanded by a senior Catholic member of the nobility the Earl of Clanricarde in his capacity as Lord President of Connaught.[14] That there were fears about the continuing loyalty of anybody who was not a Protestant is clear from the wording of a highly indignant petition of the Catholic landowners of Leinster to the Lord Lieutenant presented in 1605 to the effect that the New English were not only inventing and disseminating false allegations that their religion meant that they could not be trusted, but also hinting that they were complicit in the Gunpowder Plot.[15]

Events in Munster immediately following the Queen's death confirmed Mountjoy's fears about security. Cork, Waterford and Limerick had remained in English hands throughout the Nine Years' War, but most of their inhabitants were Irish or Old English whose livelihood based on overseas trade had suffered during the hostilities.[16] In April 1603 they made a stand by re-asserting what they saw as their traditional religious and institutional privileges egged on by the dreams and delusions of their priests. Unrest took the form of the public celebrations of the Mass, the tearing down

---

13   HMC, Salisbury Mss 14, pp.239–42.
14   CSPI 1603–06, pp.252–53, 435–36.
15   CSPI 1603–06, pp.360, 362–63.
16   CSPI 1601–03, pp 512, 551,556, 567, 583; *ibid.* 1603–06, p.36.

of fortifications constructed during the war, and denying the right of English troops returning from fighting in the far southwest of Ireland to take up quarters within their walls. At Waterford there had even been a show of reluctance to proclaim James as king of Ireland. Those involved would probably have preferred the Catholic Archduchess Isabella, Philip of Spain's sister and joint ruler of the Spanish Netherlands with her husband Archduke Albert, who had a claim to the crown of England via the Lancastrian line of the royal family. There were even murmurings that James as a Scot was ineligible to reign over Ireland.[17]

The unrest did not spread far from the three ports despite Mountjoy's initial concerns that inland towns were also affected, and it was put down with ease with few deaths in combat and none on the scaffold, but if troop numbers were to be reduced still further Ireland's defences needed to be improved. The government in Dublin suggested a way forward. It advised the Privy Council in London that unrest at Limerick had been restrained due to the presence of English troops in the town's medieval castle. It therefore recommended the building of citadels in other towns, small forts well supplied with artillery pieces located centrally where the main streets met or in a commanding position outside the built-up area with a good field of fire.[18] In addition the castles at Dublin, Limerick and Galway should be modernised, and to deter another invasion the coastal defences should be strengthened with special attention being given to the forts at Haulbowline Island and Duncannon, which guarded the estuaries giving Cork and Waterford access to the sea, whilst the old fort at Castle Park overlooking Kinsale harbour should be refurbished.[19]

The other area of concern was the north of Ireland. The walls of Carrickfergus begun in Elizabeth's reign were to be completed so as to safeguard communications with Scotland. At the same time two new forts named Charlemont and Mountjoy in deference to the Lord Lieutenant were to be constructed near Lough Neagh guarding the approaches to central Ulster from the south and east.[20] Soon afterwards it was suggested that other new forts should be established at Coleraine and Sligo. Here the concern was with the Spanish threat to land troops on an undefended part of the north Ulster coast and/or at Killybegs or Sligo Bay in the far west.

Such initiatives were expensive but necessary. The countryside was awash with 'swordsmen' who had fought for both sides in the Nine Years' War and would be only too happy to be busy once again.[21] To make matters worse the leading Irish chieftains who had been in arms against Essex and Mountjoy were still in touch with

---

17 CSPI 1601–03, p.651; *ibid.*, 1603–06, pp.33, 47, 50–51.; C. Carew Mss vi, pp.7–11.
18 CSPI 1603–06, pp.342, 491; *ibid.* 1606–08, p.411; *ibid.* 1611–14, p.127.
19 CSPI 1611–14, p.455.
20 These were places where army units were quartered in the last year of the war but seemingly behind limited and temporary fortifications. Both had been refortified by 1612: CSPI 1601–03, p.487; *ibid.*, 1603–06, pp.323, 341, 342; *ibid.*, 1611–14, p.127
21 CSPI 1603–06, pp.319, 323, 341–42, 582. Hugh O'Donnell died Spain soon after the defeat at Kinsale: *ibid.* 1601–03, pp.484, 527.

Spain through sons, brothers and cousins who were living in exile on the Continent or serving in the archduchesses' Irish regiment which could well serve as the spearhead of an invading force. Not only was it commanded by one of Tyrone's sons and largely officered by his clients and kin, gaps in the ranks of its foot soldiers had recently been filled by veterans of the Nine Years' War.[22]

Some of the anxiety felt by Lord Lieutenant and his officers should have lessened when representatives of the English and the Spanish monarchs signed a peace treaty in midsummer 1604. It also raised the hopes of the King's ministers in England that the lessening of the threat posed by the foreign power most likely to be interested in undermining English rule in Ireland would enable them to make a saving by reducing still further the size of the standing army the funding of which depended almost entirely on the English exchequer. Balancing the books had become more difficult with arrival of a new dynasty. Instead of the English exchequer having to fund one individual who, though personally quite demanding financially, showed a commendable parsimony in distributing largesse to her subjects, it had to cope with the cost of supporting a family of five. Moreover, the King and Queen were not only extravagant on their own account but also very generous towards others with money, annual pensions and lands owned by the Crown.

---

22 CSPI 1603–06, pp.25, 336, 565, 571, 579–80; *ibid.* 1606–08, p.397; *ibid.* 1608–10, pp.271–72. Amongst the officers in Mountjoy's army to take up service in Spanish regiments were William Windsor, William Newce and Christopher St Lawrence. For this see Appendices II, III and IV.

2

Slimming Down

Given the peace treaty, Tyrone's surrender and the mounting costs facing the English exchequer it is not surprising that demobilisation in Ireland gathered pace. The military establishment for the year September 1604 to August 1605 was for a force of well under 4,000 men, a third of what it had been in January 1603, with even more cuts planned for the following year. In mid 1605 Mountjoy, writing to the Dublin government from England in the final months of what was to be a fatal illness, warmly supported the idea of having the smallest army compatible with maintain security on the grounds that doing so would reduce the resentment of the Irish population and hopefully help reconcile them to English rule but with one very important proviso, namely that the Dublin government had permission to increase it to 3,000 in an emergency without having to consult the English government or the King.[1] He also emphasised that military planning should be based on present needs not on convenience or custom. Troops and companies must be quartered where they could best ensure that unrest was brought under control speedily before it spread to other parts of the island. This would necessitate the building of new forts and the refurbishment of others whilst those that were poorly situated should be demolished to save expense.

The letter fed into a full and far-ranging discussion of the army of occupation involving the army officers in Ireland, the Dublin government and the English Privy Council. It concluded that a force of 1,000 foot and 270 horse was sufficient for the army in peacetime, but the military establishment put into effect in September 1605 went further by keeping in pay just over 1,000 officers and soldiers men with a further 300 so-called wardens, retired or cashiered soldiers, acting as little more than caretakers for some of the castles and forts scattered across the island.[2] The decision seemed at first sight to be a sound one. Early in 1606 Sir Henry Brouncker, the Lord

---

1 HMC, Salisbury Mss 17, p.159.
2 HMC, Salisbury Mss 17, p.159; CSPI 1606–08, p.2.

President of Munster, boasted that, despite the serious unrest in Cork three years earlier, 200 soldiers were all he needed to keep the peace in the province.[3]

However, this was not only a halfway house. The Privy Council wanted more fundamental savings. As a consequence the pay of soldiers was cut as was the number of wardens guarding the forts. Sir Arthur Chichester, Mountjoy's deputy and eventual successor, and the Dublin government claimed that the first action would cause the soldiers in desperation to take the law into their own hands and plunder the civilian population, whilst the second threatened the security of Ireland as it would embolden potential rebels by showing that it would be an easy matter to capture some of the forts. They proposed instead a reassessment of the forts that needed to be manned with resources being moved from the south coast ports to Ulster. They also offered to go carefully through the other items of military expenditure and they were sure that economies could be achieved by removing pensions from ex-officers who were no longer carrying out any military duties.[4] But this would not be enough in the medium to long term. A letter written by Robert Cecil, now the Earl of Salisbury, stressed that although security and cost-cutting were both of the highest importance, and that the former would and should take precedence in the short run as 'whilst we must keep the soldier we must maintain him or their oppression will force a rebellion'. Note the first use of the word must. Clearly his long-term aim was to disband the standing army in its entirety.[5]

The alternative favoured by the government in Dublin dominated despite Mountjoy's advice by the New English was for Ireland to take over financial responsibility for the standing army. The economy was still severely affected by the nine years of fighting and so increasing customs duties or requiring the tenants of royal estates to pay higher rents were out of the question, but fining Catholics for not attending the Anglican church on Sundays would kill two birds with one stone. It would raise sufficient funds to pay for the army and at the same time advance the cause of Protestantism in Ireland by winning converts amongst Catholics who were unable to pay and/or were lukewarm about their religion. King James and his advisers, however, were convinced that imposing recusancy fines would antagonise the Irish and Old English landed and commercial elites without whose acquiescence security in the country at large could not be maintained. At the same time levying such fines would infuriate the wider Catholic population and thus cause widespread breaches of the peace, which might

---

3   CSPI 1603–06, pp.184, 204, 252, 387; *ibid.*, 1606–08, p.102; J. Lodge (ed.), *Desirada Curiosa Hibernica*, 2 vols (Dublin, 1772) i, p.440.
4   CSPI 1603–06, pp.342, 491, 580–82; *ibid.* 1606–08, p.411; *ibid.* 1611–14, p.127.
5   HMC, Salisbury Mss 20, p.309. The editor of the volume suggests 1608 for the letter, which is undated, but the context is clearly the cheese-paring exercise of 1606. By 1608 the security situation in Ireland had deteriorated such that the army was being increased in size.

grow in time into a countrywide uprising that could not be put down using Irish resources alone.⁶

Thus in practice Ireland was incapable of providing the funds to maintain the army and England reluctant to continue doing so. The alternative was complete disbandment, but the international situation meant that it would be dangerous to do so. The chummy relations between the British and the Spanish monarchies of the middle decade of King James's reign was still some years away. Admittedly as King of Scotland he had been a neutral in the Armada War, and he held no personal grudge against King Philip, but he had inherited Queen Elizabeth's ministers and their influence, though fading, remained a factor until the death of Robert Cecil in 1612. Moreover, there were still English troops supporting the Dutch forces fighting against Spain in the Netherlands. To make matters worse Catholic endeavours to bring about a regime change in Britain by assassination had continued into the new reign culminating most spectacularly in the Gunpowder Plot, and in the following year there was talk amongst Catholic exiles in the Spanish Netherlands about shooting James whilst he was hunting.⁷ Thus it was not beyond the bounds of possibility that Tyrone's submission and the peace treaty signed in 1604 were not the signs of a return to normality in Ireland but a stratagem on the part of King Philip and his Irish friends to create a breathing space in which to make preparations for another uprising which this time would be supported from the start by substantial Spanish military muscle. Moreover, Brouncker's boast about his peaceful province may not have been symptomatic of the dawn of a new era but instead of exhaustion caused by the bitter fighting in the last years of the previous reign and its concomitants famine, disease and death.

The year 1607 saw a return to reality when in early September the Earls of Tyrone and Tyrconnell left Ireland in secret for Catholic Europe taking their families and some of their supporters with them. Although pardoned and re-united with their ancestral lands in 1603 against the wishes of the New English whose hegemony they had so nearly overthrown, a party amongst the latter worked against them publicly and in secret via lawsuits and gossip supplied drip by drip by informants at home and in Catholic Europe. Thus traduced by their enemies at the English court and in the Irish government, the earls found King James's attitude towards them hardening. This reached crisis point when he ordered Tyrone to come to London to answer various charges. As time passed seeking safety overseas had become an increasingly sensible option as, to be fair to his enemies, Tyrone had kept up a secret correspondence with friends and potential allies abroad, yet seemingly it was a last-minute decision to leave the British Isles but a practicable one. All he had to do was join Tyrconnell, whose

---

6   CSPI 1603–6, p.580; Lenihan, *Consolidating Conquest*, pp.33–34.
7   CSPD 1603–10, p.324.

lengthy account of the ways in which he had been discriminated against is utterly convincing, and whose plans to escape from Ireland were already in place.[8]

Spain had probably been the earls' intended destination, but bad weather forced them to land in France where they were treated with great respect. The party then made for the Spanish Netherlands where Tyrone and his followers received a rapturous welcome from Irish soldiers serving under Spanish colours, from the Archduchess and the Archduke in person, and subsequently in writing from Pope Paul V. In due course they travelled to Rome where Tyrconnell died. The so-called Flight of the Earls and their reception in Europe was seen as vindicating Tyrone's accusers and it boded ill for the future. When war broke out again between the leading powers of Catholic and Protestant Europe as seemed nigh inevitable, Tyrone looked set to return to Ireland backed by foreign troops and many of his compatriots.[9]

Lord Deputy Chichester immediately asked for reinforcements. Referred to in a letter from Cecil to the Lord Deputy on 27 September less than a fortnight after the earls and their entourage left Ireland, it received royal approval a few days later. The lord lieutenants of the counties of west and central England from Cornwall to Lancashire were to raise a total of 800 foot by impressment, and these were to be sent to Ireland as soon as possible via the ports of Chester, Bristol, Workington and Barnstable.[10]

During the winter months the various county contingents duly arrived, but neither the Kings of France and Spain nor the Archduchess had any intention of getting involved militarily in Ireland at the time or in the immediate future.[11] Tension then eased and correspondence between the governments of England and Ireland reverted to discussion as to how the standing army was to be funded and the strategically important ports defended. Chichester came up with an ingenious scheme involving an initial capital outlay for the construction of new citadels and forts along the south and west coasts, but which after five years would require no further government funding. Members of the Privy Council, however, worried about building citadels at Cork and Waterford. They would be expensive to construct and unpopular with the inhabitants as in-your-face symbols of English rule. There was also no clear-cut evidence that such expensive modern contrivances were necessary for defending Ireland against internal or external threat. Would it not be better to quarter the town garrison unobtrusively in few well-built houses with a guard being kept at all times on the town gates?[12]

A completely new development was the first example of military planning affecting the three Stuart kingdoms that went beyond English men and money being used for the defence of English rule in Ireland. James I as King of Scotland had tried hard to

8   CSPI 1606–08, pp.51, 90, 93–94, 320, 364–83.
9   CSPI 1606–08, pp.631, 635–37, 654–55.
10 CSPI 1606–08, pp.273, 277, 283,360; HMC, Salisbury Mss 19, pp.277–99, 324, 348, 365.
11 CSPI 1606–08, p.351; HMC, Salisbury Mss 19, pp.260–61.
12 CSPI 1606–08, pp.276, 285–89, 304, 309, 408–09, 429, 430, 441, 452–53, 472, 475.

extend his authority over the Inner Hebrides and most particularly over the Roman Catholic Clan McDonald whose principal fortress was on the island of Islay. He had managed to chase them out of the Scottish mainland by giving permission for the Clan Campbell to take possession of the Mull of Kintyre. He now proposed to use the combined military resources of England, Scotland and Ireland to complete the job.

As the McDonalds had interfered in the affairs of Ireland through their cousins the MacDonnell sept which controlled those part of County Antrim facing the Inner Hebrides, the scheme was of some interest to the Dublin government and Chichester expressed his support for the scheme by promising to provide troops from the standing army, but the devil lay in the detail. He drew attention to ancillary costs such as making sure that the naval vessels involved were seaworthy, which raised the question of which government was to be responsible for funding the necessary repairs. There is thus a sense that he preferred the scheme to be put on ice for the moment, which is not surprising as his mind was focused on military matters much closer to home.[13]

The legal process of attainder was well under way for convicting the earls of Tyrone and Tyrconnell and their companions as traitors for having left Ireland for Catholic Europe without first asking for royal permission. Inevitably when it had gone through all its stages their landed estates amounting to several million acres would pass to the Crown. James and his advisers had no hesitation in deciding to use this windfall to solve once and for all the problem of bringing Ulster, Ireland's most unruly and ungovernable province, under stricter control by dusting down a not very successful Elizabethan scheme for developing large areas of land confiscated from noble rebels in Munster in the 1580s. Their estates had been subdivided into large units several thousands of acres in extent and leased to so-called undertakers drawn mainly from the landed gentry of the west of England, who were charged with 'planting' them with English subtenants, but the farmers of Devon and Somerset proved none too keen to settle in Ireland, and those who did discovered that the security blanket provided in theory by government troops was useless in protecting them against their Irish neighbours when the province rose in revolt in 1598.

To avoid the possibility of low demand the security issue was addressed. The subtenants were to have weapons for their personal defence in their houses, which were to be fortified against surprise attacks, and the undertakers were to ensure that they knew how to use them; existing forts were to be repaired and new ones constructed; and the towns of Derry and Coleraine were to be provided with modern defences. In addition, units of the standing army were to be stationed in the plantations as back-up should the settlers prove incapable of dealing with the problem themselves with the rest of the standing army ready to intervene as a reserve of last resort.

---

13 D. Stevenson, *Highland Warrior: Alastair MacColla and the Civil Wars* (Edinburgh: Saltire Society, 1994 print), pp.28, 38; CSPI 1606–08, pp.388, 452–55, 470, 474; HMC, Salisbury Mss 20, pp.101, 120, 192, 225.

Much of the detail was based on proposals made to the English Privy Council by Chichester within weeks of the Earls' departure, but it decided to opt for a more wide-ranging scheme by which the number of present and former army officers and Irish loyalists named as undertakers was much reduced in order to make room for English and Scottish courtiers and the wider Protestant interest which included the Anglican dioceses established in Ireland early in Elizabeth's reign, the City of London guilds and Trinity College, Dublin. When the revised scheme came to be implemented some captains in post received grants of 1,000 acres of land or more, as did eight out of the nine appointed to command the two new troops of horse and nine new companies of foot raised in response to the Flight of the Earls.[14]
    Resistance was to be expected from the Irish living on the estates of the Earls and their supporters many of whom would lose the tenancies and Chichester was initially concerned about having a major task of maintaining law and order in the plantations with an army of under 1,800 men supplemented by 100 horse and a couple of hundred Scots commanded by captains Crawford and Stewart. The pike and shot were of variable quality. Most were armed and some had suitable clothing, but few had any form of military training, and there was the usual quota of men the counties were keen to get rid of who were not able-bodied unemployed but physically unable to earn their living. These he immediately sent back home. The Scots on the other hand looked like good fighting men, but they were armed with a wide range of weapons many of which could only be described as antiquated. Nevertheless he had enough newcomers to increase the number of companies in the standing army from 18 to 27, and the settling-down process having been completed he proposed to leave Dublin for Ulster in the spring taking four companies of foot with him as a reassurance to the settlers.[15]

The threat to law and order, however, came from an unexpected quarter. Young Cahir O'Doherty, a major landowner in north-central Ulster adjacent to Derry, had been knighted by Mountjoy in 1602 and then pardoned in the following year for his father's treachery and his own misdemeanours in the Nine Years' War after making a personal appeal to King James. He was then restored to all his estates by royal order. Sir Cahir enjoyed a good relationship with Sir Henry Docwra, the garrison commander at Derry, but when in 1606 Docwra, whose appointment had been for life, sold the governorship and his company to George Paulet everything changed. Paulet accused O'Doherty of being on the fringes of a recent plot against the Dublin government planned by Lord Devlin and of leading an armed band up the coast of County Donegal to seize control

---

14 This account of the plantations is based on Lenihan, *Consolidating Conquest*, pp.10–14, 41–53 supplemented by Chichester's proposals and documents in the Carew papers: CSPI 1606–08, pp.275–78, 284, 313; C. Carew Mss vi, pp.13–22, 51–54, 235–44. See also Appendices II and III for the new captains.
15 HMC, Salisbury Mss 19, pp.277, 283, 318, 349, 373; CSPI 1606–08, pp.265, 283, 287, 308–9, 334, 360, 398. 408, 423.

of Tory Island in order to support a planned Spanish landing on the shores of Loch Foyle. Sir Cahir claimed that he was refurbishing Birt Castle, his principal residence, and he and his companions' destination had been a stand of the mature timber close to the shoreline that would provide the beams and planks his builders required.[16] This was probably not the whole story. It is understandable that O'Doherty and his men had been armed as they would be supervising work in a lawless tract of country, but his explanation as to why the carpenters he claimed to have hired to fell and roughly shape the timber on site failed to arrive, and why they were not travelling with him by boat, does not ring true.

O'Doherty was briefly imprisoned by the Lord Deputy as a warning to others, and then only released after paying a hefty bail despite Sir Richard Hansard, commander of a neighbouring garrison and much more experienced in the Irish politics than Paulet, having written strongly in his defence Sir Cahir then appealed to the King for support adding that Chichester had retained some of his ancestral lands in contravention of the decree of 1603, but the rap over the knuckles for the Lord Deputy arrived just too late to save him from crossing the Rubicon. Honour eclipsed common sense, and on 19 April 1608 he led his sept in an attack on the Loch Foyle garrisons that took them completely by surprise. First, whilst the guest of Captain Harte, who commanded Culmore Fort guarding the seaward approach to Derry, he kidnapped Harte's family and forced him to surrender the fort and the weapons stored there in order to save his life. A few hours later O'Doherty and his men attacked Derry itself whilst the garrison was asleep. Paulet, his lieutenant and his ensign who tried to fight it out were killed. The rebels then burnt the town to the ground but did not otherwise mistreat the inhabitants or the soldiers of Paulet's company who had surrendered without a fight.[17]

From then onwards it was downhill all the way. Chichester quickly got together standing army troops to march north. O'Doherty fled into the woods and bogs with a few followers and was killed soon afterwards. However, other septs took the opportunity to plunder and pillage, and several expeditions were needed to restore the peace during which the English troops used rough-handed methods to restore law and order and on a single occasion by their own admission were indiscriminate as to whom they slaughtered.[18]

There is, however, more than a slight suspicion that O'Doherty and Paulet were dupes in a plot instigated by members of the Dublin government greedy for land, as the Irishman's estate would be a handy addition to those of Tyrone, Tyrconnell and their companions which were just in the process of being carved up into convenient

---

16 CSPI 1601–03, p.95; *ibid*. 1603–06, pp.78–80; Shaw, *Knights of England* ii, p.100; CSPI 1606–08, pp.316–19, 326, 329, 337, 354.
17 CSPI 1606–08, pp.414, 420, 425, 475, 479, 481–86, 494–96, 503–14; HMC, Salisbury Mss 20, p.192.
18 CSPI 1606–08, pp.501–617, *passim*; *ibid*., 1608–10, pp.4–9, 11–13.

chunks for the numerous people keen to become undertakers. For attainder to be the correct punishment for O'Doherty he would have to be provoked into an act of violence against the Crown, but as he was on bail it would not need to be too violent, and with bad blood already between him and the governor of Derry Paulet was just the man to provoke him into an intemperate act. The army officers on the other hand were as interested in punishing Paulet as in provoking O'Doherty. Though their hunger for Irish land were typically New English, they also wanted to teach the King a lesson by bringing about Paulet's downfall and disgrace. They will have seen the King's approval of Docwra's sale of the captaincy to Paulet as an affront. He had not fought in the Nine Years' War and may never have held a military command, whereas many of their brave colleagues had lost their captaincies in the successive disbandings from 1602 onwards. Paulet was likely to make some mistake when O'Doherty took matters into his own hands. An inquiry would then follow at which Paulet's misdeeds could be brought into the open accompanied by numerous comments that this was what was to be expected of a civilian.

In the event the plot (if plot it was) proved more successful than the participants could have hoped. O'Doherty had overreacted but he was dead, and a trial was therefore unnecessary, but so also was Paulet. He could now be blamed not only for false musters (claiming he had more men under his command than was actually the case)and for arrogance and highhandedness that alienated his compatriots without terrifying or winning the respect of the Irish, and also for the burning of Derry and the three months unrest that followed. Moreover, there was little prospect of this line of argument being challenged as his junior officers were also dead. Letters from Ireland to the King and the Privy Council after the event were unanimous in condemning him for incompetence and financial malpractice, but what they did not do was suggest that O'Doherty was anything other than a traitor.[19]

King James was not deaf to the massive hint that choosing new captains for the standing army should be a matter of serious consideration not something to be treated lightly. In his response he reserved the absolute right to make such appointments, but he promised in future not to heed the advice of any person however exalted if the individual being recommended was not known to him personally. However, neither he nor the Privy Council wished the selection process to be prolonged any further than was completely necessary. and to that end he would welcome advice from Ireland. He also undertook as always to show impartiality if he was presented with several deserving candidates.[20]

---

19 Shaw, *Knights of England* ii, p.142; CSPI 1606–08, pp.389, 481, 483, 499, 528.
20 CSPI 1608–10, p.47.

3

The Perils of Peace 1609–1615

For three years after O'Doherty's uprising security remained an important issue for the Irish and the English government for reasons that were internal rather than external. Admittedly from time to time they received word of troops massing in Spain and its possessions for a descent on Ireland in support of the Earl of Tyrone, but it was low grade intelligence and treated accordingly – wishful thinking by Irish exiles and missionary priests discovered in captured correspondence, or military convoys sighted by mariners or fishermen on the high seas destined for elsewhere in Europe or north Africa, or tales brought back by Protestant merchants trading with Spain and its possessions and understandably hyper-sensitive to anything that might indicate a threat to their country and their religion.[1] However, the King of Spain had lost interest in Ireland as shown by his failure to make capital out of the Flight of the Earls, and England's involvement by proxy in war in Europe had gone into abeyance following the 12-year truce between the United Provinces and the rulers of the southern Netherlands in 1609 which King James helped to bring about.[2]

However, if the standing army was unlikely to be facing an invasion in the near future, it had an important new role to play in the plantations, but only as one element in multi-faceted plan to prevent violence breaking out between the Irish and the settlers. One measure was to remove the body of men most likely to cause trouble, the 'swordsmen' who had fought in the Nine Years' War and returned home to Ulster with few prospects of employment but plenty of time on their hands. It was not a great success. Sir Robert Stewart agreed to take 1,000 to Sweden in 1609, but 200 or so mutinied and ran their ship aground off Carlingford. They were recaptured by troops from the nearest garrison and put on board another ship, but this was wrecked

---

1   See, for example, CSPI 1606–08, pp.429, 529; *ibid.* 1608–10, pp.13–14, 393–94, 398–99.
2   D. Smith, *A History of the Modern British Isles 1603–1714* (1998), p.36. For the risk of war breaking out in 1613, see Gardiner, *History of England* ii, pp.134, 149, 165.

off the Isle of Man. They were then transferred via Scotland to Newcastle where they managed to escape but at that point the trail runs cold.[3]

The following year Sir Richard Bingley undertook to take another consignment to Sweden, but Chichester confessed that most came from other parts of Ireland. The Ulster swordsmen having no desire to leave the country had taken to the woods and the hills. Only those forced to break cover in connection with court cases or for family reasons were seized by the authorities and taken on board ship. Several years later Chichester claimed to have removed 6,000 swordsmen in total, but this seems a highly unlikely figure as there are no records of shipments after 1610.[4]

The second potential group of troublemakers were the tenants of lands formerly owned by men who had been attainted, and here again separation was seen as the best solution with men who had not supported the Crown in the Nine Years' War being forced to move to other parts of Ireland where there was supposed to be plenty of spare land. As with the transfer of swordsmen to Sweden, it did not work out well in practice for a variety of reasons the principal one being that the supply of land to be leased exceeded the demand for tenancies from English and Scottish settlers with undertakers responding by filling vacant holdings with Irish tenants and the government bewailing the fact but rarely doing anything about it. Fifty years later after the much more devastating physical destruction and famine resulting from Cromwell's reconquest of the country and the subsequent banishment of the defeated and their families to Connaught, Irish men and women were still thick on the ground in most parts of the five Ulster counties where plantations had taken place.[5]

Greater success was achieved in depriving potential rebels of one way of threatening or inflicting violence upon settlers. Instead of relying on periodic searches of suspects' persons, lands and properties for weapons most of which could be easily hidden, the English Privy Council focused on controlling the provision of gunpowder which could not be manufactured in Ireland.[6] A proclamation issued in 1604 established an English government monopoly over supply managed by the ordnance office in the Tower of London, which was only permitted to satisfy customers on instructions from the Privy Council. Thus in 1616 Sir Randal MacDonnell, a major Catholic loyalist landowner in Ulster and subsequently 1st Earl of Antrim, was allowed to purchase one hundredweight of gunpowder to supply the 40 muskets he kept in Dunluce Castle for its defence,

---

3   C. Carew Mss vi, p.49; CSPI 1608–10, pp.251, 263–64, 301, 334 etc. For a full account of their various escapades see CSPI 1611–14, pp.xxix–xxxii.
4   CSPI 1608–10, pp.458, 496, 542; *ibid.*,1611–14, p.480. The English Privy Council noted as a matter of concern that English names appeared in the lists of those leaving for Sweden. The reply was that they were pirates who had been captured: *ibid.* 1608–10, pp.265, 343, 496.
5   Lenihan, *Consolidating Conquest*, pp.42–53, citing P. Robinson, *The Plantation of Ulster: British Settlement in an Irish Landscape* (Dublin, 1984).
6   There were no sulphur mines in Ireland and it was difficult to conceal the production of saltpetre because of the foul smell.

whilst three years earlier the Privy Council released some 20 tons of gunpowder to Sir Arthur Chichester to replenish the stocks in the arsenal in Dublin Castle.[7] Future rebels would thus be hamstrung unless they managed to capture standing army supplies or were able to surreptitiously obtain some powder in advance from a friendly Catholic ruler, but a watchful eye was necessary. In 1615, for example, the Privy Council had to take measures to stop powder being shipped in small quantities from Bristol by Irish merchants as part of cargoes of miscellaneous goods.[8]

In addition, measures were taken to enhance the ability of the landowners on plantations and their tenants to defend themselves. The English government insisted that owners of parcels of lands of 200 acres or more were to construct houses on them out of stone or to refurbish existing castles. These were to serve as rallying points should their tenants come under attack and hopefully win enough time for army units to come to their aid. A survey of the plantations ordered in 1611 by a suspicious King and Privy Council was carried out by Sir George now Lord Carew, Salisbury's correspondent during Lord Mountjoy's campaigns. He found a very patchy picture. A few landowners had done all that was required of them in terms of constructing defensible houses and re-edifying castles, and in some other places work was clearly in progress. Elsewhere there was evidence of timber and other materials having been collected for building to begin the following spring, but in a disappointing number of cases there was no sign whatsoever of building activity on site.

There was insufficient time for him or his agents to ascertain how many weapons were in the settlers' possession, but a survey of part of Ulster undertaken seven years later by Captain George Alleyne on the instructions of Lord Deputy St. John to ascertain how useful the plantations would be in reinforcing the standing army in time of war gave a disappointing picture. Many landowners refused to allow their tenants to appear before him with their weapons citing tenuous excuses that almost certainly indicated that they had done little or nothing to provide them with arms for their defence. Of the men between the ages of 16 and 50 who did appear just under half were armed with muskets, calivers and pikes and perhaps 70 percent had swords, but Alleyne had good evidence of a deliberate effort to deceive him. After finishing the inspection of one area and moving on to the next, he found himself facing some of the same men carrying the same weapons.[9] On the other hand a survey taken two years later of landowners and tenants in other parts of Ulster found that the Scots at least were well armed.[10]

Urban settlements in Ulster were also charged with providing for their own defence, which meant state-of-the-art fortifications, and this applied both to new towns like Enniskillen and Omagh and existing ones like Derry and Coleraine. Uniquely in the

---

7   CSPI 1611–14, p.10; APC 33, p.53; *ibid.* 1615–16, p.540.
8   APC 34, 159.1
9   CSPI 1615–25, pp.221–26, 228.
10   CSPI 1615–25, pp.221–29.

case of Carrickfergus the King provided some of the resources for doing so.[11] The London guilds, who had undertaken to plant what had previously been known as Coleraine County, may have been hoping that he would provide a different kind of subsidy for the works at Derry if they waited long enough. In 1622 a survey of Ulster described the city as well fortified with a substantial wall, gatehouses, drawbridges, and also strong bastions and substantial gun platforms but no artillery pieces. There was no immediate response on the King's part, but two years later when a new war with Spain was in the offing and a second survey showed that nothing further had been done to defend the city against attack, he gave orders for the guilds to purchase and install 20 pieces of various calibres at their own cost. If they did not do so they were in breach of the agreement the two parties had signed in 1609 and there would be dire consequences.[12]

The standing army had been seen as playing a major supportive role as the plantations started to get under way. In the early years large armed escorts accompanied the judges on assize duty in Ulster, and the inspections of the plantations carried out by commissioners had a distinct military air with camps being constructed each night to guard against surprise attack. The first occasion when towns and country houses were preferred to sleeping under canvas was during Lord Carew's tour of the province on the King's orders in 1611.[13] Another military arrangement was more permanent. The number of companies permanently quartered in Ulster increased from 10 out of 19 to 18 out of 27, and as late as 1641 there seem to have been far more units stationed in the province than in any of the other three.[14] Moreover, whereas after 1603 they had been stationed in a cordon around the Earl of Tyrone's estates, they were now scattered across his former lands. Finally, undertakers who met with trouble in establishing their right to the land could ask for armed support but there seem to have been little demand. Only a single example appears in the official papers, and amongst the grievances against the army delivered to Chichester when the Irish parliament met in 1613 there were no complaints about its activities in the Ulster plantations.[15]

As time passed, the international situation improved and the expected trouble in the plantations did not materialise, the army was progressively reduced in size despite the slow progress of measures designed to enable settlers to defend themselves. The first reduction which occurred in October 1608 merely involved sending impressed men back to England. There was no longer a need to increase the size of all companies in the standing army to 100 officers and men as the unrest caused by O'Doherty's

11 CSPI 1601–03, pp.17, 112, 163; *ibid.* 1615–25, p.527; APC 33, pp.211, 504.
12 CSPI 1615–25, pp.368, 527.
13 C. Carew Mss vi, 218–19.
14 CSPI 1606–08, pp.1–2; *ibid.* 1611–14, p.9. For 1641 see Chapters 15 and 16.
15 CSPI 1603–06, p.436; *ibid.* 1611–14, pp.8, 48, 413–17.

uprising had come to an end.¹⁶ Three years later having completed his survey of the plantations Lord Carew was charged with ensuring that a more severe cut was implemented involving 104 mounted troops and 750 foot soldiers which would reduce the size of the army by almost a third.¹⁷

The Lord Deputy was thus presented with a *fait accompli*, but having been aware for some months that a substantial down-sizing was on the card she had taken steps to try and influence the outcome. In a letter to the Earl of Salisbury written in January 1611 he suggested that companies that were still 100 strong should be reduced in size by 50 with his own, which was 150 strong, also losing 50 men, his argument being that at the outbreak of war it would be easier to bring the army up to a competent strength by increasing the size of existing units than by raising new units from scratch. The cavalry, however, should be left alone as in an emergency it was more difficult to recruit horse than foot.

Chichester also tried to muddy the waters or cause a delay by sending the Council a report on the state of the coastal fortifications in the south of Ireland. It was perhaps bad tactics to ask for cash to finish the work when retrenchment was expected elsewhere, and all he received was a dusty reply that if the Exchequer did not have any money to spare he must use Irish revenue or borrow it. In the event the Exchequer found a small sum, which was put to good use in the summer months. By early November when the cash ran out Haulbowline was in excellent condition and very little needed to be done at Limerick and Kinsale.

The process by which the Privy Council and then the King reached their final decision about the size and scope of the cut cannot be ascertained as the minutes for 1611 were destroyed by fire, but they expected the Lord Deputy to react badly as shown by the instructions the Council gave to Carew and James's letter to Chichester penned soon afterwards. There does, however, seem to have been some attempt to soften the blow by showing that they had listened to his advice.¹⁸ He had failed to convince the members that the cavalry should not be cut, but instead of having to cashier whole companies of foot, which would have led to a more substantial savings as it removed three commissioned officers per company from the payroll, he was allowed to reduce them all in size to 50. He was also allowed to move army units and wardens from places where they were no longer needed to those where they were, but under no circumstances was this to result in an increase in the annual expenditure on the army.¹⁹

The Lord Deputy, however, was still a worried man. In letters written to the Earl of Salisbury and the Privy Council soon after Carew returned to England Chichester, having expressed great surprise that the English government had ordered a second reduction before the system of internal security based on forts and castles built by

16   CSPI 16060–8, pp.94–95, 110.
17   C. Carew Mss vi, p.178.
18   CSPI 1611–14, pp.2–3, 64, 154–55; C. Carew Mss vi, pp.68–72.
19   CSPI 1611–14, 64, 148; C. Carew Mss vi, pp.214–17.

the undertakers was properly in place, painted a bleak picture of the consequences of a third reduction using language that stopped just short of causing offence. He made much of the impact on the viability of the Ulster plantations. The stream of prospective tenants from England was already drying up and further doubts about security would prejudice the whole scheme. He would also be forced to split up his few remaining soldiers into very small bodies in order to man the port defences along the south and west coast and in Ulster and to garrison the large inland forts and castles, and such a fragmentation would make it impossible to quickly mobilise a task force capable of putting down a dangerous uprising or containing an invasion. In addition, the officers he would lose due in the slimming down would be the highly experienced ones appointed during Queen Elizabeth's reign as their commissions were worded in such a way as to make it easier to terminate them than commissions issued by King James, and to illustrate the point he added a list of the able captains forced out of the army since 1603

All he could suggest for keeping up the army at the lowest level that was practicable was for the King to reduce the number of pensions for which the Dublin government was responsible which James had granted in greater numbers than Queen Elizabeth. He should also reconsider fining adults for not attending Anglican churches on Sundays. Alternatively the composition, a form of land tax on the Irish counties established in Elizabeth's reign from which there were numerous exemptions, might be revised so as to make it more inclusive, though he admitted that there were political risks attached to all three suggestions. As for himself he had no wish to be in Ulster or indeed in Ireland when the army was reduced to a shadow of its former self. Finally, he rammed home what was perhaps his strongest argument in letters written a few weeks later. Unrest in Ireland driven by the Catholic priests would soon cause the plantation policy to be discontinued as the army would be incapable of maintaining law and order.[20]

James's reply did something to reduce Chichester's anxiety. Delighted that the Lord Deputy had accepted a reduction of over £9,000 in the army's annual cost he was not thinking of any further reductions.[21] Although this fell far short of a guarantee, the King kept his word in one respect. In 1624 the standing army was roughly the same size in terms of units, officers and men as it had been in November 1611, and thus considerably bigger than immediately prior to the Flight of the Earls.[22] To achieve this the army was seemingly kept up to strength in the normal manner. In 1613, 1616 and 1621 the English Privy Council issued orders for various counties in England and Wales to make lists of men who could be impressed and sent to Ireland at short notice. The total ran into the thousands, but this was only a precaution against the sudden

20   CSPI 1611–14, pp.145–48, 156–57.
21   CSPI, 1611–14, p.230.
22   CSPI 1611–14, pp.2, 230; C. Carew Mss vi, pp.151, 178, 218–19.

outbreak of outright war. In practice it drew on such men in accordance with need. Thus in one of the three years 300 men were sent and in the other two none at all.[23]

As ever there were concerns about the quality of the recruits. Describing the men who arrived at Chester in August 1616 the mayor and Sir Oliver St. John, who was about to set sail for Ireland to serve as Chichester's successor as lord deputy, noted that many had run away before their names could be entered in the muster roll. The contingent from Caernarvonshire had mutinied, whilst many of the recruits were too old or too feeble to be shipped. They had duly dispatched all the 'serviceable' men but did not give a number.[24] It is impossible to believe that no soldier died or become too old or decrepit for military service between 1616 and 1624 when war broke out with Spain and English reinforcements were needed to defend Ireland. All that I can conclude is that when gaps in the ranks occurred they were filled by on spot ad hoc recruiting by the captains involved, and if the occasional Catholic or suspected Catholic was signed up, the Dublin government did not see it as worth remonstrating with company or troop commander despite the possible security risk.[25]

External observers might well have seen the standing army in the middle years of King James's reign as providing good value for money. In the first place there were no uprisings that progressed beyond the planning stage. Chichester tried to capitalise out of this by making much of the one that came nearest to fruition, the so-called Great Northern or Ulster Plot of 1614 to capture Derry, Carrickfergus and Coleraine, rescue one of the Earl of Tyrone's sons who was in English hands, and massacre the settlers. It had only been nipped in the bud he claimed because his captains still had the resources to send out patrols on a regular basis to obtain intelligence and to look for malefactors. He also claimed that the plotters had only summoned up the courage to move from treasonous words to detailed planning because of the English government's neglect of the standing army. His enemies at Court, however, accused him of deliberately exaggerating the threat the plot had posed in order to squeeze more resources out of the beleaguered English exchequer.[26]

---

23   APC 33, pp.111, 286, 433; *ibid.* 34, pp.89–90, 349, 386, 697–702; *ibid.* 35, pp.65, 77; *ibid.* 38, pp.84–85, 89–91, 124.
24   CSPI 1615–25, pp.131, 136.
25   There were clearly Catholics in the army in 1628, though the Council in Ireland were ordered to recruit as few as possible: CSPI 1625–32, p.377. There were also company commanders. The Clanricarde family held captaincies throughout the period 1603 to 1642, whilst there and troop must be some doubt about the true religious allegiance of men who served in Spanish armies after the end of the Nine Years' War but were subsequently commissioned in the standing army. For these Appendices II to IV for the careers of captains Windsor, Newce, St. Lawrence and James Blount.
26   D. Stevenson, *Highland Warrior: Alasdair MacColla and the Civil Wars* (1994 edn), pp.38–41; CSPI 1615–26, pp.38, 52.

Second, the army in Ireland had played a small but effective role in an amphibious operation in the Inner Hebrides similar to the one that had been planned seven years earlier. Late in 1614, 200 men from the Ulster garrisons under the command of Sir Oliver Lambart, a veteran of Queen Elizabeth's wars, escorting three heavy artillery pieces joined Scottish clansmen and two ships of the Royal Navy in recapturing the island of Islay which had recently been overrun by renegade members of the Clan McDonald. Stevenson makes light of the matter as Dunyveg Castle quickly surrendered when part of its curtain walls fell down after two days' pummelling with roundshot, but before the bombardment could begin the troops from Ireland had spent 10 days landing the two whole cannon and the culverin onto an open shore, manhandling them across half a mile of rocks and boulders. and building platforms strong enough to bear their weight. The operation had also taken place in the depths of winter and been so efficiently managed that the troops and the artillery pieces were back in Ireland within days of the surrender.[27] Although the numbers involved had been small, this was the first example of a successful combined operations conducted by forces drawn from more than one of James I's kingdoms, and it paved the way for King Charles I's armies drawn from two or three which campaigned in Europe in the wars of the 1620s.[28] There was, however, one notable casualty. Captain Patrick Crawford, one of Chichester's company commanders, died after being hit by a musket ball or some such projectile whilst the landing was taking place

Finally, the standing army assisted the Dublin politicians in the messy business of governing an occupied country. The first meeting of the Irish parliament for over 40 years in 1613 provides a snapshot of the misdemeanours and inconveniences of the standing army as seen through the eyes of the Old English and Irish communities. The denunciation of the behaviour of the Irish government sent to the King by Catholic peers and other members of parliament after the first session contains quite a lengthy account of the army as an instrument of oppression, but the discontent was as nothing compared with the fury at the Irish government's creating a host of new borough seats just prior to the election to create a Protestant majority in the Lower House. In all of this the army's role was well-nigh invisible, but in three constituencies foot soldiers armed with muskets and halberds were claimed to have prevented Catholics from voting.

Troops were also used for collecting unpaid taxes and rents due from the King's tenants, for putting pressure on communities charged with building Protestant churches and constructing bridges, and for searching for deserters, escorting convoys from one garrison to one another, and marching across country in larger formations to deal with civil unrest or as training for going on campaign in time of war. These were run-of-the-mill activities for an army of occupation, but while the troops were

---

27 Stevenson, *Highland Warrior*, pp.45–47; CSPI 1611–14, pp.525–28, 531, 534; *ibid.* 1615–25, pp.7–8, 14, 45, 52. For the earlier operation see CSPI 1606–8, pp.388, 455–56.
28 L. Spring, *The First British Army 1624–1628* (Solihull: Helion and Co., 2016), p.viii.

away from their garrisons they relied on local sources of food and fodder. This was technically recoverable from the treasurer-at-war on the presentation of a ticket signed by the commanding officer declaring how much had been taken, but the treasurer rarely had ready cash in hand with which to discharge the debt. There was also a great fear amongst the civilian population of reprisals from the soldiers if they were challenged. This and the fact that the New English dominated the judiciary explained why the Irish rarely had recourse to the law to settle disputes with Protestants.

Chichester responded robustly to what he saw as the flimsy arguments backed by evidence that was anecdotal at best. The King, however, needed to show that he took his subjects' grievances seriously as a matter of honour and set up a commission of enquiry. Only Sir Richard Moryson, the Deputy President of Munster, showed any concern having collected money without warrant to pay for cavalry quarters, but he need not have worried as James nominated members of the Dublin government to serve as commissioners. Unsurprisingly they accepted almost all of Chichester's excuses and explanations as did the English Privy Council when they read the report three months later, but the King insisted that Chichester should do something to reassure his Irish Catholic subjects who were afraid of using the law courts because of fear of 'military men'. This looks like nothing more than a form of words that showed him to be a benevolent ruler with real regard for his subjects' sufferings, but behind it lay concern for a rise in Catholics taking the law into their own hands because they could not obtain justice.[29]

Lord Deputy Chichester, who had been ennobled as Baron Chichester of Belfast in the Irish peerage in 1613, left office two years later. The reason may have been a comment in a letter sent by Sir Richard Cooke, the Irish Chancellor of the Exchequer, to Sir Richard Winwood, one of the English secretaries of state, that many things were exceedingly out of order in the Irish government.[30] The King's permission for Chichester to resign written in late November shows that it clearly met with his approval, but otherwise the letter was full of praise for his work in Ireland, and it ended by wishing him a well-deserved rest from his labours. There is no evidence that the Lord Deputy was unhappy to leave office after an almost unprecedented length of time in charge in Ireland first as Lord Mountjoy's representative and then as viceroy in all but name. He did, however, have some concern about his future reputation. Malicious rumours were circulating, but he was hopeful that his achievements would serve to lay them to rest. Not long afterwards it transpired that the King's suggestion that he would have no objection to his enjoying a quiet retirement was an act of kindness rather than a veiled order to leave the political stage. In June 1617 Chichester received a tangible mark of James's regard when he was appointed lord treasurer of Ireland following the death of the elderly and extremely distinguished Crown servant,

---

29 CSPI 1611–14, pp.413–17, 421–22, 433, 437–41, 474–75; APC 33 1613–14, pp.426–27; C. Carew Mss vi, p.291.
30 CSPI 1615–25, pp.67–68.

the Earl of Ormond. Admittedly the post was an honorary one, but in 1622 the King chose him to head a diplomatic mission to the Holy Roman Empire when the Rhenish Palatinate, the principality ruled over by his son-in-law Frederick, was being overrun by Catholic troops, and he continued to seek his advice on military matters affecting Ireland until a few weeks before Chichester's death in February 1625.[31]

---

31 CSPI 1615–25, pp.98, 99, 115; APC 34, p.644; *ibid.* 38, p.171; *ibid.* 39, *passim*.

4

The Perils of Peace 1616–1623

The man chosen to succeed Chichester as lord deputy in April 1616 was Sir Oliver St. John, allegedly through the influence of George Villiers, James I's current favourite and the future Duke of Buckingham, to whom he was closely related.[1] However, St. John, the younger son of a prominent landed family, was well qualified for the post. Arriving in Ireland with Lord Mountjoy in 1599 after a successful military career fighting in France and the Netherlands, he was commissioned as colonel of a cavalry regiment and subsequently distinguished himself in several engagements including the battle of Kinsale. After the war he served for 10 years as master of the ordnance in Ireland followed by a short spell as Deputy President of Connaught, which broadened his administrative experience.[2]

The Villiers connection would have done St. John no harm in the struggle to succeed Chichester, and he was certainly in England in early 1616 and as such close to the centre of things when King James was making up his mind, but there is no direct evidence that he gained any benefits from his family connection during his years as lord deputy.[3] It is possible that Buckingham defended him when he came under criticism from the King and the English Privy Council as he did from time to time, but he did not support him in his claim that Ireland's security was being compromised by the reform of royal finances, the brain child of the City of London financier Lionel Cranfield, later Earl of Middlesex. Cranfield was Buckingham's protégé until they fell out in 1624 over the decision to go to war with Spain, but that was two years after St. John left Ireland.[4]

---

1   CSPD 1611–18, p.364.
2   *Oxford Dictionary of National Biography* (*ODNB*) 48, p.651; CSPI 1601–03, pp.346, 628; *ibid.* 1603–06, p.404; *ibid.* 1615–25, p.15.
3   CSPI 1601–02, pp.346, 628; *ibid.* 1603–06, p.404; *ibid.* 1615–25, p.15.
4   <www.historyofparliamentonline.org>, House of Commons 1603–1629, Members' Biographies in alphabetical order: <https://www.historyofparliamentonline.org/research/members>.

The King advised by Cranfield was intent on the Irish government balancing its books so that there was no longer any need for the English exchequer to send annual shipments of cash across the Irish Sea. This was clearly not something that could be achieved overnight, but with the Irish economy growing under the benevolent rule of James the peacemaker, the country should become amenable to paying higher taxes. He for his part would do what he could to promote acceptance by responding positively to the grievances of all communities by tackling corruption and ensuring that the legal system did not discriminate against the Old English and the Irish. To that end the Privy Council in the middle and latter part of his reign set up commission after commission charged with identifying defects in church and state and recommending improvements. In the meantime, the Dublin government dominated by the leaders of the New English community since the end of the Nine Years' War was to be prepared for the new financial regime by intermittent stoppages in treasure [as it was called] from England accompanied by instructions to fend for themselves until such time as the King had money to spare.[5]

The significance of the standing army for the finances of the Dublin government was that it was by far the biggest item of expenditure in the annual budget, and that the treasure from England was dedicated to filling the gap between what it had left when other expenses had been met and the cost of the country's defence. However, filling it when the subventions ceased would not merely involve raiding the pockets of King's Irish subjects. It was very clear that in some important respects maintaining the standing army, its forts, castles and other strongpoints was costing more than it ought, and that attention to such matters should enable a reduction to be made in the revenue needed to fund the army.

In the first place it was general knowledge that the captains, who were paid in accordance with the number of men in their companies and troops, were receiving more cash than they should by claiming for soldiers who had died or deserted and pocketing the difference. In addition, it was a scandal that funding provided to improve Ireland's coastal defences had failed to achieve its objective. In 1618 the Earl of Thomond, the recently appointed Lord President of Munster, informed the Dublin government that forts in his province allegedly fully operational at the end of 1611, were clearly not. In one case inferior wood had been used to construct the frames on which its artillery pieces rested. As a consequence, it was effectively decommissioned as the gun barrels had been removed and were lying on the ground. Moreover, the walls of Carrickfergus, in which the King had taken a personal interest because of its strategic importance for resourcing military activity in Ulster in time of war or

---

5   There is just a hint that this was partly because St. John was not allowing his advisers and officials to see all the correspondence passing between England, as he was rapped over the knuckles for excessive secrecy by the Privy Council: CSPI 1615–25, p.198; APC 36, p.93. However, the voluminous correspondence of Chichester in the Calendars and the Carte manuscripts in the Bodleian and the meagre quantity of St. John's is because the previous lord deputy's private archive survives whilst his does not.

civil unrest, were unfinished despite annual contributions from the English exchequer being paid for two years beyond the date on which the work was due to be completed.[6]

The Lord Deputy and his colleagues advised by Sir John Bodley, the engineer charged with overseeing the fortifications and reporting on progress, had answers for the charges of neglect, but how honest they were can only be a matter of surmise. However, some idea of the complexity of considerations that lay behind the stop/go progress of work on the coastal defences can be gained by looking at the citadels planned for Cork and Waterford, the principal ports on the south coast of Ireland, which were seen as the most likely places for Spanish troops to land because of the way their citizens had behaved on Elizabeth's death in 1603.

Although an upsurge in Catholic enthusiasm that might lead to the Spaniards being made welcomed did not come to the attention of the Dublin government until 1600,[7] new build citadels were recommended for Cork in 1602 and Waterford in 1603, and Bodley was charged with setting both in train, but nothing happened for some years. There was a flurry of activity early in1608, but in May of that year the Privy Council decided not to proceed. Dealing with O'Doherty's uprising and its aftermath would be expensive and take some time, and Chichester's advised that Bodley had underestimated the cost of building them. Instead the Lord Deputy was to concentrate on Haulbowline, Duncannon, Kinsale, Limerick and Galway where existing forts or castles were capable of being brought up to scratch at less cost. Only when this work had been completed was the construction of the two citadels to begin.[8]

In 1614 two years having passed since Bodley's deadline for completing all necessary work on the five coastal fortifications Chichester put a new proposal to the King, which may have been motivated by Carew's recent devastating report that Ireland would be incapable of defending itself against Spanish attack if citadels were not built at Cork and Waterford. The undertaking, he promised, would not make a substantial inroad into government revenue as it was his intention that the towns and countries of southern Ireland should pick up most of the bill, and a few weeks later James gave his permission to proceed, but in a private instruction that had not been discussed by the Privy Council.[9]

However, nothing happened for another 10 years. Presumably the Lord Deputy had been unable to devise a practicable scheme for raising the money to pay for the citadels without causing substantial unrest, but the project may have been no more than a form of words that would look good to James's English ministers at a time when relations with Spain had taken a temporary downturn, but which neither the monarch not the Lord Deputy saw as anything more than window-dressing.

6   APC 33, p.211; *ibid.* 36, p.92; C. Carew Mss vi, p.377.
7   CSPI 1603–06, pp.45, 341, 400.
8   CSPI 1600, pp.134–35, 498; *ibid.* 1601–03, p.329; *ibid.*, 1603–06, pp.45, 341, 400, 491, *ibid.* 1606–08, pp.341, 429, 430, 435, 452, 472, 526.
9   C. Carew Mss vi, pp.214–17, 310; CSPI 1611–14, pp.455, 482.

Another reason for not progressing the plan was almost certainly prudence. The English and Irish governments had not forgotten what happened at the King's accession in 1603 and both were keen not to provoke something similar at a time when they were intent on reducing Cork and Waterford's autonomy. The charters of government issued by earlier monarchs had given their citizens too much freedom to cock snooks at royal authority and they had stretched the exemptions allowed by statute law in matters of religion to the limit and beyond. Catholic mayors had taken office; Catholic religious processions attending by hundreds of people had taken place; and Protestant bishops had been treated with contempt. Cork's rulers backed down at the threat of *quo warranto* proceedings being taken against them,[10] but Waterford resisted for months until the full force of the law and the threat of several companies of foot being billeted there led to a capitulation and the loss of their charter.[11] On this occasion the citizens did not take to the streets. In its public utterances the government in Ireland was firm and forthright and moved slowly and cautiously towards its goal, but a nevertheless palpable relief can be read between the lines of the letters in which the Privy Council thanked the Lord Deputy and the Lord President of Munster for the tact and forbearance they had showed in the confrontations with Cork and Waterford

In 1624 war broke out once more with Spain and the sub-committee of the Privy Council dominated by old Ireland hands Carew, Chichester and St, John insisted that work on the citadels should begin immediately. The response of Lord Falkland, St. John's replacement as lord deputy, is instructive. He advised a softly-softly approach. It would be best to begin by re-edifying the forts at Duncannon and Haulbowline guarding the approaches to Waterford and Cork respectively, and not to begin constructing the citadels until such time as several hundred troops from England were quartered within their walls.[12]

The first sign of choppy waters ahead with respect to paying the army's wages came in the autumn 1615 as Chichester was about to leave office when the usual half year tranche of treasure failed to arrive on time. Soon afterwards Sir Oliver St. John, not yet designated as the next lord deputy, and three other men with experience of civil and military affairs in Ireland at a senior level were ordered to report in writing to the Privy Council on the places where the units of the standing army and groups of wardens were stationed and whether this fulfilled current security needs. At first sight this looks like nothing more serious than timely house-keeping, but the conclusions reached might provide the King's advisers with evidence that justified cutting the number of garrisons and thus reducing the annual expenditure on defence, a process

10 The *quo warranto* legal instrument gave the King the right to abrogate a charter in the case of an infringement.
11 C. Carew Mss vi, pp.336–42, 385; CSPI 1615–25, pp.107, 143–97 *passim*; APC 35, pp.91–92, 236, 311–12, 332–33.
12 APC 35, p.333; CSPI 1611–14, p.455; *ibid.* 1615–25, pp.512, 569–70.

that would certainly make inroads into the ranks of the wardens and possibly lead to the disbandment of some units in the standing army.[13]

Early in the new year army reform claimed its victim in the form of the treasurer-at-war Sir Thomas Ridgeway. Early in 1616 he was dismissed from office and recalled to England to explain inconsistencies in his accounts. His appointment as a baron in the Irish peerage was put on hold for nine months and two years later he was ordered to pay back almost £8,000 to cover expenditure he could not explain.[14] His replacement was Sir Henry Docwra, who unlike Ridgeway was a distinguished veteran of the fighting in Ireland at the end of Queen Elizabeth's reign, and possibly a man who already had a reputation for probity as later in his career he was described as an excellent public servant who had not made a fortune out of his position managing army finances.[15]

As was customary in the intermission between the departure of one lord deputy or lord lieutenant and the appointment of another, the two lord justices, the leading legal officials in Ireland, took charge of the government under the watchful eye of the Privy Council which, true to its policy of financial retrenchment, ordered them to keep a tight lid on expenditure. It was keen that the sum required to cover pensions, second only to the standing army as a drain on Dublin government revenue, would continue to decline. They were therefore to follow to the letter instructions not to increase the number of pensioners nor to use the death of one as the go-ahead to nominate another. They were also to exercise restraint in the issue of concordatums, that is payments made during the financial year for goods and services that could not be budgeted for in advance. Neither related directly to the standing army but there was an indirect link to both. In 1616 numerous pensioners were former military personnel from senior officers whose units had been disbanded to private soldiers who had been wounded and discharged from the army, and officers and men still serving would clearly have had expectations that this kind of financial safety net would still be in place when they retired into civilian life. Also, expenses incurred by officers featured quite prominently in the lists of concordatums that survive.[16]

Soon after leaving England in June the Privy Council reminded St. John of the need for the Dublin government to give its opinion about a cost-saving measure that had probably been sent to them by the panel appointed in late 1616.[17] It recommended the provisional decommissioning of some inland forts in Ulster and Connaught by offering the freehold to their present governors with some land attached which they could

---

13 APC 34, p.349; CSPI 1615–25, pp.87, 115.
14 <www.historyofparliamentonline.org>, House of Commons 1603–1629, Members' Biographies; APC 34, pp.391–92, 429–31; CSPI 1615–25, p.143.
15 CSPI 1625–32, p.618.
16 APC 34, pp.462–63; CSPI 1615–25, pp.12, 13, 194–96, 245.
17 St. John probably knew about the proposal well in advance as he was supposed to have served on the committee, but he may not have been able to attend its meeting as he spent the winter in England: CSPI 1615–25, 94, 115.

either farm themselves or lease to tenants the proceeds of which would be sufficient to keep the forts in a good state of repair. They could be then recommissioned in the event of an invasion or serious internal unrest, as one way of reducing expenditure on the army without reducing its preparedness for hostilities. It was for the Crown to offer the freehold of the forts.

Privy Council members did not 'dislike' the scheme but wanted more information to assure them that the forts would continue to be kept in good repair, and that there was no chance of their falling into potentially hostile hands in the future by, for example, the governor's widow marrying a Catholic. The Dublin government's enthusiastic response does not survive but its contents can clearly be seen in the Council's reply which was more than usually forthright in its language. It had expected the recommendation to apply to a small number of forts and castles, but what they received applied to all the inland forts in the two provinces including some that had been built at great expense in Queen Elizabeth's time and were still important for Ireland's defence. Moreover, the safeguards fell far short of what had been anticipated. They were also suspicious that the scheme was in reality a land grab by members of the New English elite as the Dublin government was to decide on the new owners who would not necessarily be the governors. Finally, the beneficial impact on the standing army budget would be far less than had been anticipated.

The Privy Council having spent much time on the proposal and with sufficient evidence to reach a decision declared it dead in the water. Nevertheless St. John and his Irish Council tried to argue the toss in official letters and in private correspondence in the months that followed, but the Privy Council was adamant. In October 1617 in a letter to the Lord Deputy it stated in no uncertain terms that its earlier decision still stood and would seemingly do so for all time.[18]

After this false start the Privy Council then turned its attention in the closing weeks of 1617 to malpractice in the standing army, and to this end it ordered Sir John King, the deputy treasurer of the army, and Ralph Birchenshaw, the comptroller of the musters, to appear before it in person bringing their books and papers with them. St. John tried hard to convince it that it was impossible for King to leave Ireland. Not only were his official duties too onerous for him to spare the time for a journey to London, he was also too elderly to travel such a distance at that time of the year, but the Privy Council was adamant. Sir John was given a month to complete the work he was currently doing for the Lord Deputy, but then he must be given leave of absence so that the two men could travel together.[19] This was a cunning move. Given that their areas of responsibility and expertise overlapped each would know something about the other's affairs, and if they were first interviewed individually and they told

---

18 APC 35, pp.48, 243, 333.
19 APC 35, pp.340, 388.

different stories it would be an easier task to get to the truth of the matter than if one was in England and the other in Dublin.

That need not have been the only reason for insisting on King's presence. Some members of the Privy Council may have been worried about what the questioning of Birchenshaw might reveal if he were the sole witness. There was no doubt that he would be a most informative source of information about malpractice given his 30 years' experience in keeping musters of English forces in the Netherlands, France and Ireland. The problem was the bag and baggage that went along with the acquisition of that experience. In 1600 Lord Deputy Mountjoy had described him as corrupt and a 'traitor to the Queen's profit'. Summoned to England he managed to defend himself so successfully that he was ordered to return to Ireland the implication being that he had been falsely accused by disgruntled officers whose malpractices he had uncovered. Alternatively, Mountjoy may have picked on Birchenshaw as a scapegoat to cover up the defects of his immediate superior Sir Richard Lane, the muster master general, who the Lord Deputy admired on personal grounds and wished to protect against a charge of incompetence. Having lost one battle Mountjoy counterattacked the following year this time accusing Birchenshaw of slackness in his duties, but the latter's meticulously kept accounts were sufficient to keep him in his place, and thereafter he was left alone as too dangerous to meddle with because of what he knew. It would not therefore have been surprising for old Ireland hands like Chichester and Carew to have been greatly concerned that he would see his visit to England as a heaven-sent opportunity to settle old scores if he alone had the council's ear.[20]

King and Birchenshaw spent several weeks in discussions with the Council, and clearly James, his ministers and advisers were delighted by their responses to questioning and with the quality of the written evidence they had brought with them. The outcome was a new annual establishment for Ireland in which the army remained the same size with the income streams provided for its upkeep sufficient to cover all its costs. As a mark of royal approval both officials received rewards. Birchenshaw was knighted and given greater power and responsibilities, whilst King's son Robert became Birchenshaw's deputy.[21] The document setting out the details of the new establishment does not survive, but the impact of its provisions on the standing army can be discerned in the correspondence that followed.

First much greater care must be taken to ensure that troop and company commanders were not claiming to have more soldiers under their command than was actually the case. Fears that the Lord Deputy as an army officer of very long standing would allow such a practice to continue by covering up for fellow captains gave rise

---

20 CSPD 1595–97, p.275; *ibid.* 1599–1601, pp.255, 472; CSPI 1600, pp.64, 73; *ibid.* 1600–01, pp.175–76, 249–50, 331, 449; *ibid.* 1601–03, pp.344–51, 490.
21 W.A. Shaw, *The Knights of England*, 2 vols (London: Sherrat and Hughes, 1906) ii, p.168; CSPI 1615–25, pp.192–94. Robert King seems to have succeeded Birchenshaw's son Ralph who had recently died and whose widow was awarded an annuity of £100.

to strong words from the Privy Council. St. John was to do everything possible to assist Birchenshaw in his task of ascertaining the correct number of officers and men in every troop and company by forcing recalcitrant commanders to give admittance to Sir Ralph's creatures (to use contemporary parlance) whose instructions were to produce an account of what they had seen rather what they had been told.

Second, the right of captains to live in England leaving their lieutenants with the responsibility for training and disciplining their troops and companies was to be strictly monitored in the future.[22] Permanent residence overseas would only be permitted if the captain in question had the King's consent. If they were mainly resident in Ireland but needed to leave for a short period of time for personal reasons or to perform some specific tasks for the King they must obtain Birchenshaw's permission in advance. If absentees did not have a license to leave the country or stayed away for longer than had been agreed, he was to dock their pay. This restrictive regime lasted until Birchenshaw's death in 1622 when his enemies took steps to ensure that conscientious monitoring was put in the grave with him. His office was abolished as unnecessary with responsibility for musters falling onto the shoulders of the elderly Sir John King, who only seems to have issued a small number of licenses, though the system seems to have revived during Wentworth's time as lord deputy in the 1630s.[23]

The King for his part promised that he would require the exchequer to send £10,000 every half year to Ireland to help towards the upkeep of the standing army. He made clear, however, that this was the most that the Dublin government should expect, and that it would not necessarily be paid in full or on time. To cover any temporary shortfall the Lord Deputy and his ministers were given permission to borrow up to £5,000 the security of the loan being the English government's promise to pay the debt by a certain date, but as a mark of goodwill Sir Henry Docwra, who had been visiting England, would return bringing plenty of ready cash with him to pay for what was owing to the officers and men from the year Lady Day 1617 to Lady Day 1618. Nothing was said specifically about earlier arrears other than that this was the English Privy Council's responsibility, and that the money owed would be forthcoming when it became available.[24]

Whether or not the King intended at the time be true to his word cannot be known, but in the space of three years many undertakings relating directly or indirectly to the standing army's ability to defend English hegemony in Ireland against internal and external threat had been largely abandoned. Despite the Privy Council's forthright rejection of the proposal supported by St. John to transfer the ownership and upkeep of the inland forts in Ulster and Connaught from public into private hands, the

---

22 CSPD 1619–23, p.481; CSPI 1615–25, pp.189, 425; APC 36, p.93; *ibid. 38*, pp.84–85.
23 APC 38, p.371; CSPI 1615–25, p.398.
24 CSPI 1615–25, pp.206–07, 209, 241, 254; APC 36, p.92.

King responded with indecent speed when the matter was raised again in 1620 by Sir Thomas Dutton, the scoutmaster general for Ireland, a professional soldier whose long military career had been in Europe rather than Ireland but who was also one of the King's gentlemen of the privy chamber and thus a courtier.[25] As such he was probably put up to it by James, who had ordered a new survey of the forts the previous year which focused far more on the terms of the leases issued to current custodians than on the cost of refurbishing them. The Privy Council reminded James of its earlier minute, which he ignored, but needless to say the Lord Deputy and his council were delighted. The scheme was then carried though with remarkable speed, though to be fair to the King he took notice of the Privy Council's earlier objections by retaining ownership of three of the strategically more important ones and by taking further steps to ensure that none of the rest passed into hostile hands in the future.[26] The impact on the overall spend of the Irish government was also more significant than the Privy Council had previously claimed. In 1613 there had been 23 forts in the King's ownership staffed by 335 wardens each paid eight pence a day. In 1621 there were only 12 forts and 150 wardens.[27]

Laying off almost 200 wardens had no direct impact on the troops and companies of the standing army, but it took less than a year for the English government to break the promise to send money to Ireland every half year to help pay its wages. Although the cat was not let out of the bag for some time, it is clear that very soon after agreeing to the next year's establishment the King allowed the process of financial disengagement of England from Ireland insofar as army pay was concerned to proceed. Between Lady Day 1619 and Michaelmas 1622 the English exchequer should have sent eight subventions across the Irish Sea amounting to a maximum of £80,000, but only two arrived and neither was for the full £10,000.[28] Following its instructions as to what to do in such circumstances Lord Deputy St. John and his council borrowed money on the security promised, but to its great embarrassment the £2,000 lent by Lord Brabazon in 1622 was not repaid on time by the English exchequer. The Privy Council's reply suggests that it was ready for a reproach from Dublin claiming that it had not been kept sufficiently informed about the loan, and as at the moment it had no money to spare the Lord Deputy should pay Brabazon out of the King's income streams in Ireland, which it well knew were already fully assigned to covering the cost of other items in the country's annual budget.[29]

---

25 A former soldier claimed to have fought under his command in Ireland and the Netherlands, but Dutton can only have been a junior officer in Ireland, as his name does not appear in any of the list of captains in the Nine Years' War in the Elizabethan State Papers Ireland: APC 37, p.404.
26 APC 37, pp.159, 258, 265, 338–39; CSPI 1615–25, pp.283–85, 292–93, 300, 310.
27 Moryson, *Itinerary* iii, pp.355–97; CSPI 1615–25, p.343.
28 APC 37, pp.47, 127–28, 274, 412–13; *ibid.* 38, pp.323, 426; CSPI 1615–25, pp.249, 337, 349, 394.
29 CSPI 1615–25, pp.396, 398; APC 37, pp.389–91.

All that St. John and his ministers could do in the circumstances was to write increasingly alarmist letters to the Privy Council claiming that lack of money to pay the soldiers was undermining the military competence of the army and indeed its loyalty at a time when meetings attended by large numbers of Catholic priests suggested that an uprising was being planned. To this they added the dire prediction that if nothing was done by the English government to release more funds the troops would take food and money by force from the civilian population, which would significantly increase the likelihood of the uprising gaining widespread support.[30]

Such baleful predictions reached their peak in a letter written by St. John early in 1622 soon after he had been removed from office in what seems to have been an act of exasperation by the Privy Council which chose to regard his complaints about the fitful flow of treasure from England to Ireland as evidence that he was no longer fit for the job of governing Ireland. Following a suggestion by James that he was thinking of recalling the Lord Deputy, they took him at his word and let St. John know that his time was up. The King was incensed. The way in which he had been dismissed reflected upon St. John's honour, which was not in question, The Council duly apologised, but the deed was done, and it was too late for James to do anything about it.[31]

In a final letter to the Privy Council the former Lord Deputy insisted that its contents should be likened in their sincerity and truthfulness to the words of a man on his deathbed and about to meet his Maker. He felt deeply ashamed for leaving his troops in a worse condition than any of his predecessors, and he did not know of any general who had commanded an army which had suffered so long from lack of pay. Yet despite their distress his soldiers had kept to their garrisons. They had not deserted or sallied forth committing acts of violence against the King's subjects.[32] However, the letter's impact was probably marred by the fact that St. John was clearly not on his deathbed or even on the verge of retiring from the political arena. He had not lost royal favour as James quickly made him a member of the Privy Council. Further honours followed, namely an English peerage and the post of lord treasurer of Ireland, and as Lord Grandison he served as a specialist adviser on the country's affairs. His value to the Crown in this respect increased over time following the deaths of Chichester in 1625 and Carew in 1627, and in 1630 at the age of 70 he was sent back to Ireland by King Charles I on a special mission, but the task proved too much for him and he died within a few weeks of his return to England.[33]

The Privy Council's response to St. John's final cry of despair shows a slight change in emphasis. Hitherto its replies to his letters had been almost entirely negative. Soldiers were always griping about their pay and conditions. The Dublin government

---

30 APC 37, p.339, *ibid.* 38, pp 84–85, 212; CSPI 1615–25, pp.254, 297, 311, 337, 394.
31 CSPI 1615–25, 313 (misplaced), 342–43.
32 CSPI 1615–25, p.349.
33 *ODNB*, 14, p.4; *ibid.*, 48, p.652.

knew full well that the King had no money to spare because he was honour bound to give military support to his only daughter Elizabeth and her husband who were being chased from their German principality and given Ireland's prosperity it should have offered to take responsibility for the whole of the standing army's pay. Treasonable talk was no more than wishful thinking on the part of the priests and their credulous followers, but if the government had been worried then it should have taken immediate action instead of indulging in bouts of self-pity. Finally, turning to the deplorable state of the standing army it marvelled that it was in such a condition. Given Ireland's wealth St. John and his officials could surely have found some way of providing the resources for keeping it in good shape if they had had the will.[34]

This time solutions were suggested. What the Dublin government must do was ensure that the soldiers received their pay for the current year and thus ensure that arrears did not rise any higher. In order to do so it should put a temporary stop to paying its pensioners what they were due. As this was not likely to provide sufficient extra cash for the army, it was allowed to commandeer rents and other revenues from royal estates and to collect what the Privy Council saw as debts owed to the Crown. Some people, for instance, had yet to contribute towards the royal aid levied in 1616 to help cover the cost of the marriage celebrations of the Princess Elizabeth.[35] As for the existing arrears Cranfield, now lord treasurer of England, calculated that the officers and soldiers only deserved two-thirds of what was due to them, but he promised that they would receive the lesser amount in the very near future. However, in February 1623 the deputy treasurer for the army received orders only to pay the arrears of Sir Richard Moryson, the elderly Deputy President of Munster, an instruction which remained in force until Cranfield's downfall 14 months later for putting the maintenance of peace with Spain before loyalty to the Duke of Buckingham. By that time the Dublin government's inability to fill the gap between income and expenditure was clearer than ever, but King James typically played to the crowd by blaming Cranfield for the delay. He also hinted at a more generous settlement in the future given that the English parliament had recently voted money for a war in Europe. The taxes, however, were swallowed up by preparations for that war, and so no headway whatsoever had been made in reducing the arrears which by the time of his death in March 1625 had risen to over £100,000.[36]

There is no easy way of assessing the impact of being starved of pay on either the army as a fighting force or on its behaviour towards the civilian population. Judging its effectiveness against a major uprising, an invasion or an operation elsewhere in the King's domains is out of the question as it was not called upon to fulfil any of these

---

34 APC 37, pp.267, 291–92, 332, 339, 384; *ibid.* 38, pp.84–85, 212.
35 APC 37, p.267; *ibid.* 38, pp.212, 333; CSPI 1615–25, pp.391, 394–95.
36 APC 38, pp.333, 428; *ibid.* 39, p.262.

functions during St. John's six years as lord deputy.[37] But that is not to say that the horse and foot spent their entire time on garrison duty. Breaches of law and order by small gangs of Irish swordsmen broke out occasionally in scattered localities, but they did not require the deployment of any more than a couple of companies of foot accompanied by a few soldiers on horseback. The letters of s St. John and Falkland to the Privy Council contain several reports of guerrillas killed or brought to trial and executed, but they did not claim to have nipped a larger uprising in the bud as Chichester had done in 1614. The raiding parties sallying forth and then fading back into the woods, bogs and mountains with their plunder were small and are probably best seen as brigands or men driven by hunger into poaching or cattle rustling rather than as freedom fighters. Nevertheless it was difficult for army units to hunt them down, and as the Dublin government freely admitted, their successes owed more to informers in the Catholic community than to the soldiers' perseverance and scouting skills.[38]

Historians therefore have to rely on words rather than deeds, but in the circumstances of early seventeenth-century Ireland these should not be accepted at face value. In their struggle with the Privy Council over the financing of the standing army St. John and his government describing its current state in the blackest terms was the strongest card in their hand, and it did not end with his return to England. A letter written to the Privy Council in September 1622 by Henry Cary, Viscount Falkland, his successor, claimed that the army's morale had improved in the expectation that him like Docwra several years before he would be bringing substantial funds with him, but it fell to rock bottom when he arrived empty-handed. As a consequence, some officers had refused to muster when ordered, and some of the rank and file were ready to disband whilst others had made their way to Dublin where they were likely to make their feelings known by demonstrations or worse.

It is of course possible that as a new arrival Falkland was merely repeating what his minsters and senior commanders told him, but this was almost certainly not the case as his correspondence with the Privy Council over the next 18 months included several statements to the same effect.[39] Such was the army's discontent that if ordered to assemble to meet an internal or external threat he would not expect more than a few hundred to arrive at the rendezvous and their physical appearance would be such as to make them a laughing stock. He also reported on the extreme difficulty his predecessor had faced in getting together a force 150 or so strong to restore order in County Leix where hundreds of the Moore sept had settled without permission. The reason he cited was lack of ready cash to equip the force rather than failure to

---

37 Stevenson, *Highland Warrior*, pp.48–54.
38 CSPI 1615–25, pp.126, 146–47, 249–50, 262–63, 267.
39 CSPI 1615–25, pp.394, 396, 398, 423, 474, 476, 485, 495.

obey orders, but the words he used nevertheless left open the possibility that the units chosen had refused to march unless they received some pay.[40]

The second consequence of the army not receiving its money pay on time was that it would take matters into its own hands and force civilians to provide it with ready cash and food which would drive them into the arms of the Catholic extremists.[41] St. John had vigorously argued that this stage had not yet been reached, and there is no sign of it in documents that survive in English archives for the final years of King James's reign, but some insight into how times were changing can be obtained by comparing the grievances against the army presented to Sir Arthur Chichester in 1613 discussed in Chapter 3 with those presented to the new King Charles I in 1625 and 1628.[42]

The 1625 document seemed to confirm St. John's assessment in that only one of the 15 headings concerned the misdemeanours of the army, and that was narrowly focused on bailiff-type activities such as collecting debts owed to the King. But this is not altogether surprising. The preamble and the other headings show quite clearly that it tied up with the expectations of the Old English landowning elite of the Pale that they would be called upon to play their part in the trained bands on the English model a proposal first suggested almost 20 years earlier which had been dusted down in the early 1620 with an eye to reducing the size of the standing army and thus saving money. The Privy Council was ready to give its approval to the scheme, but Viscount Wilmot, the most senior army officer serving in Ireland at the time, declared it to be too dangerous as it would provide Catholics with weapons and with training in their use.[43]

The 1628 document clearly represented the grievances of a much larger swathe of the population of Ireland. There were over 50 headings of which seven related directly to the army. Some were repeats of those addressed to Chichester in 1613, but there were two significant differences. Billeting was a new grievance, but this almost certainly stemmed from the 18 or so months when several thousand soldiers belonging to the English army were quartered in Ireland between an unsuccessful attack on Cadiz in 1625 and the more disastrous first attempt to relieve La Rochelle almost two years later. The second new grievance, however, clearly relates to the standing army. Referring to the committing of many felonies, abuses and extortions 'by the

---

40   CSPI 1615–25, p.398.
41   CSPI 1615–25, pp.376, 423, 476. The furthest he went in that direction was to suggest that if no treasure arrived by the due date he would not be surprised if the soldiers turned on the civilian population for their sustenance: *ibid.* 1615–25, p.378.
42   CSPI 1611–14, pp.413–17, 421–22, 433, 437–41; APC 40, pp.173–77; *ibid.* 43, pp.401–03, 416, 420.
43   CSPI 1625–32, p.193. Wilmot's advice on the defence of Ireland against a Spanish invasion is undated but assigned by the editor of the Calendar to 1626. I prefer 1624 or 1625 as there is no mention of the large number troops of the English army returning from the Cadiz expedition that were quartered in Ireland between December 1625 and the summer of 1627.

army already established' it asked for offenders to be prosecuted in the civil courts of law rather than presumably by courts martial, and without captains of horse and foot being present in the court room. The Privy Council on the King's behalf agreed that this type of intimidation should not continue thus accepting that there was some truth in the allegation.[44]

A hundred years after the event Thomas Carte in his biography of James Butler, Duke of Ormond, shed new light on the experience of the standing army in the early 1620s by drawing a distinction between the troops and companies commanded by Dublin government ministers, the heads of the legal profession and great landowners on the one hand, and those commanded by officers who were captains and nothing else on the other. The former were too concerned with other matters to pay much attention to their military commands and did nothing to train their troops. Also, as they were all guilty of the same neglect, they had a shared interest in not drawing attention to it, but they found money to pay their men by forgoing the rents they owed the Crown for land they had acquired in the plantations. Nevertheless, they only gave their soldiers part of what they should have received. The rest they pocketed. The latter, on the other hand, had no way of paying their men and were forced to turn a blind eye to plundering. Moreover, throughout the army soldiers took on civilian roles to make ends meet. The elite's soldiers became their captains' servants, or leased land from them and became farmers, whilst those belonging to units commanded by the remainder turned to labouring to make ends meet or to the crafts they had practiced before being pressed into the army.[45]

The extent to which Carte was describing the realities of military life in Ireland in the latter part of James I's reign is impossible to ascertain given his High Tory agenda described elsewhere, which would have been assisted by portraying the state of the army Ormond and his patron Viscount Wentworth inherited in the darkest possible colours The skills' portfolio of the impressed men, however, suggest that they would have found no difficulty in obtaining employment in the burgeoning Irish economy of the latter part of King James's reign. Nevertheless, it is worth mentioning that a survey commissioned by the English Privy Council discovered that soldiers in the company commanded by Sir John Vaughan, who was not one of the leaders of the New English elite, lived with their families in hovels under the walls of Derry with the poorest of the poor.[46]

---

44 APC 43, pp.401–20. Like the 1613 list of grievances it was a precursor to the meeting of an Irish parliament, which on this occasion did not take place. For the circumstances see Chapter 6.
45 T. Carte, *The Life of James Duke of Ormond*, 6 vols (Oxford: University Press, 1851) i, pp.91–93.
46 APC 30, p.430; CSPI 1615–25, p.367.

5

European Entanglements

In the Dublin government's attempts to defend the traditional way of funding the standing army the principal weakness was that the country was at peace and had not been faced with the threat of an invasion or a major uprising for almost 20 years. This underpinned the King's determination that Ireland should respond to the effects of his reign,[1] but from mid 1622 onwards, however, the Catholic population was showing signs of restlessness driven partly by the creeping menace of plantations as they were extended from Ulster to other parts of the island, but of greater significance was optimism that changes for the better were just around the corner.

Negotiations for the marriage of the Prince of Wales to a Spanish Habsburg princess, which had blown hot and cold for some years, seemed finally to be heading for a successful conclusion. King James hoped to receive a large dowry that would have a beneficial effect on his straitened finances, and also to secure the peaceful return of his son-in-law Frederick's ancestral lands. Having contrived as a Protestant to get himself elected king of Bohemia, which had been ruled by the Austrian Habsburgs for the past hundred years, he had been booted out by Catholic forces after a reign of less than a year, and then dispossessed of his ancestral possessions in the Rhineland by an army largely comprised of Spanish troops.

Correspondents living on the Continent and returning exiles, both ecclesiastical and lay, raised expectations in Ireland that the terms of the marriage treaty would include some form of religious toleration as well as Catholics being permitted a share in the government of the country,[2] but the enthusiasm expressed by the Spanish ambassador Count Gondomar that raised the English king's hopes for the marriage were not shared by his royal master. James's response was to try and expedite matters by abandoning a constant in his relationships with foreign powers namely refusing

---

1 APC 39, pp.156–7. For an earlier pronouncement see CSPI 1615–25, p.94.
2 A group of Catholic Old English peers had gone so far as to urge the Spanish king not to agree to the marriage treaty if James would not allow religious toleration in Ireland: Lenihan, *Consolidating Conquest*, p.72.

requests by officers serving in Catholic armies on the Continent to recruit volunteers in Ireland. This was a timely concession. The Spanish king needed to expand his army in the Low Countries as the twelve-year truce with the Dutch had just expired. It was also for James the final throw of this die. He had already allowed the Earl of Argyll and Lord Vaux to raise 8,000 men in Scotland and England respectively to assist 'a foreign prince he was in league with … his dear brother the King of Spain', but in Ireland allowing troops to be raised to support international Roman Catholicism was clearly a much greater risk to security than in James's other two kingdoms.[3]

Without consulting the Privy Council or the government in Dublin James gave permission for four captains in Spanish service, Patrick O'Donnell, Walter Delafoyd, John Maguire and Charles O'Neill, to travel to Ireland to raise companies of foot. They began recruiting soon after 1 June 1622 having shown their authorisation to Sir Adam Loftus and Lord Powerscourt, the lords justices who governed Ireland in the interregnum between St. John's departure and Falkland's arrival.[4] They did not dare stop them doing so as the officers had the King's mandate, but when letters explaining reasons for the change in policy concerning recruiting arrived three weeks or so later they wrote a well-argued but tactful response, in which they listed the precautions they had taken to avoid trouble, whilst at the same time suggesting further measures that would require royal approval.

In the first place they felt sure that the King would follow their advice and send Maguire and O'Neill packing as he had been unaware that they were grandsons of the traitor Tyrone. Second, no arrangement had been made for the captains and their recruits to leave Ireland with all possible speed despite the fact that the more time they spent there the more likely were they deliberately or intentionally to unsettle the Catholic community. Third, the King had not placed a ceiling on the number of men they were allowed to enlist. If he did not do so, they might raise a body of men that was too large for the standing army to suppress in the event of trouble. Moreover, the rank and file should not be dismissed as raw recruits and therefore of little consequence. Many would have seen military service earlier in their lives and would be well aware of the shortcomings of the standing army. All they needed was arms to become a formidable fighting force, and with good luck they would be able to supply themselves with weapons and gunpowder by surprising a garrison or two. Thus there was a risk that if nothing was done to restrain them Tyrone's grandchildren might bring about the kind of regime change the Earl had planned and failed to achieve in the final years of Queen Elizabeth's reign.[5]

The Privy Council accepted that Tyrone's descendants should be denied the opportunity to raise men in Ireland. It also approved the measures the lord justices had taken to reduce the risk to security, such as requiring the captains to spread their

3   CSPD 1623–25, pp.365, 378; APC 38, p.233.
4   APC 38, p.233.
5   CSPI 1615–25, pp.360, 363.

operations widely across the country rather than in areas with which they or their families had previously been associated, and to march the recruits to coast in bodies no larger than five. However, it was unable to persuade the King to place a limit on the number of men the captains were allowed to raise. In addition, the lord justices did nothing to force Tyrone's grandsons to leave Ireland, possibly for fear that doing so when recruiting was in full swing would result in a level of public disorder that the standing army would find difficult if not impossible to subdue.

Subsequently the lord justices accused Maguire of signing up the children of prominent landowners and merchants not to serve in the King of Spain's army but to enable them to complete their education in universities and seminaries in Catholic Europe. The Privy Council ordered them to stop him as it was against the law, but seemingly the Dublin government had qualms about doing so as it was making the same complaint six months later when the captains were about to set sail.[6]

In the autumn there was a new concern. The lord justices had expected that the recruiting operation would be over quickly and by the end of September the captains appeared to be close to completing their task, but most were dragging their feet when it came to leaving the country with their recruits. Instead they seemed happy to remain until the spring, which suggested that their real purpose in coming to Ireland was not to obtain reinforcements for their master's forces in Europe but to provide the ground for an insurrection. The new lord deputy Lord Falkland, who had just arrived, informed the Privy Council that he had responded judiciously. Rather than using the standing army units to threaten the captains in their scattered recruiting areas he had commanded them to order their men to rendezvous in the vicinity of Dublin, which was to be their port of embarkation. Once there it would be easy enough to keep an eye on them with a brigade of the standing army that was not large enough to be seen as a threat or a provocation but not too small as to be unable to take decisive action against them at the first sign of trouble.[7]

In January 1623 Falkland reported that all but one of the companies had left the country without incident.[8] However, the effects of another action on James's part aimed at easing the path towards the Spanish marriage was to cause greater concern. The Lord Deputy, prompted by the government he had inherited, made up his mind to improve the security situation by ordering Catholic priests to leave Ireland. He also set about enforcing his right to fine Catholics for not attending an Anglican church service on Sundays in order to raise money to pay the standing army's current wages. However, six months after giving the go-ahead for collecting recusancy fines, King James came round to seeing this as an obstacle to the successful conclusion of the

---

6   APC 38, pp.287, 331; CSPI 1615–25, pp.393–94. The Privy Council's first letter is a reply to a letter or letters from the lord justices that no longer survive which clearly went into more detail about their fears and their subsequent actions.
7   CSPI 1615–25, pp.393–94, 396.
8   CSPI 1615–25, pp.398, 423, 428.

marriage negotiations and told him to stop. Such a slap in the face for the defenders of English hegemony was seen by the Catholic population as a sign of things to come and they reacted accordingly. By the autumn of 1623 mass was being celebrated in public; Catholic sermons preached in the open air were attracting thousands of people; and Catholics living in corporate town were claiming the right to serve as mayors. Such a surge in confidence on the part of the Irish and the Old English was also encouraged by rumours that negotiations over the marriage were very close to reaching a successful conclusion or had already done so, and there was nothing the Lord Deputy dare do about it for fear of offending the King and Buckingham – by then a duke – to whom he owed his high office.[9] However, having visited Spain to try and expedite matters, the Prince of Wales and the Duke changed their minds probably before leaving for home. Despite agreeing with gritted teeth that the children of the marriage would be brought up as Catholics until the age of 13 knowing how badly this would be taken back in England, there was no commensurate guarantee that Spain would ensure that the Elector Palatine regained the territory in Germany that he had lost because of his Bohemian adventure.[10]

When news of this setback reached Ireland, it was not quite the end of the matter insofar as the hopes of the Catholics were concerned, as King James did not finally give up hope of the Spanish marriage until after the New Year. As late as 17 February 1624 the Privy Council reminded the Lord Deputy that the King's instruction to show leniency towards Roman Catholics remained in force, though he was to suppress tumultuous and disorderly proceedings.[11] When expectations were finally dashed a few days later, however, an insurrection fuelled by disappointed hopes failed to materialise. Nevertheless, the sea change in international relations that followed soon afterwards caused the security of Ireland to rise to the top of the political agenda in both London and Dublin.

The breakdown of negotiations between two royal families over a marriage treaty rarely had serious consequences, but in this case it did. First, James had been hoodwinked into abandoning his rightful role as the leader of Protestant Europe by the Spanish ambassador's hints that the dowry brought by the bride would solve his financial problems for once and for all. Diplomacy having failed his only hope of restoring his son-in-law to his rightful inheritance was to use force. However, the King remained a reluctant warmonger, and focused his military planning on Germany in the hope that this would not involve open conflict with Spain. Unlike his son and his leading minister he was totally opposed to a multi-theatre war on land and sea like that fought in the last years of Queen Elizabeth's reign.

9   APC 38, p.370; CSPD 1623–25, pp.423, 428, 432–33, 454–55, 473.
10   Richard Cust, *Charles I: A Political Life* (Harlow: Pearson Longman, 2005), pp.31–36.
11   APC 38, p.178.

Second, public opinion in England was ripe for another armed conflict with Spain as shown by the joyous celebrations on the safe return of the Prince and the Duke and the aggressive mood in the English parliament which James summoned in February 1624 to advise him on how to proceed regarding the Palatinate.[12] This is not surprising. The behaviour of the Catholic forces in Germany and Bohemia and the Spanish king's generals' vigorous conduct of the war against the Dutch, which had resumed in 1621, looked like the beginning of a new attempt at imposing Catholic hegemony on the rest of Christian Europe. Bedazzled by the myth that England had brought the first attempt to a halt by its victory in the Armada War James's subjects saw it as the country's duty to go to the defence of lesser Protestant powers on the Continent, but there was a strong feeling in Parliament that success was most easily achieved not by a campaign in Germany but by using the navy to prevent the arrival in Europe of silver from the New World without which the military and strategic plans of Spain and its allies would necessarily grind to a halt.

Taking advantage of the national mood, Prince Charles, who had felt humiliated by his treatment in Madrid and was determined as a matter of honour to defend the rights of his sister and her husband, persuaded Parliament with Buckingham's wholehearted support to vote taxes for a Protestant crusade. They also encouraged it to bring about the downfall of Lord Treasurer Cranfield, the leader of the pro-Spanish faction in the English government, on a charge of financial malpractice.[13] His disgrace gave great satisfaction to Lord Falkland, who had been humiliated by commissioners answerable to Cranfield, who had undermined his authority in many spheres of government. It was also good news to Lords Carew, Chichester and Grandison, who were now living at court, and who with their wealth of experience dominated the new sub-committee of the Privy Council entrusted with putting James's three kingdoms onto a war footing.[14]

For the three distinguished veterans of the Nine Years' War and the soldiers and administrators in Ireland charged with maintaining the Protestant hegemony there, the fear that King Philip IV would respond in the same way as his father had done 25 years earlier and much more promptly if King James's hope for a limited war in Germany was frustrated by enthusiasm in England for a naval war with Spain. The threat to the flow of bullion from the New World was now much greater than in the 1590s because of the increase in the size of the Dutch fleet, which would doubtless undertake joint operations with the English aimed at intercepting the ships carrying it to Europe. However, by landing troops in Ireland and inciting a nationwide insurrection the Spanish king would force King James to starve his navy of resources

---

12   Journal of the House of Lords (JHL) iii, pp.209–10, 235–66, 244–45.
13   Cust, *Charles I*, pp.31, 36–39.
14   CSPI 1615–25, pp.511–14, 570; APC 38, pp.371–72. For their membership of the Council of War see APC 39, pp.1–2; CSPD 1625–26, p.9. One of the charges against Cranfield was that he had neglected Ireland: CSPD 1623–25, pp.216–19.

thus hamstringing preparations to intercept the treasure fleet before it docked at its home port of Cadiz.

In so far as the defence of Ireland against a possible Spanish invasion was concerned the sub-committee's priority was strengthening the standing army. On 6 July 1624 it advised the King that a near trebling in size from 1,350 foot and 170 horse to 3,600 foot and 400 horse was imperative with the foot being raised in the English counties by impressment and the horse by recruiting volunteers, but it was not until 24 November that James gave orders for impressment to begin, and it took another four months for the foot soldiers to begin crossing the Irish Sea.[15] The limited evidence about the cavalry that survives tells a similar story: a notice about transportation sent to the ports of the west coast of England in December 1624; authority for treasure to be sent to Ireland to pay the wages of the newly levied horse and foot in mid March 1625; a suggestion that some of the horse may have been raised in Ireland but with one new troop certainly shipped there from England as their captain paid for it.[16]

The long delays between authorisation and implementation and between implementation and embarkation were not because impressing men for service overseas was something new that was encountering teething problems.[17] Admittedly defending Ireland was not the only call on England's surplus male population in 1624, and the 12,000 or so men the King considered necessary for regaining his son-in-law's lost lands could not be provided by London and the counties of the east and the south alone thus causing midland and western counties to be commandeered.[18] Nevertheless the numbers required from the counties charged with raising men for Ireland were not unrealistic, as shown by correspondence between the governments in London and Dublin. Indeed in April the Lord Lieutenant of Lancashire successfully raised several hundred more than the King had ordered to replace men lost at sea.[19] Shipping them to Ireland was also unproblematic. There is no evidence that the west coast ports from Liverpool to Barnstaple had insufficient vessels to perform the task at what was not exactly short notice.[20]

Finally, although the military adventure on the Continent took precedence over sending troops to Ireland, with the former leaving England at the end of January

15   APC 38, p.496; CSPI 1615–25, pp.541, 549; *ibid.* 1647–60, p.136.
16   APC 39, p.496; CSPI 1625–32, pp 541, 549; *ibid.*, 1647–60, p.136.
17   Earlier in the reign the lord lieutenants in Wales, the Midlands and the counties facing the Irish Sea from Cornwall to Cumberland had raised foot soldiers by that method to fill up the ranks of the standing army.
18   CSPI 1615–25, pp.511–12.
19   The disaster is discussed at the beginning of Chapter 6.
20   Orders for shipping to transport the recruits and their equipment were issued to the ports concerned by the Privy Council on 18 and 25 February. The troops were to be at the ports by 20 March and they had landed in Ireland within a very few weeks: APC 38, pp.470–73, 485.

and the latter two months later, the two operations appear not to have got in one another's way apart from in Devonshire, which uniquely was charged with raising men for both.[21] There is also no evidence that the demand for captains to command companies in the 10 regiments of foot raised for Germany left insufficient applicants for units to serve in Ireland.[22]

The ostensible reason for the slowness in sending soldiers overseas was lack of funds as on this occasion supplying the infantry with uniforms and paying for their maintenance until they left the country was the responsibility of central government not the counties that raised them. As usual revenue from the taxes approved by Parliament in the spring was slow to come into the body ordered to receive it. The lord lieutenants were therefore under strict orders not to begin the process of impressment until they heard from the Privy Council that money was available.[23] This, however, was almost certainly an excuse as in previous wars London merchants and financiers regarded parliamentary consent to the raising of a new tax as a sufficient security for lending the Crown money. Considerations both military and political bore a greater responsibility for the delay.[24]

First, there was a difference of opinion amongst the King's advisers as to how the impressed men were to be incorporated into the standing army. Should they be assigned to existing companies or to units raised from scratch? It can be inferred from the proposals emanating from the Council of War that it favoured new units, but others quickly pointed out that increasing the number of companies from 27 to 71 would have important consequences for a government strapped for cash.[25] Insofar as pay for the private soldiers was concerned, there was nothing to choose between the two options, but creating so many new units would entail the commissioning of well over 100 additional captains, lieutenants, and ensigns, which would clearly have a significant effect on the cost of fighting the war.[26]

Incorporating the recruits into existing units would also speed up the process of changing civilians into soldiers as they would be trained in army discipline, drill and fighting with pike and shot alongside serving soldiers and by serving commissioned and non-commissioned officers. Admittedly if the new formations were commanded by former serving officers, they might lag less far behind the older units than if they were commanded by gentlemen volunteers with friends at Court, and it was surely this consideration that lay behind Lord Chichester's plea that military experience

21   CSPD 1623–25, pp.378, 384; APC 38, pp.469–74; Spring, *First British Army*, p.143.
22   At least 60 names were proposed for command of companies in Ireland by one supplicant and about half of them had recent military experience: CSPI 1615–25, pp.551, 555–56; *ibid.* 1647–60, p.46–47 but not those on pp.48–49 who were men who wished to serve in the Palatinate.
23   APC 38, pp.352, 371–72; CSPI 1615–25, pp.511, 513.
24   APC 38, pp.371–72, 403, 440–41, 471.
25   This issue was raised in early July: CSPI 1615–25, p.517.
26   These figures are derived from Spring, *First British Army*, pp.255–56.

rather than importunity should be the prime consideration in choosing commanders to serve in Ireland.[27] However, employing former officers would not necessarily be a panacea. Although there were many alive in 1624 who had fought in Elizabeth's wars in France, the Netherlands and Ireland, this was no guarantee that those who applied were still fit for active service and motivated by a late burst of enthusiasm for army life rather than by the financial rewards of commanding a company. Moreover, even if an officer was fit and genuinely keen on returning to his former career, his military knowledge might well be 20 years out of date.

In early August 1624 the King informed the Privy Council that he had decided on a compromise. He accepted the advice that the standing army should be increased from 1,350 foot and 200 or so horse to 3,600 foot and 400 horse. There were to be nine new companies of foot and the 27 companies in the standing army were to be increased in size from 50 to 100 officers and men.[28] There was a similar compromise with the horse, but this was not agreed until 10 January 1625. The six existing troops were to be doubled in size from 25 to 50 officers and men, and 25 were to be added to Falkland's troop of 25 which had probably been raised by top-slicing the others. In addition a new troop 25 strong was to be created for Lord Cromwell.[29]

But James's declaration about the infantry was not the end of the story. The English Privy Council and the Dublin government expected that it would be quickly followed by the naming of captains to command the new companies and troops, but this was to prove a protracted and very frustrating process, and not principally because of the large number of applicants. Although numerous names were put forward for command of the companies of foot, almost all came in a rush at the very end of the selection process.[30]

The fact of the matter was that King James was dragging his feet because he still had hopes of avoiding outright war with Spain, but if he sent reinforcements to Ireland it would suggest that he was preparing for one. Further evidence of his not wanting to alarm the Spanish king is also to be found in his decision that the fleet should not put to sea in 1624, which Richard Cust has seen as effectively crippling the war effort.[31] Another reason, however, may have been a struggle between the King on the one hand and his son and the Duke on the other over the control of military patronage.

27 CSPD 1623–25, p.334.
28 CSPD 1623–25, pp.322, 360, 363.
29 CSPI 1615–25, p.555.
30 CSPD 1623–25, p.308; CSPI 1615–25, pp.555–56. Two of the lists were compiled in early January 1625. The third list is not dated but the editor of the Calendar suggests December: *ibid.*, 1615–25, pp.551–52; *ibid.*, 1647–60, p.50. The editor of the 1625 addenda in the 1647–60 volume ascribes several earlier lists to the army in Ireland, but there is enough internal evidence to show that they comprised applicants for commissions in the army being raised to reconquer the Palatinate. For the Palatinate army list see Spring, *First British Army*, pp.220–24.
31 Cust, *Charles I*, p.42.

The right of nominating new captains for service in Ireland was something that James had jealously guarded throughout his reign with only minor concessions being made following O'Doherty's rebellion. Buckingham and Prince Charles, however, were keen to control appointments for no better reason, it seems, than a desire to extend the boundary of their patronage still further, which was already very extensive through Buckingham's position as lord high admiral.

The first move came from Lord Deputy Falkland, who owed his appointment to the Duke and therefore clearly owed him a favour.[32] On 17 July, three weeks before James informed the Privy Council how many new companies and troops were to be raised for service in Ireland, he asked the King's permission to nominate the captains via correspondence with Lord Conway, the senior secretary of state. James was not willing to delegate but instead of a rebuke, which would have been very appropriate in the circumstances, he brought Falkland into the selection process following in the spirit of the guidelines he had put in place after the sack of Derry in 1608.[33]

In late September the King sent the Lord Deputy a list of nine names five of whom eventually received commissions to command the companies destined for Ireland.[34] The Lord Deputy's response does not survive, but after this display of royal clemency he took the unwise step of appointing his eldest son Lucius as captain of a company in the standing army without first asking for royal approval.[35] To make matters worse the young man may have been only 15 years of age and without any military experience, and he was to follow in the footsteps of Sir Fulk Conway, a distinguished veteran of the Nine Years' War, who had just died. To cap it all Conway had been the secretary of state's brother, who later correspondence suggests was hoping to succeed him.

Realising that he had made a very serious faux pas and feeling that the King might become personally involved Falkland apologised profusely for his earlier request for the right to nominate all the new captains, his excuse being that he had acted on the word of Lord Chichester and Lord Treasurer Cranfield that the King would not be averse to delegation. It was to no avail. He had presumed too much for the second time in six months and felt the heat of the King's displeasure. Young Lucius's appointment, which required a royal commission before it became effective, was put on hold. Three months later the company was still being described in the minutes of the Privy Council as formerly Sir Fulk Conway's, but in due course the Prince of

32 Cust, *Charles I*, pp.42–44. The best direct evidence of a struggle over appointments in the companies going to Ireland is in a letter written by Lord Conway, the senior secretary of state. In it he asserts that the dispute was between the King and Prince Charles, but this is scarcely surprising as the person to whom he was writing was the Duke of Buckingham: CSPD 1623–25, p.400.
33 CSPI 1615–25, pp.520, 539, 541, 548.
34 CSPI 1615–25, p.524. They were Sir Faithful Fortescue, Sir Arthur Tyringham, Lord Dunkellin, and captains Charles Price and Edward Thynne.
35 CSPI 1615–25, p.548.

Wales, who succeeded his father as king in late March, signed Lucius's commission presumably as Falkland was one of Buckingham's 'creatures'.[36]

James made it known that Falkland was out of favour in another way. Although the Lord Deputy was commander of the standing army by virtue of being lord deputy, the King kept him in ignorance of almost every decision made about putting Ireland on a war footing. His letters were not discussed in the Privy Council; and he received no orders concerning the army between June 1624 and the King's death apart one written in February requiring him to see that the old and the new companies were treated equally in terms of pay.[37] Falkland made his disappointment known, but experienced courtier as he was he sought to build bridges and scotch rumours that he might be dismissed by setting his sights on obtaining a minor mark of royal favour, namely permission to decide the order in which the forts of the south coast were to be repaired.[38] He did not get a reply and it was no use asking for Buckingham's support as he too was out of favour for speaking in support of a naval war with Spain.[39]

As autumn passed into winter the *impasse* over the officers for Ireland dragged on. The Privy Council made its concern known to the King, whilst the Dublin government worried that the reinforcements would be arriving in Ireland with nobody to command them.[40] The final blow in the fight with Buckingham and Charles came in December with James's rejection of all but one of the names put forward by the gentlemen of the bedchamber, a group notorious for being Buckingham's creatures.[41] However, the storm finally blew itself out early in the new year two months before James's death in what looks remarkably like a compromise rather than a collapse of will on the King's part as his health deteriorated.[42] The biggest plum of all, however, fell to Buckingham whose half-brother Sir Edward Villiers was created Lord President of Munster with a company and a troop under his command, the Earl of Thomond having died late in the previous year.[43]

There is insufficient evidence to identify who amongst the new captains was a king's man and who was favoured by Charles and Buckingham, but there was at least one who was acceptable to all parties, namely Charles Price who was one of Buckingham's clients and also named in the list the King sent to the Lord Deputy in September, but they were a mixed bunch insofar as their background and military experience

---

36 APC 38, p.473. James's sensitivity about commissions in the standing army is apparent in another bid for vacant captaincy made six weeks earlier: CSPD 1623–5, p.316.
37 The date when the new king signed the commission is not known as no army list survives for the period March 1625 to August 1629, but Lucius lost his company when his father left Ireland in virtual disgrace.
38 CSPI 1615–25, pp.484, 548, 570.
39 Cust, *Charles I*, p.42.
40 CSPI 1615–25, pp.541, 548, 549, 551; CSPD 1623–25, p.400; APC 38, p.403.
41 CSPI 1615–25, pp.555–56; Cust, *Charles I*, pp.9, 37.
42 CSPI 1615–25, p.541; *ibid*. 1647–60, p.48; APC 39, p.403.
43 CSPI 1615–25, p.568.

were concerned. The officers commanding the new troops of cavalry as stated above were Falkland himself and Sir Thomas Stafford, the illegitimate son of George Lord Carew, lord president of Munster under Lord Mountjoy. Falkland and Stafford may have briefly held commands in Ireland in the Nine Years' War, but Falkland is best seen as courtier and Stafford as a bureaucrat who had served for many years as an official in the royal armoury and probably owed his captaincy to his father's influence as a member of the Council of War.[44]

Of the new captains of foot three, Sir William St. Leger, Sir John Ogle and Sir Robert Yaxley, had had lengthy experience serving in the English forces in the Netherland. Of the remainder Charles Price had probably had some direct military experience as he was described as Captain Price well before receiving his commission in the standing army, though he could have been a train band officer. Sir Arthur Tyringham, however, was probably not one of the Duke's followers but instead a disappointed courtier with little or no military experience who was intent on changing his career. Neither treated their new command as a sinecure as both were in the good books of the reforming Lord Deputy Thomas Wentworth in the 1630s.[45] The sixth and seventh companies look like examples of inappropriate exercise of patronage. Lord Dunkellin was the son of the Catholic Earl of Clanricarde, who had loyally served Elizabeth and James first as a senior army commander and then as lord president of Connaught. The other was Richard Preston, a long-standing Scottish favourite of King James, who had recently been granted the prestigious Irish title of Earl of Desmond.

The eighth captain was Sir Faithful Fortescue, the nephew of Lord Chichester, who had commanded the castle at Carrickfergus for the past 10 years or so, and on whose behalf Chichester had made a special plea for a captaincy in a letter written to Lord Conway asking him to have a word in Buckingham's ear.[46] Nothing is presently known about the ninth captain, Edward Thynne, except that he had not served in Ireland as a company commander under either Elizabeth or James and was not a close relative of the Longleat family, but as with Charles Price the fact that he was described as Captain Thynne before receiving his commission shows that he had had at least some military experience at an appropriate level.[47]

---

44   CSPD 1623–25, pp.316, 454, 478, 486; CSPI 1615–25, p.555; *ibid.* 1647–60, pp.46, 136. Lord Cromwell had declined the offer of a troop, presumably because of his commitment to the Palatine expedition: Spring, *First British Army*, p.221. For Stafford see Appendix IV.
45   Desmond was a Scottish courtier and favourite with no known military experience. He was also well over 50 years of age as his father had died in 1571. He was deprived of his company before February 1627 but then restored. He was still in command in April 1628 but died later in that year: CSPI 1625–32, pp.204, 326. For Tyringham's career as a courtier see <www.historyofparliamentonline.org>, House of Commons 1604–1629, Members' Biographies. See the website and the appendices for the subsequent military careers of Price and Tyringham and for Price's friendly relationship with Wentworth.
46   CSPD 1623–25, pp.334, 371; CSPI 1615–25, p.548.
47   CSPI 1615–25, p.524.

6

The Duke of Buckingham's Wars 1625–1628

The English recruits, ordered to be at their ports of embarkation by 20 March, duly converged on Chester, Liverpool, Bristol, Barnstaple and Milford Haven. Their shipment to Ireland was completed over the next three months marred by a major disaster, the foundering in April of five ships sailing from Liverpool to Carrickfergus each carrying 100 men impressed in the six of the seven counties of north-west and north-east England the exception being Yorkshire. Two managed to beach themselves on Anglesey but the rest sank in the open sea with the loss of over 300 lives.[1] They were quickly replaced by William Stanley, Earl of Derby, the Lord Lieutenant of Lancashire and Cheshire, who had raised by far the largest contingent, and by late September there were almost 3,700 officers and soldiers in Ireland with just over 100 temporarily absent and some 50 or so sick.[2] Two months later Falkland reported that he had five short of 4,000 men under arms.[3]

The Lord Deputy used this access of strength to prepare for an internal uprising, which he saw as being followed by a Spanish invasion rather than the other way round, reasoning that king Philip would readily send troops to aid a community already in revolt but be less keen in getting involved in 'blowing up a bubble not already stirred'.[4] Stationing himself at Kilbeggan, Lord Cromwell's house in the dead centre of Ireland, with a force of 200 foot and about 20 horse drawn from nearby garrisons to save expense he was well placed to put down the first signs of trouble and before it could spread. He was also training the foot twice a week so that they would be first rate soldiers by the time they returned home.[5] The bulk of his remaining infantry he kept in Ulster where most of the standing army units had been stationed from 1608 onwards keeping an eye on the former lands of the Twilight Earls and their leading

---

1 APC 39, pp.467–68. 473–74; *ibid.* 40, pp.20–22, 76; CSPD 1625–26, pp.3, 5, 8, 54.
2 CSPI 1625–32, pp.41–42; CSPD 1625–26, pp.8, 157.
3 CSPI 1625–32, p.50.
4 CSPI 1625–32, p.39.
5 CSPI 1625–32, pp.34–35.

supporters. This made good sense as it was there that the Irish army in exile, the regiment in the Spanish Netherlands commanded by Tyrone's son, was likely to try to land

The south coast of Ireland was the other major area of concern, as it was a closer destination for an attack coming from Spain, and as mentioned above the Lord Deputy had every intention of using about a third of the new recruits to strengthen his garrisons there, Cork and Waterford being a particular concern given their behaviour in 1603. In the opinion of the old commanders advising the King it was essential to build citadels there capable of accommodating hundreds of men and bristling with artillery to deter the enemy, but Falkland had argued that starting work before the standing army was up to full strength would be too much of a provocation to the citizens given their past record. Instead he had proposed refurbishing Duncannon and Haulbowline, the small forts guarding the mouths to the estuaries that gave the two ports access to the sea, but this caused difficulties as the English government was reluctant to shoulder the cost. However, military engineers claimed that Haulbowline was poorly placed to bombard incoming troop transports, and that a new fort should be constructed closer to Cork on the foundations of one erected in the days of King John. As for the citadels Falkland's local military advisers favoured one that made use of a section of Waterford's town's walls, which would be unproblematic as the King had yet to re-issue the city's charter and was therefore at liberty to do what he wanted without fear of a legal challenge. Cork was a different matter altogether. The fort built overlooking the road to Kinsale in Queen Elizabeth's reign would be ideal, but it had been torn down in the riot that followed King James's accession. Houses and a lime kiln had then been built on the site by the citizens presumably using the stone and timber from which it had been constructed. The furious response from London was that Falkland should force them to pay for the cost of rebuilding it, but he appears to have considered such a course of action politically dangerous. Instead it was to be paid for out of government income and a loan from the Earl of Cork. Work on the citadels was approved in June 1625 but did not begin on King John's fort not until six months later after the Privy Council had carefully examined a detailed plan of the site and totted up the cost.[6]

Weapons were apparently not a major issue insofar as the foot were concerned. The new companies and the recruits for the existing companies would be supplied with pikes and calivers before leaving England but 300 additional firearms would be much appreciated as a reserve, but many more would be required if, as planned, the English and Scottish settlers in Ulster were to be trained in their use. Gunpowder was another matter. There was sufficient in the magazines for peacetime purposes but not for war.

---

6   CSPI 1615–25, pp.512, 569–70; *ibid.* 1625–32, pp.2–3, 19, 28, 70–71, 80, 102; APC 40, p.274.

The Tower of London should therefore supply Dublin with several hundred additional barrels as a matter of urgency.[7]

Making sure that there were sufficient artillery pieces for offensive and defensive warfare was a serious concern. In Ulster uncertainties about whether the London companies or the English government was responsible for purchasing cannon meant that towns like Derry were under-provided, but elsewhere there seem to have been enough for the present needs. However, the 20 years of peace since the end of the Nine Years' War had taken their toll. The heavy wooden carriages essential for moving siege artillery around the country had rotted away, and there were similar problems with the cannon defending the forts and walled towns as the Earl of Thomond had discovered some years before. Many lacked the wooden frames needed for keeping them steady when they were fired, and gun platforms were sometimes not strong enough to support their weight.[8]

Pay, however, remained the most important issue, and one that would worsen as the army increased in size. Sir Henry Docwra had brought some pay with him for soldiers newly arrived from England, but there was no provision for their further supply, and no money for the old companies had arrived in the country since 1622 following the policy put in place by Lord Treasurer Cranfield despite the fact that he had been sacked in the meantime, but there was no sign of a change in government policy. The total cost of the armed forces would therefore have to be covered by the King's Irish revenues, which were totally inadequate for that purpose. All the Lord Deputy could do was turn a blind eye to the mounting arrears and order the various troops and companies to live off the land by requisitioning food in the places where they were quartered. It was also noted that some soldiers were using their initiative and making ends meet by working for their living. It is therefore scarcely surprising that Falkland feared that if forced to put together a field army to suppress a serious uprising or to deal with the threat of an invasion standing army soldiers might refuse to leave the places where they lived which afforded a modicum of financial security for themselves and their dependents.[9]

---

7 CSPI 1615–25, pp.510–12, 527, 529, 543, 548, 569–71; *ibid.* 1625–32, pp.26–28, 50, 52–53, 82–83.
8 CSPI 1615–25, pp.368, 379, 381, 527, 529; *ibid.* 1625–32, pp.28, 71, 79, 84; APC 40, pp.240–41.
9 APC 39, pp.495–96; CSPI 1625–32, pp.20, 26, 50–51, 450. A letter dated April 1625 in page 2 of the 1625–32 Calendar tells a different and even more dire story, but the contents show that it was written in early 1626 as it refers to soldiers who had taken part in the Cadiz expedition in the previous autumn. However, it does make clear that money to pay the new units had run out some months previously. A document from about the same time refers to soldiers as chiefly artificers and labourers, married and unmarried: CSPI 1647–60, p.317, whilst another shows that soldiers in garrison towns were better placed for finding casual employment or borrowing money than those stationed in forts: *ibid.* 1625–32, p.53.

The first invasion scare came in late October 1625. In a war with the King of Spain the United Provinces were the British King's ally, but relations were not as close as they had been in the Armada War. The Dutch were now strong enough to stand on their own feet militarily thanks to commercial success. Moreover. such success had brought them into conflict with English merchants in the Far East, the Baltic and the Mediterranean. Nevertheless, joint naval expeditions were mounted in the autumn of 1625, one against Dunkirk in the Archduchess Isabella's domains (her husband Albert having died in 1621), the other against Cadiz, Spain's principal port for trading with the New World.

Dunkirk's significance was that it was the base from which numerous privateers preyed on shipping passing through the Channel and the North Sea. The aim was to destroy the 'Dunkirkers' by blockading the port and then sending in fireships to force them to weigh anchor and sail straight into the maw of a Dutch fleet supported by English auxiliaries waiting just off the coast. But the weather intervened. On 13 October the allied ships were driven off station and badly damaged by a storm, thus setting the enemy free to go on the rampage. They immediately sailed off into the North Sea, and to the alarm of the English government intelligence from the Netherlands insisted that 22 ships carrying 400 or possibly 4,000 Spanish soldiers were heading for Ireland intent on landing on the shores of Loch Foyle.[10]

The Privy Council tried to warn Falkland of the danger he was in, but such were the delays in communicating between London and Dublin in times of bad weather that the news did not reach Ireland for almost a month. Once he heard the Lord Deputy reinforced the garrison at Derry with troops from the standing army supported by a company of foot and a troop of horse from Scotland, though the arrival of the latter was apparently on the initiative of their commander Sir Robert McLellan rather than in response to a government order. In his reply Falkland continued to show little confidence in the commitment of the forces under his command, but he was confident that the reason why the Dunkirkers had not arrived was that they had been scattered by a great storm that raged in the Atlantic from 19 to 21 November as they tried to round the north of Scotland.[11] But the truth of the matter was that there had never been a cause for concern. The Dunkirkers only had 12 ships at sea in the late autumn. These sailed no farther north than the coast of Northumberland where they had sent some weeks harassing fishing boats searching for herrings, a staple of the Dutch diet in the seventeenth century, but reliable intelligence indicated that all but one had returned to harbour by 20 November.[12]

Knowing that he would not be facing an invasion in 1625 Falkland ordered the standing army units to return to their home garrisons, but it was clear to him, his advisers in Ireland and the Council of War in London that even with the reinforcements

---

10   APC 40, pp.213–14; CSPI 1625–32, p.50; CSPD 1625–26, pp.125, 127.
11   CSPI 1625–32, pp.45, 50–51.
12   CSPD 1625–6, pp.140, 144, 148, 154.

he had received earlier in the year his troops had neither the numbers nor the morale to protect English hegemony in Ireland against all eventualities. Several plans for keeping Ireland safe in the future were put to the Privy Council or directly to the King during the first two years of the war with Spain. Those written by Sir James Perrott and Captain Thomas Chamberlain, showed sound knowledge of the problem but the solutions they proposed were unrealistic.[13] A third, written by Lord Wilmot, was thoughtful in terms of the dire strategic situation and the ways in which it should and should not be tackled. It has been ascribed to 1626 but was probably written between late 1624 and late 1625 or when Wilmot was commander-in-chief in Ireland three years later, as it makes no mention of the large number of so-called fleet soldiers returning from Cadiz, who were stationed in Ireland between December 1625 and August 1627.[14]

The most thoughtful proposal written in the form of a memorandum can be confidently dated to the winter of 1624–25.[15] Its principal point was that the plantation policy had so alienated many hitherto loyal Catholics that even if it was immediately brought to an end it would take some time for the damage to be repaired. In the meantime an army of between 5,000 and 6,000 foot and 500–600 horse was absolutely vital to protect Ireland against invasion. Superiority in mounted troops was easily attained and essential for containing the enemy as large numbers of horses could not be transported easily by sea, but if nothing was done and Spanish troops landed in any numbers, there was only one option. The lord deputy with no more than 2,000 foot and 200 horse under his command must shut himself up in a fortified port town and ensure that the harbour was kept open for reinforcements arriving from England.

There were also some more detailed recommendations concerning the army once it had been increased to the strength, namely arming some of the cavalry with carbines rather than pistols thus converting them into what in the seventeenth century were known as dragoons. Time was the essence if an uprising was to be put down before it got out of control, but infantry could not respond quickly enough whereas mounted troops armed as infantry could. However, to fight the Spanish most of the standing army horse must be rearmed with two pistols instead of a single pistol and a stout staff which were only suitable for dealing with mobs of poorly armed rioters. The writer also recommended the purchase of light field pieces like those currently in use in the

---

13 CSPI 1625–32, pp.46–51, 68–69, 187; *ibid.* 1647–60, pp.84–86.
14 CSPI 1625–32, p.193. 1624 seems the most likely as he refers specifically to the disarming of Catholics in England which was taking place at that time. There were also several proposals that only survive as abstracts one of which shows a very clear knowledge of the strengths and weaknesses of the governors of the forts manned by the standing army: CSPI 1625–32, pp.71–76.
15 *Ibid.* 1625–32, pp.46–48. It was endorsed as received on 11 November.

United Provinces to protect the general's quarters whilst on campaign and to harass the enemy if they were encamped or in retreat.[16]

The memorandum was not signed but members of the Council of War, officers serving in the standing army, and senior members of the Dublin government can be ruled out as they would have known that the army was already 4,000 strong. However, the writer was clearly somebody with considerable knowledge of the country and a goodly measure of military experience. The deep hostility towards the plantation policy points to a leading Catholic nobleman the prime candidate being Richard Bourke, Fifth Earl of Clanricarde, who had fought a successful campaign against plantations in that part of Connaught where his estates were situated. He had also served with great distinction at the battle of Kinsale, and subsequently as Lord President of Connaught, but had retired in 1616 and was spending his retirement in Surrey managing an estate belonging to his wife.[17] It is also significant that he was invited to a meeting with the King and other advisers to discuss Ireland's security on 29 or 30 October, and if my reasoning is correct, the memorandum was his reflection on the discussion that had taken place.[18] But all the buzz of activity concerning the defence of Ireland was to a large extent overtaken by events as the recommendation in all the reports that the army must be enlarged was about to be achieved albeit fortuitously but for an indeterminate length of time.

In addition to the 15,000 or so men impressed in the autumn and winter of 1624–5 to recapture the Palatinate and to strengthen the standing army in Ireland, 10 additional regiments of foot were raised in the following summer for an attack on Cadiz. The aim was to sack the town and destroy its shipping in a repeat of the success of the 1596 expedition commanded by Lord Howard of Effingham and the Earl of Essex, but also to capture the fleet carrying treasure from the New World which was fast approaching the shores of Europe. Both operations failed and to make matters worse a storm in the Bay of Biscay scattered the ships carrying the army back to England. In consequence part of least 50 companies of foot ended up landing on a stretch of coast between Waterford in the southeast to Killybegs Bay in the far northwest. The officers expected that their soldiers would quickly return to England, but they were to remain there for the next year and a half. The presence of so many more English soldiers in Ireland was however a mixed blessing for the Dublin government as it was now required to supply sustenance for a force well over three times the size of the peacetime standing army with no significant financial assistance from England.[19]

---

16 After the invasion crisis of October–November 1625 there was serious discussion as to whether Clanricarde should be ordered to return to Connaught, though his religion was seen as an issue: CSPD 1625–26, pp.45, 71.
17 CSPI 1625–32, p.144; Lenihan, *Consolidating Conquest*, p.72.
18 CSPI 1601–03, pp.267–69; *ibid.* 1603–06, p.105; *ibid.* 1625–32, p.71; CSPD 1625–26, p.133.
19 CSPI 1625–32, pp.194–95,.222.

The Lord Deputy could see confirmation of his anxieties in the months that followed the arrival of the 'fleet soldiers'. There were mutinies and the forcible plundering of civilians by the army units newly arrived in Ireland; attacks on troops and by troops in Cork; and a minor uprising in central Ireland that it took quite a time to suppress.[20] However, although there were intelligence reports in the late summer that military and naval forces assembling in Spain's Atlantic ports were destined for Ireland, King Philip was too busy elsewhere in Europe to launch an invasion in 1626. There was also some reassurance that the country's internal peace would continue following protestations of loyalty and promises of support for Ireland's defence from the Catholic aristocracy, but could they to be taken at their word?[21]

In September 1626 Charles I informed the Privy Council and the Dublin government of his plan for defending Ireland against a Spanish attack once the fleet soldiers had left. The army's wartime establishment was to be raised from 3,600 foot and 400 horse to 5,000 foot and 500 horse, and the entire expense was to be borne by Ireland with the Crown's existing subvention from its Irish sources of income such as customs duties being supplemented by nationwide tax that would fall on Protestants and Catholics alike.[22] At the same time the King accepted the justice of some of the grievances of his loyal Catholic subjects and responded by suggesting complete or partial solutions succinctly summed up as The Graces, which in commercial terms would also have benefited the New English.

Negotiations between Lord Falkland and an assembly or quasi-Parliament of the Irish nobility and gentry took place in Dublin in the months that followed, but finance proved a stumbling block with the representatives claiming that Ireland could not afford the sum required to bridge the gap between royal revenue and the cost of maintaining the enlarged army, whilst the Lord Deputy claimed that they were rich enough to do so because of the growth in the Irish economy since the end of the Nine Years' War. As an alternative the representatives suggested that the army should be reduced in size with the slack being taken up by trained bands in every county commanded by members of the Irish aristocracy both old and new. There was some support amongst Charles's advisers in England for such a militia in the Pale where the Old English were the principal landowners, but the New English in Ireland and senior officers in the standing army were horrified. As there were insufficient Protestants living in most districts to fill up their ranks, trained bands would provide Catholics with weapons and training in their use, and if a major insurrection broke out or the

20   CSPI 1625–32, pp.59–61, 88, 112–15, 118–20, 130, 132, 142, 144, 148–49, 155–56, 163, 169; APC 40, pp.392–93.
21   See for example CSPI 1625–32, pp.126, 142, 144, 202.
22   CSPI 1625–32, pp.130, 148–49, 156; APC 41, p.295.

Spaniards invaded in force, even the most loyal might come under intolerable pressure from priests and family to change their allegiance.[23]

The result was an impasse, and on 2 May 1627 Falkland broke off negotiations. A few days later before the news reached England a meeting of the Privy Council chaired by the King had showed that it too had lost patience at the lack of progress. After initially agreeing to wait a few days for a report from a panel of experts on Ireland it dismissed the assembly as unfit for purpose as the longer it lasted the more extreme became the demands of its members. Charles nevertheless was adamant that an army of 5,000 foot and 500 horse must be stationed in Ireland for its defence, and that the cost of maintaining must be met by the Dublin government alone. As it was obvious to all that his Irish revenues fell far short of being sufficient, Falkland was to hold secret talks with leading members of the Irish peerage and come up with a recommendation as to how the rest of the money, some two-thirds of the total, might be raised.[24]

The firmness of Charles's stand is in accordance with his usual behaviour in the face of opposition to his policies, but there was also a sense of urgency. In the late spring of 1627 England's military resources were being stretched to the limit and beyond. The King was committed to providing assistance to the Dutch and to his uncle the King of Denmark, who fighting the Habsburgs in support of the Elector Frederick and Elizabeth his sister, whilst he himself was still at war with Spain. Charles had also drifted into war with France from late 1626 onwards, and as a result was committed to mounting another very expensive amphibious operation in Europe, but this time without Dutch assistance. Its object was to support Protestants in the port of La Rochelle who were being besieged by an army commanded by the French king.[25]

Nobody was more aware of the extent and the burden of the King's wartime commitments than the Duke of Buckingham in his role as de facto military and naval supremo of Charles's three kingdoms. Running a war on several fronts could only be managed by tapping into new or dormant resources, and Ireland was the obvious place. Within a fortnight of the meeting that had terminated the negotiations with the assembly, the Privy Council ordered Ireland to provide soldiers for what was to be the first expedition to relieve La Rochelle. Half were to be veterans of the Cadiz expedition who had some experience of amphibious warfare, the rest volunteers from the population as a whole. Removing the fleet soldiers from Ireland had been under review for some time, but the second initiative was something new whose origins lay in a proposal made by Sir Ralph Bingley in March 1627 suggesting that two regiments each 1,000 strong could easily be raised in Ireland for the King's wars. It

---

23   CSPI 1625–32, pp.110, 193, 441–42.
24   CSPI 1625–32, pp.229, 231; APC 42, pp.264–65.
25   The sense of urgency caused by the military situation may also perhaps be seen in the Privy Council's demand that the Irish should hurry up choosing their delegation to meet the King

met no opposition from the Dublin government as it would be of interest to the 'idle swordsmen', who lord deputy after lord deputy had seen as a threat to law and order, and also to young potential troublemakers from the Catholic community who might well leap at the chance of acquiring fighting skills even if it meant spending time in an army that was predominately Protestant.

However, although reducing the forces defending the country by removing the fleet soldiers would lessen the financial burden on the population, it increased the likelihood of a Spanish invasion being successful followed by the end of English rule. That this would have been a cause of great anxiety to Protestants is obvious, but some papists would have been disturbed by the Protestant Archbishop of Armagh's speech in the assembly just before it was sent packing. The King of Spain's army would regard Catholics as collaborators who had not gone into exile but worked with the English in the government of Ireland, and if the country was overrun they were as likely as the Protestants to lose their lands, their possessions and even their lives.[26] They were therefore keen to keep talking in secret.

The behind-the-scenes negotiations led by the Lord Deputy came into the open on 26 June 1627 when the Irish government met with some of the Catholic lords in the presence of a large audience of 'gentlemen of quality'. There the Lord Deputy accepted on the King's behalf a petition asking for permission to send an elected delegation representing all three Irish communities to talk to Charles in person about how to maintain an expanded army. Nevertheless he reminded them that if the delegates saw themselves as the assembly's successor, and therefore empowered to give their consent to a tax to help support the standing army, the people who had elected them stirred up by their priests might not be of the same mind.[27]

On 30 September the Privy Council wrote to Falkland on the King's behalf expressing grateful surprise at developments in Ireland and giving retrospective and enthusiastic approval to the method by which the delegates were being elected.[28] The reaction is difficult to believe, but there is no record of the experiment being discussed in the Council's minute book. It beggars belief that Falkland would have allowed such a highly significant and unprecedented political development without a nod of some kind from England. If he had gone ahead regardless, his enemies at Court and in the governments of the two kingdoms would have informed on him to the King before the elections got underway, and he would have been out of a job in weeks. It is much more likely that it was the Privy Council that had been kept in the dark and not the monarch, as this was not the first or indeed the last time that the early Stuart kings took important decisions without first asking for its advice.[29]

26 APC 42, pp.264–65; CSPI 1625–32, p.229. Much of the rest of the account given here reflects the discussion in Lenihan, *Consolidating Conquest*, p.73.
27 CSPI 1625–32, pp.221–22, 245–46.
28 APC 43, p.59.
29 For other examples of this see Cust, *Charles I*, pp.125–26.

The formations that left Ireland to serve in the first expedition to La Rochelle bore little resemblance to the ones that had landed there in the winter of 1625–6. In the first place the veterans of the Cadiz expedition were considerably fewer in number.[30] This was partly due to death and desertion, but also because the Lord Deputy had incorporated two companies into the standing army under new captains to strengthen the military presence in the bandit country where Connaught, Leinster and Ulster met. There were also important changes in command for the units that remained. First Falkland reduced their number such that there were only 10 companies left by the spring of 1627 four of which were sent to England under their existing captains – Willoughby, Vaughan, Pelham and probably Michael Williams who died soon afterwards – to help form a regiment of 10 companies for Sir Peregrine Bertie.[31]

The remainder stayed in Ireland, and the companies commanded by the elderly Sir Richard Aldworth and Sir George Flower were placed on the standing army establishment. The last four were incorporated into Sir Richard Bingley's own regiment, which was then completed by recruiting volunteers with no regard being paid to their religious allegiance. Their captains could apply to serve in the regiment if they so wished, but only Captain Lewis Williams did so. Of the rest William Stewart may have been commissioned as major in a Scottish regiment which failed to make it to France. Nothing further is known about Captain Crispe, whilst Captain Elphinstone was in command of a company in Sir Thomas Morton's regiment in 1628. His name does not appear in Spring's list of the captains in that regiment who fought in France in 1627, but Lieutenant Robert Moore claimed to have served under him in the first expedition to La Rochelle.[32]

A second of Bingley's regiments was to have been raised from scratch from Irish volunteers by Sir Piers Crosby, a landowner with Old English ancestry, and although he himself was a Protestant at the time there is little doubt that many if not all of the rank and file were Catholics and probably swordsmen given their subsequent behaviour on and off the battlefield. None of the company commanders are known

30 CSPI 1625–32, pp.145, 240.
31 The army establishment in October 1629 included four companies that had taken part in the Cadiz expedition. Three were commanded by Sir George Flower, Sir Charles Coote and Sir John Netterville. The fourth by a process of elimination was George Herbert's as the other two captains in that part of the list were men who had taken over the Cary family companies after Lord Falkland's recall to England in August: CSPI 1633–47, p.534. For further details see Appendix IV.
32 APC 42, pp.294–95; CSPI 1625–32, pp.194–95. The detailed provisions for creating the three regiments mentioned in the Privy Council minutes are self-contradictory. Spring has read it one way and I another, but I am convinced that the passage relating to Bertie's regiment only makes sense if the word there in line 24 was here in the original. In such circumstances the four specified companies from Ireland would be supplemented by men from the Cadiz expedition who had landed in England to create a full regiment. For Elphinstone, Sibthorpe, and Stewart see CSPD 1627–28, p.512; CSPI 1625–32, pp.266, 273, 307.

to have served in the standing army or the Cadiz expedition, but this was because his instructions were that all should be Irish.[33] How many of them were papists is uncertain, but Lieutenant Colonel John Butler almost certainly was as he joined the patriotic uprising in autumn 1641.[34]

Reorganising and recruiting took some time, but Bingley's and Crosby's regiments were shipped straight from Ireland to the French coast in early September. They had very different fates. Fort Saint-Martin, which guarded the seaward approach to the La Rochelle, had been under siege by Buckingham's army for the past three months. Having beaten off an attempt to storm it on 27 October, the garrison counterattacked the following day driving the British from their entrenchments. Bingley's regiment lost its colonel and four other company commanders, but the regiment under Crosby's command, which seems to have been in reserve, performed in exemplary fashion. Had it not successfully defended a bridge which Buckingham's troops had to cross to reach the safety of their ships, what was a very humiliating and costly rout could easily have ended in the capture of the entire army.[35]

What was left of the expeditionary force then returned to England, which meant that the military presence in Ireland was now much weaker than it had been in the early summer. A solution, however, eventually emerged from the face-to-face negotiations between the King and the elected representatives of his Irish subjects who had left for England in December 1627. An important stage was reached on 20 March 1628 when the Irish delegation informed the King that they were willing to approve a tax on freehold land and goods modelled on the English lay subsidy that would raise the sum of £40,000 a year for three years provided the exact wording of the Graces could be agreed. Two months later the deal was struck. An Irish parliament was to meet in November to approve the military arrangements, to turn the Graces into law, and to sort out any problems in implementing both which had emerged in the meantime. Falkland, however, had permission to start collecting the tax at once. The King's reasoning was that the Dublin government would be losing some of its income from traditional sources such as custom duties immediately as a result of his agreeing to the Graces, but that it would be several months before the Irish exchequer received any benefit from the subsidy.[36]

The provisions for increasing the troops defending Ireland to 5,000 foot and 500 horse had involved a series of compromises designed to allay the fears of Catholics and Protestants alike. The cavalry, which had increased from eight to 11 troops by mid 1627, required no extra recruits but Catholic troopers were to be replaced by

---

33   APC 42, p.294.
34   The major, Sir Thomas Esmond, came from a Protestant family, the lieutenant colonel John Butler from a vehemently Catholic one: CSPI 1625–32, pp.235, 303, 382.
35   The most detailed recent account of Crosby's regiment's role in preventing total disaster is to be found in Spring, *First British Army*, pp.194–99, but lack of other evidence means that it is based almost entirely on Crosby's first-hand but self-serving account.
36   CSPI 1625–32, pp.327, 590.

Protestants. As for weaponry they would continue to be armed with a single pistol and a stout staff. Bringing the infantry up to the right number was a different matter altogether. Fourteen hundred new recruits were required all of whom were to be raised by impressment in England. Seven hundred were to fill gaps in the ranks of the existing 40 companies – the 27 of 1624, the nine raised in 1625 and four made up of fleet soldiers – and to replace Irish soldiers who had joined the ranks during the war. Henceforth only four were allowed per company to serve solely as guides and interpreters. The rest of the recruits were to be placed in seven new companies commanded by a cross-section of Old English, New English and Scottish landowners

The infantry were to be armed with pike and shot in the customary ratio but only 10 of the shot per unit were to have muskets possibly because the shorter barrels of the calivers made them more appropriate for combat in the woods and scrub of contemporary Ireland. They were also less expensive. Another feature explicable more by tradition than by the Irish landscape was for each company to include a small number of men described as targets. Their role seems to have been that of skirmishers, but instead of the customary bow and arrows and darts they were armed with a pistol, whilst retaining the small wooden shield from which they took their name. The impressment, however, was put on hold until the autumn because the English government claimed it could not afford the cost of feeding the recruits whilst they were waiting to set sail for Ireland. The price of meat and cereals were unusually high in June 1628 because of diseases affecting cattle and the previous year's bad harvest.[37]

Implementing the agreement in full ran into difficulties within weeks. Falkland duly issued writs for parliamentary elections, but he was reminded that the constitutional arrangements between England and Ireland instituted by Poynings Law (1493) required him first to obtain the Privy Council's approval of the legislation that was to be put before the Irish Lords and Commons. The election was therefore postponed, but Falkland, having begun collecting the subsidy, continued to do so,[38] and then less than two months later the English government had second thoughts about impressing 1,400 foot soldiers for service in Ireland. Instead it declared itself satisfied that the country would be more secure if the 10 companies of Sir Piers Crosby's regiment, which had not been chosen for the relief expedition to La Rochelle in May, were shipped there instead. This change of heart was almost certainly because the recruiting operation from 1624 onwards had drained the pool of men in England eligible for impressment to such an extent that there were not enough to supply an inactive theatre of war like Ireland when soldiers were needed for a third expedition to relieve La Rochelle planned for the autumn and also to strengthen the force being prepared

---

37   CSPI 1625–32, pp.338–39, 341, 342–43; APC 43, p.401. The company commanders were to be the Earl of Westmeath, Lord Killeen eldest son of the Earl of Fingall, Robert Lord Dillon of Kilkenny West, Andrew Stewart son or grandson of Lord Castle Stewart, Sir Lucas Dillon, Sir Adam Loftus and Captain Arthur Forbes: CSPI 1625–32, p.343.
38   Lenihan, *Consolidating Conquest*, p.74; CSPI 1625–32, pp.378–79, 384, 386; CSPD 1627–28, p.512.

in the Netherlands to assist the King of Denmark whose lands were being threatened by a German Catholic army. However, there was subsequently a slight change of plan. In August only 700 officers and soldiers landed in Ireland, two companies having been sent to Portsmouth under Lieutenant Colonel John Butler possibly to reinforce the garrison there rather than to form the nucleus of a new Irish regiment; but after the failure of the third expedition to break the French naval blockade in October, followed by the surrender of La Rochelle to the French King immediately afterwards, they too were shipped to Ireland via Bristol.[39]

The Dublin government was most unhappy with the change of plan. In the first place the seven nobles and gentlemen chosen to command the new companies would be mortally offended at being treated in such a cavalier manner. Second, Crosby's regiment was not the well-disciplined formation it had described in a letter to the Privy Council in 1627 as it set sail from Ireland. Although it had done well against the French, it would not necessarily perform in a similar manner facing an invasion or charged with suppressing an uprising of fellow Catholics. To make matters worse many of the rank and file were criminals who the Lord Deputy had freed from prison provided they were willing to serve under Crosby.[40] Finally, the regiment had been guilty of violence against civilians when quartered in Essex on its return from La Rochelle, though only after being severely provoked by ridicule and ribaldry during its celebration of the feast of St. Patrick.[41] It was therefore probably not a coincidence that the Privy Council took every precaution to ensure that its march across southern England towards its port of embarkation was conducted in such a way as to avoid any further trouble.[42]

Buckingham's war with France fizzled out soon after he was assassinated at Portsmouth on 23 August 1628 whilst putting the finishing touches to the third La Rochelle expedition. Not only did this remove the driving force from the English side for securing parliamentary acceptance of the Graces, it also revived the fortunes of the faction in the Court and Privy Council that favoured friendship with Spain which had been largely inactive since Cranfield's disgrace, but now began flexing its muscles.[43] Amongst the first to suffer was Lord Falkland, who was brought down by accusations that he had falsely accused an Irish sept of treasonable activity with the aim of seizing their lands in County Wicklow. Although his council wrote in his support, he had made too many enemies in England and Ireland by carrying out his

---

39 APC 44, pp.58, 76, 81, 85–86, 188, 303; CSPI 1625–32, pp.374, 376–77, 385, 395; CSPD 1628–29, pp.253, 317; CSPI 1633–47, p.534; *ibid.* 1647–60, p.106. For the dispatch of armed assistance to Denmark see APC 44, pp.10, 93–94, 195.
40 APC 44, p.115; CSPI 1625–32, pp.376–77, 385, 395.
41 Spring, *First British Army*, p.238.
42 APC 44, pp.81, 86.
43 Cust, *Charles I*, pp.76–77, 180.

patron's instructions, which had first alienated the New English by courting the Old English and then the Old English by going back on the agreement to summon an Irish parliament.[44]

First mooted in April 1629 Falkland's dismissal was confirmed by the King in a most gracious letter written in early August. Charles congratulated him on his success in keeping Ireland quiet in time of war, but he and his son Lucius were relieved of all three of the captaincies they held in the standing army. This was humiliation on a grand scale given the experience of his immediate predecessors. Chichester had continued to command a company of foot and a troop of horse in the standing army until his death nine years later, whilst Grandison in 1629 was still a captain of horse and foot. Although both had been soldiers first and foremost whereas Falkland and Lucius had not, such treatment was seen by the Cary family as a reflection on their collective honour, and this induced Lucius to challenge his successor as captain to a duel. It was not a wise move. Sir Francis Willoughby had been a soldier for many years and was to remain active for another twenty. He would therefore have been a formidable opponent despite being wounded in the foot at La Rochelle, but he was not looking for a fight. Sir Francis assured Lucius that he had not applied for the captaincy, and when the news broke he was as surprised as the Carys. The King followed this up by putting the young man in prison for a few days to allow his anger to subside. Lucius then apologised, and his apology was accepted. The King may thus have saved his life, and he repaid the debt in full measure 14 years later when as Second Viscount Falkland and First Secretary of State he died fighting bravely for his monarch as a volunteer at the First Battle of Newbury.[45]

---

44 CSPI 1625–32, pp.416, 422–26, 445, 447.
45 CSPI 1625–32, pp.474, 480, 503; APC 46, pp.239, 247. There is a spirited account of the incident in Lady Theresa Lewis, *Lives of the Friends and Contemporaries of Lord Chancellor Clarendon*, 3 vols (London: J. Murray, 1852) i, pp.189–94.

7

Lord Wilmot as Army Commander 1629–1632

Responsibility for governing Ireland in the King's name until a new appointment was made rested as was customary on the shoulders of the lord justices. At the time of Lord Falkland's recall these were Richard Boyle, Earl of Cork, a New English landowner and reputedly the richest man in Ireland, and the Lord Chancellor Sir Arthur Loftus, but as it was a time of war, and neither had any recent military experience, Charles appointed Lord Wilmot as general of the standing army.[1] But there was a second reason. The lord justices were bitter enemies but Wilmot with extensive experience of civil and military government in both England and Ireland had the skills to serve as the voice of reason and hopefully persuade them to put animosities to one side in the interest of good government, but he would not have the authority to insist that they did so.

Born in about 1570 into an Oxfordshire gentry family Charles Wilmot was a veteran of the Nine Years' War. Knighted in 1599 he was sufficiently senior in rank and reputation by the end to be entrusted with the command of mixed brigades of over 1,000 men with which he won minor battles against Tyrone's allies. In fact it was the return of his brigade from a successful expedition into the far southwest of County Kerry that had helped to spark off the unrest in Cork in April 1603 described in Chapter 1.[2]

A military reputation was a diminishing asset with peace coming over the horizon, and in the first stage of the slimming down of the army in Ireland just before James I's accession to the throne Wilmot lost his troop of horse. The annual pension he received as a recompense was small, and his subsequent appointment as governor of Kerry yielded him nothing financially. It also made him an enemy in the shape Sir Henry Brounker, the Lord President of Munster, who saw his appointment as a lessening of his authority. In late 1607 Wilmot voluntarily surrendered his company of foot to another officer in return for an increase in his pension and appointment to

---

1 CSPI 1625–32, pp.460, 466, 474–75, 502.
2 CSPI 1603–06, pp.22, 38, 43; Shaw, *Knights of England* ii, p.245.

the Lord Deputy's council in Ireland. Returning to England he set about making a career at court aided in its later stages by Robert Carr, Earl of Somerset, James's favourite in the middle years of his reign. This culminated in his appointment as Lord President of Connaught in 1616 in succession to the Earl of Clanricarde together with the promise of the command of the first company to fall vacant, but his rise had not been devoid of friction. Five years before he had been granted the right to succeed Sir Richard Wingfield as marshal of the standing army. This caused some anxiety to Lord Deputy Chichester because of the jealousies it caused amongst other former senior commanders in the Nine Years' War, though he had no concerns about Wilmot's competence.[3]

Viewed initially with suspicion by Buckingham, who had replaced Carr in King James's affections by 1617, Sir Charles experienced a bumpy ride in his fortunes for the next 10 years with the award of an Irish peerage in 1621 being counter-balanced by a serious attempt by Sir Charles Coote, one of the Duke's 'creatures' (as followers were often described at the time), to remove him from office for financial irregularities surrounding improvements to the defences of the town of Athlone, the administrative hub of the province which guarded a strategically important bridge over the River Shannon.[4]

Wilmot had his chance to get into Buckingham's good books when the wars of the 1620s required men of experience to make the military machine work. Little used at first, his skills as an administrator were displayed in 1627 when he had the responsibility for overseeing troops arriving at Plymouth to reinforce the expedition commanded by the Duke which was trying to relieve La Rochelle, and he was fortunate that his reputation was not tarnished by the debacle on the Isle of Rhe at the end of October briefly described in Chapter 6. Delays were caused by the late arrival first of supplies from London and then of the Earl of Holland, who was to take command of the reserve corps. Finally, when the transport vessels and their naval escort left Plymouth contrary winds made it impossible for them to sail out of the English Channel and into the Bay of Biscay. As a result they were still off the Cornish coast when ships carrying the Duke's shattered army passed them in the opposite direction heading for home.[5]

---

3   CSPI 1611–14, p.57.
4   This account of Viscount Wilmot's life is very largely taken from the biography of members of the English parliament in the *History of Parliament* volume for 1603–29 but supplemented by more accurate information about his various military commands in the Domestic and Irish State Papers. I place Wilmot's return to England early in King James's reign which is several years before the date given by the author of the biography on the grounds that he did not hold a command in the standing army between late 1607 and his appointment as lord president of Connaught in 1616: CSPI 1606–08, pp.252, 269, *ibid.*, 1608–10, pp.329, 366, 367, 384; *ibid.* 1615–25, p.11.
5   CSPD 1626–27, pp.374–75, 395–414, 424–25, 447. 451–52.

Wilmot's brief as commander of the standing army was to hold the fort until a new lord deputy was appointed, but it took over two years for the King to decide who to appoint and another year and a half for the person chosen to arrive in Dublin during which time the size of the standing army and its finances came yet again under scrutiny. The hostilities with France having already ended and the war with Spain showing every sign of going the same way, the time had come for a move towards a peacetime establishment following the precedent of the Nine Years' War when the slimming down began two years before the signing of the peace treaty with Spain. A start had been made in September 1629 a month or so before Wilmot arrived in Ireland when the companies of foot were reduced in size from 100 to 50 officers and men but with care being taken to ensure that the best soldiers were retained.[6] None of the companies was disbanded, but the cavalry were cut from 11 troops to nine and the spare horses and pistols shipped back to England. This gave Wilmot a force of 3,000 or so officers and men, but this was still twice as many as Lord Falkland had had under his command in 1624 prior to war being declared.

The first comprehensive roll call of the captains in the standing army since that date is headed 'A list of the army in Ireland of horse and foot as they are now established'.[7] It is undated but internal evidence is such that it can be confidently ascribed to late August 1629: the companies were only 50 strong and, members of the Cary family no longer held any of the captaincies.[8] Its purpose was almost certainly to inform Wilmot of recent changes, as he had been absent from Ireland for the past two years, but it would serve a useful purpose as the starting point for discussions about where the next blow of the axe would fall. Further reductions were not mentioned as such in Wilmot's commission or in the instructions given to the lord justices by the Privy Council, but it is implicit in the latter's reminder to the Dublin government that it was responsible for covering the entire cost of the army but that in the previous year the revenue it had raised for that purpose had fallen short by some £10,500 resulting in pay arrears rising to £60,000.[9]

First came the nine troops of cavalry followed by 50 companies of infantry subdivided as follows: 25 of the 27 companies that had been existence before the war with Spain; Sir William St. Leger's followed by the other eight raised in England in 1625; Sir Pierce Crosby's regiment, 10 companies strong, and two of the four so-called supernumerary companies made up of soldiers from the Cadiz expedition who had not been drafted into the first expedition to relieve La Rochelle. In last place came the two missing companies of the pre-1625 standing army (those of Sir John Borlace and

---

6   CSPI 1625–32, p.466; APC 45, pp.79, 106.
7   CSPI 1633–47, p.534.
8   CSPI 1625–32, pp.476, 480.
9   CSPI 1625–32, pp.270, 446, 466, 471–74; *ibid.* 1647–60, pp.135–36. The arrears appear to be on the small side but presumably Cranfield's calculation of what was owed had become set in stone.

Sir Francis Willoughby who had succeeded Lord Falkland and his son) and George Herbert and Sir John Netterville commanding the other two 'fleet' companies.[10]

A second army list like the first is undated but it is ascribed by the editor of the Calendar of State Papers to the year 1630.[11] Its heading is 'List of the army in Ireland as they now stand', and the clear inference is that it represented the second stage of the return to a peacetime establishment that would come into force in October and last until September 1631. It shows the standing army reduced to below the level of 1624 in the case of the infantry, that is 25 instead of 27 companies each 50 strong, some 1,250 men. The captains are named, and all were commanding units that were in existence before the start of the war with Spain. Thus, two companies of the old standing army; the nine companies raised d in England in 1625, the four supernumeraries made up of 'fleet soldiers', and Sir Piers Crosby's Irish regiment, were to be disbanded in their entirety, but the cavalry was to remain intact with nine troops of varying sizes.

However, a comparison of the two lists suggests that they must have been compiled at almost the same time, namely the late summer of 1629 as Sir Henry Moryson, who was dead by early 1630, was still apparently in post. However, despite the authoritative words in the title, and the fact that the sheet on which it was written contains a note in the secretary of state's hand to the effect that the King had amended it, the second list cannot be the army in Ireland in 1630 'as it now stands'. Wilmot described it in December of that year and in January 1632 as comprising 2,000 foot, whilst the King in a letter to the newly appointed lord deputy Thomas, Lord Wentworth, later Earl of Strafford, in February 1632 gave the same figure and the number of companies as 40.[12] All I can suggest is either that a decision was taken and then rescinded, probably following a vigorous fightback by the top officials in Ireland, or that originally the document consisted of two pages the second of which has since been lost. This is by no means unfeasible as the addendum section of the Calendar of State Papers Ireland for 1647–60 includes several examples of stray pages that can be married up with others in the volume for 1625–32.

Whatever the status of the second list with its authoritative heading, proposals to reduce the army in Ireland below the level of October 1629 were very much in the air, and a major reduction did take place in the summer of the following year when Crosby's regiment left the scene. As shown above the Dublin government had been

---

10 This was certainly so in Netterville's case: CSPI 1647–60, p.180. Herbert had succeeded his father Sir Edward in command of 13 troopers in 1625, but the unit had disappeared from the army list by 1629 as had his father's name from the list of pensioners. George had presumably been given the company of foot in compensation as well as a baronetcy. For this see Appendix IV and CSPI 1625–32, p.526; *ibid.* 1647–60, pp.80, 273, 325; *ibid.* 1660–63, pp.36, 147.
11 CSPI 1625–32, pp.595–96.
12 CSPI 1625–32, pp.588, 649–50; Knowler, William, *The Earl of Strafford's Letters and Dispatches*, 2 vols (London: W. Bowyer, 1739), i, p.62.

horrified at the decision that it should be added to the establishment and had tried its best to change the Privy Council's mind. It failed, but it did not see that as the end of the matter. For the next two years it marshalled argument after argument to undermine the regiment's reputation and rationale. Because of doubts about the loyalty of its officers and men placing its companies in garrisons around the country was out of the question. The corollary was that it had to be quartered in country areas in contravention of the King's declaration in the Graces, and as it marched from one location to another its soldiers behaved in an aggressive way towards the civilian population. Moreover, it was by far the most expensive item in the army budget, and the money saved by disbanding it could be profitably employed in fitting out ships and establishing new forts on the coast to guard against raids by Spanish naval vessels, Dunkirkers and pirates. Finally, for reasons of security it had been disarmed and so would be of no use whatsoever in an emergency.[13]

The first move in the process that would lead to the regiment's elimination came in February 1630 when Lord Justice Cork wrote to the King's new secretary of state Viscount Dorchester praying that God would put it into Charles's mind to disband it as it had no military value and was no more than an 'eating army'. The matter was put to the Irish committee of the English Privy Council whose report made to the King three months later fleshed out the arguments, and on 26 June Charles he ordered the lords justices to disband the regiment in its entirety. However, he was concerned about the threat to public order should this all happen at once. Instead they were to reduce it gradually, a process that was completed without incident before the establishment for 1630–1 came into force on 1 October.[14]

By the autumn the protracted peace negotiations with Spain were edging towards a successful conclusion and the peace treaty was duly signed at Madrid in November 1630. There had, however, been a last-minute scare that a large fleet King Philip was assembling on the coast of Portugal was destined for Ulster, but its destination was Brazil where soldiers carried by the Dutch fleet had recently overrun the province of Pernambuco.[15] The Dublin government thus had no need to fear a Spanish invasion in the foreseeable future, but the threat to internal security remained with the return into the community of the 900 or so men trained in the practices and weaponry of modern warfare whilst under Crosby's command. Sir Piers tried to lessen concern by undertaking to recruit a thousand or possibly several thousand men to serve in Europe the core of which would be soldiers of his former regiment. The beneficiary was to be Gustavus Adolphus King of Sweden, who had just begun his incursion into Germany

---

13   CSPI 1625–32, pp.376, 385, 419, 421, 427, 441, 450, 540.
14   CSPI 1625–32, pp.513, 540, 551, 576.
15   HMC, Cowper Mss i, p.416; CSPI 1625–32, pp.586, 587.

which stopped the Catholic resurgence in its tracks, but good Protestant as he was and keen not to tarnish his image as ideologically untarnished he refused the offer.[16]

Further shrinkage was possible even to the point of extinction. Those members of the Dublin government who thought yet another disbandment would be misconceived would not have been reassured by a long and rambling missive from the Privy Council written a few days before news reached England that the war with Spain was over, which looked to the future whilst rapping the Dublin government over the knuckles for past neglect and for faction fighting getting in the way of the prudent management of its finances. Insofar as the army was concerned, it was congratulated on its success in disbanding Crosby's regiment, but in future annual income should be dedicated to paying the army in the current year and not to settling pay arrears for which some other stratagem must be devised. The Privy Council were convinced that Cork and Loftus would succeed in achieving economies, but the sting was in the tail. Its Irish committee, now heavily under the influence of Lord Falkland who had been found not guilty of the charges made against him, had described the standing army as 'but a name and no strength to defend the Kingdom', and it was duty bound to investigate the allegation. The Dublin government knew that if found to be true, there were only two alternatives, a costly and time-consuming restructuring or a revival of the trained band initiative which would have the added bonus of removing the problem of financing a standing army for good and for all.[17]

A climate conducive to reform involving a national militia was encouraged by a letter sent by Lord Cork of his own volition to the Privy Council before its letter and news of the peace had reached Ireland. Looking to the future he was highly optimistic. The control great Irish landowners like the Earl of Tyrone had enjoyed over their tenants was a thing of the past; the Old English landowners and merchants had seen the commercial benefits of peace; and a few more years of prosperity would enable the government in time of crisis to draw upon a very strong force of armed loyalists from all three communities, the Catholic Irish having been 'reformed in manners and religion'.[18]

Wilmot's involvement in the debate as to how the English hegemony could best be defended is well hidden. Throughout 1630 he had been in correspondence with the Privy Council primarily on matters relating to the interface between the military and the political spheres of government. Soon after taking up his post he claimed to have succeeded in persuading the lord justices to patch up their quarrel. He had also confined units of the army to their garrisons in accordance with the King's promises to the Irish delegation during the negotiations over the Graces and had put down a very

---

16 CSPD 1631–33, pp.55, 113, 129–31; CSPI 1625–32, pp.608, 615, 629; HMC, Cowper Mss, i, p.438.
17 APC 46, pp.133–35; CSPI 1625–32, p.110.
18 CSPI 1625–32, pp.589–90.

serious pro-Catholic riot in Dublin.[19] His greatest achievement, however, had been to browbeat the Dublin corporation into accepting troops being quartered in the city as protection for the lord justices. Knowing from Waterford's experience that their charter would provide no defence against the New English control of the judiciary, it had also agreed with some reluctance to provide food, fuel and candles for the soldiers.[20] He was, however, silent about the militia but there is no evidence that he had changed his mind forcibly expressed a few years before.[21]

The last of Wilmot's letters for the year written to the Privy Council in early December two days before the Earl of Cork's (and like his before news of the treaty of Madrid reached Ireland) is full of bravura but the context was the ongoing war with Spain not the defence of the English hegemony thereafter. Its primary purpose was to calm the nerves of the people in London. The fleet massing on the coasts of Portugal was not bound for Ireland. Indeed the whole idea of a Spanish invasion was ridiculous until such a time as a flame had been lit in Ireland, and even if there was serious unrest in the future Spain's military commitments elsewhere and the habitual caution of its rulers meant there was little likelihood of a Catholic invasion. If, however, King Philip decided to chance his arm, the outlook was dire. His men would fight to the best of their ability, but he only had gunpowder for muskets and calivers sufficient for two days' fighting.

Anybody reading the letter could not avoid the conclusion that the general was insisting that a full-scale uprising that was not quickly extinguished would be beyond his capacity to suppress.[22] Thus, although he did not say it in as many words, he was arguing that it would be unsafe to weaken the standing army still further as he would be unable to use force to nip an insurgency in the bud. There was no mention of what a militia might contribute. But it was the Earl of Cork not Wilmot who led the counterattack against the adoption of the English model based on county militias.

A month later the lord justice decided that he had given the Privy Council the wrong impression in his previous letter. The standing army must not be reduced in size. Although the great lords were no longer a threat, there were large numbers of idle young men who were, and if there was an uprising the Dublin government could not rely on the English settlers. On past record they would flee in the face of a serious uprising rather than stand and fight for their farms, which reads like a massive indictment of the military potential of the men who would be serving in the trained bands should they be established.[23]

---

19   CSPI 1625–32, pp.479, 488–89, 504; APC 45, pp.258–59, 320–22.
20   CSPI 1625–32, pp.498, 500, 504.
21   CSPI 1625–32, p.193.
22   CSPI 1625–32, p.588.
23   CSPI 1625–32, p.597. The editor of the Calendar gives the date of June 1631 to an undated letter containing a rumour that the army was to be disbanded, but it was almost certainly written six months earlier as it refers to Lord Mountnorris having recently left for England to answer charges against him before the Privy Council. The summons to

The January letter seems to have done the trick for the moment. There is no record of a resolution about the size of the standing army being reduced still further in the minutes of the English Privy Council for early 1631, whilst the last mention of such a concern in Ireland was at the beginning of March.[24] However, early in the following year and well before the new lord deputy Wentworth left for Ireland he would have received a powerful memorandum from Richard Hadsor, a senior civil servant working there, recommending an army of less than 1,000 men and trained bands in every Irish county.[25] At about the same time Secretary of State Sir John Coke had on his desk a memorandum on the shortcomings of the officers and soldiers of the standing army suggesting instead trained bands on the English model with a few hundred professional soldiers guarding the magazines where their arms and ammunition were stored. It may have been written years before, but Coke had written on it 'points to be thought upon'.[26]

Wilmot's outgoing correspondence in 1631 differed markedly from that of the previous year in that there was far less of it, and it contained little of substance, which suggests a lack of commitment. He was very concerned about the fate of his son Henry who had killed a man in a duel, and peace with Spain meant that the army was not likely to be called upon to defend the Protestant interest in Ireland for some years to come, but another factor was probably the growing awareness that he would not achieve what had probably been his ambition since 1610 if not earlier, namely to finish his career as lord deputy. There is some evidence that this was still alive in 1630 when he had commented adversely on the failure to make an appointment: the lord justices were about to fall out again in a way that would be not only embarrassing to the English government but also frustrating to their officials who looked to them for leadership. In a more direct criticism of Cork and Loftus he complained bitterly about his own lack of authority which prevented him carrying out reforms in the army.

In a letter written to the Privy Council in March 1631 Wilmot's earlier enthusiasm showed distinct signs of having evaporated, a sign that he was no longer in the running for lord deputy. He had written a long letter of advice on the army three months earlier. The context had admittedly been the ongoing war with Spain, which had now come to an end, but he had not received a reply which was a clear indication that he was no longer regarded as a person of importance. However, to show that he was still a conscientious servant of the Crown he offered two constructive pieces of advice for the peacetime army, the appointment of a well-educated chaplain for the troops and of an experienced military engineer to supervise the fortifications.[27]

---

appear before the Council was issued on 10 November 1630: *ibid.* 1647–60, 165; APC 46, pp.133–34, 136.
24   CSPI 1625–33, p.602.
25   CSPI 1625–32, pp.680–81.
26   HMC, Cowper Mss i, pp.456–57.
27   CSPI 1625–32, pp.603–04.

As time passed and it became increasingly clear from rumours that were circulating that Wentworth would be the new Lord Deputy Wilmot apparently kept his feelings to himself if his surviving outgoing correspondence gives the correct impression, but when writing to Lord Cottington, a member of the Privy Council, in January 1632 a few days before learning officially of the King's decision he expressed his disappointment. However, having got it off his chest, his principal concern was that Wentworth's arrival would be quickly followed by a reduction in the size of the standing army. In a constructive gesture he volunteered to perform any task Wentworth wished to give him. This might have elicited some gesture of gratitude on the part of his successor as commander of the standing army, but he spoilt it with a short burst of sarcasm. He did not doubt that the new man would be able to fill the gap between the revenue raised in Ireland to support the army and the true cost by using the last 10 months of the subsidy approved by the delegation which had negotiated with the King in 1628, an achievement he and everybody else knew full well had eluded the lord justices in previous years. He also showed resentment at the way he had been cast aside: he had no wish to remain in Ireland any longer than was necessary having spent 40 years labouring there.[28]

The lord general's wish was soon granted. In July 1632 the King ordered him to tender his resignation and to return to England, though he stayed there longer than both had intended because Wentworth was not ready to move to Ireland until 1633. Wilmot's last recorded act was to sign a letter to the English Privy Council in November 1632 warning that Archduchess Isabella's officers were surreptitiously recruiting in country districts for her army in the southern Netherlands with one officer having the gall to try and ship his soldiers to the Spanish Netherlands through the port of Dublin.[29]

The King also required him to provide a memorandum of advice on the army for the Lord Deputy before leaving. What form this took cannot be ascertained, but the fact that it does not appear amongst Wentworth's correspondence does not mean that it was not written, as the new Lord Deputy was quite capable of tearing it up in a fit of rage. However, some of the comments about Ireland in the letter to Cottington would clearly have passed before Wentworth's eyes as the only copy is in the new lord deputy's papers. However, they were no more than platitudes. The only revelation was that soldiers were being used to enforce payment of the subsidy, but this cannot have come as a surprise.[30]

---

28 CSPI 1625–32, pp.532, 545, 566, 599, 603–04, 623; APC 46, p.99; Knowler, *Strafforde's Letters* i, pp.61–62, 63.
29 CSPI 1625–32, pp.670, 677.
30 Knowler, *Strafforde's Letters* i, pp.61–62, 67–70.

During Wilmot's watch the Dublin government was only faced with a single actual threat to the security of the realm and one against which the first line of defence was not the standing army but the English navy. Throughout the wars of the 1620s much of what was described as pirate activity around the coasts of Ireland was commerce raiding by privateers sanctioned by letters of marque granted to civilians by the kings of France and Spain and the Archduchess Isabella. This warfare by proxy was often carried on in cooperation with Irish seamen and shipowners who best knew the coastal waters and who had been damaged financially by wartime restrictions on trade with southern Europe. Such activity lessened considerably following the peace treaties signed in 1629 and 1630 but did not die out completely. Two royal naval ships therefore continued to patrol the Irish Sea and the Western Approaches.

Early in 1631 intelligence gave the Dublin government and the Privy Council notice of raiders from the north coast of Africa attacking coastal settlements in Spain, Portugal and the Bay of Biscay in search of slaves. The captains on patrol were warned, but when the raiders struck the ship commanded by Sir Thomas Button was patrolling the seas between Chester and Dublin hoping to intercept an Irish pirate operating out of the Isle of Man, whilst the other was tied up at the quayside at Kinsale unable to go to sea because Captain Hooke had not received cash from the English government to buy victuals for his crew.

After a probing attack on Berehaven near Cork that went well, two galleys from North Africa carried out an assault on the small port of Baltimore further to the west under the cover of darkness and captured over 100 men, women and children. The responsibility for the defence of Munster rested on the shoulders of Lord President Sir William St. Leger, but his superiors in London and Dublin agreed that he did not have the resources to protect every community under his jurisdiction. The spotlight therefore fell upon Button and Hooke. Their ultimately successful attempts to avoid blame lie outside my remit, but soldiers from the standing army were used to strengthen the coastal garrisons in the immediate aftermath of the raid, and St. Leger was ordered to provide musketeers for the navy. They were needed for close combat with the enemy galleys as the naval vessels' principal artillery pieces lacked flexibility when the distance between them closed.[31]

St. Leger's own suggestion was to build beacons at intervals along the coast to give advance warning of unfamiliar vessels off the coast. The lord justices and lord general Wilmot were in full agreement, but they urged him to make sure that this early warning system was properly supervised at the local level. Frequent false alarms would cause unnecessary panic in the short run followed by turning a blind eye to lighted beacons thereafter, which might well prove disastrous if the pirates were busy elsewhere for a number of years. They were also happy with his proposal to

---

31 An interesting proposal for constructing ships with oars and sails capable of dealing more effectively with North African pirates was put to the government in Dublin in 1632 or thereabouts: CSPI 1647–60, p.68.

distribute arms amongst the civilian population of Baltimore but insisted that they should only be given to loyalists who were to pay for them, and that a record was to be kept of who had what. The scheme looked fine on paper, but there are doubts about whether it was put into effect once the immediate danger had passed. It took eight months for St. Leger to submit his proposals and then only after receiving intelligence that new attacks on the Irish coast were being prepared. Moreover, Lord Deputy Wentworth made no mention of beacons having been erected in any of the extremely lengthy letters he sent to the King and his ministers between 1633 and 1639 on every conceivable aspect of the government of Ireland.[32]

32   CSPI 1625–32, pp.598, 616, 617–18, 621–24, 627–28, 649–50, 658–59; CSPD 1631–33, pp.285, 385.

Part II

The New Commander-in-Chief

8

Army Reform under Lord Wentworth: Preparing the Way

The official announcement in January 1632 that the new lord deputy would be Thomas Viscount Wentworth promised interesting times ahead. For the past three years he had imposed his authority on the counties on the far side of the river Trent as Lord President of the Council of the North and shown the King that he was an able and conscientious administrator, single-minded in the pursuit of clearly defined goals, and a good chooser of men to serve under him. An authoritarian by conviction he was also capable of employing the highest level of persuasiveness in speech and in writing when putting his case or defending himself against attack. In the parliaments of the 1620s as Sir Thomas Wentworth, and well before becoming a royal minister, he had shown not only an ability to influence opinion in the House of Commons, but also the confidence to be constructively critical when speaking about the King's foreign policy and the means being used to finance it but without losing control or abandoning the deference a loyal subject owed to his monarch.[1]

With those who opposed his views or stood in his way it was a different matter. The body language in paintings of Wentworth during the 1630s strongly suggests a grim determination and a self-confidence bordering on arrogance. To my untutored eye this is most evocative in the portrait of the minister at work painted at the end of the decade. The depiction of his face with its glaring eyes and slightly flared nostrils suggests pent-up anger which he often unleashed when bullying lesser mortals or denouncing men close to the King whom he saw as his enemies, whereas the expression on his secretary's face clearly shows apprehension about what might happen next. Although not directly facing Wentworth he could clearly see the hunched shoulders and one

---

1   The most authoritative accounts of Wentworth's life are to be found in *ODNB* 61, in Cust, *Charles I,* and in J. Adamson, *The Noble Revolt: The Overthrow of Charles I* (London: Weidenfeld and Nicholson, 2007).

hand forced down on the arm of the chair in which he was sitting as a sign that his master was about to leap to his feet in an outburst of rage.[2]

Wentworth's aspiration was to become the King's chief minister and exclusive adviser like his contemporaries the Count Olivarez in Spain and Cardinal Richelieu in France. A spell as a reforming lord deputy would provide the final stepping-stone, but first he had to win his spurs by providing a solution to the most fundamental problem that had faced good government in Ireland for over a decade, namely how to create an army that was fit for purpose without it being a drain on the English exchequer. Once he had achieved this he could expect the King's unwavering support in implementing the rest of his reform programme which would be followed in due course by a triumphant return to England and supreme power. However, Charles's experience of being dominated by his father and avoiding being dominated by Buckingham made him determined after the Duke's death to keep ultimate authority in his own hands. Wentworth was therefore kept at a distance until the autumn of 1639 when the poor performance of the King's forces in the First Bishops' War against the Scottish Covenanters forced Charles to recall the Lord Deputy.[3]

Wentworth's predecessors had focused on trying to persuade the English government to reinstate the biannual convoys of treasure whilst resisting further cuts in the strength of the standing army with reform very much on the back burner as it would require additional resources. He, however, was convinced that he had the political skills necessary to make Ireland pay for the full cost of both the army and the reforms that would follow provided that the peace with King Philip lasted, though for most of his time as lord deputy this was not a concern as Charles's Privy Council continued to be dominated by the pro-Spanish faction.[4] More worrying when reform commenced was his lack of experience in military matters, which had extended no farther than being responsibility for the trained bands of the seven counties under the Council of North's jurisdiction. He therefore prepared himself during the 20 months between being appointed as lord deputy and setting sail for Ireland by listening and learning. In his own words he 'dived into the minds of the ablest Irish here with whom I have had good relations since Lord Chichester's time', most particularly Lord

---

2   National Portrait Gallery, Viscount Wentworth with Sir Phillip Mainwaring by Sir Anthony Van Dyck 1640. There are several versions in which the facial expression has been toned down as, for example, in the late copy at Dunham Massey owned by the National Trust. The original is reproduced in full colour on the NPG's website.

3   Cust, *Charles I*, pp.171–72; M. Braddick, *God's Fury, England's Fire* (London: Allen Lane, 2008), pp.84, 134–35; M.C. Fissel, *The Bishops' Wars: Charles I's Campaigns against Scotland 1638–1640* (Cambridge: University Press, 1994), pp.28–30, 39.

4   Knowler, *Strafforde's Letters* i, p.93 for the first of his many suggestions for improving Ireland's economy such that the King's income from customs duties would increase (though not at England's expense).

Wimbledon, who had had a long and distinguished military career but one that had ended ignominiously in 1625 with the expedition to Cadiz.[5]

Lord Falkland would presumably not have counted amongst the ablest in Wentworth's eyes, but the King ordered the former Lord Deputy to give Wentworth a full report on the government of Ireland as he had left it and what his future plans had been, but all that survives in Wentworth's incoming correspondence is a letter received just after he arrived in Ireland the curiously written contents of which are best discussed later in the chapter.[6] However, he would certainly have heard of the difficulties he would face in other ways as Falkland was extremely vocal before and after being dismissed about the limitations on the lord deputy's powers which had made it impossible for him make headway in solving Ireland's problems, and ultimately in protecting himself against his enemies in Ireland and at Court.

Clearly despite Wentworth's conscientiousness in preparing himself for army reform the task he faced would be a formidable one. This was not only because the Roman Catholic landowners and merchants and the communities they represented were full of resentment at being cheated out of a parliament to confirm the Graces, but also because of the entrenched attitudes of the leading members of the Dublin government with whom he would have to work. Although their behaviour towards one another on the personal level was infused by enmities stretching back over many years, they were New English almost without exception and could be expected to sink their differences albeit temporarily if his proposals threatened their community's interests.

To make things worse the new Lord Deputy was a complete newcomer whose lack of experience of Ireland compared most unfavourably in the eyes of the New English elite with that of the Lord Justices Cork and Loftus. Moreover, he had no family, friends or acquaintances living there who could form the nucleus of a pro-Wentworth faction in the Dublin government to argue the toss. Admittedly he brought a few trusted men with him who were eventually to rise to high ministerial rank, but they could only be appointed when vacancies occurred, the first two being Christopher Wandesford, created Master of the Rolls in May 1633, and George Radcliffe, whom the King chose to serve on the Lord Deputy's council in October. Both had worked with Wentworth for some years on the Council of the North and both like him were Yorkshiremen.[7] Thus initially the Lord Deputy was reliant very largely on his own political skills to make headway with programmes on which he and his council did not see eye to eye.

---

5   C. H. Firth, *Papers relating to Thomas Wentworth, First Earl of Strafford* (London: Camden Society n.s. 53, 1895), p.3; Knowler, *Strafforde's Letters* ii, p.198.
6   Knowler, *Strafforde's Letters* i, p.102.
7   <www.historyofparliamentonline.org> 1604–1629, House of Commons, Members' Biographies. Wentworth had previously sent Radcliffe to Ireland presumably to serve as a reliable informant about the problems he would face when he arrived there: CSPI 1625–32, p.675; *ibid.* 1633–47, p.11.

Wentworth saw from the start that the only way in which he could secure the authority to implement his reforms was for it to be absolutely clear that he had the total and unconditional support of the King, and that patronage in terms of appointments in the government and the army flowed solely through him as de facto viceroy. In a document written a few weeks after his appointment he presented the Privy Council with 11 propositions to extend and formalise the lord deputy's powers in areas that had caused frustration to his predecessors. They were duly discussed in Wentworth's presence and sent to the King for his approval accompanied by highly favourable comments on every one. Within days Charles gave his consent and ordered that the propositions should be entered into the Council's register of decisions taken 'to the end that they may be constantly observed'.

Only two of the propositions related directly to the standing army and both focused on the importance of the lord deputy having sole and exclusive powers to recommend new captains with the King merely signing the commissions His justification was that if officers were chosen in any other way, and most notably by representations made to the King at Court which he knew nothing about, it would weaken the respect he needed for his reforms to be accepted and also dash the hopes of more deserving men with whom he knew he could work. Second, Charles would no longer insert a clause into a captain's commission allowing it to pass to a family member on his death or resignation. If the practice continued well-qualified men would be passed over for promotion with no guarantee whatsoever that those who took over the troop or the company possessed the necessary abilities or commitment to be worthy of a captaincy in the army. What Wentworth did not touch on was captains being allowed to sell their captaincies. This was presumably based on the presumption that the King would refuse to issue a captain's commission to the purchaser if the lord deputy advised him that the man in question was ill-qualified to serve at that rank in the army.[8]

If Wentworth's claim that he had Charles's total confidence was to be recognised and respected, he also needed to ensure that lying tongues at Court did not turn the King against him when his response would take weeks to reach him. He knew that he could rely totally on the support of the King's favourite churchman, William Laud, Archbishop of Canterbury from 1633, whose ideas on strong government were almost identical to his own, their watchword being Thorough, which meant that they would leave no stone unturned in the pursuit of the efficient government of church and state provided, of course, that the King was in agreement. Nevertheless the opportunities for his enemies to tell tales against him without his knowledge were numerous. Dublin government ministers and officers of the standing army as well as members of the Old English and Irish aristocracy often went to England either on the King's business or for private reasons, and this would give them opportunities to blacken his name. Charles's belief in his new lord deputy could also be influenced by full-time courtiers with extensive land holdings in Ireland post 1608 who would be only too

---

8   Knowler, *Strafforde's Letters* i, pp.65–67.

happy to spread rumours of a negative nature should they learn that Wentworth's reforms threatened their interests.

Wentworth took what precautions he could. First, he ensured that his communications with the King would not be accidentally garbled or deliberately misrepresented by gaining Charles's agreement for them to reach him via a single, utterly trustworthy member of the Privy Council, namely Sir John Coke, the senior secretary of state, unless the contents were of a financial nature. In that case the recipient was to be the lord treasurer, the Earl of Portland, the senior member of the pro-Spanish faction amongst the King's ministers.[9] Wentworth also persuaded the King to order Lord Mountnorris, the vice treasurer in the Dublin government, to return to Ireland. Wentworth's stated reason was that he needed him to serve as a go-between with the Old English aristocracy who held him in high regard because of his past opposition to the collection of recusancy fines. However, Mountnorris was a potential rival well versed in political intrigue who had helped bring about the recall of Lord Falkland, and whose loyalties were determined exclusively by his vaunting ambition, which probably extended as far as lord deputy. To make matters worse his opinions were listened to as he was held in high esteem by the King and some of his English ministers because of his financial shrewdness.[10]

The Lord Deputy's fears about stabs in the back may also explain the King's order in May 1633 that captains of units in the standing army should return to Ireland or else lose their commands. Admittedly a similar injunction had been issued several times in the past, but this time it singled out those officers living in London and its environs,[11] but there was no reason why their absence from their units was more likely to result in slackness and ill-discipline than that of men living at a distance from the capital.

These precautions would clearly not block every avenue by which opinion hostile to Wentworth reached the King, but he was lucky in one very important respect. By the mid 1630s there were few distinguished former standing army officers living out their retirement in England, who also had places on the Privy Council where their opinions about his rule in Ireland would have been listened to with respect. As mentioned above Lord Chichester and Sir George Carew had died during Falkland's watch and Lord Grandison in 1630. Lord Danvers, the former Lord President of Munster and now Earl of Danby, sat on the Irish Committee of the Privy Council but could probably be counted on not to speak out against Wentworth as Danvers' niece and heiress was married ,to Sir Edward Osborne, his utterly loyal second-in-command who was presiding over the Council of the North in his absence.

Lord Falkland may initially have been pleased to learn that Wentworth was to be his successor as lord deputy as he had assented to the 11 propositions when they came before the Privy Council, but by the time Wentworth set foot on Irish soil in the

---

9   Knowler, *Strafforde's Letters* i, pp.67, 68.
10 Knowler, *Strafforde's Letters* i, p.73; Lenihan, *Consolidating Conquest*, p.77.
11 Knowler, *Strafforde's Letters* i, pp.84–85.

summer of 1633 he appears to have changed his mind. The letter of congratulations he sent to Dublin on the Lord Deputy's safe arrival reads as if words of goodwill and the offer to send him advice in secret were uttered through gritted teeth, but possibly this was because of what he saw a breach of courtly etiquette on Wentworth's part. To me it reads like a response to a letter of thanks from the Lord Deputy for facilitating his appointment which he had failed to write because two of the four paragraphs were taken up with hints that Falkland deserved his gratitude for making Dublin Castle more habitable and for appointing an excellent comptroller of the household.[12] As such it probably only added to Wentworth's suspicion that Falkland was his chief enemy at Court as it was rumoured that he had expected to be reinstated as lord deputy when the Wicklow case against him collapsed even though the King had already appointed Wentworth. However, Wentworth's anxiety was quickly laid to rest. Within days of sending the letter Falkland was in his grave having fallen from a stand at Theobalds Park while watching the King hunt.[13]

Thus the most senior former officer in the standing army still alive was Viscount Wilmot who, although sharing the lord presidency of Connaught with Lord Ranelagh, was living in London. Given Wentworth's mindset and the strong note of disappointment at not being chosen as lord deputy in Wilmot's letter to Lord Cottington mentioned in the previous chapter, it is highly likely that he would have envisaged the former general spending his retirement causing trouble at Court in the hope that by bringing about the new man's downfall he might at the second attempt gain the appointment he coveted.

Attack being the best form of defence, Wentworth set about diminishing the former lord general's reputation immediately on arriving in Ireland by describing the condition of the standing army as utterly deplorable. He then allowed Sir Charles Coote to revive the charge of peculation in relation to the refortification of Athlone, and as the legal case proceeded he ensured that it achieved the greatest publicity by being heard in an English rather than an Irish court of law. Wilmot's humiliating requests for Wentworth to be merciful fell on deaf ears and that was not the end of the matter. When in 1638 it was proposed that Wilmot should become governor of Newcastle at a time when differences between King Charles and his Scottish subjects might need to be resolved by force Wentworth briefed against him and seems to have succeeded in prevented his appointment.[14] Later he managed to persuade the King to freeze Wilmot's income from his lord presidency until such time as a final verdict was given in the Athlone case. However, if the Lord Deputy had intended to follow up a guilty verdict by depriving Wilmot of his troop of horse, he was too late. Wilmot

---

12   Knowler, *Strafforde's Letters* i, p.102.
13   Knowler, *Strafforde's Letters* i, p.163; CSPD 1633–34, p.220.
14   CSPI 1633–47, p.23; *ibid.* 1647–1660, p.323; CSPD 1633–34, pp.129–30; *ibid.* 1637–38, p.607; Knowler, *Strafforde's Letters* i, pp.79, 96, 138; Firth, *Papers relating to Thomas Wentworth*, p.9.

was still in nominal command in the spring of 1642. Wentworth's enmity, however, extended beyond the grave. The former lord general was still experiencing anxiety over the Athlone business in July 1641 two months after the former lord deputy's execution.[15]

Wentworth also set his sights on humiliating the Earl of Clanricarde, who was still living quietly in England and had no unfulfilled ambitions involving Ireland.[16] Why then did Wentworth bother? The answer almost certainly lies in his wish to further ingratiate himself with the King combined with his obsession with the principle of Thorough. Connaught was the only substantial part of Ireland where plantation had not taken place largely due to Clanricarde's influence at Court. Wentworth went ahead regardless using strong-arm tactics to browbeat juries into acknowledging that much of the land rightfully belonged to the King rather than to the existing landowners whose titles were then declared to be defective. County Galway, where Clanricarde's estates were mainly situated, put up a stronger resistance but Wentworth overcame this in the end signalling his contempt for traditional authority by lodging without permission in Clanricarde's house and lying on one of his sumptuous beds whilst still wearing his riding boots.

The Lord Deputy also set his mind against the Earl's estates being exempt, a policy favoured by others of the King's counsellors because of the Bourke family's loyalty to the Crown over many years despite being openly Roman Catholic. Halfway through the legal process that preceded confiscation and plantation the old earl was sufficiently roused to do something about it, but soon after arriving in Ireland he suddenly died. This was very convenient for the Lord Deputy, but the charge that he had poisoned him did not stick and the impassioned plea made by the new earl that the attack on the Bourke family estates was a shabby way to repay his father's lifetime of service cut no ice in Wentworth's Ireland. In the end, however, Charles forced a measure of leniency on the Lord Deputy claiming that to have seized any part of the Bourke family estates would be a dishonourable act.[17]

Wentworth's behaviour towards those he saw as actual or potential enemies looks like over-reaction verging on paranoia, but he had some reason for behaving as he did after his first experience of New English politics. Immediately after his being named as lord deputy the Dublin government tried to ensure that he played no part in decision-making concerning the financing of the standing army after the direct taxation agreed to by delegates from all three communities came to an end. The King

---

15   Knowler, *Strafforde's Letters* ii, pp.205, 341; HMC, Cowper Mss ii, p.287; Sir John Temple, *The Irish Rebellion* (London: S. Gillibrand, 1646), p.26.
16   He did so in the case of Lords Mountnorris and Esmond, but both had been implicated in personal attacks on his mental or physical health. For this see Appendix IV.
17   Lenihan, *Consolidating Conquest*, pp.78–81; CSPD 1635, pp.452–53; CSPI 1633–47, p.119.

opened discussion as to how the army was to be funded by asking the lord justices for their advice in a letter written on 12 January 1632, which was sent to Ireland in the same package as the announcement of Wentworth's appointment. A month later they wrote to the new lord deputy on the King's instructions describing in considerable detail the problems he would face in governing the country but they considered that finding money to pay the army was not one of them. They had already sent their advice to Lord Treasurer Portland, who they assured him 'will make it known to you and therefore we need not enlarge ourselves therein to your lordship'. Moreover, such was the urgency of the task that they intended to put the new financial arrangements in place before he arrived in Dublin.[18] He had thus been effectively side-lined.

The letter to Portland no longer survives but it is clear from subsequent correspondence that it was overwhelmingly in favour of filling the gap between the revenue the Dublin government received and the cost of maintaining the standing army by fining Catholics 12 pence every time they failed to attend an Anglican church service on a Sunday. The justification was seemingly watertight. Direct taxation of Ireland as a whole had aroused bitter opposition in the Protestant community once the war with Spain was over. Keeping several thousand men permanently in arms in peacetime was only necessary because of the Catholic threat at home, and as the Old English and Irish communities were responsible for it they should pick up the whole of the bill. The lord justices also claimed that Catholics would be happier paying recusancy fines than direct forms of taxation. Moreover, their collection could begin immediately without the need for further consultation or decision-making either informally as in 1628 or formally in a new session of the Irish parliament. A statute legalising the levying of fines for non-attendance had been passed by an Irish parliament in the second year of Queen Elizabeth's reign.

In April the English Privy Council with Wentworth in attendance discussed the Dublin government's recommendation for the standing army to be funded from fines imposed on Catholics for recusancy. It accepted the logic of the argument but put off making a final decision until it had seen more evidence. Would such fines provide a more reliable revenue stream than any other option, and were the two Irish Catholic communities as antagonistic towards direct taxation as the lord justices claimed? To avoid any uncertainty about its ruling it ordered that it should be copied into the volume the Dublin government used for keeping a record of the instructions it received from England. Finally interested parties were to have the right to read the ruling with their reactions being recorded as this would provide a more informed picture of Catholic opinion than the lord justices' say-so. The support of Catholic landowners was essential for the peaceful collection of fines in most parts of the country, but if their opinion had been misrepresented they would not agree to cooperate; the steady stream of revenue required to pay the standing army year on year would diminish; and the cost of the army would increase as the government would be obliged to enlist more

18 Knowler, *Strafforde's Letter*s i, pp.62–63, 69.

soldiers in order to enforce payment. On the same day, however, King Charles sent a personal message to the lord justices which showed a much stronger commitment to their scheme for funding the army based on sheer necessity. Getting sufficient money to pay the troops was the top priority as otherwise the soldiers would run riot. The Dublin government was therefore to be ready to collect recusancy fines as soon as the last proceeds from the subsidy reached the Irish exchequer, and to the lord justices it looked as if they were only one short step away from outright approval.[19]

Although so close to achieving their objective the lord justices and their supporters needed to be on their guard as their description of the Catholic communities' preferring recusancy fines to direct taxation was wishful thinking at best. They therefore kept the Privy Council's ruling under wraps, but Wentworth was onto the case. Convinced on grounds of common sense that the Catholic communities were most unlikely to look favourably upon a measure that struck at their faith as well at their pockets he decided to take discreet soundings of his own. In July or thereabouts he secretly gave orders to Sir Piers Crosby, the colonel of the regiment raised in Ireland for the first La Rochelle expedition, to 'test the pulse' of the Catholic communities. When he discovered on Crosby's return that prominent Catholics were bitterly opposed to paying recusancy fines but willing to continue paying the subsidy for a further 12 months and thereafter to give formal assent in Parliament for it to be levied for several more years. The only conditions they made were that Protestants and Catholics were to be taxed at the same rate, and that the Graces were confirmed by statute. Unsurprisingly Wentworth persuaded them to petition the King so as to make it quite clear where their preference lay. By early October he had also obtained the King's tacit content that recusancy fines would not be collected until after he arrived in Ireland.[20]

Rumours of what was afoot woke the Dublin government up and it took immediate steps to keep the King onside. Its agents began quietly collecting recusancy fines in County Wicklow presumably to provide concrete evidence of the effectiveness of the scheme in raising money, whilst Lord Cork wrote a long letter to Charles on 21 November claiming that it was the only practicable way of paying the army's wages bill.

Aware that all was not signed and sealed and wanting to give Cork the chance of avoiding serious trouble Secretary Coke wrote to him in early December explaining that his personal view was that it would be unwise to try and impose recusancy fines at short notice because the popish priests would stir up their flocks against the collectors. Cork's response was to go onto the attack by pointing out the danger of extending the collection of the subsidy beyond the date agreed in 1628. The fact that the Catholics gave their approval did not make it legal *ipso facto* as the Protestants had not given their consent to its continuation.[21]

---

19   Knowler, *Strafforde's Letters* i, pp.71–72, 77; CSPI 1625–32, p.659.
20   Knowler, *Strafforde's Letters* i, pp.73, 74–77.
21   HMC, Cowper Mss i, pp.481–83.

Three weeks later the fat was properly in the fire. News of what was happening in County Wicklow was public knowledge as was the failure of the lord justices and their council to permit open access to the Privy Council's ruling. The royal response penned by Coke rapped the lord justices very firmly over the knuckles. They were to stop collecting recusancy fines immediately and to allow anybody who wished to have access to the ruling. Although couched in diplomatic language, the description of the lord justices' actions as being 'contrary to our express pleasure' with the follow-up that 'our service and ministers here have suffered very much trouble' as a result made Charles's anger abundantly clear. Cork's response two months later shows that the Dublin government had obeyed but with bad grace. The battle was lost but not the war. Collecting recusancy fines had the support of the 'better and conformable party'; there was strong evidence of Protestant opposition to paying another year's subsidy in County Fermanagh; and in a petition against doing so from County Cavan appeared the disquieting notion that it was illegal for taxes to be raised with the consent of the great ones of the realm but without the people having first been consulted. [22]

At the time Wentworth claimed not to have made up his mind as to how the army should be funded once the final tranche of the subsidy had been collected. As he stated in different circumstances, he was opposed to making decisions until he had had the chance to examine the problem at close quarters, and even when he did reach Dublin in July 1633 he merely repeated Secretary Coke's argument against immediately collecting recusancy fines as this would pose a threat to Ireland's security, but his first impression of the troops under his command was that they were in no state to collect money by force or to deal effectively with the riots that were most likely to ensue.[23]

The icy silence that greeted Wentworth at his first formal meeting with his council when he asked for its advice as to how the army should be funded given that the Catholic communities were bitterly opposed to paying recusancy fines masked fury at being thwarted but also a determination to stand firm in the hope that if they did so the Lord Deputy would eventually be forced to come round to their point of view through sheer exhaustion and a barrage of recrimination from the King and the Privy Council about lack of progress. There were, they claimed, no practicable alternatives. However, the Lord Deputy, far from being discouraged or intimidated, derived some amusement from the reaction to his response that the Privy Council refused point-blank to bail the Dublin government out by providing money fill the gap between the annual cost of the standing army and the funds the Irish exchequer had available. At that point the Council pricked up its ears as it left the Lord Deputy with only two choices. He could go for the trained band option and reduce the size of the army to a few hundred men which would entail the disbanding of many troops and companies or the captains themselves would have to make some contribution towards their soldiers' pay. In either case those members of the Council who were also captains

22 HMC, Cowper Mss i, p.486; *ibid.* ii, p.4; Knowler, *Strafforde's Letters* i, pp.88, 150–51.
23 Knowler, *Strafforde's Letters* i, pp.75, 94, 97–98.

would be substantially out of pocket, and this would cause the solid front to collapse as what the leaders of the New English had in common that in this case would be driving them apart was love of money.[24]

By the end of 1633 at the very latest Wentworth had come round to the view that the best way of funding the gap between the King's revenue in Ireland and the annual cost of the army was to continue raising money by direct taxation, but that this must be approved by the Irish parliament, a body which had not met since 1615. This was congenial to the councillors who had refused to contemplate anything other than recusancy fines as it would give them a good chance of organising the Protestant members to throw out the proposal, or at the very least cause such an uproar by goading the Catholic peers and MPs that government business made no progress leaving the Lord Deputy with no option other than dissolution. Wentworth did not express his view openly but allowed the suggestion of a new to come from the Council, which he duly passed on to the King. Surprisingly Charles, whose experience of the English parliaments in the first years of his reign had been dire, merely asked for Wentworth's opinion rather than dismissing the suggestion out of hand.

The Lord Deputy was sensitive to Charles's worries about surrendering prerogative powers through Parliament endorsing the Graces in return for Catholic votes, but the King was reassured by the tactics Wentworth intended to employ which would ensure that concessions of that nature would be unnecessary. When Parliament met, the subsidy bill would be the first item of business, and he would muster Catholic support for it by giving vague promises that parts of the Graces dear to their hearts would be approved in a second session to be held later in the year, whilst the New English MPs would vote in favour to show that they were no less loyal subjects of King Charles than the papists.[25]

The Irish parliament duly met at Dublin in July 1634, and the Lord Deputy's plan worked like a dream.[26] Legislation approving six subsidies to be collected over four years were quickly approved and the Lord Deputy brought the session to an end just as the Catholics were starting to ask questions about the timetable for endorsing the Graces. When Parliament met for a second session in the autumn, the Catholic MPs tried to get their demands satisfied by obstructing government business whereupon Wentworth successfully called on New English support to frustrate them. Having secured the passage of two important government bills he declared that such was the impasse between the two blocs that no further government business could be transacted. He then dissolved Parliament before the session became too disruptive, but he had the revenue stream he needed to pay the standing army in full for the next few years with a little extra to help with the army reform.[27] The King was as pleased

---

24 Knowler, *Strafforde's Letters* i, pp.100, 115.
25 Knowler, *Strafforde's Letters* i, pp.99, 115, 134, 159, 182–87, 194–95.
26 Knowler, *Strafforde's Letters* i, pp.184, 231.
27 Cust, *Charles I,* p.204; CSPI 1633–47, pp.70, 100.

as the Lord Deputy, and from then onwards allowed Wentworth to carry forward his military agenda with little interference from the Privy Council and not much from the King.

When the Lord Deputy paid a brief visit to the Court two years later, he delivered a very long account to the Privy Council in the King's presence of his achievements in Ireland in all spheres of government since 1633 and of his plans for the future. In his opinion he received an extremely positive response, but he did not receive the honours he expected. Wentworth made his view known to Charles claiming he needed the lord lieutenancy, an earldom or something equivalent to cause his many critics in England and Ireland to back off and let him get on with the business of reform, but Charles replied that if he had bestowed a reward of such magnitude upon him it was likely to have caused even greater envy and bitterness and given an extra boost to the rumour mill and to schemes for his entrapment or humiliation. The fact that as monarch he paid no attention to the tales he was told should be sufficient reassurance that Wentworth had nothing to fear, and there were further words of advice for a minister he described as a friend: 'for a statesman, a courtier or a lover it made good sense not to make a defence or an apology before being accused'.[28]

28 Knowler, *Strafforde's Letters* ii, pp.8–9, 16, 17–21 27–28, 32, 33.

9

Army Reform under Lord Wentworth: Implementation

The changes in the standing army between 1634 and 1639 were without question instrumental in creating an effective fighting force and thus an important new asset for the Stuart monarchy, but it must be understood that some of the military doctrines that underpinned Wentworth's reforms were already in place, namely the prioritisation of cavalry over infantry in the defence of English hegemony in Ireland, the quartering of army units in castles, forts and the larger towns rather than the countryside, the strict control of the trade in gunpowder, and the importance of stationing troops in Dublin to protect the seat of government against surprise attack.

The Lord Deputy's first impression of the forces under his command when he finally arrived in Ireland in July 1633 was that they were 'extremely out of frame, an army rather in name than in deed whether you consider their number, their weapons or their discipline'. Later in the year in correspondence with Secretary Coke he was even more forthright. The horse and foot were 'in a dreadful state', a verdict based on evidence emerging from an inspection of every army unit carried out on his orders by the muster master Sir Robert King and three professional soldiers two of whom had no recent connection with the standing army. Each was allotted a province, and in due course Wentworth received four independent reports rather than one written jointly. This was presumably in the interest of speed, but it might also have served to reduce the chances of King, a very experienced political operator, persuading the others to tone down their input so as to cover up the neglect and malpractices of fellow senior members of the New English community who happened also to be captains in the army.

The distrust Wentworth felt for King is very apparent in one document in which he described Captains Blunt, Farrer and Fortescue as honest and impartial, but all he would say about King was that as a Crown employee he could be relied upon to be reasonably honest for fear of losing his job should it turn out that he had strayed too far from the truth in order to protect his friends. It is also probably significant that Blunt and Farrer, the outsiders, were given Ulster and Munster where the risk to internal security was the greatest. Fortescue had responsibility for Leinster, the largest province though perhaps significantly not the one where his company was stationed, which left King with Connaught where army units were thin on the ground thus ensuring that if he tendered a very favourable report it would do little to offset the horrors the others found elsewhere.¹

The reports were in the Lord Deputy's hands by late January. Taken together they confirmed his first impressions, but the political support from England for army reform was not immediately forthcoming.² No sooner was he taking comfort from the death of Lord Falkland than the old troublemaker struck a blow from beyond the grave against his authority and his *amour propre*. In early 1632 having managed to convince the King of his innocence of the charges against him the former lord deputy persuaded Charles to reappoint him as captain of a company of foot in the standing army and to undertake that following the precedent of Lord Chichester's and Lord Grandison's troops of horse it would pass to a family member after his death, namely Lorenzo his second son. Wentworth, however, had promised Henry Percy, brother of the Earl of Northumberland with whom he was trying to make a political alliance, that he should have command of the next troop or company to fall vacant having, he claimed, received the King's consent before he left for Ireland.

On hearing that Charles had commissioned Lorenzo to succeed his father, Wentworth fired off letters in quick succession to the Lord Treasurer of England, Lord Cottington, and Secretary Coke arguing passionately that the appointment undermined his control over appointments in the army agreed in March 1632 which he saw as essential for the successful delivery of the sweeping reforms he had in mind. Moreover, on the wider stage of early Stuart politics his being overruled showed friend and enemy alike that his credit with the King fell short of that of Lord Newburgh, a minor member of the English government, who had successfully championed his nephew's cause. If the King did not relent a principle would be established that fishing at Court for preferments in Ireland was fair game for all. To make matters worse a 'boy' with no military experience whatsoever was completely the wrong sort of person to be put in charge of a formation that needed to be brought up to scratch. Finally, the King's decision to ignore one of the principles for the future government of Ireland which he had accepted less than two years before undermined the credibility of all the rest.

Charles refused to be moved claiming that he was honour bound to appoint Lorenzo given the promise he had made to his father. Bombast had not worked, and Wentworth's next logical move was to find persons of influence able to support his case. Aiming for the top he first consulted the lord treasurer, but Portland had no

1 Knowler, *Strafforde's Letters* i, p.132.
2 Knowler, *Strafforde's Letters* i, pp.96, 117, 132, 138, 194–97. For Farrer and Blunt see Appendix IV. For a collection of documents covering Sir Faithful Fortescue's very long career see Thomas Fortescue, Baron Clermont, *A History of the Fortescue Family in all its Branches* (London: Ellis and White, 1880), pp.169–99.

recollection of the King agreeing to give a captaincy to Henry Percy. He therefore swallowed his pride and sounded the retreat claiming that he had welcomed Falkland's son to Ireland, but Lorenzo remained an irritant, the reminder of a battle lost. In 1636 the Lord Deputy described him as a vain young man who needed to learn his duties to his soldiers and his betters. Three years later he claimed that a young man, who can only have been Lorenzo, had caused him more trouble than the rest of his captains put together.[3] In 1640, however, he promoted him to major in preference to captains who had more seniority. This suggests that Lorenzo had suddenly improved in his estimation though it may merely have been a means to an end, namely to provide him with a justification for kicking him out of the army when he showed that he was not up to the job.[4]

Not long after the Cary setback the Lord Deputy received a second rebuff. In a frosty communication dated 16 January 1634 the King informed him that he had been told that there were no cavalry horses left in the standing army, and that there were none in Ireland that could be purchased or requisitioned. He therefore gave him permission to make purchases in England but only after obtaining licenses issued by the Marquis of Hamilton as Master of Horse allowing exemptions from laws forbidding the export of horses, and only after following advice on what kind of horse to acquire. He was also not to apply for too many as they were a strategic asset. Finally the King noted that Irish hobbies, which had often been exported to England in olden days, were nearly extinct.

None of the responsibility for this could be laid at Wentworth's door, but Hamilton not he was to be in charge of the programme for encouraging the breeding of hobbies, whilst the licenses would make it possible for him to closely monitor the purchase of cavalry horses for the standing army with the authority to say yea or nay to individual purchases. There is no record of what happened next in the Lord Deputy's surviving correspondence, but men far less prone to take offence would have seen the whole episode as a major humiliation. This suggests that the King's source of information turned out to be false, but Wentworth would surely have seen it as a sneaky attack on his competence and a sly dig at the research that he had boasted about conducting before leaving for Ireland. He therefore added Hamilton's name to the list of his enemies at Court and waited patiently for the chance to get his own back. This came five years later when he rubbished the Marquis's management of an early stage in the armed confrontation between the King and his Scottish subjects.[5]

Given these blows to the confidence he had in his relationship with the King it is scarcely surprising that Wentworth postponed the implementation of army reform

---

3   Knowler, *Strafforde's Letters* i, pp.117, 128–29, 138–40, 142–43, 144, 161–63, 205, 228; ibid., ii, pp.15, 295.
4   See Appendix V.
5   CSPI 1633–47, p.38; Knowler, *Strafforde's Letters* i, p.158. Neither the King nor Wentworth mentioned hobbies or the shortage of horses for the cavalry in their correspondence concerning army reforms in the first months of 1634: *ibid.* i, pp.195–97.

until after the meeting of the Irish parliament in the summer, though he certainly wrote about it claiming in one place that the captains were shaking in their shoes at the prospect, but when it was all over they would thank him for it. In another he provided considerable detail about his plans most of which the King found acceptable,[6] but Charles continued to interfere in matters great and small concerning the army. In the lead-up to the meeting of the Parliament, for example, he opposed Wentworth's proposal for getting as many officers as possible elected to the Lower House to help ease the passage of the subsidy bill. Instead they should be spending their time training their soldiers so that they were better able to maintain law and order, but on this occasion Wentworth went his own way. At least a third of his captains who were not peers and therefore ineligible to sit in the Lower House were elected as MPs.

The Lord Deputy's success in persuading the Lords and the Commons to vote substantial sums of money to help fund the army for the next four years ought to have ensured that from then onwards he faced less interference from the King and the Privy Council. To that end he invariably took care to consult Charles before undertaking any important initiative that might impact on army finances and this was normally an effective ploy, but Charles continued to meddle from time to time in what were essentially technical matters or those that reflected adversely on the reputation of the royal armoury in the Tower of London.

Wentworth's plans for army reform, which he carried out between 1634 and 1639 can be conveniently grouped under three headings – the structure of the army and its weaponry; unit and group training; and personnel, though there was such an overlap between them that complete separation is impracticable in much of the discussion that follows. His starting point was the reports of the four inspectors and his own investigations summed up in a memorandum sent to the King in January 1634. The overall condition of the cavalry was 'very mean'. In the first place the troopers were poorly armed: Their pistols, one per man, were of poor quality and the wooden staff they carried instead of a second pistol was 'more a trouble to themselves than an offence to an enemy'. Second, lack of stabling meant that were quartered here and there in the countryside around the place they were charged with policing in time of peace and defending in time of war. This hindered their coming together as a unit for training purposes. Also being scattered made it difficult to respond to a surprise attack as the troopers were at risk of being picked off one by one as they tried to reach a prearranged assembly point. Third, many of their captains lived miles away, and in the case of Sir John Kingsmill hundreds of miles away, leaving discipline and training to junior officers who might well possess neither the force of personality not the inclination to attend to such duties.[7]

6   Knowler, *Strafforde's Letters* i, pp.144, 194.
7   Knowler, *Strafforde's Letters* i, pp.158, 195.

Concerns about weaponry also applied to the infantry. Pikes were not long enough, upper body armour was in short supply, and the shot were very largely equipped with calivers which had a smaller bore and a shorter barrel than muskets and a shorter range, and although ideal for skirmishing or operating in difficult country against similarly armed guerrillas, they were less effective in other circumstances and most particularly on the field of battle. Theoretically formations of soldiers armed with calivers were capable of delivering impressive barrages but only at ranges of less than 100 yards. Moreover, the low muzzle velocity of their weapons meant that they were unable to inflict heavy losses on well-armoured horse or foot other than at point-blank range. Musket balls in contrast could punch a hole through armour at 200 yards, and it had been common knowledge that muskets were the superior weapon since the publication of Sir Roger Williams's *Briefe Discourse* four years before the start of the Nine Years' War.[8]

As for the artillery the weaknesses noted in earlier reports had not been addressed, and Wentworth quickly came to the conclusion that it was essential to persuade the current master of ordnance to retire. Lord Caulfield was old, infirm, unskilled in military matters, and rarely left his estate to attend to official business. As his replacement he recommended Sir John Borlace, who had at least 20 years' experience fighting in the Low Countries and was committed to finishing his military career in Ireland having taken charge of a company in the standing army in 1629. The King agreed to the appointment of the new master of ordnance provided Caulfield was happy to resign. He and Borlace quickly reached an agreement for a handover by which neither would be out of pocket, and within weeks of the King's signing the commission the Lord Deputy was proposing that Borlace should use his contacts in the United Provinces to obtain military hardware which was cheaper and of higher quality than that which the royal armoury could provide. The King, however, continued to insist that lead shot and gunpowder intended for the standing army should be ordered from the Tower of London and not purchased overseas.[9]

Finally, Wentworth's report showed that the local militia planned in the mid 1620s had been introduced in Ulster where a Lieutenant Graham was licking the civilian soldiers into shape, but although 14,000 strong and entirely British (that is English or Scottish as opposed to Irish) they were 'a company of naked men' armed with no more than 7,000 swords, 3,000 pikes and 2,000 assorted firearms.[10] Thus the only element missing from the appraisal of the means by which what was now the Protestant hegemony was to be made safe was the south coast forts and citadels, but this was a minor consideration after the work that had been done during Buckingham's wars and the good relations between Great Britain and Spain which the King and Wentworth

---

8 Sir Roger Williams, *A Briefe Discourse of Warre* (London: Thomas Orwin, 1590), p.37.
9 CSPI 1633–47, pp.55, 77–78; Knowler, *Strafforde's Letters* i, pp.195–97, 247. Both were opposed to gunpowder being manufactured in Ireland: *ibid.* ii, p.87.
10 Knowler, *Strafforde's Letters* i, pp.194–99.

were determined to preserve. There were, however, proposals in 1634 and 1638 to convert Kinsale harbour into a naval base for operations against Moorish pirates.[11]

The context for reform had been established during Wilmot's time as lord general., namely that a standing army of 2,000 foot and 400 horse was large enough to safeguard Ireland' security, and that this should paid for out of the King's sources of revenue in the country with a strict eye being kept on expenditure and on eliminating waste and corruption. Whether Wentworth was of the same mind in 1633 concerning the size of the army is uncertain but if he was not he kept it well under wraps. Indeed he made it clear that he was on board with regard to cutting costs by making a small personal contribution. On his acceptance of the post of lord deputy the King gave him permission to create a new troop of horse for himself by taking men from the eight troops in the 1632 establishment. This would not have added to the army's pay bill, but the appointment of a new lieutenant and cornet and several non-commissioned officers would certainly have done. When, however, Sir Thomas Dutton died in 1634 following a drunken celebration attended by former 'Low Country officers' Wentworth took over the captaincy of his troop and removed his own from the establishment. The troopers who had been seconded returned to their former units thus bringing them back to full strength but Wentworth cashiered Dutton's lieutenant, who he replaced with his own. The rest of Dutton's officers must have experienced the same fate thus producing a small reduction in army expenditure, but he did not hold the lieutenant responsible for what he had earlier described as the worst troop in the army. Instead he found an equivalent position for him in the lord president of Munster's troop as the replacement for a man who had not stepped foot in Ireland for more than five years.[12]

The first substantive change in the size of the army came about in 1635 following military planning to prevent an uprising in the county of Galway. So far that part of Ireland had resisted plantations due to the influence of the Earl of Clanricarde, but when plantations were forced upon the county on the grounds that this was essential for increasing royal revenue in order to pay for the upkeep of the army, Wentworth foresaw breaches in law and order. He therefore recommended moving the two companies of foot quartered there commanded by Clanricarde and his son Lord Dunkellin to another part of the country and replacing them with eight companies and a troop of horse to be stationed around the port of Galway and its refurbished fort. He also proposed raising an additional 200 horse which were to be added to the strength of the existing troops thus avoiding the cost of appointing new officers.

In the event there was no uprising but Wentworth, having convinced Charles in advance that the annual pay of the new recruits could be met without asking the English exchequer for funds, organised the newly raised horse in a different way.

---

11   CSPI 1633–47, pp.90, 93, 181.
12   Knowler, *Strafforde's Letters* i, pp.306–07.

Fifteen or so troopers were indeed added to each of the existing eight troops, but a ninth troop was created for Sir Robert Dillon, an Old English Protestant convert and member of the lord deputy's council, whose interventions during the sessions of the 1634 parliament had had a most beneficial effect.[13]

Thereafter the Lord Deputy's main focus remained on the cavalry rather than the infantry. In 1638 four more units were raised making a force of 1,000 horse divided into 13 troops with the possibility of a fourteenth being created in time of war if the escorts of the four provost marshals were combined into a single unit.[14] But the horse were no longer armed as they had been in 1633. Wentworth had replaced the staff with a second firearm, which was almost certainly a carbine, a gun with a larger bore and a longer barrel but as with a pistol the gunpowder was fired by a spark from a flint rather than by a lighted match. Carbines caused less damage at point of impact than muskets with their even longer barrels, but the latter being matchlocks were impracticable for use on horseback.

The addition of a carbine with its greater firepower and range to the troopers' weaponry rather than a second pistol made more sense tactically as it was possible to employ them as dragoons. In the mid seventeenth century dragoons served in armies on the march *inter alia* as advance guards for seizing control of pinch-points such as a bridges and mountain passes. Having dismounted their carbines had sufficient stopping power to enable them to keep the foe at a distance until the infantry arrived in strength. Carbines would also be more effective than pistols in the caracole, the tactical manoeuvre in which the standing army cavalry was almost certainly being trained by their officers the charge in close order sword in hand having scarcely if at all penetrated training regimes in the 1630s.[15] Finally weapons that were shorter barrelled but still had considerable firepower were useful for soldiers storming towns where muskets would be an incumbrance on account of their size, the greater complications in firing them, and the need to react instantly to the dangers that lay in the warrens of streets beyond the walls with which they would almost certainly not know about in advance.

However, the evidence that the standing army was thus equipped is equivocal. The King ordered the Tower of London to supply it with 440 carbines musket not pistols bore to replace the staffs in January 1635 whilst Wentworth sent Colonel Russell to the Low Countries in the same year to purchase another 500, but three years later, having described his light horse as carbines rather than harquebusiers, the word most commonly in use for light horse, he used the term pistol a couple of paragraphs later

---

13   Lenihan, *Consolidating Conquest*, pp.72, 73, 78; Knowler, *Strafforde's Letters* i, pp.260, 262, 453–54, 476.
14   CSPI 1625–32, p.595; Knowler, *Strafforde's Letters* i, p.476; *ibid.* ii, p.199; TNA, SP 63/257, f.50.
15   The charge appears first to have been used by Swedish cavalry in Germany from 1630 onwards: K. Roberts, *Cromwell's War Machine* (Barnsley: Pen and Sword, 2005), p.150.

to refer to their principal weapon.[16] All I can suggest is that his correspondent would have known that the carbine was nothing more or less than a long-barrelled pistol with a large bore rather than that he was informing him that he had re-equipped his troopers having found carbines unsatisfactory.

Wentworth's other major innovation was to my mind a vanity project characteristic of the enthusiastic amateur. By 1638 he had changed his own troop from harquebusiers to heavy cavalry the current term for which was cuirassier and was thinking of raising a similar troop for his second-in-command. Like the light horse cuirassiers were equipped with two firearms and a sword, but they were clad in full armour to the knee and mounted on bigger horses. Unsurprisingly fitting out troopers as cuirassiers was a very expensive business, and such units were of limited use in mid-seventeenth century warfare. They were often present on the battlefield as the last reserve under the general's personal command where their huge momentum once they got under way could well resolve an impasse in which their target remained stationary. But these were rare occurrences. For the rest of the time the cuirassier units were an idle and costly incumbrance as they were unsuitable due to their lack of flexibility for other tasks for which cavalry were more commonly used such as scouting, raiding enemy quarters, escorting their infantry through difficult country where there was chance of an ambush, responding to unexpected encounters with the enemy whilst on the march or encamped for the night, and most importantly after a battle had been won causing disorder and carnage amongst the retreating enemy and thus lessening the chance of their army quickly reforming. Not surprisingly cuirassiers were well on the road to military obsolescence by the late 1630s.[17]

Nonetheless despite all the attention the Lord Deputy paid to men fighting on horseback Wentworth was critical of his cavalry in the lengthy report he wrote for the King in the autumn of 1638. When he arrived in Ireland he discovered that Lord Wimbledon was not exaggerating when he claimed that there was not a single officer in command there who knew how to train a troop of horse. Five years later he congratulated himself on insisting that troopers were trained on a daily basis. He was confident that their commanders' knowledge had increased considerably, but he was ashamed to admit that their mounts were not as strong or as highly prised as he would have wished. This he attributed to the traditional structure of army pay by

16   CSPD 1634–35, p.2; *ibid.* 1638–39, pp.147, 193–94; Knowler, *Strafforde's Letters* i, pp.196, 391; *ibid.* ii, pp.53, 59–66, 78, 111, 197–99, 203–04; C.H. Firth, *Cromwell's Army*, Chapter 5, and most especially pp.131–32; Roberts, *Cromwell's War Machine*, pp.58–64.
17   Roberts' highly knowledgeable account of cuirassier units describes them as being far less redundant in mid-seventeenth century warfare than I do, but he was writing exclusively about their use on the battlefield: *Cromwell's War Machine*, pp.59–60. In the closing minutes of the battle of Naseby Fairfax's lifeguard led by the general showed what cuirassiers were capable of doing by causing the last of the King's infantry formations still standing to lose cohesion and disintegrate: C. Firth and G. Davies, *The Regimental History of Cromwell's Army*, 2 vols (Oxford: University Press, 1940) i, pp.45–46.

which cavalry received less pay than infantry, which meant that they scarcely had sufficient funds to supply their mounts with fodder. He could not therefore expect more of them in terms of commitment unless the matter was addressed. For this he needed royal approval even though it was a minor problem as he could afford to pay them more thanks to the growth in the Irish economy and the consequent increase in the yield of customs duties, but to protect himself against a downturn in overseas trade he proposed to establish a cash reserve by utilising funds in the 1638 establishment dedicated to increasing the number of foot soldiers.[18] The King accepted his argument, but there was another reason why the cavalry were not in better shape. The horses were spooked by the noise of battle ranging from drumbeats to cannon fire. Animals needed to be trained not to react to noise by taking flight. Once the cavalry as a whole were bolder, they would be an invaluable asset to the army, and he intended to make it illegal for a trooper to sell a battle-hardened horse without having first obtained his permission.[19]

Throughout Wentworth's time as lord deputy the standing army infantry consisted of 2,000 officers and men divided into 40 companies.[20] This he considered was sufficient for peacetime purposes, and such was the experience of the officers and the proficiency of the rank and file (for which he had nothing but praise) that he was confident that every company could be doubled the size in time of war with the new recruits being brought up to speed through experiencing at first hand the discipline and training of the regular soldiers with whom they were billeted. His only concern in 1638 was with their weaponry. They now had sufficient body armour and their pikes were of the right length, but they were still largely armed with calivers. This was partly the King's fault, though Wentworth was too astute to say so. The Lord Deputy had tried to change Charles's mind about muskets, but the most he would agree to was for the soldiers' calivers to be remodelled with proper stocks, longer barrels, and a common bore. Wentworth did not press the point apart from informing the King that it would be impossible for the gunsmiths to standardise the bore, but possibly during his visit to London in 1636 he managed to persuade him to allow them to be replaced by muskets. There then followed a delay caused by differences amongst the lord deputy's military advisers as to whether to opt for muskets with barrels four feet long or bastard muskets with shorter barrels. However, the matters had recently been resolved and all the shot would be rearmed with full-size muskets by Easter 1639. He

---

18 Knowler, *Strafforde's Letters* ii, pp.197–201.
19 This comment appeared in a slightly earlier letter, but it is not the sort of problem that was easily addressed: Knowler, *Strafforde's Letters* ii, pp.91–92.
20 This was not the opinion of Francis Windebank, Coke's companion as secretary of state in the English government, who opted for a higher number in a document in which he gave the correct number of cavalry units. However, Wentworth was adamant that he had only 2,000 foot in 40 companies: CSPD 1638–39, p.63, Knowler, *Strafforde's Letters* ii, p.197. Possibly Windebank did not know of the saving the Lord Deputy made on the infantry that was used to guarantee higher pay for the cavalry.

proposed to buy these in Holland rather than from the royal armoury for the same reasons he had previously refused to acquire swords from that source: Dutch weapons were cheaper and of better quality. As for the calivers he would not sell or destroy them. In a future conflict they would be useful for equipping skirmishers.[21]

Artillery was something in which the lord had originally taken considerable interest but once Sir John Borlace was in post he rarely mentioned it in his correspondence. This was not a device for hiding a big hole in the reform programme. Instead having delegated the matter to an expert who he had appointed and trusted it would be tedious to report in detail on progress. It was also a sensible rhetorical ploy not to do so. By taking a laid-back attitude he could reassure the King and the Privy Council that anxiety over the army was not a state of mind but focused on areas for improvement. Also, as he knew that reform of the artillery was going very well, he could hold it in reserve for when he might need it to counterbalance less satisfactory progress in another area of military reform or to silence a critic on the Privy Council who had noticed the failure to provide regular updates and thought it seasonable to draw it to the King's attention.

The excellence of Borlace's achievement a master of ordnance was revealed in the autumn of 1639. Using Irish resources alone he had assembled a train of artillery ready to set out on campaign which included 34 brass cannons made up of four full culverins, two demi culverins and 28 drakes with almost 200 horses to pull them. In addition several hundred carts were available for carrying barrels of gunpowder as well as spare wheels, axletrees and timber for repairing the gun carriages. As for munitions Borlace had plenty of gunpowder of the right composition for use in artillery pieces, 100 cannonballs, and 25 case shot for each of the culverins, and 50 cannonballs for each of the drakes.[22] Wentworth had also persuaded a master gunner to move to Ireland from the Netherland but was concerned that he would not stay for long as his pay had not been provided for in the army establishment for 1639–40.[23]

The training programme the Lord Deputy instituted for all units within a year of arriving in Dublin required horse and foot to be drilled regularly by their captains to an acceptable level. Previously the monitoring of military preparedness had formed an element in the muster masters' list of duties, but it was a minor consideration compared with ensuring that the number of officers and men every captain claimed to have under his command was correct, and that all of them had in their possession the weapons they were supposed to have.

---

21 Knowler, *Strafforde's Letters* i, pp.196, 200; *ibid.*, ii, pp.91–92, 200, 233–35; CSPI 1633–47, p.209; Firth, *Papers relating to Thomas Wentworth*, p.7; CSPD 1636–37, p.305.
22 CSPD 1625–26, p.266; APC 45, p.91; *ibid.* 1630–31, p.37; Knowler, *Strafforde's Letters* i, pp.114, 306, 307; *ibid.*, ii, p.199; TNA, SP63/257, f.51.
23 Knowler, *Strafforde's Letters* i, p.197.

The check on numbers by the muster masters continued, but from 1634 onwards everything else changed. Every captain was to receive a list of defects in his unit that must be addressed within six months. Otherwise there would be dire consequences. However, only two captains are known to have been sacked, and in neither case was it for military incompetence. Lord Mountnorris had persuaded his brother to trip Wentworth up when he was in agony with gout, whilst Lord Esmond had been involved in spreading a rumour that the Lord Deputy had killed a sick prisoner in a fit of rage.[24]

The second stage was for every unit to visit Dublin for a month's training in groups of three, one troop of horse and two companies of foot, over the course of the next two years, a process in which the Lord Deputy would be directly involved as he intended to be present [25] As an example of what he expected of his captains he began regularly drilling his own troop of horse and company of foot on a green space just outside the city clad in black armour and astride a black horse with a black feather thrust into his helmet and it seems likely that this was in progress when so many company and troop commanders were attending the second if not the first session of the 1634 parliament A military display of this nature had apparently been quite usual when Sir Arthur Chichester was lord deputy, but it caused amusement to at least one observer given the two men's very different military credentials, though he was careful not to use the word pretentious to describe a blatant piece of theatre.[26]

Moving troops backwards and forwards between their garrisons and Dublin merely for training purposes could have been a cause for concern as it was in contravention of an understanding between the King and the Irish and Old English elites that army units would remain in their quarters until there was an emergency, as on occasions in the past soldiers on the march had seized food and fodder without paying for it and plundered and assaulted country people who put up a resistance.[27] In Wentworth's opinion however route marches were an essential part of the training of officers and soldiers in the reformed army. In the event of a serious uprising or an invasion they needed to be fit enough to cover large distances quickly either in defence of the capital or to join other units at a rendezvous within striking distance of the threat.[28] Moreover, unlike in the past when money had been in short supply his officers paid for the food and fodder they requisitioned. That the system was working by the autumn of 1638 was shown by the fact that the only recent example of violent behaviour during a cross-country march had been between soldiers in Lord Grandison's troop, and it had not involved any members of the civilian population.[29]

---

24 See Appendix IV.
25 Knowler, *Strafforde's Letters* i, pp.195–96.
26 HMC, Appendix to the Third Report, p.283.
27 See an account of the Graces in Chapter Five.
28 Knowler, *Strafforde's Letters* i, p.247; *ibid.* ii, pp.17–18, 19–20, 22; CSPI 1633–47, pp.102, 133, 164, 193.
29 Knowler, *Strafforde's Letters* ii, pp.198, 254, 262.

Before that time Wentworth had raised the training programme to a higher level by requiring numerous units to assemble at Dublin at the same time so that they could experience fighting in larger formations, which took the form of mock battles conducted in his presence. In 1638, for example, he had ordered all 40 companies of foot to be present for an entire month apart from six who were excused because of the bad weather they had experienced the previous year during their march to Killybegs Bay in the far northwest of the country where there were rumours of ships unloading troops and military supplies.[30]

Nearly all the evidence for the structure and success of these training sessions comes from the Lord Deputy's self-promoting reports to the King, but in 1637 a participant put words on paper. In July directly after the event. George Rawdon, Lord Conway's estate manager and lieutenant of his company in the standing army, sent a letter to his master who at the time was serving in the fleet. Units were exercised twice a week in mock battles watched carefully by the Lord Deputy. He also required the infantry officers to meet every day in the Parliament House in Dublin, the largest open space under cover, to practice drill as a company of foot with the former Low Countries officers Sir John Borlace and Sir Robert Farrar as captain and lieutenant. As an encouragement Wentworth presented prizes of silver plate on a daily basis to the most proficient officers, but he also entered into the spirit of things by joining the ranks in what he surely saw as a means of both instilling group solidarity in units that spent the rest of their time in virtual isolation from the rest of the standing army and preparing them for a campaign culminating in a face-to-face confrontation with an enemy. Some flavour of the camaraderie created can be found in Rawdon's closing remarks. Sir Arthur Blundell, who was acting as the senior non-commissioned officer, threatened to prick two officers, Lords Moore and Lecale, in the buttocks with his halberd if they did not perform their drill successfully. This was a punishment for making him drunk so many times. Reading between the lines they had probably been sniggering about the mistakes he was making whilst struggling with a hangover, though Lord Moore may have been in a peevish mood having been ordered to take part despite being a cavalry commander.[31]

The inspection and training of the horse and foot at Dublin for a few weeks in the summer even given the Lord Deputy's watchful eye and fearsome temper could achieve little on its own. For the rest of the year it was the troop and company commanders' knowledge, expertise and commitment which would determine whether good practice became embedded. Wentworth was clearly aware of this, but were the changes in the captaincies made during his watch focused on employing men with considerable prior

---

30 Knowler, *Strafforde's Letters* ii, p.198.
31 CSPI 1633–47, p.164. This may look like an infantry/cavalry set-to, but Lecale did not receive a commission as troop commander until 1638.

military experience who were the most likely to make a success of turning their new commands into effective fighting units?

Hardacre has claimed that the types of men Wentworth appointed to replace the veterans of the Nine Years' War were very similar to those chosen by his immediate predecessors Viscount Falkland and Lord Justices Cork and Loftus.[32] Sons succeeded their fathers or other family members as troop and company commanders, whilst government ministers and major purchasers of land in Ireland were rewarded with captaincies by virtue of that fact as were close relatives of the Lord Deputy. But the evidence Hardacre used may be misleading as it was drawn very largely from Wentworth's letters and papers, which were never intended to provide a comprehensive account of changes in army personnel.

The people to whom the Lord Deputy wrote about matters affecting the army were the King and a small number of royal ministers and advisers living in England, and unsurprisingly he only mentioned things that would be of interest to them or about which they needed to be briefed if his honour and reputation were likely to come under attack at Court or in the Privy Council. Anecdotes about the ups and downs of people his correspondents knew personally or by repute were often included if the letter's content was none too serious, but there was no reason whatsoever for mentioning men unknown to them unless there had been an altercation about their appointment.

A more informed picture of the additions to the officer corps that occurred in Wentworth's time as lord deputy can be achieved by comparing the army lists of 1629, 1639 and 1641 using the evidence to be found in other sources as well as that in Wentworth's correspondence to try and understand what was happening, though with care being taken not to include appointments made in the years 1629–32 and 1641 when lord justices governed Ireland on the King's behalf. This shows that only 13 of the 31 new appointments were mentioned in the Lord Deputy's correspondence, and that nine of these were cavalry captains, a clear imbalance between the number of units of horse and foot, though not altogether surprising given that five new troops and no new companies were created between 1635 and 1639.

Of the 10 new captains of horse none were promotions from lieutenant within the standing army and none was old enough to have fought in the Nine Years' War. Three are known to have had extensive military experience outside Ireland and two no military experience whatsoever. Of the remaining five none appear in Laurence Spring's lists of officers who fought in the British armies in Buckingham's wars, though it is possible that they could have spent the time in the Netherlands or in another European army. The most likely of these is Wentworth's brother George whose first appointment had been as a provost marshal, a common appointment for ex-soldiers.[33]

---

32 P. Hardacre, 'Patronage and purchase in the Irish standing army under Thomas Wentworth, Earl of Strafford 1632–1640', *J. Society of Army Historical* Research 67 (1988), pp.34–45, 94–104.
33 TNA, SP63/257, f.50.

This is not conclusive evidence about the doctrine Wentworth favoured covering senior appointments in the standing army cavalry, but in his second confrontation with the King over a captaincy his views on who should and who should not be in command of a troop of horse are very clear indeed.

In January 1639 the King informed the Lord Deputy that Lord Kirkcudbright, the former Sir Robert McLellan, had decided that he was too old for active service and recommended Robert Maxwell, who was not only his lieutenant but also his son-in-law, as his successor. Wentworth, however, had interviewed the young man and found him arrogant and ill-mannered, a supporter of the Scots who were in dispute with the Crown, and clearly the social inferior of the other cavalry captains with whom he would have to work. He also held him personally responsible for the discipline of the troop, which was by far the worst in the army. On these grounds he would not have appointed him as a corporal of horse.

The King responded by choosing George Fielding, the new Earl of Desmond, to replace Kirkcudbright. He could not be faulted on social grounds, but in a longer and frankly ill-tempered response Wentworth argued that he was almost as unsuitable as Maxwell. First, although the commission the King had issued required Desmond to live with his troop, the Lord Deputy suspected that he would only do so for a few months and then find some excuse for returning to Court leaving responsibility for training and disciplining his men to his lieutenant, and as army commander he was totally opposed to command being exercised by proxy. Moreover, given the condition the troop was in it needed a firm hand exerted by somebody whom the troopers would respect and instinctively obey. A young courtier was therefore most unlikely to be the man for the job. Then over the next thousand words he made it clear again and again that he only wanted to fight the King's enemies in the company of officers who understood their profession. Finally, in what was almost certainly a reflection on Lorenzo Cary he claimed that experience had taught him to fear the consequences of appointing a young gentleman 'of tender years'.[34]

The King did not reply directly but delegated the task to Sir John Coke. The letter Coke wrote to Wentworth does not survive, but Wentworth's response does. Before hearing of the King's wish for Desmond to command the troop, he had already appointed a very suitable successor to Kirkcudbright, but he now understood that he was getting into deep water when he learned that Charles had given the Queen the right to choose a replacement for Kirkcudbright. In the event this did not make Desmond's appointment unstoppable. In a friendly letter to the Lord Deputy Henrietta Maria gave her wholehearted support to the officer Wentworth had chosen and assured him that what had happened would not lessen her regard for him.[35] So unlike in 1634 the Lord Deputy got his own way. The reason why the Queen was content was almost

---

34 Knowler, *Strafforde's Letters* ii, pp.294–96.
35 CSPD 1638–39, p.185; CSPI 1633–47, pp.206, 209; Knowler, *Strafforde's Letters* ii, pp.272–73, 294–96, 329, 378; HMC, Cowper Mss ii, pp.206, 209.

certainly because he had chosen someone who was suitable in every way at a time when the King was considering making war on his Scottish subjects. He was neither a self-made career soldier with bags of experience but no class, nor a courtier or the son of some great man untutored in the art of war, but Thomas Cromwell, Fourth Baron Cromwell in the English peerage and from 1628 Viscount Lecale in the Irish peerage, a man whose military service in Europe and in the standing army stretched back at least 15 years.[36]

But what of the new infantry captains? In 1638 Wentworth described them somewhat ominously as a gallant company of gentlemen, but not all would necessarily have belonged to families entitled to bear a coat-of-arms. A captain's commission in the army gave the appointee the right to assume the title of gentleman ex officio along with new attorneys and aldermen in corporate towns.[37] Of the 21 appointed between the beginning of 1632 and the end of 1640 16 were members of the peerage or the landed gentry or were government ministers or their sons, but at least eight had seen military action and probably as many as 12. Of the remaining five whose origins are obscure it is likely that all were professional soldiers as given the competition for captaincies in the standing army men without connections in high places were unlikely to be appointed if they did not possess well-attested prior military experience. Thus the composition of the officer corps in 1640 does not suggest that the de-professionalisation of the standing army beginning in the 1620s when the veterans of the Nine Years' War were fast disappearing from the scene had continued or gathered during Wentworth's time as lord deputy but may to some extent have gone into reverse.

Thus officered, trained and equipped the standing army was ready not only to successfully besiege towns, castles and forts in Ireland held by rebels or foreign troops, but also to take on a field army in a conventional battle, and the ratio between pike and shot of one to one was not badly behind the times. Admittedly the New Model Army at its birth 10 years later had a ratio of two musketeers to a single soldier armed with a pike, but the depiction of a company being drilled for battle in William Barriffe's

---

36 Cromwell had commanded a regiment in Mansfeld's expedition in 1624 and accompanied Lord Wimbledon to Spain, and the Duke of Buckingham on the first La Rochelle expedition: Spring, *First British Army*, pp.196, 221. He had also been captain of a company of foot in the standing army in Ireland for nearly 10 years the command of which he gave up in 1639 in order presumably to give his whole attention to his new troop. There is some circumstantial evidence from his other appointments such as that of Sir John Borlace in 1638 that the Lord Deputy was opposed to officers commanding two units in the standing army: Appendix IV.
37 William Harrison, *A Description of England 1577* cited in M. Wanklyn, Landownership and Allegiance in Shropshire and Cheshire at the Outbreak of the English Civil War, University of Manchester Ph.D. thesis (1976), p.127.

Military Discipline printed in 1635 depicts a formation of 64 pikes its flanks protected by two bodies of 32 musketeers.[38]

The standing army was, of course, tiny compared with armies under the command of rulers on the Continent, but there is also evidence that Wentworth was intent on increasing the size of the army at the outbreak of war. In 1639 he purchased an extra 3,000 muskets after the order for those to equip the standing army had been placed. These were to be kept in his arsenals at Dublin and elsewhere together with the same number of pikes in preparation for the arming of 6,000 additional foot soldiers drawn from the plantations which would be used to expand the existing 40 companies from 50 to 200 officers and men. He would thus possess a decent sized army fully capable of fighting with or intimidating the King's enemies wherever they were when combined with the 1,000 horse he already under his command.[39]

---

38 D. Blackmore, *Destructive and Formidable: British Infantry Firepower 1642–1765* (Barnsley: Frontline books for Pen and Sword, 2014), pp.10–11, 23–24.
39 CSPI 1633–47, p.209; Knowler, *Strafforde's Letters* ii, pp.197, 200.

10

The Coming of War

The Lord Deputy's plans for the standing army would have required a few more years to be fully implemented, but he was not allowed the time. King Charles's confrontation with his Scottish subjects came to a head over his attempt to force them to use a new prayer book. However, from the start of the reign there had been friction. The war with France in the 1620s had been unpopular for breaking the trading links with Scotland's traditional ally in past wars against England. Charles had also antagonised the landed elite by proposing to claw back lands granted by the Crown as far back as 1540. It also took him eight years after his father's death to find the time to travel to Scotland for his coronation, though to be fair he had been at war with Spain for six of those years. The visit was not a success. Charles had been arrogant. Unlike his outgoing father he clearly preferred the company of the courtiers he had brought with him to that of the Scottish nobility. He had also insisted that the coronation service followed a programme that was essentially English in terms of its structure and the language and ceremonies used. In Scottish eyes it had more than a whiff of Roman Catholicism about it, which had ceased to be the dominant form of Christianity in Scotland following the reformation of the 1560s. In its stead was a Presbyterian Church purely Calvinist in doctrine with a system of government that was democratic rather than hierarchical. Altogether it was something in which Protestant Scots took great pride. The King in his turn had been disturbed, even offended, by the lack of reverence and order he had seen in Presbyterian services, and when he returned to England he decreed that a prayerbook should be written for universal use in Scotland. This was to include a more structured form of Sunday worship that was less dependent on ex tempore sermons and with ceremonial aspects more in line with English practice, which retained elements that could be perceived as vestiges of Catholicism. Four years later the storm broke.

The Scottish ministers of religion were ordered to begin using the new prayerbook on Sunday 23 July 1637 despite the misgivings of the Scottish Privy Council which rightly feared trouble. The upshot was civil disorder in many parts of the country involving all classes with powerful images that had resonances for many years to come such as the market trader Jennie Geddes hurling a stool at the head of the dean who was presiding over the service in St. Giles's Cathedral.

The events of 23 July and the weeks that followed were not a one-off demonstration of dislike followed by grudging acquiescence. In fact the prayerbook conjured up a perfect storm of fury against what was seen by many as an attack on Scotland's religion, liberties and independence. It had been prepared mainly by English clerics, enforced by royal degree without consulting the General Assembly, the Scottish church's governing body, or the Scottish Parliament, and it contained instructions and forms of words that could be interpreted as re-introducing Roman Catholicism by the back door. Over the next few months the storm developed into a hurricane when the King not only failed to take measures to appease his Scottish subjects as his Privy Council there wanted, but went on the attack against the promoters of petitions against the prayerbook and the Scottish bishops they held responsible for it. The latter, having been reinstated during King James's reign, had stepped over the line from administrators into arbiters of doctrine and ceremonial. If the protests continued, he would regard those involved as traitors.[1]

To zeal for the true church was thus added fear for the future. For the protestors the only recourse was to organise themselves, which gave rise to the so-called National Covenant, by which those who opposed the changes pledged themselves to 'labour by all means lawful to recover the purity and liberty of the gospel as it was established and professed before the aforesaid innovations'.[2] The National Covenant was clearly a challenge to royal authority in North Britain in that it paved the way for an alliance of patriots determined to protect Scotland's religion and liberties.

The Covenanter movement came into being on 1 March 1638 when the document was signed in Edinburgh by numerous noblemen and lesser landowners, and then by nearly 300 ministers and the lay representatives of Scottish towns and cities. From the capital its endorsement spread to the provinces where all classes of parishioners committed themselves to its aims by signing it in public often in their own churchyards.[3] The King's response was to refuse to compromise over what he saw as a plot conceived as long ago as 1625 by a faction of the nobility but dressed up as a grievance over religion in order to win massed support, but it took him some time to make up his mind how to proceed. However, on 20 June he described his strategy for military action against Scotland should it be necessary, and on 1 July he informed the English Privy Council that unless his Scottish subjects immediately distanced

---

1 M. Braddick, *God's Fury, England's Fire: A New History of the English Civil Wars* (London: Allen Lane, 2008), pp.26–33; Cust, *Charles I*, pp.223–29. For a recent account of Jennie Geddes, see *ODNB* 23.
2 S.R. Gardiner, *Constitutional Documents of the Puritan Revolution 1625–1666* (Oxford: University Press, 1979), p.132.
3 Cust, *Charles I*, pp.229–30; Braddick, *God's Fury, England's Fire*, pp.33–36; Robert Baillie, *Letters and Journals 1637–1662*, D. Laing (ed.), 3 vols (Ballantine Club: Edinburgh, 1841) i, p.62.

themselves from the National Covenant he would impose the prayer book on them by force. Within weeks arms manufacturers in the Netherlands were receiving orders for weapons and armour from both England and Scotland; the Covenanter leadership was compiling a list of Scottish professional soldiers serving in European armies who might be willing to come home in the event of an invasion; and the King was preparing to place garrisons in towns close to the Scottish border to deter an invasion.[4]

Up to that point Ireland had not been involved in the Anglo-Scottish spat. Wentworth had deliberately kept his thoughts to himself, although it has been argued that he was already having worries about security issues surrounding the numerous Scottish settlers in the Ulster plantations.[5] Nevertheless his incoming and outgoing correspondence throughout 1637 and for the first half of 1638 was obsessively concerned with financial matters and securing the downfall of Lord Chancellor Loftus. The Reverend George Garrard kept him intermittently informed from London about goings-on in Scotland and reactions at Court,[6] but he does not seem to have known about the suggestion made in June by the Marquis of Hamilton, who was serving as the King's representative in Scotland, that Irish military resources could be used to cause trouble for the Covenanters by inciting clan-on-clan warfare in the Inner Hebrides the details of which are discussed later in this chapter.

The first inkling of the prayerbook rebellion impacting directly on Ireland was in a letter from Randall MacDonnell, the Catholic Earl of Antrim, written in London on 17 July 1638 prior to his leaving for Ireland asking for Wentworth's assistance in defending his Irish estates against Archibald Campbell, Lord Lorne. Encouraged by the Covenanters' use of armed forces against Catholic supporters of Charles I in Scotland, Lorne was preparing to add the MacDonnell's Irish lands to his clan's ex-MacDonnell possessions in the Inner Hebrides, which had been granted to the Campbells by King James following their conquest by units of the standing army in 1614–15 as described in Chapter 2. Antrim's request was for a secure store of weapons to be established at Coleraine for which Wentworth held the key but which he would allow Antrim's tenants to use for their defence if Scottish troops landed in Ulster. A week later the Lord Deputy received a flurry of communications from England. Archbishop Laud wrote warning him to be wary of the Ulster Scots; the Earl of Northumberland, now his close though nervous political associate, was in a state of near panic because the English government was totally unprepared to fight a war; whilst the King wanted to know what he could expect from Ireland in terms of military support against the Covenanters. Charles's request was apparently delivered

---

4 Cust, *Charles I*, pp.227–28; J. Wheeler, *The Irish and British Wars 1637–1654* (London: Routledge, 2002), pp.18–19; HMC, Cowper Mss ii, p.196; A. Woolrych, *Britain in Revolution 1625–1660* (Oxford: University Press, 2002), pp.105–6; Gardiner, *History of England* viii, p.314; C.V. Wedgwood, *The King's Peace* (London: Collins, 1955), p.218.
5 Knowler, *Strafforde's Letters* ii, p.189; Stevenson, *Scottish Covenanters and Irish Confederates*, pp.12–14.
6 Knowler, *Strafforde's Letters* ii, pp.117, 129, 167, 181.

by word of mouth only, but the gist can be inferred from the Lord Deputy's letters written to the King on 28 July and 11 August and to Sir John Coke on 10 August.[7]

The Lord Deputy promised Archbishop Laud that he would be wary and tried to calm Northumberland down by outlining a strategy that could bring the Covenanters to their knees. In his written response to the King he was very careful in his use of words. Although he would immediately obey any future command to fight the Scots using what military resources he could muster, he made it very clear that he had the gravest misgivings about a premature declaration of war. The 2,000 foot and 600 horse currently in the standing army were not sufficient to guarantee Ireland's security given the situation facing him in the summer of 1638.[8] Not only was there the strong chance of unrest in the recent plantations in Munster and Connaught he was also worried about some of the settlers in Ulster who had welcomed extreme Presbyterian ministers fleeing from persecution by the Scottish bishops and about whom he had been recently in correspondence with Laud. However, he thought that he might be able to assemble a body of 3–4,000 volunteers and impressed men living in Ireland most of whom would be English who, having been licked into shape by a dozen or so able captains and lieutenants from the standing army, could be shipped to England as an army corps under the command of two of his most experienced officers, Sir Francis Willoughby and Sir Robert Farrar. Catholic Irish recruits he thought would also fight well against the Covenanters, but he had the usual misgivings about the threat to Ireland's security of men trained in the use of arms overseas returning home and teaching others. He would, however, be unable to supply the recruits sent to England with weapons. As for the standing army he would station most of units in Ulster to deter an uprising by the settlers or an invasion commanded by Lord Lorne, and if the province did not become the seat of war he might well find it operationally feasible to make raids on the west coast of Scotland and thus tie down troops that would have otherwise have strengthened the Covenanter field army facing an English invasion.

Wentworth devoted less space to rubbishing the Earl's proposal, but he dealt with it first before the King's concentration lapsed in the hope of discrediting Antrim before he became a object of concern to the Dublin government. But he had no need to worry. Charles was not yet interested in the Earl's wider schemes for the MacDonnells to carry the war to the enemy which are described later in this chapter. His only instruction was to keep an eye on developments. This Wentworth promised to do but he had no confidence in either the Earl's ability or his military clout. He also suspected Antrim's true intentions given that he was a grandson of the Earl of Tyrone. Finally he feared that establishing an arms store at Coleraine close to the lands occupied by Scottish settlers and secured only by a lock would encourage them to help themselves to weapons if war broke out between England and Scotland leading to a second front opening up in Ireland.

---

7   Knowler, *Strafforde's Letters* ii, pp.184, 185–89, 197–201, 203–04.
8   The 400 additional horse mentioned in Chapter 9 had yet to be raised.

In other respects the letters that Wentworth wrote to the King and also to Secretary Coke were mainly concerned with the state of the standing army and with arguments for increasing the strength of the cavalry as discussed above together with the first tentative plans for increasing the number of foot soldiers should serious fighting break out in Ireland. The Lord Deputy also had two recommendations designed to lessen still further Antrim's potential to disturb Ireland's tranquillity. To prevent Catholic hopes being raised and Scottish settlers being tempted by an arms store at Coleraine, the calivers made available by the rearming of the infantry with muskets should be placed in a magazine under his control from which they could be distributed to English settlers, and by implications Irish loyalists, in times of war or civil unrest. Second, he warned the King that Antrim was likely to lobby vigorously for his brother to be given command of one of the new troops of horse. Given his religion and his ancestry this would cause great offence to all the English in Ireland, both New and Old.[9]

The King's response was largely positive. He accepted Wentworth's concerns about arming the Catholics and giving a captaincy to Antrim's brother, and he left the decision about the establishment of an arms store at Coleraine to the Lord Deputy's discretion and that of his council, but he praised the Earl for his generosity and nobility and urged the Lord Deputy not to ignore him when he arrived in Ireland. He should behave towards him exactly as he would towards any other member of the Catholic nobility.[10]

However, in the middle of Wentworth's very long letter to Coke written on 10 August were two paragraphs of immense consequence for his future and ultimately that of the King. For most of the time the Lord Deputy's focus was on keeping the standing army in Ireland as a defence against an invasion or an uprising, but he also gave an inkling of his plans for the future, which envisaged it playing an offensive role as an instrument of royal will when this was challenged by rebellious subjects anywhere in Great Britain.[11]

Wentworth's reasoning ran as follows. In the future it will be '…necessary that his Majesty breed up and have a seminary in some part or other of his dominions, a truth which perchance the present time shows plainly to every eye'. Moreover, Ireland was best fitted to fulfil that role as it would be easiest to transport troops from there by water 'to answer the several occasions of the three kingdoms'. He then went on to take another swipe at his immediate predecessors as the King's representatives in Ireland. If the reforms he had instituted had been imposed immediately after the end of the Duke of Buckingham's wars the groundwork would already have been laid, and 'the Crown might have taken hence at this time officers to command an army of 20,000 men in every part of Christendom'.[12] This left open the possibility that they could

9   Knowler, *Strafforde's Letters* ii, pp.200, 204.
10 Knowler, *Strafforde's Letters* ii, p.211.
11 Knowler, *Strafforde's Letters* ii, p.198.
12 Knowler, *Strafforde's Letters* ii, p.198.

have been used to recover the Elector Palatine's lost lands in Germany, but it did not rule out the possibility that they might have been be employed much closer to home against the King's subjects who opposed his policies which they saw as a threat to their liberties

Finally, in a letter to the Earl of Northumberland intended for the King's ears if not his eyes Wentworth described what he saw as the only practicable strategy for defeating the Covenanters, which steered a middle path between the bleak pessimism of the Earl himself and the foolhardy optimism of ministers such as Lord Cottington and Sir Francis Windebank.[13] The King must not allow his authority to be reduced by making concessions to the Covenanters, but for the present he must temporise so as to avoid going to war ill-prepared and suffer the inevitable consequences. He should therefore open negotiations with the Covenanters in the hope of causing splits in their ranks, but if these failed as well they might, he should do all he could during the breathing space they provided to raise, train and equip a large army.[14] And that was the policy Charles adopted. Impressed it seems by Wentworth's advice not to fight the Scots in 1638 he directed the Marquis of Hamilton, who was still in Scotland, to win support there by talking about what he hoped would be seen as genuine concessions. However, despite the Lord Deputy's hints that he would like to return to England and thus be closely involved in the preparations for war, Charles decided to keep him on the side-lines to be used as a weapon of last resort.

The Marquis's wheeling and dealing came closest to success on 22 September with his first announcement of the concessions Charles was prepared to make, which included the summoning of a General Assembly of the Scottish church over which he was to preside as the King's representative. From then onwards, however, it was downhill all the way. A close examination of the language used in the printed version did nothing to allay concern about Charles's long-term aims, and the result was a major push by the Covenanters to obtain the assembly's consent to measures that would protect Presbyterianism against royal interference in the future including doing away with Scottish bishops. When he saw that the Covenanters' programme had the support of the majority, Hamilton tried to send the assembly packing, but the representatives refused to budge whereupon he gave up his mission and returned to England in mid December.

The Covenanters then set about creating Fortress Scotland. Parts of the country not wholeheartedly for the Covenant like the lowlands beyond the river Tay centred on Aberdeen were secured by force, whilst in the far southwest of the mainland closest to Ireland where support for the Covenant was very strong Lord Lorne began raising troops for a field army. Well before Hamilton returned to London it was clear to him

---

13 Knowler, *Strafforde's Letters* ii, pp.185, 186; Cust, *Charles I*, p.231.
14 Knowler, *Strafforde's Letters* ii, pp.181–86, 190–93.

and to Charles that war was inevitable, and the process of incorporating the standing army into the King's strategy for conquering Scotland began in earnest. In late October a memorandum presented to the King suggested that it should be expanded to almost 10,000 men and that it should play a part in defeating the Covenanters by launching an attack on their exposed west flank, namely the coastline between Ayr and the mouth of the river Clyde. This had the advantage of requiring only a short sea voyage and an even shorter march overland to gain access to the Scottish Lowlands and the country's principal centres of population. The writer's identity is not known but it was clearly neither the Earl of Antrim whose possible assistance did not receive a mention nor the Lord Deputy as the numbers given for the standing army in the text were several months out of date.[15]

When Hamilton was first in Scotland Wentworth's letters were concerned less with matters relating to Ireland, both civil and military, or harassing or rubbishing his political enemies real or imaginary and more with the military potential resources of the counties that fell within his jurisdiction as president of the Council of the North. However, he had begun to drop small pieces of advice about strategy for defeating the Scots whilst humbly admitting to his lack of active military experience, which he acknowledged in his letter to the King written on 28 July.[16] A small tactical retreat from his previous position that the standing army must remain in Ireland to curb internal unrest was appropriate, but one that would serve not only as a sign of his commitment to a war against the Covenanters but also clear evidence of the success of his military reforms.

In almost his first comment on how to respond to the Covenanter threat the lord deputy had emphasised the need to tie Scottish troops down by a vigorous defence of the royal fortresses in Scotland, Edinburgh and Dumbarton castles. Both were close to the sea, and he saw them as capable of being reinforced by troop transports protected by the royal navy, but in his naivety about military matters he underestimated the difficulties, and when hostilities commenced in the spring of 1639 both garrisoned fell into Covenanter hands almost immediately.[17]

Wentworth then urged the King to strongly fortify the frontier by placing troops and munitions in Berwick-on-Tweed and Carlisle defending the east coast and the west routes from England into Scotland. This would most easily be done at Berwick. It was a port which could be supplied by sea from the naval base at nearby Holy Island; it already had a small garrison of regular troops; and it had modern fortifications

---

15   CSPD 1638–39, pp.63–64. The writer was probably a privy councillor or a civil servant with no immediate knowledge of what was happening in Ireland. He knew that the establishment for 1639–40 allowed the Lord Deputy to raise companies over and above the 40 in the standing army but not that the King had given Wentworth permission not to do so but to use the money saved to increase the cavalry officers' pay.
16   Knowler, *Strafforde's Letters* ii, p.188.
17   Knowler, *Strafforde's Letters* ii, pp.192, 235; CSPD 1638–39, p.4; Stevenson, *Scottish Covenanters and Irish Confederates*, p.31.

constructed during Queen Elizabeth's reign. However, the garrison must be increased in size as the Covenanters would see its capture as a great propaganda victory as it was the only part of Scotland to remain in English hands at the end of the interminable wars between the two kingdoms from the thirteenth to the sixteenth centuries.

Carlisle on the other hand was defended by nothing more substantial than a medieval stone wall and a castle both of which were in a poor state of repair, and the city had for many years not been geared up to supplying a large garrison with bread and beer. Admittedly it was very close to the Irish Sea but it lacked a harbour deep enough for the unloading of large ships. Troops and supplies would therefore have to be fed through Whitehaven and Workington over 40 miles to south, but between west Cumberland and Carlisle lay difficult country where convoys might easily be ambushed by Scottish raiding parties.[18]

Nevertheless on 22 October when he could see that Hamilton was making little headway in creating divisions within the Covenanter leadership the King wrote to his Lord Deputy in a way that was more characteristic of a supplicant than a monarch, In a personal letter rather than in a paragraph in one of Coke's he asked Wentworth whether he would be willing to alter his stance about the standing army and dispatch 500 foot soldiers to Carlisle to serve as a garrison together with some artillery pieces if he could spare them.[19] Wentworth's response was over the top in terms of enthusiasm. He agreed to provide a regiment comprising five companies 100 strong from the infantry serving in the standing army. He proposed the distinguished veteran Sir Francis Willoughby as colonel with Sir Henry Tichborne and Sir Arthur Blundell as field officers and George Blount and Phillip Wenham as commanders of the fourth and fifth companies. All were captains in the standing army and all except possibly Wenham had had combat experience before being commissioned.[20] His only request in return was for a troop of cavalry raised in England to be attached to the garrison. Otherwise intelligence gathering and foraging in the surrounding countryside would out of the question.

The Lord Deputy assembled the regiment's rank and file by taking 13 or so soldiers from every company and replacing them with pressed men on the ground that this would cause less least disruption than selecting five fully formed companies and

---

18   Knowler, *Strafforde's Letters* ii, pp.191, 261–2, 268, 275, 298. Strafford preferred Whitehaven, which was five miles further away, presumably because a stone pier had been erected there very recently permitting coal to be exported from the Cumbrian coalfield to Ireland: CSPI 1633–47, p.12; O. Wood, 'West Cumbria Coal 1600–1982', *Cumberland and Westmoreland Antiquarian and Archaeological Society* extra series xxiv (1988).
19   Knowler, *Strafforde's Letters* ii, p.228.
20   Knowler, *Strafforde's Letters* ii, p.233; TNA, SP 63/257, f.50. Tichborne and Blundell were long-standing company commanders having been in post since about 1620, whilst Wenham seems to have succeeded his brother Sir Thomas as late as 1638: CSPI 1615–25, pp.10, 343. Blount, who had been used by the Lord Deputy as a de facto inspector of the army in 1633, probably acquired a company soon afterwards. For their previous active service see Appendix IV.

re-garrisoning their former quarters with raw recruits. On the other hand he would guarantee that no company suffered in matters affecting command and control as a result of top-slicing by ensuring that the most each would lose was a single commissioned or non-commissioned officer. He also promised that the regiment would be equipped entirely with muskets and 12 months' supply of gunpowder, bullet and match, and that given they were to be in garrison the ratio of muskets to pikes should be seven to three rather than one to one. Finally, he asked and was granted permission to impress 500 men to replace the soldiers going to Carlisle, but he undertook to cashier them when Willoughby's regiment returned. It would, however, take him nine weeks to prepare it for embarkation given the time of the years and the distances and disruption involved that top-slicing would involve.

In the event it was four months before the regiment left for England. Interestingly much of the time was taken up with training which the Lord Deputy supervised in person. Some would have been necessary in order to give the new companies the chance to shake down and to as well as to bring up to scratch the 50 men Wentworth been obliged to impress to replace soldiers of Scottish nationality sent to Carrickfergus by some of his captains, but to be cynical the time taken suggests that even the best men were not as well trained as Wentworth had claimed in his letters to the King and Secretary Coke. However, good courtier that he was he took care to keep the King directly or indirectly informed about progress and the reasons for the delay.[21]

Willoughby's regiment left Carrickfergus for Whitehaven on 31 March 1639. In its absence Carlisle had been garrisoned by the Cumberland trained bands in case the Scots, believed to be massing close to the border, mounted a surprise attack. Wentworth then set about exploiting the propaganda value of having part of the standing army stationed in England as shown by the instructions he sent to Willoughby on his arrival at Carlisle. The regiment was to be exercised twice a week in the use of arms. The officers were to ensure that the men were kept in good order and not allowed to live a life of idleness which could well lead to debauchery. To that end they were to be employed in building work, namely as pioneers improving the city's defences. His expectations were that the Carlisle garrison would be seen to be behaving more gallantly than any other regiments facing the Covenanters, and that if his advice was followed to the letter it could well be ordered to join the main body of the King's army due to rendezvous near Berwick so that its drill and discipline could serve as an example to the rest of the infantry.[22] But all that proved to be a pipe

---

21 Knowler, *Strafforde's Letters* ii, pp.233–34, 254–55, 278–79, 287, 290, 292, 306, 309, 312; HMC, Cowper Mss ii, p.205.
22 CSPD 1639, p.9; Knowler, *Strafforde's Letters* ii, pp.310, 312, 315–17, 320. Wentworth proved to be correct, but Willoughby successfully argued against part of his regiment being moved to York: *ibid.* ii, p.330.

dream. The regiment remained at Carlisle where it was a marvel to many, but they were mainly local worthies.[23]

As Charles I and his Scottish subjects prepared to fight one another in the First Bishops' War, and well before Willoughby's regiment left for Carlisle, the Earl of Antrim was being discussed as somebody capable of making a major contribution towards the strategy for defeating the Covenanters. This was first mentioned in elite Catholic circles in Scotland as early as April 1638 in the interest of preventing the Covenanters overrunning the whole of Scotland before an army could arrive from England. The reasoning that behind it was that the MacDonnell sept and its allies in Ulster and the west of Scotland were so numerous as to be capable of mounting an offensive against the lands occupied by the Earl of Argyll and other members of the Campbell family and their tenants in the Highlands and Islands. This distraction would make it impossible for the most powerful of the Presbyterian clans to join the Covenanter army, which would be much to the advantage of the King's cause.[24] There was, however, no mention at the time of the Lord Deputy or the standing army.

The first official suggestion of Antrim causing a rumpus in the west of Scotland and of the standing army being involved can be found in a letter written by the Marquis of Hamilton to the King in June 1638:

> the Earl of Antrim may be of use in this business (subduing the country by force) for he is beloved by divers of his name, and hath some pretensions to lands in Kintyre, Islands and Highlands and will no doubt repair to Ireland and bring such forces with him as will put those countries into that disorder, and chiefly if the deputy can spare any of the army there to join with him, as I hope that part of the country will do us but little hurt.

Charles was interested, but the instructions issued to Wentworth six months later and the discussions that followed envisaged the standing army merely supplying Antrim with weapons:

> I should be glad if you could find some way to furnish the Earl of Antrim (though he be a Roman Catholic) with arms, for he may be of much use to me at this time to shake loose upon the Earl of Argyll.[25]

---

23 Knowler, *Strafforde's Letters* ii, pp.315, 316, 330, 346–47, 352, 354; HMC, Cowper Mss ii, pp.237, 238, 244.
24 Cust, *Charles I*, p.231 citing P. Donald, *An Uncounselled King: Charles I and the Scottish Troubles 1637–41* (Cambridge: University Press, 1990), pp.71, 87–89.
25 S.R. Gardiner, 'The Hamilton Papers' (London: *Camden Society* n.s. xxvii, 1880), pp.12–13; Knowler, *Strafforde's Letters* ii, p.275.

Wentworth's response was that Antrim's plans were overly ambitious. He might be able to raise a substantial body of men, but he needed money to turn them into an army and that was something he clearly did not possess. He would be happy to sell him military hardware surplus to his own requirements, but to provide anything more would imperil Ireland's security. The size of the gulf between the Earl and the Lord Deputy, however, only became fully apparent in late March 1639 when Antrim asked for twice as much gunpowder as there was in the Dublin arsenal, large numbers of muskets, and a dozen pieces of field artillery. This raid on his patiently accumulated military resources Wentworth flatly rejected to Antrim's face with his council lined up behind him. He then wrote a long and tightly argued letter to the King demolishing one by one the Earl's proposals for converting his aspirations into reality.[26]

In a letter written on 11 April the King remained enthusiastic about Antrim's scheme but two days later Secretary Windebank wrote that after receiving Wentworth's response to the Earl's requests he had changed his mind about whether Antrim would be capable of effecting a landing in Scotland in the 1639 campaigning season, but he was not to discourage him.[27] Windebank, however, had jumped the gun. Charles, having reached York on his way to join his army at Berwick, had changed his mind. Wentworth was to give Antrim what resources he could short of a contingent from the standing army but not to allow him to leave Ireland until the war on the Anglo-Scottish border was under way and then only after he had received the King's order to do so.[28]

The twists and turns in the demands, charges and counter charges made by Antrim and Wentworth during April, May and June do not merit a place in a monograph on the standing army as Antrim wanted nothing more in terms of personnel than some skilled soldiers to train his men before they set sail and a couple of experienced officers to command them. I also have no intention of speculating about whether or not the Earl would have succeeded in causing havoc in the Western Highlands and the Inner Hebrides had the Lord Deputy given him the resources he requested, or the extent to which Wentworth's unwillingness to cooperate was rooted in first rate evidence that Antrim was being economical with the truth or his habit of rubbishing somebody whom he saw as a rival for the King's ear.

It is, however, possible to knock firmly on the head the allegations made by many historians that Wentworth had plans for the standing army to fight in the war against the Covenanters in 1639, and that the King was as committed to the notion.

---

26 Knowler, *Strafforde's Letters* ii, pp.305–06.
27 Knowler, *Strafforde's Letters* ii, pp.275, 278, 289, 304, 335, 363, 365. In April 1639 he agreed to contribute 300 soldiers towards strengthening the garrison of Dumbarton castle, but it surrendered within days and well before orders could be sent for him to do so: *ibid.* ii, pp.313, 324–25.
28 Knowler, *Strafforde's Letters* ii, pp.319, 322–23. For the beginning of Wentworth's fightback see *ibid.* ii, p.338.

Using the standing army for an incursion into the Highlands and the Islands or the lowlands around Glasgow was clearly not in Wentworth's mind when he wrote on 28 July 1638 and again on 11 November suggesting that a force 3,000 strong should be stationed in the royal fortress at Dumbarton and thus cut Glasgow and its port off from the sea. This was exactly the size of the standing army in November, but if he had shipped it to Scotland in its entirety he could not have defended Ireland against insurrection or invasion, which as he frequently reminded the King's ministers was his first and foremost duty as lord deputy. Antrim's scheme having not yet seen the light of day, the clear implication is that Wentworth expected Charles to provide the 3,000 men, their equipment and their pay, a point that was driven home by his statement that he would be able to supply them with food and fodder. If he had thought that Ireland could have contributed anything more substantial to the operation he would have said so.[29]

In the same month Wentworth mentioned the possibility of raising 3,000 to 4,000 men in Ireland to help the war effort most of whom would be English by birth, but these were clearly to strengthen the King' forces on the Scottish border not to take part in an invasion of Scotland from Ireland. Although their destination was not made fully clear at the start, of the letter, later on he stated that he could not provide them with arms which they must be supplied with when they 'reached that side', which can only mean England.[30]

A letter from Sir Henry Vane, acting secretary of state in Coke's absence, to the Lord Deputy written on 13 April 1639 is totally irrelevant.[31] It reads like an order for a large number of soldiers from the standing army to be made ready at very short notice to land in Scotland, and as such seems to be the basis for Stevenson's claim that Wentworth's men were to be part and parcel of Antrim's plan of attack. However, the number stated was identical to the number of men the Earl was proposing to ship to the Inner Hebrides, which points to some confusion in Sir Henry's mind rather than anything involving the standing army.[32]

The only occasion when the King either requested Wentworth to provide a large number of soldiers from the standing army for service in Scotland or asked for his advice as to its feasibility was in late May when cold war between England and Scotland was hotting up. There is no record whatsoever of this in the Lord Deputy's incoming and outgoing correspondence carefully copied down by Knowler, but Wentworth's forthright response can be found in passages on the second page of a letter to Sir John Coke dated the 30th.[33] What else Wentworth was to supply to accompany the

---

29   Knowler, *Strafforde's Letters* ii, pp.188, 235.
30   Knowler, *Strafforde's Letters* ii, p.188.
31   Stevenson, *Scottish Covenanters and Irish Confederates*, pp.26, 27–28.
32   Knowler, *Strafforde's Letters* ii, pp.305–06, 312–13, 319, 335, 357.
33   It was probably delivered by Sir Henry Spottiswood, the son of a High Church bishop in the Church of Ireland, who arrived in Dublin on 30 May: Knowler, *Strafforde's Letters* ii, p.353.

troops and where they were to land is not revealed, but he refused to contemplate anything beyond further strengthening the standing army in Ulster to deceive the Earl of Argyll a stratagem which he and the King had talked about since the autumn of 1638.[34] And having so many soldiers in Ulster in June 1639 would have added advantages. Not only would it be a further incentive for supporters of the Covenanters living there to keep their heads down, it would also help to browbeat the Ulster Scots into swearing an oath of loyalty that he was about to impose on them.[35] [36]

The letter mentioning an invasion of Scotland had clearly come as a great surprise to the Lord Deputy as the second page begins with the statement 'That 1,000 of the army more (than Willoughby's regiment) are expected to be landed on the other side startled me much and I dare not advise it in any respect'. He then described his worries about unrest or potential unrest in almost every part of Ireland: Presbyterian Scots in Ulster on the verge of rebellion; unrest in Munster and Connaught stemming from recent plantations; the burning of Englishmen's houses in parts of Leinster; and a gang of 40 freebooters on the loose in County Donegal. The principal restraint on unrest turning into something much worse was the standing army which if kept at the existing level of 3,000 horse and foot would enable him to keep the peace, but if he were to advise the King to reduce it by a third, he would deserve to have his head chopped off when the whole country descended into uproar. Moreover, there was no military logic behind sending 1,000 soldiers to serve in Scotland as they were too few to act as a deterrent or distraction and, though he did not say so, highly likely to be lost for good given the much larger force the Covenanter could bring against them.

He did however offer something of a compromise. Once he had Charles's permission to do so he would march into north Ulster at the head of the rest of the standing army, join forces with the units already there at their camp adjacent to Carrickfergus, and ensure that Covenanter spies and informants could see that there were sufficient ships in harbour to carry 3,000 men to Scotland accompanied by a naval escort prepared to chase away or sink the ship bristling with guns the Earl of Argyll had recently purchased in the United Provinces to guard the west coast. This having been done it would make Ulster secure against anything planned by the Earl of Argyll by making it impossible for boats from the Scottish west coast ports to put to sea.[37]

Wentworth's letter was followed several days later by two more addressed to the King. The first written by the Lord Deputy's council repeated much of what he had said on 30 May relating to the threats to Ireland's security of draining Ireland of

---

34 Knowler, *Strafforde's Letters* ii, pp.188, 309, 337.
35 Knowler, *Strafforde's Letters* ii, p.338.
36 The final touch was for the Lord Deputy himself to visit the army encampment if deemed necessary, but he appears from his outgoing correspondence to have spent the whole of April and May at Dublin Castle or at Fairwood Park, his private residence just outside the city: Knowler, *Strafforde's Letters* ii, pp.320–60.
37 HMC, Cowper Mss ii, pp.229–30; Stevenson, *Scottish Covenanters and Irish Confederates*, p.27; Knowler, *Strafforde's Letters* ii, p.406.

troops. The second from Wentworth himself focused on strategy. Charles was asked not to permit the naval vessels stationed off the north-east coast of Ireland to sail to the island of Skye on what he saw as a whim of the Earl of Antrim. If they did so, Ulster would be in danger of plundering raids from the Scottish west coast ports and Argyll might attempt an invasion despite the odds against it succeeding given the number of standing army units he would be facing.[38]

Whether or not the King would have accepted Wentworth's advice in the letter written on 30 May is irrelevant. He did not receive it until 8 June, and by that time the context had changed.[39] After a brief and humiliating excursion into Scotland four days before Charles had decided that the Covenanters were much better prepared for war than he was, and that it was too risky to fight a campaign on the Borders in 1639. He therefore accepted the enemy's offer of negotiations and a truce, the so-called Pacification of Berwick, was signed on 18 June.[40] Wentworth and many others were convinced that it would not last but initially some of the King's advisers had high hopes that if he visited Edinburgh he might be able to cause divisions in the Covenanter leadership and thus enhance his chances of achieving a victory by political means. However, Charles had had doubts from the start. In a letter to Wentworth written on 23 June he quoted an old Scottish proverb to the effect that if you make friends with an enemy you should put two locks on your door.[41] He had not forgotten that both his father and Mary Queen of Scots had been kidnapped by some of their leading subjects. Even so the Lord Deputy felt it necessary to try and strengthen the King's resolve by dropping hints about the danger of his being forced to make significant concessions in order to regain his freedom if the Covenanters refused to allow him to leave Scotland.[42] A second war was therefore very much on the cards with Wentworth in pole position to supervise the preparations in both England and Ireland thanks to the wise strategic advice he had given to the King in 1639.

---

38 Knowler, *Strafforde's Letters* ii, pp.357–60.
39 HMC, Cowper Mss ii, pp.229, 231.
40 Cust, *Charles I*, pp.247–49.
41 Knowler, *Strafforde's Letters* ii, p.361.
42 Knowler, *Strafforde's Letters* ii, pp.372, 376.

11

Planning a New War

The standing army had played a significant support role in an Anglo-Scottish war that never properly caught fire by garrisoning Carlisle and by its heavy presence in Ulster reducing the possibility of an armed confrontation there between the earls of Antrim and Argyll. The Lord Deputy's assessment of the feasibility of Antrim's proposals had proved right, but this was not ultimately accepted by the King until several weeks after the Pacification of Berwick when the experienced professional officer Sir Henry Bruce, whom Charles had chosen to lead the Earl's expedition to the west coast of Scotland, returned to Court and confirmed that preparations were so behindhand that an attack on the Clan Campbell in 1639 was out of the question.[1]

In his letter to the Lord Deputy written on 23 July the King could not admit that he had been hoodwinked by the silver-tongued earl, but he dropped his first hint that Wentworth's time in Ireland might be coming to an end. He wanted them to have a face-to-face talk about how best to defeat the Covenanters, but the Lord Deputy was to conceal the purpose of his visit to England by explaining to interested parties that it was for personal reasons not reasons of state. The implication was that the visit would be a short one, but within a few weeks Charles was urging the Lord Deputy to hurry up, with no time limit being set to his stay in England and provision being made for Lord Justices Wandesford and Dillon to govern Ireland in his absence. The chance of open warfare with the Covenanters was increasing by the day, and Wentworth's political and administrative skills were needed to ensure that the armed forces operating along the Scottish border were better prepared than they had been in the summer.[2]

Antrim's duplicity being brought into the full light of day was not the only reason why royal regard for the Lord Deputy's abilities increased during 1639, but the fact that it had done so was not entirely due to his own efforts. Luck had also played its part in that Henry Rich, Earl of Holland, who Wentworth rightly saw as his principal enemy

---

1 Knowler, *Strafforde's Letters* ii, pp.363, 372.
2 Knowler, *Strafforde's Letters ii,* pp.356, 372–73, 374–75, 378.

at Court, had blotted his copybook.[3] Commissioned to the Lord Deputy's disgust to serve as second-in-command of the army assembling near Berwick he had advanced from Coldstream as far as the outskirts of Kelso, a distance of some eight miles, with a force of horse and foot only to fall back hurriedly into England with his troops in some disorder after mistaking the size of the Covenanter army facing him.[4] On the other hand Wentworth's men based at Carlisle had earned some credit by staying put when a larger force of Covenanters stationed themselves at Dumfries. Moreover, there had been no criticism of their behaviour towards the civilian population in the city or the surrounding countryside.[5]

Wentworth also gained some mileage out of a military initiative which he first saw as circumventing if not undermining his authority as lord deputy. In March 1639 the Protestant Earl of Barrymore was commissioned by the King to raise a regiment in Ireland 1,000 strong for service in the English army fighting the Covenanters. All that was required of the Lord Deputy was to provide ships to transport it to England, but he would have suspected the venture was a deliberate slight as Barrymore was the Earl of Cork's son-in-law. In typical fashion when faced with something that looked like the work of his political enemies he went on the attack informing the King that the methods used by Barrymore's agents for raising troops in Munster had caused alarm and unrest. He also accused them of recruiting men who were English by birth and were needed in Ireland to help fill gaps in the standing army. However, the regiment was raised quite quickly, and Barrymore's men duly landed at Workington in mid July, but by that time the truce had been in force for several weeks and they were promptly shipped back to Ireland and disbanded seemingly without disturbing the peace.[6] By then Wentworth had slightly changed his tune. He had clearly been responsible for the success of the shipping arrangements and for overseeing the disbandment and could therefore afford to be magnanimous which went as far as expressing sympathy for Barrymore who had spent large sums of his own money but gained nothing in return. Such behaviour towards a possible enemy pawn showed a statesmanlike quality the Lord Deputy had not previously displayed, but he took the opportunity to make capital out of the whole episode with a Parthian shot aimed at preventing the like happening again. The raising of men for wartime service in the modern age was

---

3   See, for example, Knowler, *Strafforde's Letters* ii, pp.123, 187, 284, 337; Edward Hyde, Lord Clarendon, *The History of the Rebellion and Civil Wars in England*, W.D. Macray (ed.), 6 vols (Oxford: University Press, 1888), book ii, paras. 48, 81.
4   C. Terry, *The Life and Campaigns of Alexander Leslie, Earl of Leven* (London: Longman 1899), pp.69–70. For the most stimulating account of Holland's expedition see Wedgwood, *The King's Peace*, pp.271–72. For *schadenfreude* on Wentworth's part see Knowler, *Strafforde's Letters* ii, p.382.
5   Knowler, *Strafforde's Letters* ii, pp.333, 346, 354; HMC, Cowper Mss ii, pp.237–42.
6   CSPD 1639, p.210; CSPI 1633–47, pp.210, 213; Lenihan, *Consolidating Conquest*, p.69; Knowler, *Strafforde's Letters* ii, pp.342, 425; HMC, Cowper Mss ii, pp.229–30, 237, 238.

better placed in the hands of the government rather than that of 'these Irish lords' representing the past.[7]

Whether the arrow struck home cannot be ascertained, but evidence for Wentworth's enhanced reputation in the King's eyes can be found elsewhere. Charles, for example, was delighted by the success of the so-called Black Oath imposed by the Lord Deputy on all Scots over the age of 16 living in Ulster from the end of April 1639 onwards, which required them to renounce or denounce the National Covenant on pain of being heavily fined.[8] According to the Lord Deputy and Covenanter sources many avoided the oath by returning to Scotland. After some hesitation about how to proceed against those who did so, Wentworth decided to let them go presumably on the grounds that it would rid Ireland of potential rebels. However, at least one of the army officers involved in administering the oath found it irksome and by implication distasteful.[9]

Probably the most important factor in Wentworth's favour was that almost from the start he had shown a better grasp of how the Covenanters might be defeated than the King's gung-ho advisers at Court. His first effort in a letter written in July 1638 to Earl of Northumberland, by then Lord High Admiral, had contained an unrealistic assessment of the English navy ability to land troops at Leith in preparation for an assault on Edinburgh.[10] A similar flight of fantasy appears in a letter to the King written in November, but from then onwards with increasing boldness he argued for a Fabian strategy of non-engagement to allow time for a well-equipped, well-trained and well-motivated army to be in place on the Scottish border before fighting began.[11] He had also urged the King to keep Berwick and Carlisle as full of soldiers as possible on the grounds that the Covenanter forces would not dare to advance any farther into England in 1639 without first capturing them. If they bypassed them on the way south their communications with Scotland would easily be broken as the Scots did not have a navy to defend ships carrying provisions.[12] However, although the logic was impeccable based as it was on manuals on the martial art in print and on current

---

7   Knowler, *Strafforde's Letters* ii, p.342.
8   Knowler, *Strafforde's Letters* ii, pp.336–38, 343–46, 354, 356, 367; CSPI 1633–47, p.220.
9   Stevenson, *Scottish Covenanters and Irish Confederates*, pp.18–19; Knowler, *Strafforde's Letters* ii, p.324.
10 Knowler, *Strafforde's Letters* ii, pp.191–92. Wentworth described his advice as private. If Northumberland used it in discussions about strategy with anybody else it should not be attributed to him.
11 Knowler, *Strafforde's Letters* ii, pp.235, 268, 278, 292, 313, 324, 355; HMC, Cowper Mss ii, pp.229–30.
12 HMC, Cowper Mss ii, pp.229–30; Knowler, *Strafforde's Letters* ii, pp.189–91, 324, 325–8. 356, 364, 377. See also Wedgwood, *King's Peace*, pp.272–73. The only offensive operation Wentworth advocated was sending the English cavalry, which were far superior in numbers to those the Covenanters could muster, into the Scottish Lowlands in September to disrupt the harvesting and thus cause unrest due to shortages of food during the winter months.

practice in the war in the Low Countries, the Earl of Leven, the Covenanters' general, ignored convention and went his own way in the 1640 campaign.

Wentworth's enemies fought back against his rise to power. The charge that he was mentally unstable having struck a prisoner in a fit of temper was still being bandied about with the Lord Deputy trying to pin down and eliminate (metaphorically), the chief gossipmongers Sir Piers Crosby and Lord Esmond, the former the colonel of the Irish regiment in the late 1620s and the latter a captain in the standing army, the governor of Duncannon Fort, and a veteran of the Nine Years' War. They were both heavily fined for slander in the English courts of law in May 1639, whereupon the King reduced the figure by a substantial amount, whilst Lord Mountnorris, who Wentworth suspected was behind the plot against him, was seemingly absolved from blame. Crosby and Mountnorris were hand in glove with the Earl of Holland, who was also involved in trying to frustrate Wentworth's long-running campaign to punish Lord Justice Loftus in the law courts for various financial and legal malpractices. The matter was not finally resolved in the Lord Deputy's favour until the following November, but then only after a setback six months previously when Charles had been persuaded to allow the old man to return to Ireland to find evidence to strengthen his defence.[13]

At the same time the Lord Deputy's credentials as a military administrator were being brought into question. As Lord President of the Council of the North and ex officio Lord Lieutenant of Yorkshire he came under attack with regard to the county's trained bands whose 12 regiments of foot were intended to form the largest corps in Charles's army assembling at Berwick. On the one hand the deputy lieutenants were claiming that his obsession with training and rearming in previous years had been so expensive that they dare not impose another levy on the county to cover the cost of mustering the regiments and marching them to the rendezvous. This caused considerable delay and when some of the companies arrived at Berwick they were described as not being combat-ready, thus showing that their expensive training had been a waste of money. They were also surly and unwilling to obey orders. However, although Wentworth could do nothing to protect the Yorkshire muster master against the King's wrath, he managed to make capital out of the whole episode as it showed that an effective army could not be created by merely calling out the county militias. Their poor training stemmed from the fact that it was time-honoured practice for such soldiers to avoid actual fighting by hiring substitutes who would probably not have received any training in discipline, drill or the use of arms. Moreover, as civilians trained band soldiers were not subject to martial law, and to make matters worse commitment to fighting the Scots was being undermined by arguments that they were

---

13 See CSPI 1633–47, pp.211, 214–18 and CSPD 1638–39, pp.113–14, 410 for Crosby, Esmond and Mountnorris; CSPI 1633–47, pp.189–229 and Knowler, *Strafforde's Letters* ii, p.389 for Loftus.

a local defence force and could not be required to operate let alone fight outside the boundary of the counties where they lived.[14]

Thus there was no major chink in the Lord Deputy's armour for his enemies to exploit, and one powerful weapon in his hands – the project for raising an armed force on the cheap advocated by Holland and his friends at Court had clearly failed and Charles had seen it with his own eyes when he visited Berwick in June. Indeed he probably heaved a sigh of relief to see the back of the trained band army as the terms of the Pacification of Berwick required them to return to their home counties and stand down. This left him with no more than 1,000 thousand or so professional soldiers under arms, Willoughby's regiment at Carlisle and the garrison at Berwick, but for the moment that was not a worry as by the terms of the Pacification the Covenanter army was also to be reduced to a token force. Moreover, he had regained Edinburgh and Dumbarton castles with the right to regarrison them if he so wished.[15]

It was clear to the Lord Deputy that in order to impose his will on Scotland Charles needed to revert to the customary way of preparing for war. namely raising an army from scratch which was equipped, paid, and maintained by taxation approved by the English parliament and commanded by experienced officers. He must also ensure that it was trained for battle as quickly as possible and charged with implementing a strategy that was realistic. However, Wentworth's return to Court did not mean that Charles immediately put him in charge of preparations to fight the Covenanters. It took three months for the King to overcome his aversion to summoning an English parliament and an Irish parliament to finance the war in the conventional way, and it was only then that the honours that the Lord Deputy craved came his way, namely promotion from Viscount Wentworth to Earl of Strafford in the English peerage and from deputy lieutenant to lord lieutenant in Ireland, a post unfilled since the death of Lord Mountjoy in 1606.[16]

The toing and froing was summed up in a letter from the Lord High Admiral's secretary in London to the commander of the fleet in the Downs. In November 1639 Wentworth was 'great at court' and promising significant military assistance from Ireland against the Covenanters. Nothing, however, had been decided about the coming war though various matters were 'consulted upon very diligently and often'. What eventually backed the King into a corner was evidence that the Covenanters were making contingency plans for the next round of hostilities. Although they continued to respect the terms of the truce, they retained the services of professional soldiers who

---

14 J.T. Cliffe. *The Yorkshire Gentry from the Reformation to the Civil War* (London: Athlone Press,1969), pp.313–14; CSPD 1639, p.247. For the military value of men hired as substitutes, see CSPD 1639–40, pp.362, 489. The muster master was Sir Robert Farrer, one of Wentworth's most respected officers, who had retained the office despite being commissioned as a captain in the standing army six years before: CSPD 1638–9, p.410; Knowler, *Strafforde's Letters* i, p.355.
15 Wheeler, *The Irish and British War*, p 29.
16 A. Woolrych, *Britain in Revolution* (Oxford: University Press, 2002), pp.128–9.

had joined the army in 1639 from the Protestant armies on the Continent; soldiers disbanded in August were keeping up their training schedules in their own localities on an informal basis; and funds were being collected voluntarily or by force to finance a new war.[17]

Unfortunately Wentworth's letter books tell us nothing about the period between his landing in England and the King's decision to issue writs for an English parliament. Moreover it is not possible to see into his mind by reading the letters he wrote to the King immediately before leaving Ireland presumably so as not to brief his enemies in advance of face-to-face discussions in the Privy Council. They contain no recommendations about how the next war against the Covenanters should be conducted apart from a comment that the resources he controlled as lord deputy would be at the King's disposal, but others speculated that this would take the form of military hardware. On 18 November Secretary Windebank calculated that an army of 35,000 men would be required to defeat the Scots which could be supplied in part by requisitioning 4,000 muskets and 4,000 pikes in the Dublin Castle arsenal.[18]

The lord deputy's departure seemed to leave the standing army in a limbo, though he had every intention of returning once he had sorted out the King's business in England. The problem was that neither of the lord justices who governed Ireland in his absence had sufficient military experience to move the reform programme forward. Christopher Wandesford, his long-standing friend, was a lawyer. Robert, Lord Dillon, heir to an Old English earldom, a Protestant convert and a member of the lord justice's council since 1632, had commanded a troop of horse in the standing army since 1635, but his was almost certainly a political appointment. I have found no evidence that he served in the wars of the 1620s, and he was too young to have fought in the Nine Years' War. With war in the offing the day-to-day management of the standing army needed therefore to be delegated as in the time of Cork and Loftus, but on this occasion the King did not appoint a general to take charge as this would have been seen as an insult by Strafford, as we must now call him. His correspondence with the King, the Lord High Admiral and successive secretaries of state shows that he had come to regard himself as expert in the military art from grand strategy to the training of soldiers with his disclaimers nothing more than exercises in false modesty. Instead hands-on management of the standing army was put into the hands of a triumvirate. Two members, Sir John Borlace, Master of the Ordnance, and Sir William St. Leger, Lord President of Munster, had many years of active service and of military

---

17 Clarendon State Papers ii, pp.81–82; CSPD 1639–40, pp.98, 362. For the professionalism of the Scots' preparation for war in the first six months of 1640, see D. Stevenson, *The Scottish Revolution 1637–44: the Triumph of the Covenanters* (Newton Abbot, 1967), pp.194–201; Wheeler, *Irish and British Wars*, p.29.
18 Knowler, *Strafforde's Letters* ii, pp.371–72, 376, 378, 387; CSPD 1639–40, p.109.

administration at a senior level behind them.¹⁹ The third was James Butler, 12th Earl of Ormond, who in military terms was their superior officer having been appointed by Wentworth as lieutenant general of cavalry in the standing army in 1638.²⁰

Ormond's appointment seems remarkable as his only military experience was serving for a few months on the Duke of Buckingham's staff just prior to his assassination and three years command of a troop of horse in the standing army (not nine as Carte claimed). However, given the sentiments of the time it was not so. Leadership qualities were supposed to pass down from generations to generation through the blood and were encouraged by training in swordsmanship and other martial skills desirable in a nobleman plus education in the mighty deeds of their ancestors, and the frequently expressed expectations of family, friends and tenants.²¹ But Ormond's ancestry and education did not quite fit the bill. Admittedly the last earl but one had been a general in Queen Elizabeth's army in Ireland, but Wentworth's earl was the great man's great nephew not his direct descendant. His father and grandfather had been more renowned for their Catholic zeal which his father had developed through clandestine contacts with the Habsburgs, but when the latter was drowned at sea when James was a child Lord Thurles, which he then became, was taken to London where he converted to Protestantism and spent his teenage years in the archbishop of Canterbury's household. However, to be fair to the Lord Deputy, he took time to make up his mind about the young earl, and although Ormond's career took off like a rocket in the late 1630s it was not until five years after settling in Ireland having married the heiress of another of the great Irish landed families that Wentworth became fully convinced that he was a man of ability with whom he could work, and as a first step he persuaded the King to add him to his council in Dublin.²²

Looking after the standing army for the first six months was unproblematic and unaffected by Wentworth's promotion to lord lieutenant and Wandesford's subsequent appointment as lord deputy. It is of course possible that the absence of administrative material in the English and Irish state papers, the Ormond manuscripts and Knowler's edition of Strafford's letter books may be the result of a pruning operation involving the removal of documents a year or so later that were incriminating when Strafford was on trial for his life. However, there are sound reasons for believing that business was slack. First the triumvirate did not have to go to the trouble of moving troops around the country, as Strafford's training programme took place in the summer

---

19 For Lord Dillon, eldest son of the Earl of Roscommon, see CSPI 1625–32, 282, 326; *ibid.*, 1633–47, 117; Knowler, *Strafforde's Letters* i, p.476.
20 Knowler, *Strafforde's Letters* ii, pp.203–04.
21 Sir Thomas Smith, *De Republica Anglorum* (Cambridge: University Press, 1906 edn), pp.31–32.
22 This brief account is largely taken from Carte, *Life of Ormond* i, pp.1–20; Knowler, *Strafforde's Letters* i, pp.260, 378; CSPI 1633–47, p.93; Bodleian, Carte Mss i, f.104. Carte states incorrectly that Ormond acquired a captaincy to 1631: *Life of Ormond*, book i, p.18. It did not happen until 1636: Bodleian, Carte Mss i, f.114.

months.²³ Second, security was less of a concern than it had been. The threat of an attack by the Earl of Argyll on Antrim's estates or a revolt by Scottish settlers in support of the Covenant had ended with the Pacification of Berwick, and a Spanish invasion was out of the question given King Philip's mounting problems in Europe and in the Americas. Unsurprisingly rumours of Catholic exiles plotting to overturn English hegemony in Ireland ceased to be of interest to anybody other than the English ambassador in Spain, Sir Arthur Hopton, who continued to send ill-documented scare stories about the movements and intentions of the sons and grandsons of Tyrone and Tyrconnell to the English and Irish governments probably in order to justify his position.²⁴ However, the seemingly light workload for the triumvirate in the surviving documentation for the first six or so months of its existence was very much the calm before the storm.

What upped the tempo in early 1640 was that conflict with the Covenanters became more and more certain as time passed with Ireland being involved from the start. Although the Lord Deputy had vehemently opposed the standing army becoming heavily involved in the 1639 campaign, there is sufficient evidence to show that he also took the longer view by making provisions for it to be expanded in an emergency to a force of between 8,000 and 10,000 men. In March 1637 when there were rumours of war with Spain he had written to the King describing how he might quadruple the size of the infantry and 16 months later when using force to suppress the Covenanter movement first became a serious issue he proposed adding 150 men to each of its 40 companies of foot. He had also made provisions from the autumn of 1638 for the over-provision of weapons for the standing army beginning with the calivers being put into store rather than destroyed or sold when the muskets to re-equip the infantry arrived from the United Provinces. Moreover, the process was not brought to a halt by the Pacification of Berwick, as in the early months of 1640 Strafford decided to purchase another 2,000 arms for the foot and 1,000 for the horse. However, plans for increasing the size of the King's forces in Ireland by focusing on the standing army and its existing units was dropped. Instead the additional weapons were to equip a new army to operate overseas whilst the standing army remained in Ireland to safeguard the country's security which was to be raised in the country by impressment a precedent for which having been created the previous year when preparing Willoughby's regiment for the journey to Carlisle.²⁵ There was, however, one change made soon after the proposal was agreed. The original plan was clearly to raise and train new horse, which is confirmed by the purchase of pistols and swords

---

23 It would have been foolish to choose another time of the year, given the bad experience of a company sent across country in the autumn of 1637 to a possible landing place presumably because of a short-lived rise in military tension with Spain: Knowler, *Strafforde's Letters* ii, p.198.
24 Knowler, *Strafforde's Letters* ii, pp.69–85.
25 CSPD 1638–9, pp.63–64; Knowler, *Strafforde's Letters* ii, pp.64, 188, 200, 281, 319, 341, 363.

from the Netherlands, but it was abandoned presumably because this would take too much time. Instead the entire standing army cavalry were to be shipped overseas to support the New Army.

There is thus a reasonably clear paper trail from 1637 to 1640 with respect to the size of the New Army and the weapons it required. What is less clear was where Wentworth would find the infantry. Initially when Spain was seen as the enemy he had hoped to find sufficient men in the plantations, and they would have been primarily if not exclusively English and Scottish Protestants. Later when the confrontation between the King and the Covenanters became his principal concern he was still hopeful of a fair number being drawn from the New English community, but before he left Ireland with another war in the offing he had clearly come round to the view that this was too optimistic. He did not say it in so many words in correspondence with the King, but it would have been clearly visible to Charles when he read his comments on Lord Barrymore's recruiting methods in Munster. Moreover, it was self-evident that draining Ulster of English Protestants would make it difficult to defend the province should Argyll's clansmen land there on the outbreak of hostilities with Scotland whilst it was notorious that protestants were very heavily outnumbered by papists in Connaught, which left only Leinster.

The logical conclusion is that Strafford knew in 1640 that he would be heavily dependent on Ireland's Catholic population for recruits for the New Army. This he justified in various ways none of which could be described a convincing at first sight such as that the Irish disliked the Scots and would fight well against them, and that although the many Catholics amongst them could not be trusted to keep the peace in Ireland, they would happily obey orders overseas when they would be less under the influence of their priests. He may also have taken some comfort from memories of veterans of the first La Rochelle expedition like Sir Robert Farrer and Sir Francis Willoughby of the conduct of Sir Piers Crosby's regiment in covering the army's retreat, but he would not have acknowledged it as he was currently suing Crosby for slander.[26]

The strategic issue as to where and how the New Army should be deployed against the Covenanters seems cut and dried. Carte writing 100 years after the event stated that it was to land on the west coast of Scotland and modern historians have accepted his contention without question.[27] However, there were a number of other possible

---

26 Knowler, *Strafforde's Letters* ii, pp.188, 342.
27 Carte, *Life of Ormond* i, pp.184–85. The source cited in page 36 note 121 of Stevenson, *Scottish Covenanters and Irish Confederates*, does not refer to New Army troops landing in Scotland, and neither does that cited by C.V. Wedgwood in *The King's Peace*, p.328. Amongst the many historians who mention the planned assault on the west coast of Scotland in 1640 in the books in my bibliography, are Cust, Wheeler, Reid, Kenyon and Ohlmeyer, and Lenihan. Fissel seems to have understood the role of the New Army in the

scenarios such as landing at Whitehaven or Workington and invading Scotland from the south or marching across country from the Cumberland ports to the east coast where the New Army might be absorbed into the royal army or else allowed to operate independently which I do not doubt would have been Strafford's preferred option. In fact Carte was wrong largely because there were nigh insuperable problems involved in landing a large army safely and quickly anywhere on the Scottish mainland facing Ireland. Only in the panic situation of the Scots being about the cross the border into England in mid August 1640 did Strafford toy with the idea of an attack on mainland Scotland but his correspondence clearly shows that it would only be feasible if the campaign in the north of England was a prolonged one, which of course it was not.

What an invading army required was a well-appointed port with a deep-water channel extending from the sea as far as its quays to enable large ships to unload the soldiers, horses, military supplies, and heavy artillery they were carrying directly onto *terra firma*. The only places that qualified were Dumbarton and Ayr. The former, although dominated by the royal castle which was in friendly hands thanks to the Pacification of Berwick, was disabled as a port in May by the sinking of two large ships in the Clyde estuary which effectively cut it off from the sea. Moreover, the survey of Dumbarton Castle undertaken early in 1640 showed that it was too small on its own to serve as an army base and establishing one in the town would run up against massive problems as it and the surrounding countryside had no affection for the King but were firm supporters of the Covenanters.[28]

Admittedly Strafford showed some interest in Dumbarton when forced to stay in Chester for a few days in early April 1640 laid low by an attack of gout whilst in transit between Dublin and London, but his concern was to secure a naval escort for 100 men from the English army waiting in the Wirral to be shipped there to reinforce the garrison. The amount of space he allotted to the matter in his correspondence seems out of proportion to its military significance, but it may have been the natural response of a man of his temperament to a spell of enforced idleness, though he had genuine concerns about the lack of a naval escort for the troop transport which without it would be in danger of being intercepted and sunk.[29]

Ayr was a different proposition. It had a good trade with France and was well used to the coming and going of seagoing vessels. It may also have been an open town whose medieval defences if it had any were viewed as too dilapidated to be worth the Covenanters placing a garrison there, but the surrounding area was heavily pro-Covenant, and it cannot be doubted that plans would have been made for its defence should enemy forces from England or Ireland show any interest in seizing it.

King's strategy in 1640 by the direction of the arrow on his map of the operations planned, but this may have been due to the mapmaker as the port of embarkation is depicted as Dublin rather than Carrickfergus: *The Bishops' Wars*, p.40.
28 CSPD 1639–40, pp.504–05; *ibid.* 1640, pp.198–99.
29 CSPD 1639–40, pp.504–05; Knowler, *Strafforde's Letters* ii, pp.391, 400, 404–07.

However, the most telling argument against Ayr being the destination for the New Army was that it was mentioned only once in the surviving documentation from the English side relating to the Second Bishops' War, and then only in a throwaway remark by Lord Conway in late August 1640 justifying his decision to abandon Newcastle to the Covenanter army without a fight.[30] Moreover, he named it in the context of a plan by which Ireland was to provide 10,000 rather than 8,000 foot for the war against the Scots. This suggests that a landing at Ayr was something being discussed in early April before he left London for Newcastle as governor and garrison commander that was subsequently rejected.[31]

The only other alternatives were either to transfer the army from large ships onto vessels that could unload at a smaller port when the convoy reached the Scottish coast or to land the soldiers and horses together with their artillery, gunpowder, and other military supplies directly onto an open shore. The first had several significant drawbacks. Transhipment could only be undertaken in a flat calm and the process would be so protracted that Covenanter forces could well have captured the landing place well before sufficient men and material had been brought ashore to defend it, whilst transferring horses and heavy artillery pieces from boat to boat would be almost impossible. The second option was even more impracticable as it would require large numbers of flat-bottomed boats to carry the army from its assembly point at Carrickfergus to the Ayrshire coast. The Earl of Antrim had had a number constructed in 1639, but many more would be required for a sea-crossing by more than double the number of men Antrim had intended to ship to Scotland. The extra boats would also have taken a long time to construct as Cromwell would discover in 1651 when trying to move troops across the Firth of Forth to bypass the Scottish defences at the pass of Stirling.

Cromwell's venture was ultimately successful though it took eight months from start to finish, but his sailors only had to pilot their boats across two miles of open water to reach the far shore.[32] Strafford's landing craft would need to travel 10 times the distance, which would take at least a day in the best conditions rather than an hour or so, and during the voyage they would have to cope with several tides and the prospect of changeable weather for which flat-bottomed boats even if supplied with draught boards to act as temporary keels would find it almost impossible to sail to the landing point without being driven off course. The Mull of Kintyre was, of course, closer than the Ayrshire coast, but landing there would be operationally crass as Strafford's men could easily be bottled up in the narrow peninsular by Covenanter troops guarding the pinch point where Kintyre connects to the mainland proper.

30 Clarendon State Papers ii, p.99.
31 On 16 April he was at Hull on the way north by sea: CSPD 1640, p.43.
32 M. Wanklyn, 'Cromwell's Generalship and the Conquest of Scotland 1650–51', *Cromwelliana*, series 3, no. 4 (2015), pp.37–46.

It can therefore be argued with considerable confidence that a large-scale amphibious operation against the west coast of Scotland was so problematic that the initial intention of the King's advisers must have been for Strafford's men to make landfall in England, and for the first six months of the year this is strongly supported by a number of pieces of evidence. On 2 March the King ordered Strafford to return to Ireland and summon a parliament to approve taxes to pay for the raising of an army of 8,000 foot and 1,000 horse to join the English army at Berwick to wage war on his rebellious Scottish subjects.[33] The shortest route would be from Carrickfergus to the Cumberland ports with Carlisle serving as a safe haven until such time as the hostilities began. This would explain why in the previous month the English Council of War ordered the construction of additional bread ovens and malt houses in the city and then storehouses for two months' supply of food and drink.[34]

This can have had nothing to do with the Willoughby's garrison which had been in Carlisle for almost a year and not been reinforced. It can only have been to prepare for the arrival of a much larger force, and there is some circumstantial evidence of the enhanced strategic importance of Carlisle in the fact that Sir Nicholas Byron, a more senior though less experienced officer, replaced Sir Francis as governor in January 1640.[35] Finally the New Army was to be strengthened by two regiments of foot and at least three troops of horse raised in England, which would not have been the case if it was to have been absorbed. Into the royal army. It was also stated in no uncertain terms in April that the forces raised there were to join those raised in Ireland in Cumberland rather than at York where King Charles's army was due to assemble indicating that the New Army was to operate independently along the west coast route between England and Scotland.[36]

33 CSPD 1639–40, p.391.
34 CSPD, 1639–40, pp.354, 375, 399.
35 CSPD 1639–40, p.321.
36 Knowler, *Strafforde's Letters* ii, pp.400, 402, 405; CSPD 1640, pp.470, 472; Adamson, *The Noble Revolt*, Chapter 1. See Appendix V for the officers listed in the two regiments.

12

The New Army and the Old Army

It was Strafford's drive and his ministers' success in influencing the borough elections that turned the New Army from aspiration into reality. The King having decided that an Irish parliament should meet before the English one the Lord Lieutenant left London early in March 1640 and travelling via Chester arrived in Dublin just after the first session had begun. Within a week the two Houses had approved four subsidies, which were deemed sufficient to maintain a force of 8,000 foot and 1,000 horse for a year and a half. Having sketched in the arrangements for raising the New Army, he set out for London to work his magic on the English parliament, but success in Dublin proved to be a false dawn. Bad luck in the form of the bout of debilitating gout referred to in Chapter 11 meant that his journey took longer than anticipated, and the session was well under way by the time he arrived at Westminster. As a result the government request for taxation to fund a new war with Scotland was put to the MPs and peers by less skilful advocates. The House of Commons insisted that redress of grievances should precede supply whereupon Charles sent the Short Parliament packing. Strafford was disappointed but gave the advice that as his subjects had refused to approve taxation to support the war effort, the King was free to use any means he liked to raise and fund an English army to fight the Covenanters.[1]

Clearly Strafford expected to command the New Army in person in his capacity as Lord Lieutenant, but its formation was the responsibility of the triumvirate. According to Carte he nominated the Earl of Ormond to take charge during his absence with the other two members relegated to subordinate roles. This seems to make sense as it could be argued that although Ormond had no direct experience of warfare and only a short spell commanding troops in peacetime, he had shown himself to be an able parliamentarian in 1634 and again in 1640, and political skills were what were required to combine the disparate elements of the New Army into an effective fighting force: former soldiers and raw recruits; many Catholics and a few Protestants; Old English, New English and native Irish; and officers ranging from

---

1   Lenihan, *Consolidating Conquest*, p.87; Cust, *Charles I*, pp.250, 259–60.

professionals with years of combat experience to rank amateurs who happened to be chosen because of their distinguished ancestry or their exalted position in the Dublin government. It is, however, likely that Carte was misinformed. Although Ormond was lieutenant general of cavalry in the standing army, this did not allow him to assume the same rank in the New, and he was not appointed as Strafford's deputy until mid August when his return to Ireland was put on hold by the illness of the Earl of Northumberland.

Carte describes Ormond as playing a major role in putting flesh on the bones of the orders issued by Strafford for raising the New Army. This may have been so but having signed the necessary paperwork he was a man without a role until it was ready to set sail. In the intervening period the two professional members of the triumvirate set to work turning aspiration into reality. It is clear from a letter St. Leger sent to Ormond that he was happy to have responsibility for assembling the army at Carrickfergus and training it. Nothing is known about Borlace's state of mind, but he appears to have gone about preparing the train of artillery for war with some alacrity, which involved solving a crucial and seemingly unexpected logistical problem. The horses said to have been available in October 1638 to move it by road failed to materialise. His response was to immediately commandeer sufficient ships to carry it from Dublin to Carrickfergus where it had arrived by early August.[2]

When Ormond requested permission to return to his principal seat at Kilkenny Castle in May because his wife was ill and expecting a baby, Wandesford gave his consent, but the young Earl soon became restless and asked for the right to ride at the head of the forces assembling at Dublin when they set out on their march to Carrickfergus, but the Lord Deputy had different ideas. Speed was of the essence in readying the army for combat, and this was likely to be impeded by the third member of the triumvirate with no clear function but sufficient military knowledge to interfere with proceedings. In addition, given Ormond's ancestry and his closeness to Strafford, he was likely to be the first port of call and possibly the mouthpiece for disgruntled officers, administrators, and civilians.[3]

Wandesford consulted his Council of War, which resolved that he should follow the Lord Lieutenant's original instructions to the letter. St. Leger was to be in charge at Carrickfergus until Sir John Borlace arrived with the artillery and the munitions. The Master of the Ordnance would then 'command in chief there' until the Lord Lieutenant

---

2   Carte, *Life of Ormonde* i, p.195. T. Whitaker, *The Life and Correspondence of Sir George Radcliff*, (1810), 251. Carte's actual words were 'commander-in-chief of all the forces of the Kingdom in the absence of the Earl of Strafford'. This was clearly different from acting commander of the standing army, which he was by virtue of his commission as lieutenant general of horse.
3   It is most unlikely that Ormond would have meddled intentionally, but he was most likely to have been the recipient of complaints against St. Leger which he might feel duty bound to support.

returned from England.⁴ All of this neatly correlates with Carte's comment that Ormond's presence was not required at Carrickfergus until then when the triumvirate would revert to their normal positions in the army hierarchy as commanders of the infantry and the artillery under Strafford as captain general with Ormond becoming lieutenant general of cavalry as the units he would be commanding were those he had commanded in the standing army.⁵ Below them would be Sir Thomas Lucas and Sir Thomas Armstrong as commissary general and adjutant general of horse, and three infantry brigadiers Sir John Borlace, Sir Henry Bruce and Sir Charles Coote.

The most surprising omission from the highest echelon of command in the New Army was Sir Francis Willoughby after almost 30 years military experience in Europe followed by another 11 years as captain in the standing army during which time he had steadily risen in repute. In 1638 Wentworth chose him as the man best qualified to command recruits to assist the King against the Covenanters. In the following year he promoted him to colonel and then to major general, and thereafter he served the King as an assiduous and well-regarded commander of the standing army garrison at Carlisle. However, he may then in Wentworth's eyes have become too keen on self-promotion through direct contact with senior members of the English government like Sir John Coke rather than relying on the Lord Deputy to liaise with them on his behalf. There is no hint of tension in the surviving correspondence between Willoughby and Wentworth in the first weeks of his time in Carlisle, but the letters come to an abrupt end in May 1639. This was not in itself suspicious as Willoughby was now under the command of the English commander-in-chief, but this was the Earl of Arundel, with whom the Lord Deputy had previously crossed swords, and Arundel's second-in-command was the Earl of Holland.⁶

The first sign of the Lord Deputy's displeasure came in July when he mentioned in an aside in a letter to Sir Henry Vane, soon to be Sir John Coke's successor, that he had made some disparaging remarks about Willoughby in earlier correspondence. It was clearly a recent development as in May when Vane suggested that he might be replaced by Sir Nicholas Slanning, who was bringing some artillery pieces to Carlisle by sea from royal fortresses in Cornwall, Wentworth had sprung to his colonel's defence and managed to prevent it happening. Unfortunately, the letter containing the criticism no longer survives and Wentworth's language is so gnomic that it is impossible do any more than guess at what he wrote, but the implication is that, although he had

---

4   Carte, *Life of Ormonde* i, p.199; Whitaker, *Sir George Radcliffe*, pp.251, 253.
5   He wrote to Radcliffe on 11 June of his intention to return quickly to Ireland, and there is no suggestion whatsoever that this was a change of plan: Thomas Whitaker, *The Life and Original Correspondence of Sir George Radcliffe* (London: Longmans etc., 1810), p.201.
6   Knowler, *Strafforde's Letters* ii, p.188; TNA, SP 63/257, f.50: HMC, Cowper Mss ii, pp.237–42; CSPI 1633–47, pp.304, 306, 315.

disapproved of Willoughby's behaviour, he did not doubt that he had the experience and the commitment to serve the King competently in the first bout with the Scots.[7]

In December 1639, however, Wentworth moved from words to deeds when he sacked Willoughby as major general of the standing army, and the King accepted his decision to appoint Sir William St. Leger in his stead. This may well have been because he needed somebody at that rank on the spot at a time when tension with Scotland was rising. A month later, however, came a second humiliation. To Willoughby's bitter disappointed he was replaced as governor of Carlisle.[8] The governorship was not in Strafford's gift, but in that of the Earl of Northumberland, the newly appointed captain general of the English army, with the King having the last word. Strafford counted Northumberland as a friend and the King as his patron and so he was well placed to make representations on Willoughby's behalf, but there is no evidence that he spoke in his favour to either of them.[9] In what looks like a further sign of disfavour Willoughby's field officers and captains were sent back to Ireland with him but not the rank and file, which suggests that there had been some dissatisfaction about the way in which the soldiers had been commanded, but the more likely reason was is that they were needed to serve as officers in the New Army

After waiting some weeks somewhat impatiently for Byron to take up his post, Sir Francis returned to Ireland with no preferment higher than that governor of Limerick castle where his standing army company was stationed. A few weeks later he was commissioned as colonel of foot in the New Army but of the eight regiments of foot to be raised in Ireland his was the sixth in order of precedence, and he was not appointed commander of the brigade to which it was assigned. Instead Strafford chose Sir Charles Coote, who had a similar length of service in the standing army as Willoughby but no experience of fighting on the Continent. He had, however, one important advantage in that he had long been Wentworth's creature having been the first person to accuse Lord Wilmot of financial misdemeanours at Athlone, and in 1640 he was still actively pursuing the matter in the law courts as the Lord Deputy's agent in all but name, whereas Sir Francis had apparently been punished for deciding to strike out on his own.[10]

To make matters worse Willoughby was in acute financial difficulties having spent large sums of money on the fortification of Carlisle on the King's orders for which he had not been paid. All that he had been promised in compensation was a place on the Lord Deputy's council, but nothing came of it until after the Earl's trial and

---

7   Knowler, *Strafforde's Letters* ii, pp.423, 426; HMC Cowper Mss ii, p.229.
8   CSPI 1633–47, p.229; CSPD 1640, pp.26–27, 106, 132–33; *ODNB* 9, pp.363, 369.
9   It may or may not be significant that Byron replaced Willoughby on the same day that Wentworth became Earl of Strafford and lord lieutenant of Ireland: CSPD 1639–40, pp.321–23, 349.
10 Bodleian, Carte Mss i, f.182; Whitaker, *Sir George Radcliffe*, pp.238–89. For their careers in the standing army see Appendices II–VI.

execution.¹¹ Not surprisingly Sir Francis wrote to Secretary of State Windebank in May 1640 to let him know how he felt. He did not have a disloyal bone in his body, but he felt humiliated by the low regard in which he was held by his superiors who ignored him but promoted men 'whom I hold far inferior to me in point of soldiership'.¹²

Willoughby's experience contrasts strongly with that of another brigade commander, Sir Henry Bruce. Admittedly he had been colonel in the Cadiz expedition when Willoughby was a rank lower, but he had never been a major general and he had not previously held a command in Ireland. But this was somebody else to whom Strafford owed a debt of gratitude, as it was his report to the King on military preparations in Ulster that put paid to Antrim's scheme for attacking the Earl of Argyll's estates in the Highlands and Islands in 1639. Even Sir Robert Farrer had been honoured in the appointments to the New Army. Wentworth had chosen Willoughby in his stead as commander of forces that might be sent from Ireland to England in the summer of 1638. He had then angered the King during the First Bishops' War who held him responsible for the poor appearance and lack of commitment of the Yorkshire trained bands of which he was muster master. Although not a full colonel as he had been in the Duke of Buckingham's army in 1628, Strafford had done the next best thing by making him lieutenant colonel of his own regiment of foot, which given the Lord Lieutenant's manifold responsibilities and poor health meant that Farrer would be its commanding officer in all but name.¹³

During the New Army's short life of 14 months' anxiety in King Charles's three kingdoms about its composition and its future strategic role can be traced though contemporary documents such as the deliberations and declarations of the parliaments of England, Scotland and Ireland, newsletters and other private and official correspondence, and pamphlets published in London and Edinburgh, but tracking down information about the army itself is bedevilled by the lack of administrative documents and gaps in the flow of letters between the governments of England and Ireland.

Historians have relied on Thomas Carte's biography of the Earl of Ormond to fill in the gaps . They have also very largely respected the tale he told of the creation and composition of the New Army and of the impact these had on the standing army given his access to the archives at Kilkenny Castle which he cited from time to time. However, given his High Tory agenda mentioned in an earlier chapter, Carte cannot necessarily be taken at his word, but fortunately there is just enough evidence in documents dating from the years 1640 and 1641 for some of his more important statements to be tested. These include lists of army officers; the correspondence of Sir

11   CSPD 1640, pp.132–33; CSPI 1633–47, pp.306, 315.
12   CSPD 1640, p.132.
13   Bodleian, Carte Mss i, ff.182–85; *ODNB* 59, p.455; Knowler, *Strafforde's Letters* ii, p.188.

George Radcliffe, Strafford's friend and confidant; and materials relating to the New Army's disbandment in the National Archives at Kew.[14]

The eight infantry regiments raised in Ireland for the New Army were each to be 1,000 strong divided into 10 companies. Carte's description of them as designed to be raised in specific provinces is confirmed by the army lists: the first and the third, Strafford's and Lord Dillon's, in Leinster; the second and the sixth, Sir William St. Leger's and Sir Francis Willoughby's, in Munster; the fourth and the fifth, Sir Charles Coote's and Sir Henry Bruce's, in Connaught; and the ninth, Sir Henry Tichborne's, in Ulster. The tenth regiment's recruiting area was not specified in the draft which Strafford brought with him from Ireland, but appears as Leinster and Munster in the fair copy in the Clarendon papers in the Bodleian.[15] The reason why the Dublin government let Ulster off lightly was probably because it made good sense not to drain the province dry of men of a military age who were not Scottish by descent. A *levee en masse* of loyalists, Catholic as well as Protestant, English as well as Irish, would be needed to reinforce the standing army units stationed there should the Earl of Argyll attempt a landing, which Strafford may have known was to be the Covenanter leadership's response should the New Army leave Ireland's shores.[16].

Carte asserted that the New Army was quickly raised, and this is confirmed by several pieces of contemporary evidence, the most immediate being a letter of lord deputy Wandesford to Sir George Radcliffe written on 21 June which stated that those soldiers who had been ordered to assemble at Dublin before marching to Carrickfergus had duly arrived, and being 'very near their number' were being allocated to specific companies. His remark that some captains had taken on too many volunteers, a matter that could easily be addressed, serves as confirmation that the cavalry officers were the culprits as the infantry were all impressed men.[17]

At this point it is necessary to separate the infantry from the cavalry. Having described the way in which the foot soldiers were impressed on a county-by-county basis using commissioners charged with collecting the subsidy, Carte explained how they would be kept in order given that they would be very largely Catholics. This was to be done by drafting in 1,000 men from the standing army, which he asserted was entirely Protestant in composition down to the most lowly of the private soldiers, a notion that has been dismissed as false on several occasions in previous chapters. Clearly the figure of 1,000 included both officers and men who were successful as 'being invested with authority or in a state of superiority over the rest of the new army [they] had it absolutely in their power'.

---

14 Bodleian, Carte Mss i, ff.182–86.
15 See Appendix V and Ian Ryder, *An English Army for Ireland* (Southend-on-Sea: Partizan Press, 1987), p.41.
16 Stevenson, *Scottish Covenanters and Irish Confederates*, pp.36–37.
17 Whitaker, *Sir George Radcliffe*, p.253.

In total 36 of the 40 standing army captains were thought worthy of serving as officers the New Army, 29 in regiments to be raised in Ireland and the rest in the two to be raised in England. The four who were not were Sir John Vaughan and Sir George Flower, who were almost certainly too old for active campaigning, and the new Earl of Clanricarde and Lord Ranelagh, Lord President of Connaught, whom Strafford regarded as his enemies. There was, however, no consistency in the way in which they were embedded into the New Army with the Lord Lieutenant's regiment having nine Old Army captains as company commanders and the second and tenth only one each.

A similar pattern applies to the captains of the Old Army promoted to colonel, lieutenant colonel or major. Eight of the 10 colonels were Old Army captains with the remaining two very well experienced professionals. Seniority was certainly not the criterion, but status may have been important. One of the regiments raised in England was to be commanded by Sir Thomas Wharton, a new standing army captain but the brother of the Philip 4th Baron Wharton in the English peerage, whilst Lord Dillon, who was a senior minister rather than a soldier and with no experience of commanding infantry, was colonel of the 2nd Regiment but had the added advantage of being the Earl of Roscommon's heir. Service in the Carlisle garrison seems to have been a bonus. Of the five company commanders two became colonels in the New Army and two field officers.

Few of the new captains appear to have been lieutenants in the standing army, though it had not been normal practice for such junior officers to go up a rank when their company commander left. Only two can be clearly identified, Sir Francis Willoughby's son William in his father's regiment who had undertaken an incognito spying mission to Edinburgh in 1639, and John Savage in Sir Henry Tichborne's who deserved a long-service award, but there may have been more as lieutenant's names rarely appear in administrative papers surviving for the standing army in the 1630s.[18]

There is, however, no more evidence than Carte's word that the 900 or more non-commissioned officers and private soldiers needed to complete the transfer from the standing army actually made the move. They are not mentioned in any of the documents relating to the raising of the New Army whilst those dating from a year later when it was being disbanded tell a completely different story.[19] Thus with the standing army backbone for the New Army as described by Carte disappearing from the scene, the Catholic element in the New Army infantry rises from 88 percent to almost 100 percent, and what made it worse was the fact that at least 10 of the New Army captains were Catholics many of whom were to fight for the patriot cause against English hegemony only a couple of years later.

The contribution of the standing army cavalry to the New Army is simplicity itself. Carte is largely silent about it, but the army lists show that it was to have three regiments of horse, the lieutenant general's own with seven troops and two

18 Knowler, *Strafforde's Letters* ii, p.271; CSPI 1625–32, p.444.
19 For this see Chapter 13.

commanded by the Earl of Ormond and Sir Thomas Lucas with six each making a total of 19. The names of the officers for the first and the second regiments and for the first three troops of the third are given in full, and it is abundantly clear that the 13 troops belonging to the standing army were drafted in lock, stock and barrel. The confessional composition of the New Army horse, however, is impossible to ascertain. It almost certainly contained Catholics recruited when the five new troops were raised in the 1630s without an input from England.[20]

It is also clear that two of the three troops that were not drafted in from the standing army were to be raised in England, but unlike the two infantry regiments thus designated they saw the light of day. In August 1640 when the Covenanter invasion of Northumberland was under way they were dispatched from County Durham to Carlisle in case a second attack was about to be launched down the west coast of England, but they were quickly recalled when it became apparent that the enemy forces were exclusively focused on the east coast route.[21] Thus a tiny component of the new army under Strafford's command became operational, and Lucas's troop in the end found its way to Ireland where it fought with the Earl of Ormond against the patriots.

The timetable for raising the New Army and turning it into a force capable of fighting the Covenanter army on equal terms was exceedingly short, and it was impeded by shortages of physical resources none of which could be supplied immediately. Ireland had to import most of its woollen cloth, and so there was insufficient material available to make some of the items of clothing required. Also, as had been described above, heavy horses had to be purchased in England to pull the artillery pieces needed in siege warfare. As for weapons there were plenty of firearms for the infantry, but additional items had to be procured in the Netherlands the most important in terms of quantity being swords, half armour for pikemen, and musket rests.

Impressment according to Carte involved a careful check by army officers on the suitability of the men chosen before they were allowed to leave for Carrickfergus, which must have been a time-consuming business.[22] The new soldiers then spent a month being trained in the use of their weapons and in the drill necessary for effective

---

20 See below Chapter 15.
21 CSPD 1640, pp.460, 462, 481, 570–71. Lord Conway claimed the two infantry regiments were cancelled in early August: Clarendon State Papers ii, p.106. The other non-standing army troop, that of Major Barry, was in the second regiment, but it does not appear to have been raised in Ireland as it was not mentioned at the time of the New Army's disbandment in May 1641: TNA, SP63/257, f.50; Temple, *The Irish Rebellion* (London: R. White for S. Gellibrand, 1646), p.27.
22 Carte, *Life of Ormonde* i, pp.195, 197; Bodleian, Carte Mss i, ff.179–81; Knowler, *Strafforde's Letters* ii, pp.395, 402, 404; P. Edwards, *Dealing with Death* (Alan Sutton, Stroud, 2000), p.186.

fighting in formation. Sir William St. Leger was very satisfied with the outcome, but July stretched into August as they waited for the military supplies from the Netherlands to arrive.[23] Leaving Ireland was also problematic. The ships that had carried the train of artillery from Dublin to Carrickfergus had apparently been discharged as Strafford issued new orders on 17 August for vessels to be acquired suitable for carrying the soldiers, horses, cannon and their associated paraphernalia across the Irish Sea.[24]

To make matters worse the planned financial support for the New Army fell short of expectations. Money was needed immediately to assist in the raising of the regiments but revenue raised by the first subsidy was slow coming into the Irish exchequer.[25] Strafford put his trust in a loan to bridge the gap negotiated in London on his behalf by the English government, but when the King dissolved Parliament the city merchants and financiers refused to play ball blaming the effects of a downturn in overseas trade on their ability to lend. However, as with some of the MPs and peers who were later to form the backbone of the parliamentary party in the English Civil War, movers and shakers in the city fearful for their religion, their liberties and their fortunes were coming round to the view that a Covenanter victory would be the first step on the road to greater security.[26] Nevertheless the subsidy revenue did eventually arrive before the troops mutinied and for the next nine months the New Army received some if not all of its pay.

The subsidies, however, were only supposed to supply enough revenue to cover the army's wages and some basic foodstuffs. There was nothing in the Irish government's budget for 1640 to supply what was lacking in terms of weaponry and clothing as described above, but also for gunpowder and tents and for cash to hire shipping. This was to be the English exchequer's contribution towards the costs of making the New Army operational agreed in advance of the meeting of the Irish parliament, but the precise sum of money was not specified in the correspondence that survives. Strafford suggested that £50,000 in cash provided by the English exchequer would suffice at a pinch £10,000 of which was needed immediately to pay for the items mentioned in the last but one paragraph, though the headline figure was eventually reduced to £40,000.

How much of the cash arrived in Ireland as opposed to being authorised by the English Privy Council or used for paying off debts incurred in England is uncertain. However, the delay caused concern. In late July Secretary Windebank wrote that although Strafford had permission to return to Ireland, he would not do so until he received the money the New Army needed. However, the first tranche did not see the light of day until after 24 August as on that date the ships carrying the military supplies from the Netherlands were still anchored in the Thames estuary.[27] They did

23 Bodleian, Carte Mss i, ff.214, 231.
24 Whitaker, *Sir George Radcliffe*, p.253., Bodleian, Carte Mss i, f.228.
25 Whitaker, *Sir George Radcliffe*, p.255.
26 Cust, *Charles I*, pp.251–60; Adamson, *The Noble Revolt*, pp.45–48.
27 Knowler, *Strafforde's Letters* ii, pp.399, 401, 402; CSPI 1633–47, p.242. Fissel claimed that almost all of it did arrive: *Bishops' Wars*, p.147. Contemporary correspondence, however,

indeed arrive at Carrickfergus a few weeks later, but by then the prospect of the New Army fighting for the King against the Covenanters in 1640 had lessened and was soon to disappear altogether because of the way in which events played out in the north of England during August and early September.

At the root of the matter lay the English government's difficulties in assembling an army, though military planners were reassured throughout June and July by intelligence reports from Lord Conway at Newcastle and Sir John Conyers at Berwick. Although the Covenanters had stationed a force just across the border, it was only a few thousand strong, and its intention was not to invade England but merely to browbeat the King into agreeing to begin discussions for another truce. On 10 August, however, Conway was supposed to have changed his tune. The latest word out of Scotland was that the Covenanters were about to cross into England with an army 20,000 or so strong, which was far larger than the troops the King's commanders had assembled at York or moved forward to Newcastle. The news reached London a few days later and panic ensued scuppering Strafford's plans to return to Dublin.[28] The Earl of Northumberland collapsed under the strain and the King commissioned the Lord Lieutenant to deputise for him as general of the English army facing the Scots.[29]

Conway was castigated then and has been since that time for his gullibility in trusting the word of individuals coming out of Scotland rather than setting up some form of intelligence gathering service of his own. In a long letter he sent to Secretary Windebank after the dust had settled he vigorously defended himself. The English army was ill-prepared to face an invasion, but this was not his fault. The blame lay with the complacency displayed by those members of the English government charged with raising it, a totally valid point. Whilst the Covenanters had kept their army of the First Bishops' War ticking over in preparation for the second, the King's English ministers and council had not only the task of raising a completely new army but had spent hours talking about it but done nothing positive apart from ordering more weapons. To make matters worse soldiers they had sent into the north of England were ill-motivated at best, and at worst regarded the Covenanters as fellow soldiers in the fight against creeping Roman Catholicism. Indeed at least two regiments had lynched officers suspected of being papists whilst on their march to York. Moreover,

---

      suggests that even if this was so it too late in the day: CSPD 1640, pp.45, 495, 512; Whitaker, *Sir George Radcliffe*, pp.199, 203, 211.
28 CSPD 1640, pp.562, 567, 570–71, 573.
29 His illness seems to have coincided with the news arriving. On 11 August he had well enough to send a long letter to Lord Conway which focused on preparing for hostilities: CSPD 1640, pp.572–74. It has been suggested that the illness was feigned as Northumberland had not wanted to fight the Scots: Wedgwood, *King's Peace*, pp.344–45; Adamson, *Noble Revolt*, p.50.

when regiments of foot arrived there and found there was no money to pay their wages, they threatened to mutiny.[30]

Recent scholarship has largely exonerated Conway's intelligence reports about the invasion threat on the grounds that the Covenanter leadership did not finally make up its mind to invade England until the first week in August. It was also the case that Conway had mentioned the possibility of a Scottish offensive in letters to the Earl of Northumberland from 3 August onwards, and Northumberland's replies showed that he had understood what he had been told. However, as Strafford pointed out in a letter written to Conway on 15 August, his principal fault had been to lull the Privy Council into a false sense of security by grossly underestimating the size of the Covenanter army the English troops would be facing.[31]

On 20 August the Covenanter regiments crossed the Tweed at Coldstream 10 miles from the coast thus bypassing Berwick. They then marched slowly through Northumberland making friends as they went by their orderly conduct and their leaders' skilful use of anti-Catholic propaganda. On the 28th they brushed aside a heavily outnumbered English force at Newburn just to the east of Newcastle and soon afterwards occupied the town without a fight. Having decided that discretion was the better part of valour Conway had escaped taking 4,000 or so troops in the garrison there with him. The Scottish cavalry did not pursue them for fear that the ensuing bloodshed would turn English indifference or opposition towards the war into a demand for revenge. Instead the Scots fanned out across the rest of Northumberland and County Durham, but Cumberland and Westmoreland remained in English hands with Carlisle still defended by soldiers of Strafford's standing army.[32]

To prevent the Covenanters coming any farther south and forcing the English army either to fight a battle they were bound to lose or to make a disorderly retreat into the Midlands the King responded positively to a Covenanter proposal for a truce, but it took six weeks for the terms to be agreed. During that time there was every prospect of the unofficial ceasefire breaking down, but the suggestion that Strafford dusted down the idea of New Army attacking the west coast of Scotland and thus forcing the Covenanter army to fall back across the border and defend its heartland is

---

30   *Clarendon State Papers* ii, pp.99–110; Wedgwood, *King's Peace*, p.339; CSPD 1640, pp.461, 468, 490, 581, 570–71, 587–88.
31   Adamson, *The Noble Revolt*, pp.43–44, 48; *Clarendon State Papers* ii, pp.99–110; CSPD 1640, pp.562–63, 573, 587. Sir John Conyers at Berwick had also warned the Court on 30 July though he did not himself believe the intelligence: *ibid.* 1640, p.533.
32   CSPD 1640–41, pp.40–41, 50, 61; *Clarendon State Papers* ii, pp.98–99, 106–09; *Hardwicke State Papers* (London: W. Strahan and T. Cadell, 1778), pp.146–77. For the longest secondary account of the engagement at Newburn and the operational difficulties facing Conway, see Fissel, *The Bishops' Wars*, pp.54–58, but the English retreat and the Scottish occupation of the whole of Northumberland and Durham apart from Berwick is not covered.

problematic.³³ This is what Conrad Russell has written concerning a meeting of the King and his advisers in October, but a very detailed account written by somebody present at the meeting reported that he said no more than that he might in the past have brought an army of 10,000 men over from Ireland had the King provided him with the shipping.³⁴

There is, however, no doubt that Strafford changed his mind about attacking Scotland from Ireland when he learned the size of the Scottish army and its true intention. It is confirmed by a letter Ormond on 17 August described in detail in the next paragraph but to place the decision any earlier than this as Carte does is misconceived. As late as 22 July Secretary Windebank was writing as if the army was still to land in Cumberland, and if there had been change in strategy in early August it is remarkable that the Earl of Northumberland did not mention it in letters written to Lord Conway at Newcastle in the days before illness struck him down.³⁵

On the other hand the King's decision on 3 August to commission Strafford as captain general of all the forces in Ireland with authority to make war on the Covenanters and to appoint a deputy looks relevant but may not be. If his existing powers as lord lieutenant only gave him the authority of captain general in Ireland itself, it was as necessary for an invasion of Scotland from England via Cumberland or Berwick as it was for a descent on Scotland from the sea. It tells us nothing about a change in strategy.³⁶

The 17 August letter the contents of which Carte described at length, Strafford acknowledged Ormond as his deputy, but what is most interesting is that it contained detailed instructions for preparing for a landing on the open shore in Scotland, and one that was likely to be opposed. Vessels needed for unloading horses into shoal waters were to be procured, and the flat-bottomed boats which the Earl of Antrim had had constructed in 1639 were to be seized and brought to Carrickfergus to serve as landing craft for foot soldiers and also as floating batteries for firing on the enemy when they tried to prevent the New Army gaining a foothold on Scottish soil.³⁷ However, although the letter clearly indicated a change in strategy it did not necessarily mean that the expedition was to leave Ireland immediately. Instead it was designed to ensure that all was ready when the Lord Lieutenant did return to Ireland, which would presumably be after the Earl of Northumberland had made a full recovery. In fact the text alone is more than enough to show that Strafford's plans were not for an immediate attack. His principal concern was that the soldiers at Carrickfergus should

33 Cust, *Charles I*, p.266 citing C. Russell, *The Fall of the British Monarchies* (Cambridge: University Press, 1995); CSPI 1633–47, pp.292–93. Russell's source seems to be the report of a meeting of the King's council at York in October cited in the next foot note, but if so he recorded it incorrectly.
34 HMC, Marquis of Abergavenny etc. Mss, p.137.
35 CSPD 1640, pp.496–574.
36 Carte, *Life of Ormond* i, pp.208–09; CSPD 1640, p.495.
37 Carte, *Life of Ormonde* i, p.208. The Bodleian reference is now Carte Mss i, ff.229–30.

set about constructing extensive fortification around the place where his transport fleet would be laid up during the winter. However, this did not necessarily mean that Strafford intended the invasion of Scotland to be postponed till the spring. He may have made a contract with the ships' owners by which, having landed the New Army in Scotland, they were to return to Carrickfergus so as to be able to bring the troops back again after they had crushed the Covenanters. The justification for building the fortifications would be that in the meantime the ships would be protected against a spoiling attack on Ulster by the Earl of Argyll in response to the New Army's landing in Scotland.[38]

Two other sources should probably not be regarded as evidence of a drastic but realistic change in strategy affecting the New Army. On 24 August an order was issued for 100 soldiers from Ireland to go to the relief of Dumbarton Castle then under siege by the Earl of Argyll, but the plans for landing on an open shore in the letter written on the 17th and Strafford's knowledge of Dumbarton's shortcomings as an army base suggest that it was no more than a morale booster for the King's supporters in Scotland who would be discouraged if the castle surrendered to the Covenanters.[39]

The second document is ambivalent at best. On 12 September Strafford issued a new instruction which was for the Earl of Ormond to leave Kilkenny Castle for Carrickfergus immediately to take charge of the army. This looks as if an invasion of Scotland was imminent and as such marries up with the proposal he put to the Privy Council as recorded by Conrad Russell that he could order the New Army to set sail in days, but it is more likely that it was because according to Carte he was about to send a delegation from York to report on progress in preparing for the Scottish expedition, and that his deputy should be at Carrickfergus to greet it. In the event, however, Ormond did not leave home. The problem was that he did not have the authority to use martial law to maintain discipline in the army, and this was deteriorating as soldiers turned to burglary to relieve the boredom of having little to do. With some difficulty Strafford obtained the requisite authority from the King and sent it to Ormond whereupon the Earl set out from Kilkenny in mid November 1640 to take up his command.[40]

---

38 Stevenson, *Scottish Covenanters and Irish Confederates*, pp.35–37.
39 Bodleian, Carte Mss i, f.237.
40 Whitaker, *Sir George Radcliffe*, pp.204, 210. Carte, *Life of Ormond* i, pp.208–09. There is no evidence that Strafford's delegation ever arrived in Ireland.

Part III

Passing into Oblivion

13

The Demise of the New Army

The formal truce between the Covenanters and the King was signed at Ripon on 26 October, but there were very significant differences from the previous year. First it was no more than a ceasefire.[1] The English and the Scottish armies were not disbanded but continued to face one another along the line of the river Tees with the King responsible for paying the daily expenses of both in terms of soldiers' and officers' wages. This would necessitate the calling of another English parliament as his normal sources of income had fallen far short of keeping the English army in pay, and this time he would have to respond to his subjects' grievances as he needed the two Houses to pass legislation authorising the collection of large sums of money via taxation with the London merchants providing the bridging loans between parliamentary approval and the revenue being collected. If he refused the English army would disintegrate. The Scottish army would then continue its march south unopposed, or if it was able to subsist in Northumberland and Durham, cut off London's supply of fuel from the Newcastle coalfield thus causing an uprising in the capital aimed at deposing the King and replacing him with somebody who was more congenial. The prime candidate was his sister Elizabeth and her family of dispossessed Palatinate princes and princesses who were not only not under the influence of Catholic or quasi-Catholic advisers but also the clear victims of international Roman Catholicism.

Meanwhile the New Army prepared to go into winter quarters in Ulster. Orders to that effect were issued by Strafford throughout October and November, and they were what one would have expected from a general mindful of the need to preserve his army after the end of the campaigning season so that it would be ready to spring into action when hostilities resumed. The infantry, who had been under canvas during the summer, were dispersed into billets in the coastal towns, but with a large garrison still stationed at Carrickfergus to defend the harbour and the area where the shipping would be anchored or laid up during the winter against attack by land or sea. Finally, with an eye to the revenue the Dublin government would have available to pay the

---

1   CSPD 1640–41, p.166.

New Army troops, which had been severely affected by the Irish parliament reducing the rate at which the subsidy was assessed,[2] half the infantry were to be laid off during the winter. The rest were to have their pay cut, which he justified on the grounds that they would be effectively in garrison rather than on the march.[3] Such precautions were militarily more detailed than would have been case had the army been stationed in a rear area, but Ulster remained in the front line as the most likely first response of the Covenanters to the collapse of the truce would be to send the Earl of Argyll and his clansmen to Ireland to cause havoc.

However, Strafford's days were numbered. He was no longer the King's principal adviser, though his efforts to put a strategic plan in place to defeat the Covenanters were recognised by the award of the Order of the Garter. He spent six weeks after the conclusion of the treaty of Ripon preparing the English army for a long stay in Yorkshire, and he agreed with the advice of Charles's other counsellors that a parliament must be called to vote money for the maintenance of it and the Scottish army for fear that the first would disintegrate and the second march on London. However, he was under no illusion that a majority of the MPs in the House of Commons with strong support in the House of Lords would hold him to account, and that the leadership was in the hands of the very men who had been in correspondence with the leaders of the Covenant for several years and shared many of their ideas about defending Protestantism and the liberties of the subject. When the new parliament met on 9 November Strafford had completed his task in the north, but his hopes of returning to Ireland were dashed. Instead the King called him to London where he was arrested on Parliament's orders to answer a whole range of charges relating to his rule in Ireland as lord deputy and lord lieutenant and in England as Lord President of the Council of the North and as the King's principal adviser in the Second Bishops' War.[4] He was also to be accused of advising the use of the New Army to quell unrest in England.[5]

The chummy relationship between the Covenanter leadership and their English allies, the so-called junto who took control of much of the business of the new English parliament from the beginning, meant that the days of the New Army were numbered. Its purpose had been to fight the Covenanters. Now a third Bishops' War was totally out of the question, and it was therefore redundant. However, in the winter of 1640–41 the junto was preoccupied with other matters, most notably the trial of Strafford, and although lip-service was paid from time to time to the army's disbandment, it was

---

2   CSPD 1640, pp.254–55; CSPI 1633–47, pp.247, 249, *ibid.* 1647–60, p.231–82.
3   Bodleian, Carte Mss i, f.307; Whitaker, *Sir George Radcliffe*, pp.220–21.
4   The best account of Strafford's feelings in the autumn of 1640 as his plans and his influence on the King collapsed are in to be found in letters to his friend Sir George Radcliffe: Whitaker, *Sir George Radcliffe*, pp.202–23. The best narrative remains the second edition of C.V. Wedgwood's biography of the Earl, but it should be updated by consulting observations in Adamson, *The Noble Revolt*, which has an excellent index.
5   J. Rushworth, *Historical Collections of Private Passages of State*, 8 vols (London: D. Browne, 1721 reprint), iv, p.1261.

the Dublin government, which was no longer under the thrall of Strafford and his minions, that showed the greater interest in doing so. Christopher Wandesford, the lord deputy Strafford had nominated, had died suddenly in December. According to Carte the King decided that it would not be opportune to name Ormond as his successor given the way in which the Earl's military career had blossomed under the aegis of the Lord Lieutenant.[6] Instead Ireland was to be governed for the time being by the lord justices Robert, Lord Dillon and Sir William Parsons. Parsons' sympathies lay with the junto, but Dillon was not only closely associated with Strafford's autocratic rule but also linked to him personally by the marriage of his eldest son to the Lord Lieutenant's sister. A delegation of Old and New English peers and commoners, who were in London preparing to give evidence against Strafford, advised Charles that Dillon would be unacceptable to Irish public opinion, and within a fortnight he had appointed Sir John Borlace in his stead.[7]

Internal security continued to be the main preoccupation of Ireland's rulers. The Catholic soldiers in the New Army were the most obvious threat, but the hope was that they would obey their Protestant officers provided they received their pay when it was due. That, however, was an increasingly worrying problem with the major decline in revenue from the subsidies and custom duties, the government's other principal source of income, producing almost a third less in early 1641 than they had done in the second quarters of 1638 and 1639.[8]

It was not long before familiar anxieties found voice. Philip Wenham, who had served in the Carlisle garrison whilst retaining his captaincy in the standing army, and Sir George St. George, captain in the Old Army and major in the New, reported that they were finding difficulty in getting their orders obeyed because of delays in providing the troops still quartered at Carrickfergus and adjacent parts of Ulster with pay and victuals.[9] At about the same time George Rawdon, Lord Conway's estate manager in Ulster, advised his master that there was a shortage of money to pay the army.[10] These were teething problems and the lord justices solved the problem temporarily by using every possible source of revenue to keep the New Army happy whilst cutting back on as many other sources of expenditure as possible. But this could not go on forever. In February 1641 the lord justices wrote to Sir Henry Vane, the senior Secretary of State, that the Irish exchequer would be empty within three days,

---

6 Carte, *Life of Ormond* i, pp.243, 245.
7 Dillon and Parsons had been suggested by the King in 1639, but Strafford preferred Wandesford to act as lord deputy: CSPI 1633–47, pp.222, 247–8. For the short-lived alliance between members of the Irish, Old English and New English elites in 1640–41, see Lenihan, *Consolidating Conquest*, p.89.
8 Sir John Temple, *The Irish Rebellion*, p.14; CSPI 1625–33, p.27; *ibid.*, 1647–60, p 234.
9 Bodleian, Carte Mss i, f.298.
10 CSPI 1633–47, p.247.

and if the English government did not do something about it the troops would soon start plundering the civilian population. A similar message was sent in March with the additional information that the pay of the standing army companies on garrison duty, now usually referred to as the Old Army, was a year and a half in arrears. However, the English House of Commons, which had absolute control over the purse strings, ignored the hint that financial contribution would solve the imminent threat of unrest in Ireland.[11]

On 10 April the lord justices and the Council wrote again to Secretary Vane. By scrimping and saving they had managed to find some money for New Army pay, but the soldiers of the two armies were coming into conflict with one another with one being paid and the other not. However, there would soon be a level playing field when there was no money to pay either. Moreover, their authority was being challenged. Already soldiers visiting Dublin had seized foodstuffs from the weekly market under their very eyes. In consequence stall holders were on strike, and this threatened to cause unrest amongst the civilian population unable to purchase food and other essentials.

Later in the month Sir Arthur Loftus, who as deputy treasurer was the principal financial official in the Irish government, wrote in despair to Vane that the New Army had not been paid for three weeks, and that the rank and file were beginning to systematically plunder civilians. He ended that section of what was a very long letter about Ireland's troubles with the forthright declaration that the New Army was a useless expense and should be disbanded as quickly as possible.

Later Loftus raised the spectre of a more dangerous threat not just to law and order but to English hegemony in Ireland as other interests were intent on taking responsibility for security. Some prominent people in Connaught (who by implication were Catholics as there were very few Protestant settlers in that province) were about to offer to pay for the costs of maintaining the New Army for a year provided that it was settled into quarters in every part of the country. But they were wolves in sheep's clothing. Once the army had been dispersed individual units might well be ordered by their paymasters to browbeat or even attack isolated Protestant communities in their immediate neighbourhoods, and Loftus was not alone in his fear for the future if the Dublin government was forced by financial penury to accept the proposal. The Protestant officers in the New Army were also alarmed. They asserted that whilst it remained in north-east Ulster it was possible to exert a good measure of control over the Catholic rank and file. Under any other arrangement this would be impossible.[12]

The increasingly desperate pleas coming from Ireland were not totally ignored in London as demands for its disbandment of the New Army were made in Parliament from time to time in the winter of 1640–41. There was, for example, a brief flurry of interest in the Commons between 31 December and 7 January, and in both Houses

11 CSPI 1633–47, pp.260, 267.
12 CSPI 1633–47, pp.270–71, 279; *ibid.* 1647–60, p.243.

between 13 and 19 February, but such was the lack of urgency on the second occasion that it took the Commons four weeks to reject the Lords' proposal that 2,000 officers and men should be retained to strengthen the standing army and thus make Ireland more secure.[13] Other matters such as the trial of the Earl of Strafford were of a much higher priority. In such circumstances Ireland could hardly said to be forgotten as many of the witnesses against his rule came from the Irish, Old English and New English communities. Possibly the MPs and peers, who were beginning to take over the business of government in areas other than finance from the Privy Council, thought that if the New Army mutinied and ran amok, the Earl of Argyll would easily be able to land a large body of Campbells in Ulster to bring an end to the violence before it got completely out of control.

The issue that eventually placed the fate of the New Army centre stage had nothing directly to do with Ireland. In King Charles's other two kingdoms security, which seemed to have been restored by the treaty of Ripon and the meeting of the English parliament, no longer looked as assured by the following spring. Peace negotiations proceeded at a snail's pace as did Strafford's trial; unrest grew in the English army in the north as grievances mounted about the more favourable treatment given to the Covenanter army in terms of pay and resources; and fears grew of a devilish plot by the Pope, the Jesuits and the kings of France and Spain to undermine by stealth and then supplant the reformed religion and the constitution in all three kingdoms. However, the absence of international sabre-rattling directed at the British Isles increasingly suggested that the two Catholic kings would wait for something to happen before becoming involved. The first blow would therefore be an uprising of papists in England master-minded by the King's 'evil advisers', the Queen and the Catholics or crypto Catholics at Court and in the provinces, with the military muscle being provided by the New Army.[14]

New security measures began to be implemented in December 1640 with Parliament persuading the King to expel Catholic officers from his army in Yorkshire.[15] In mid February members of the English House of Commons tacked a request for the disbandment of the New Army onto an initiative for petitioning the King to expel designated Catholics from Court and to require all weapons in the possession of

---

13   JHC ii, pp.61–64, 82–84, 91, 93, 99, 103–04; JHL iv, pp.167, 187. Adamson implies disbanding the army was an active issue in the first three months of 1641. However, the absence of entries concerning the disbandment in the journals of both Houses suggests strongly that there was little enthusiasm for taking such an action at that point in time, and the silence of John Pym, the junto's principal spokesman on the Commons, in response to one attempt to sway the House in favour of disbandment is surely significant: *Noble Revolt*, pp.190–91, 200, 201, 207, 277.
14   For a succinct but many-sided appraisal of the Catholic menace, see Adamson, *The Noble Revolt*, pp.288–89.
15   JHC ii, pp.34, 39–40, 43, 57–58; HMC, Egmont Mss i, p.122.

Catholics to be confiscated.[16] Pressure of other business meant that they made little progress, but measures to protect the King's realms against Catholic aggression soon took on a new urgency.

For some months the procedure by which the London mercantile community provided bridging loans had run smoothly, and on 1 March the Commons duly sent a delegation to the city to ask for £100,000 the repayment of which would be guaranteed by the yield of subsidies already approved by Parliament. After three weeks' discussion the reply came back that the loan would not be forthcoming until Parliament provided better security. The citizens were chary about lending money. Their cash reserves were low because of the downturn in trade caused by the war, but there were other considerations that could be addressed almost immediately that would reassure everybody worried about Catholic plotting. The Earl of Essex then took up the matter in the House of Lords. The city's wariness stemmed from Parliament's slowness in dealing with the great grievances of the kingdom and in bringing to justice those responsible for them.[17]

On 31 March delegation headed by the lord mayor reassured the two Houses that money would be forthcoming if Parliament shifted its ground. Their response delivered on 3, 6 and 8 April was somewhat lacking in precision, but there would be no delay in executing justice or in redressing grievances, and the loan would be used specifically for paying money owed to soldiers who were being disbanded. It did however offer to dedicate additional subsidies to the payment of the loan and to ask the King to receive a deputation of MPs and peers, who would ask him to agree to the three anti-Catholic provisions and, it can be inferred, point out to him the inevitable consequences of the loan not materialising.[18] Charles did not respond immediately, and when he did five days later his reply to the House of Lords was clearly intended to cause delay.[19] The Houses could not reasonably expect him to decide how the New Army was to be disbanded given the more important issues facing him at that time. He was also of the opinion that all three armies raised in 1640 should be disbanded at the same time following the signing of a peace treaty as that was the normal practice.[20]

---

16 JHC ii, pp.85, 91; JHL iv, p.162.
17 JHC ii, pp.94, 111.
18 JHL iv, pp.202–06, 209; JHC ii, pp.116, 117.
19 There were rumours that the King was taking his time in the hope of finding a way to use the New Army to save Strafford's life, but the only evidence that this was his reason is a remark made by the Earl of Antrim at the start of his statement to the Commonwealth officers in 1650 that the King asked him to ask Ormond not to carry out the disbandment. However, Antrim's account of the first occasion on which he tried to sound out the Earl, namely the day on which the fourth session of the Irish parliament met, was far too late to have saved Strafford. It is also impossible to see how such a ploy if it had succeeded would have done anything other than hasten his death. Sir Richard Cox, *Hibernica Anglicana*, 2 vols (London: H. Clark for Joseph Watts, 1689–90) ii, pp.207–08..
20 JHL iv, p.216.

Busy with the trial of the Earl of Strafford neither House responded immediately but on 23 April the citizens of London, impatient with yet more delay, took direct action. Several thousand marched on Parliament carrying a petition with 20,000 signatures allegedly attached linking acceptance of the three demands formally to the granting of the loan.[21] This gave the MPs and the Lords the impetus to increase the pressure on the King, and on the 27ththey demanded a quick response.[22] Charles's reply delivered on the 30th was not particularly constructive. With regard to the New Army he was 'already upon the disbanding', but there were difficulties and he would not be adverse to receiving Parliament's advice and assistance in overcoming them.[23] This was not a lie. In March he had promised Major John Barry, one of the Catholics removed from the English army in December, that he would permit him to take soldiers from the disbanded New Army to serve the King of Spain.[24]

The following day Charles addressed members of both Houses from his throne in the House of Lords Seemingly he was more emollient as he desired and craved Parliament's assistance in carrying out the disbandment, but his words were taken by those present as indicating that he was still committed to a simultaneous disbandment with one MP reporting him as 'desiring and requiring your assistance for disbanding all the armies'.[25] Within a week, however, the English Privy Council had found a way around all the practical difficulties of disbanding the New Army and persuaded the King to agree by decoupling it from the other two demands.

What probably pushed Charles over the edge was fear of the London mob his attempts to move his wife and children to a place of safety having failed. In conversation on 3 May with Eusebius Andrews, one of the King's informants, John Lilburne, the London mob's hero and the future Leveller spokesman, had stated that 50,000 men and women would descend on Whitehall Palace the following day. They would be armed and in search of justice the rumour being that this would be either against Strafford or the King.[26] In the event it was Strafford who paid the extreme penalty at the executioner's block on Tower Green on the 12th.

On 7 May the Lords reported to the Commons that the King had given orders for the infantry of the New Army to be disbanded immediately, and that he had named eight colonels who were to recruit 1,000 men each for service in the armies of countries whose rulers were in a friendly relationship with his dominions. They also estimated that the disbandment would cost £10,000, which could be raised by

21 Rushworth, *Historical Collections* iv, pp.233–34; Woolrych, *Britain in Revolution*, p.177.
22 JHL iv, p.227.
23 JHL iv, pp.230–31.
24 HMC, Egmont Mss i, p.129.
25 JHL iv, p.232; HMC, Marquis of Abergavenny etc. Mss, p.140. Although Charles had been saying something similar about disbanding the army for weeks, Adamson's account of the reaction to the speech as causing horror is very convincing: *Noble Revolt*, pp.276–77.
26 Braddick, *God's Fury, England's Fire*, pp.135–38; Woolrych, *Britain in Revolution*, pp.178–82; HMC, Marquis of Abergavenny etc. Mss, pp.140–44.

borrowing money from private individuals accompanied by a promise that it would be repaid three months later. If this was a hint that the loan should be guaranteed by the English parliament, it fell on deaf ears. The Commons received the report the next day, but there was no further mention of the New Army in the journal of either House other than brief reports on the progress of the disbandment until the King's arrangements for ridding Ireland of its former soldiers came under scrutiny two months later.[27]

The Dublin government was left with the task of disbanding the New Army whilst the King gave permission for a number of colonels to take the soldiers abroad to serve in the armies of the French and Spanish kings. With no money coming from England all it could do was identify five men who it thought would be willing to loan money at very short notice to pay the officers and soldiers their wages for April and May on the understanding that the proceeds of the last of the subsidies granted in 1640 would be available to reimburse them at the beginning of September. A fortnight later, however, the lord justices admitted that they were at least £3,000 and possibly £6,000 short of the mark. One man could not afford to lend money; another had not replied; and a third, though very likely to oblige, was temporarily out of contact. By 1 June, however, when disbandment was well under way, they had managed to borrow £8,000, which would be enough to give the rank and file 10 shillings each with the remainder being presumably reserved for the officers' pay. This they thought should be sufficient, but the revenue raised by the final instalment of the subsidy approved in March 1640 would not be available for honouring the loans as it was needed to pay the standing army which was already 18 months in arrears. As for the former soldiers of the New Army they were to surrender their weapons on being discharged (which would be put in safe storage for the King's future use) and return to their homes to wait for the call to re-enlist for service overseas.[28]

The lord justices in the meantime worked on instructions for the colonels based on those devised in the early 1630s to ensure that officers recruiting for foreign rulers caused as little disruption as possible to normal life The veterans were to be enlisted in their communities by the colonels' agents and to proceed to their ports of embarkation in small groups. They were allowed free passage across country but must pay for their food and drink whilst doing so, and once there they were to be quartered in the suburbs or the surrounding countryside not within the town or city walls. The colonels were to be responsible for feeding them whilst they were waiting to embark and not to provide them with weapons until they were on the high seas.[29]

27 JHC ii, pp.137, 141; JHL iv, p.239.
28 JHL iv, p.239; CSPI 1633–47, pp.281, 289.
29 CSPI 1633–47, p.297.

The Earl of Ormond as Strafford's deputy had the job of disbanding the New Army and in mid June he reported that it was no more. Both he and the lord justices expressed their profound relief that discharging the rank and file, the most dangerous part of the operation, had gone without a hitch. There had been no reports of violence against civilians, and the outrages which had happened in the spring had been through desperation at having no means of subsistence when the money the government had to pay wages ran out. However, the officers had not been paid their arrears in full as it had not been possible to borrow the full £10,000 but given their excellent record in training and disciplining the foot soldiers in difficult circumstances they deserved nothing less than the full amount.[30]

Having completed his task the Earl reverted to being acting commander of the standing army by virtue of his commission as lieutenant general of cavalry, but this would not be for long as the King had appointed the Earl of Leicester as Lord Lieutenant of Ireland within days of Strafford's execution. Second-in-command was clearly not enough, and the tone and contents of the letters he wrote to the King during the summer show that he was angling for something more distinguished, but the most Charles would do was express his extreme gratitude for the way Ormond had commanded the New Army and supervised its disbandment with just the hint of a commensurate reward at some future date. His only instructions were to do what he could to prepare Ireland for possible involvement in a new war, but this time in Germany in support of a Protestant alliance.[31]

Generals, colonels and field officers who held commissions in the New Army returned to being mere captains in the standing army as we must now call it, though they would not experience a loss of income as during the time of their secondment they had only been paid as captains. Sir Thomas Lucas had the best prospects as master of the ordnance designate, but it remained a half-post as Sir John Borlace showed no interest in retiring completely. Lucas did however have a strong chance of a captaincy in the standing army. When the disbandment of the New Army changed from possibility to probability in the spring of 1641 he and his troop of horse were transferred to Ireland from the north of England on the grounds that its services were needed should there be any trouble with the infantry. The troops of horse which had been drafted into the New Army from the standing army were full of Catholics who might not be prepared to obey orders to disperse their fellow soldiers by force.

The King subsequently declared that when one of the existing captains of horse in the standing army died or left his command for whatever reason, his troop should be disbanded thus creating a vacancy for Lucas and his men, but once the tidying-up after the disbandment had come to an end changed circumstances meant that Charles was unable to honour his pledge.[32] Lucas's troop then seems to have been disbanded

---

30 CSPI 1633–47, pp.292, 295–96, 302; Carte, *Life of Ormond* v, pp.248–51.
31 Carte, *Life of Ormond* i, p.269; *ibid.* v, pp.248–54; CSPI 1633–47, p.302.
32 CSPI 1633–47, pp.292, 323; CSPD 1640–41, pp.318, 321.

in August or September but it was reformed in the immediate aftermath of the patriotic uprising. This suggests that the disbandment took place in Ireland rather than England and that many of the troopers had not left for the mainland before 23 October.[33]

Orders to be followed by Catholic foot soldiers of the New Army at their disbandment had their re-enlistment been clearly laid down, but a question mark hangs over the fate of officers and soldiers seconded from the standing army. Insofar as the troops of horse were concerned there is no doubt whatsoever that they were reinstated *en bloc* after the disbandment as they appear under the same officers in Sir John Temple's list of the standing army at the outbreak of the patriotic uprising in the following October. As for the two troops raised in England, they were disbanded sometime during 1641.

As mentioned above the officers commanding companies in the New Army also returned to their commands in the standing army, but in none of the documents describing the disbandment of the rank and file of the New Army and their re-enlistment is there any mention of the near 1,000 soldiers Carte claimed had been transferred from the standing army into the New Army at its birth. Similarly nothing was said about the fate of the men impressed into the standing army to replace them who would have been expelled from its. ranks in June 1641 to make way for the seconded soldiers and would have been owed substantial sums of money in pay arrears. Absence of evidence cannot be regarded as anything more than highly suspicious, and it is indeed possible that the return of the infantrymen to their units was such a humdrum matter that it was not worth mentioning. However, if this had been so, the number of soldiers to be recruited into the armies of France and Spain after the disbandment should have been 7,000, but the figure of 8,000 is repeated again and again in contemporary documents.[34]

There can only be two explanations for the figure of 8,000 and both are highly implausible. First, the draft from the standing army into the New Army in April 1640 was made up of Catholic soldiers rather than Protestants, but this completely contradicts Carte's explanation of the reason why they were seconded. Second, the Dublin government considered that the Protestant soldiers in the New Army as well as the Catholics were best employed in service overseas after the disbandment, as swordsmen who had fought on both sides in the Nine Years' War had been. a menace to law and order for some years afterwards. However, if this had been in the lord

---

33 CSPD 1641–43, pp.55–56; Temple, *The Irish* Rebellion, p.26. Lucas's troop reappeared in November 1641 and was not usually referred to as having been raised after the uprising: CSPI 1641-3, p.771; HMC, Ormonde Mss o.s. i, pp.126, 129, 134; *ibid.* o.s. ii, p.11; Sir John Gilbert, *History of the Confederation and the War in Ireland 1641–1653*, 7 vols (Irish Archaeological and Celtic Society: Dublin, 1882) i, pp.230–32

34 See above for the raising of the 8,000 foot and Carte, *Life of Ormond* v, p.248 and CSPI 1633–47, pp.281, 292 for their disbandment.

justices' minds, the prospect of a near full regiment of Protestants serving in the army of a Catholic king when they would have been invaluable in bolstering up security at home or assisting in the recovery of the Palatinate would have caused an uproar in both the English and the Irish parliament.

14

Disbandment and its Consequences

The transformation of the New Army personnel into soldiers swearing allegiance to a foreign ruler began in a straightforward manner. First, the demand for new recruits in Europe was buoyant. Despite serious negotiations taking place at Ratisbon to bring the fighting in Germany to an end after 20 years, France was at war with Spain and King Philip was also facing nationalist uprisings in Portugal and Catalonia which needed to be put down by force, as well as pursuing the interminable war with the Dutch. Second, the qualifications of the eight colonels named by the King on 7 May – Sir James Dillon, Theodore Taaffe, Garrett Barry, John Barry, Lorenzo Cary, William Wintour, Christopher Belling and John Butler – were not a problem. Carte described those he named as men known for their merit, loyalty and integrity. Whether this was indeed the case cannot be proved one way or the other, but they could not be described as lacking in experience. At least six and possibly all eight had previously served on the Continent. Subsequently five had been field officers and above in the New Army and two in the English army facing the Scots. Third, despite Catholic officers being expelled from the English army in December 1640, the fact that at least seven of the eight were Roman Catholics does not seem initially to have been seen as a problem.[1]

There was admittedly a hiccup right at the start. Lorenzo Cary, the only possible Protestant amongst the eight colonels, and the one whose experience of warfare overseas had almost certainly been aspirational rather than actual, returned to his standing army company in garrison at Galway. Much less is known about Wintour, who disappeared from the record at the same time, but his appointment may have been seen on reflection as too confrontational because of his family ties with the Queen's secretary Sir John Wintour, who was regarded as one of the King's 'evil advisers'.

---

1   CSPI 1633–47, pp.281, 330; Carte, *Life of Ormond* ii, p.271; JHC ii, p.40. Carte only gave the names of seven colonels, five from the original list and the two replacements mentioned below. He ignored the eighth, Sir James Dillon, almost certainly in order to continue the fiction that there were only 7,000 Catholics in the New Army infantry regiments.

Replacements, however, were quickly found, namely George Porter and Richard Plunkett, and it is they who appear on Thomas Carte's list of the colonels given their commissions by the King on 13 May.[2]

A much more serious problem was that only one of the eight was immediately available. John Barry, for example, was stranded in London because he was temporarily too strapped for cash to travel to Ireland. Christopher Belling, however, was ready to start recruiting, and by the end of June he and his soldiers had left for France having behaved impeccably from start to finish.[3] The only disquieting factor was a report taken very seriously by the lord justices. Two former New Army officers, Major Thomas Searle and his lieutenant William Flower who could understand Gaelic had witnessed an impassioned speech made by a Catholic priest to a body of 30 or 40 recruits for Belling's regiment on their march to their port of embarkation. He had been trying to persuade them to remain in Ireland as 'there might be use for them soon'.[4]

Recruitment for service in Europe became a political issue in England on 8 July when the House of Commons heard that 14,000 soldiers all of whom were Catholics were being raised in Ireland by officers employed by foreign Catholic monarchs who were not considered to be friendly towards England. This was reported to the Lords and questions were raised about the wording of their commissions, but the matter was then put on a backburner whilst the two Houses dealt with more important items of business such religious reform, protecting England against the machinations of the King's evil advisers, and giving the final touches to the peace treaty with Scotland. However, mentioning it was sufficient to ensure that when the so-called Ten Heads or Propositions for improving the security of the realm against Catholic attempts to destabilise it was increased to 15, one provision related to consultation in the future about the issuing of commissions, which might in due course give Parliament a veto over the King's exclusive control over appointments in the armed forces.[5] Charles accepted the old and the new propositions on 21 July, whereupon the Lords and the Commons lost interest in Ireland for a few weeks whilst they concentrated on other matters.

---

2   *Life of Ormond* i, pp.268–89; CSPI 1633–47, p.330. Plunkett from a distinguished Old English family had served in Catholic armies overseas, whilst Porter, the son of King Charles's friend and adviser Endymion Porter, was a captain in the English army in 1640 who had been discharged as a Catholic some months before.
3   HMC, Egmont Mss i, p.136; Carte, *Life of Ormond* i, pp.268, 271; M. Hickson, *Ireland in the Seventeenth Century* (London: Longman, 1884) ii, p.336 (letter from the lord justices' council to Secretary Vane, 30 June 1641); CSPI 1633–47, pp.297, 307; Gilbert: *Irish Confederation* i, pp.58–63, 217–19.
4   CSPI 1633–47, p.308.
5   JHL iv, pp.320–22; JHC ii, pp.185, 202–03, 217. Fourteen thousand was indignantly denied at the time, but if one adds the numbers given in commissions issued to officers wanting to recruit soldiers in Ireland who were not formerly in the New Army the 8,000 quickly becomes over 11,000: CSPI 1633–47, pp.312–40.

The Irish parliament then took up the running.⁶ In late July it ordered the lord justices to ban the transport of troops overseas. Ten reasons were cited ranging from Spain being the traditional enemy to the damage that would be done to the Irish economy by so many men being taken out of employment in farming and manufacturing.⁷ However, the speaker of the House of Lords decided that he must refer the matter to the English parliament either because he disapproved of it or because there was doubt as to the Irish parliament's right to issue such an order. He sent a letter to his namesake, and there was some discussion between the Lords and the Commons on 6 August during which the peers proposed that 3,000 or 4,000 New Army veterans should be allowed to leave Ireland for Europe, but taking a decision was apparently postponed.⁸

On 9 August the King responded to the anxieties of his parliaments by reducing the scale of the exodus. He revoked the commissions of the seven remaining colonels and issued new ones allowing four of them to recruit 1,000 veterans each for service in the King of Spain's armies. The English House of Commons immediately asked for a discussion with the Lords as despite having agreed to consult about commissions Charles had acted unilaterally. It soon transpired that there had been a misunderstanding. He had apparently taken the proposal they had taken to the Commons as tacit approval.⁹ Clearly there was anger at his action, but nothing happened for the moment. The four colonels therefore went ahead with the Dublin government's active support whilst the Spanish ambassador set about hiring ships.¹⁰

On 20 August leading members of the junto had an interesting conversation with a Mr. Walsh who had up-to-date information about the raising of forces in Ireland for service in the French and Spanish armies. What Walsh said was nor recorded,¹¹ but a few days later the two Houses issued an order banning troops leaving the country and requiring the navy to put the ships the Spanish ambassador had hired under guard to ensure that they did not leave the Thames estuary. A letter to that effect was sent to the lord justices, and on 9 September the two Houses passed an ordinance confirming their decision attached to which was a lengthy paper justifying their action. This drew heavily on the case made by the Irish parliament, but it reduced the number of reasons to three. A pause would give time for the King to make an agreement with a Protestant ruler to incorporate the veterans into his army; if allowed to go to Spain they could very well return in due course as the spearhead of an invading army; and it would be a major discouragement to the Protestant cause in Germany if the military

6 JHC ii, pp.212–18; JHL iv, pp.321–3.
7 Index to the Journal of the Irish House of Commons, vols 1–11 (Dublin: J. Bradley, 1765), p.66; Cox, *Hibernia Anglicana* ii, pp.70–71; Carte, *Life of Ormond* i, p.270.
8 JHL iv, pp.339–345; JHC ii, pp.240, 242.
9 JHL iv, pp.363–64; JHC ii, pp.253–56.
10 CSPI 1633–47, pp.331, 338; JHL iv, pp.390, 394–95.
11 JHC ii, p.266.

manpower at the disposal of Catholic rulers was increased by 4,000 trained soldiers on the instructions of a Protestant king.[12]

These explanations sound unconvincing to twenty-first century ears, but this is partly the effect of hindsight. What Parliament did not know was that Spain would not be in a position to send an expeditionary force to Ireland for many years because of King Philip's commitments in Europe mentioned above to which was soon added an uprising in southern Italy. In addition the military situation in Germany had changed since June. The peace talks at Ratisbon were on the verge of collapse. The English position had been that peace would only be acceptable if the Elector Palatine was restored to his ancestral lands, but despite favourable noises coming from Spain its Catholic allies would have none of it. As a result the junto and its Scottish friends were in serious discussion about sending in a British army to recover them by force.

A war in Europe might well be initially popular in England where anti-Catholic sentiment was being fanned for all it was worth by the junto as a means to an end, namely putting intolerable pressure on the King to agree to their entire slate of constitutional and religious reforms, but past experience had shown that public opinion was as changeable as a weathervane. First, it would expect a quick victory, but this was even less likely in 1641 than it had been 17 years earlier when the first attempt had been made to put pressure on the Catholic powers over the Palatinate by force of arms. An advance into the Rhenish Palatinate from the west could only make progress with the wholehearted support of the United Provinces, but the Dutch had not been enthusiastic about accommodating Mansfeld's army in 1625, and since then relations with England had soured due to commercial rivalry in the Baltic, the North Sea and the Far East.

Second, as the Venetian ambassador advised his government after taking extensive soundings amongst his many contacts in commercial and political circles in London, it would be heavy going asking Parliament to approve another very heavy round of taxation immediately after the peace treaty with the Scots had ended almost a year paying the wages of the two armies in the north of England. Moreover, there was no guarantee that the initial demand would not be followed by many more if the first campaign was inconclusive.

The dangers of committing England to a major military undertaking in Europe with all the uncertainties about its outcome must have been obvious to professional soldiers in the junto's ranks like the Earls of Warwick and Essex, and experienced politicians like John Pym and John Hampden cannot have been blind to the impact on public opinion of a stalemate or a humiliating reverse like those suffered by English armies during the Duke of Buckingham's wars. If on the other hand the underlying aim of the whole business was to use preparations for war as a way of wresting control of the armed forces of England and Ireland from the King that fell short of actually sending an expedition to Europe, there was the risk of dashing expectations and

---

12   CSPI 1633–47, pp.327, 330; JHC ii, pp.266, 275, 284–87; JHL iv, pp.381–82, 393–94.

attracting charges of political cynicism. In such circumstances it would be surprising if some at least of the junto had not reasoned that there was a cheaper way of achieving it that was much closer to home, far less expensive to resource, equally acceptable to their Scottish friends, and involving little of the risk of fighting a campaign in the Rhine valley.

Six weeks after the 9 September ordinance was passed by the English parliament there was a major Catholic uprising in Ireland aimed at overthrowing the Protestant hegemony. The planning and execution were the work of a group of predominately Irish landowners aided by professional soldiers some of whom were Old English the two communities being united by fears for their lands, their liberties and their faith following the political upheavals in England and Scotland over the past year during which their hopes had first been raised and then dashed.

Senior members of both communities had eagerly joined the New English in the winter of 1640–41 in taking revenge on the Earl of Strafford for the ways they had been tricked and their differences exploited during his rule, and their grievances formed a considerable part of the charges levied against him. However, after they had served their purpose, the junto performed a cynical volte-face and gave its unwavering support to the New English. As a result the King's previous agreement to confirm the Graces was put on hold, the final court of appeal in legal cases was moved from Dublin to London, and hopes of challenges to existing landholding that had enabled plantations to spread being ended was dashed. To make matters worse the junto's exploiting of anti-Catholic sentiment to further its constitutional and religious aims had reached such a pitch that by the autumn Catholics in Ireland could see their religion being suppressed in the near future by English and Scottish troops, their parliament becoming totally subordinate to the English parliament, and the lands of those who would not convert being confiscated and handed over to Protestants. An early resort to arms looked like the only way of preventing the demise of Catholic Ireland and one that given the context is completely understandable and, dare I say, theologically justifiable as a just war.[13]

What the ordinance had not done was order the former New Army soldiers to return to their towns and villages and the colonels and their agents and recruiting officers to return to Europe. As a consequence the rank and file in at least two of the regiments stayed together close to the ports under their new commanders.[14] But something not far short of panic grew amongst the latter: they had spent the Spanish

---

13 Lenihan, *Consolidating Conquest*, pp.89–93.
14 For John and Garret Barry see below. Plunkett was directly involved in planning the insurrection and it can be assumed that he kept his men together for this eventuality, though there is no empirical evidence. George Porter, on the other hand, having no real connection with Ireland, claimed to be out of pocket along with the other colonels but he may not have left England. In the English Civil War, when he had reached the dizzy rank

king's money to no effect and were running into debt themselves, whilst the veterans' hopes of overseas employment had been disappointed. How the troops were fed cannot be ascertained. There does not seem to have been an outbreak of plundering, but in the case of one regiment it would have been impossible. John Barry's was billeted in ships lying in Dublin Bay until fears of multiple deaths through starvation forced the government a few weeks after the uprising to allow the soldiers to come ashore, disband and thereafter presumably fend for themselves.[15]

The involvement of the regiments and their officers in the uprising seems unquestionable but the evidence is slim. First the only person to specifically link the veterans with the uprising in Ulster was Lord Montgomery, and that was in a letter written immediately afterwards, whilst nothing of that nature appeared in the extensive outgoing correspondence of the lord justices and their council in October, November and December.[16] A false lead is provided by the term the Colonel's Plot to describe a scheme for an uprising in the summer that did not take place, which implies that they and their regiments had an interest in joining the patriots but only one of the 10 colonels named in documents dated 7 May and 8 August was named as a participant in the events of 22/23 October This was Richard Plunkett, and by a process of elimination his men were likely to have been those identified by lord Montgomery as being active in Ulster, though Plunkett himself was miles away supervising the arrangements for the capture of Dublin Castle. The best case of direct involvement of New Army veterans in the uprising can be made for Garrett Barry's regiment which refused to disperse when ordered to do so by the lord president of Munster when the Ulster uprising was well under way. Their colonel subsequently became general of the patriotic forces in Munster, but whether or not his regiment joined the patriots and maintained its corporate identity in their army has yet to be ascertained.[17]

The most surprising element in the run-up to the Ulster uprising to my mind is that the English parliament led by the junto, having created circumstances that were likely to provoke Irish Catholics into a rebellion of desperation, and despite warnings from the King and also from the lord justices culminating in a letter from Sir William Parsons to Sir Henry Vane on 3 August,[18] was seemingly oblivious to the need for

---

    of major general, he was described by Lord Goring as the best company but the worst officer who served the King.
15 Carte, *Life of Ormond* i, p.344.
16 HMC, Ormonde Mss, n.s. ii, pp.2–49.
17 CSPI 1633–47, pp.341, 351, 357: HMC, Egmont Mss i, pp.144–45, 203. The British Civil War Project claims that both Plunkett's and Garrett Barry's regiments joined the patriot armies, but it does not provide any evidence: <http://www.bcw-project.org>. Colonel John Barry's men on board the ships in Dublin Bay were suspected of being ready to garrison the capital once the castle had been captured, but nothing was proved.
18 Hickson, *Ireland in the Seventeenth Century* ii, p.339.

enhanced security measures when there were 7,000 trained Catholic soldiers in the country who only required arms and ammunition to be transformed into a formidable army.

An exception was Sir Simons D'Ewes, the most prolific diarist of the first years of the Long Parliament, who wrote 'I often foretold what I feared'.[19] The wording implies very strongly that he had talked to others rather than just to his conscience, but if this was so nobody had been listening. In the journals of the Two Houses there is only a single direct reference to the security of Ireland posed by the former soldiers of the New Army in the three and a half months between the eight colonels' commission being raised as a matter of concern and the news of the uprising reaching London. In late August a delegation reporting to the Commons on a meeting of a joint committee of the two Houses which had been discussing what was to become the ordinance of 9 September recommended that the Lower House should ask the Upper House to 'consider some course for preventing any inconvenience that might arise by the Irish soldiers that are levied and in one body in Ireland'. There is, however, no record in the Lords' Journal of any proposals being made to deal with the matter either before the parliamentary session came to an end 13 days later or at the start of the new session which began on 20 October.[20] .

Contemporary or near-contemporary discussion of the first few days of the patriotic uprising unsurprisingly focused far more on who or what was responsible and on the horrors that followed and not on why security measures were not in place to prevent it or at least to extirpate it before it got out of control. Admittedly Sir John Temple, who was closest to the events, blamed the lord justices for stationing the units of the standing army in garrisons scattered from one end of Ireland to the other rather than in larger concentrations in areas where trouble might occur, but this had been the practice from the end of the Nine Years' War onwards and the Dublin government had not weakened the concentration of companies in Ulster where trouble was most likely to occur.[21]

Academic historians acknowledge with a fair degree of puzzlement that the junto was more to blame for ignoring the threat posed by the recruits and the officers commanding them once they had been ordered not to leave the country. Their explanations none of which can be described as convincing or even particularly illuminating, can I suspect be seen as the final flowering of the version of English

---

19 This entry in D'Ewes's diary is quoted in A. Fletcher, *The Outbreak of the English Civil War* (London: Arnold, 1981), p.136.
20 JHC ii, p.275. JHL iv, p.381. Official confirmation that the Irish parliament was in favour of putting a stop to the scheme had reached the English House of Lords on 4 August. It was discussed on the following day with support being given to 3,000 recruits leaving for Spain, but there had been no further progress in either House: JHL iv, pp.339, 340.
21 Edmund Borlace, *A History of the Execrable Irish Rebellion* (London: Brome, Clavell and Chipwell, 1680), pp.7–11; Cox, *Hibernia Anglicana* ii, pp.71–76; Temple, *The Irish Rebellion*, p.27.

history usually described as Whig which studiously ignored bad press concerning progressive elements from Simon de Montford onwards who they saw as preparing the way however unwittingly for the eventual triumph of parliamentary democracy. Gardiner implied that ignoring Ireland was a gamble. When it failed and Ireland burst into flames the junto regretted persuading Parliament to forbid the transfer of troops to Europe, but the decision was morally sound in that the purpose had been to avoid harming the Protestant cause by strengthening the King of Spain's armies. C.V. Wedgwood, on the other hand, blamed lack of knowledge of Irish politics amongst the King's leading opponents in Parliament, and the fact that they were distracted at the time by fears of plots in England and Scotland to overturn the political and religious achievements of the past four years. More recently Conrad Russell sidestepped trying to explain the junto's failure to understand the impact that its antiCatholic propaganda in England was likely to have on Ireland with the phrase 'sublime blindness',[22] whilst Woolrych was content with describing the uprising as something unforeseen. Gentles' sole but entirely valid comment was that forcing the New Army veterans to remain in Ireland was an event with ironic consequences.[23]

Adamson building on what was no more than an aside in Gardiner's account of the events of 1641 has produced the most penetrating analysis of what was in the minds of the junto in the late summer of 1641 and shown an acute awareness of the European context for the two months' havering over whether the veterans should or should not be allowed to leave Ireland. He does not dodge the charge that its leaders were partly to blame for the uprising, but like many of his predecessors he sees this as a sin of omission summed up in phrases such as their being paradoxically insensitive to opinion in Ireland, and that there are few clearer examples of the Law of Unintended Consequences.[24] He does, however, see the junto's exploiting the business of what to do with the New Army veterans as part of their drip-drip campaign to deprive the King of his prerogative powers over the armed forces, but he stops short of considering that its leaders were guilty of a sin of commission. It is certainly worth suggesting arguable that doing nothing about the security of the Protestant hegemony whilst threatening the Catholic communities with extinction might have been driven by the hope that some form of unrest would result which required immediate military intervention, and which could provide the justification for wresting military authority from the King on the grounds that his 'evil advisers' had some role in the Irish conflagration.[25]

---

22 Gardiner, *History* x, p.10; Wedgwood, *King's Peace*, pp.467–68; C. Russell, *The Causes of the English Civil War* (Oxford: University Press, 1990), p.129.
23 *Britain in Revolution*, p.188; *The English Revolution*, p.42.
24 Adamson, *Noble Revolt*, pp.367, 376, 677.
25 The nearest Adamson gets to this is the statement that the junto seem not to have seen the consequences of forbidding the recruits to leave Ireland, but he then goes on to explain it in terms of lack of accurate intelligence coming from Ireland, insensitivity, and obsession with maintaining good relations with Scotland via plans to intervene militarily in the war in Germany: *Noble Revolt*, p.376.

Thomas Carte dismissed the 'public reasons given' by Parliament for keeping the veterans in Ireland and discounted two others, namely the desire of the junto to humiliate the King in the eyes of the other rulers of Europe and accepting without question the advice of its 'creatures' in the New English community sitting in the House of Commons like Sir John Clotworthy whilst ignoring the fears of the Dublin government. Instead Carte was strongly of the opinion that the junto did not take the security issue on board because it was in their interest for trouble to break out in Ireland that would require English military assistance:

> the heads of that faction wished that some disturbance or insurrection ... might happen in that kingdom (Ireland) to distress his Majesty and thereby afford them a favourable opportunity and greater means to execute the measures they had formed.[26]

Although it is important to be wary of Carte's pronouncements because of his Tory bias, I feel that on this occasion he was closer to the truth as the germ of the idea can be found in the Earl of Clarendon's Autobiography in which he claimed that, whilst many people saw the uprising as a means of binding up the wounds in the English body politic and reconciling king and parliament, the absence of surprise he observed in the faces of members of the junto indicated that they 'had fomented and contrived this rebellion in order to carry forward their plans for the further changes in the English constitution and the Church of England.'[27]

But if the junto had been at best turning a blind eye to the possible effects of its actions or at worst indirectly encouraging an upsurge of violence in Ireland, can any of the blame be laid at the King's door? It is now accepted that the document the patriot leadership flourished mightily in the first weeks of the insurgency giving royal approval for the coup was a forgery.[28] It also goes without question that the King tried to warn the lords justices of an impending Catholic uprising in the spring of 1641, and that during June, July and August he was making every effort to discourage plotters with measures designed to move the veterans of the New Army out of the country as expeditiously as possible. Less well known to English historians is that on first hearing about the uprising he made every effort to send military hardware to Ulster from Scotland where he was in residence between 14 August and 18 November, whereas the slowness with which England responded to the uprising was not his fault. It was the direct consequence of his delegating executive authority to Parliament during his absence.

---

26 Carte, *Life of Ormond* i, pp.272–73.
27 This passage is printed as a lengthy footnote in Macray's edition of *The History of the Rebellion and Civil Wars in England* i, p.409.
28 To the disappointment of at least one historian: Woolrych, *Britain in Revolution*, p.199.

The only direct evidence that the King was thinking about remobilising the New Army in the months before the patriotic uprising dates from almost 10 years after the event and the source was the Earl of Antrim. He was in deep financial difficulties after the death of his wife the dowager duchess of Buckingham, and he hoped to win the sympathy of the republican regime by blackening the King's character. Propaganda-wise it was on the back foot following the publication straight after Charles's execution of *Eikon Basilike*, an alleged personal testament in which the King's ghost writer effectively exonerated him from all the crimes against his subjects of which he had been accused at his trial.

The controversy over the validity of his claims is too complex to reproduce here. It can be read in the pages of Ohlmeyer's biography of the Earl and in Perceval-Maxwell's responses.[29] I must say that I incline towards Ian Gentles's recent verdict that on past record the Earl should not be believed,[30] but I do wonder if the tale Antrim spun had its origins in moves to provide an the Irish corps for the British army to recapture the Palatinate mentioned above, the reason for contacting Antrim being for him to sound out the Catholic aristocracy.

The King had already committed himself to removing 4,000 New Army veterans from Ireland, which Parliament had yet to reject, and he may have seen the remaining 3,000 as making a major contribution despite their being Roman Catholics. Presumably they were not as committed to their faith as those busy signing up with the four colonels and could only be stirred into action by threats and inducements from their ancestral lords. This sounds like building castles in the air, but there is clear evidence that Charles was taking steps to bring Ireland into line with England and Scotland. In August he informed the Earl of Ormond by word of mouth of the country's intended role in the Palatine project. Ormond replied in a letter written on 6 September which was woolly enough for him not to be accused of being presumptuous for assuming that he was about to be given command of the Irish contingent. No sooner had he sent his response than clearer instructions arrived from Edinburgh under the King's name to which Ormond sent a reply on the 20th which had to be carefully worded. He had not been offered the command for which he had hoped, but he wanted to make sure he kept the door open for the King to be able to change his mind at a later date.[31]

That Antrim would be a useful intermediary is obvious from his loyalty to the Crown, his Catholic faith and his ability to make a doubtful line of argument credible, but he found the men he met interested only in the forthcoming uprising. The advice he gave was for them to focus exclusively on capturing Dublin Castle, the

---

29 A good starting point is J. Kenyon and J. Ohlmeyer (eds), *The Civil Wars: A Military History of England, Scotland and Ireland 1638–60* (Oxford, 1998), p.29.
30 *The English Revolution*, p.51.
31 Carte, *Life of Ormond* v, pp.252–54 (The King to Ormond 2 September 1641; Ormond to the King 6 and 20 September 1641).

seat of government, but like fools they compromised with disastrous consequences for thousands of men, women and children living in Ireland in 1641.[32]

---

32   Cox, *Hibernica Anglicana* ii, pp.207–08.

15

The Patriotic Uprising

What rapidly developed into a countrywide insurrection had been intended as a swift and surgical *coup d'etat*. The extent to which the plundering and massacre of Protestants that followed was intentional is a matter of debate which falls outside the remit of this book, but there is a measure of agreement in the present age on three points. Violence against civilians, though extensive, was less than supporters of the English hegemony claimed at the time and subsequently; Protestants responded very quickly by massacring Catholics but on a lesser scale; and although the coup could not have been bloodless, the way in which the predominantly civilian backlash against the English settlers rolled out was because the latter were seen as the beneficiaries of the Dublin government's years of repression, legal chicanery and broken promises. They were thus surrogates for the New English ministers and civil servants who could not be brought to account because the coup did not go according to plan.

The attack on the English instruments of repression, the Dublin government and the standing army, was to take place without warning on the night of the 22nd and the morning of the 23rd of October. Secrecy was essential. Otherwise it was doomed to failure as the assailants had few firearms and next to no gunpowder all of which would need to be captured in the first few hours before the enemy had time to gather their wits. The operation was to be two-pronged. The first was to seize Dublin Castle and secure its arsenal which contained most of the arms and ammunition that had formerly belonged to the New Army, and then to fan out across the city and capture or kill the lord justices and as many members of their council as possible in their lodgings before they had a chance to organise an appropriate response. The second was to inflict immense damage on the standing army in Ulster where it was at its strongest.

Although the men charged with storming the castle would only be armed with swords and daggers, the plan had every chance of success. The assailants, many of whom had been serving soldiers, would enter Dublin in ones and twos on the 22nd and early on the 23rd dressed as civilians heading for the weekly market. Gaining control of the castle soon after first light would be relatively easy, as it was to all intents and purposes undefended, the standing army company quartered there having been removed by the lord justices earlier in the year in response to claims that stationing soldiers in the city contravened a clause in its charter of self-government. What served as a garrison in late 1641 was a body of no more than 11 retired soldiers described officially as wardens and unofficially as 'ould silly men'. The lord justices' bodyguard, a company of halberdiers 40 strong, served in theory as a kind of reserve. They too were mostly ex-soldiers but armed as their name indicates with weapons that were of some use in close combat but in other respects obsolete.[1] To make matters worse the castle gates were never closed whilst access could also be gained at all hours by means of a staircase leading from the street into the outer bailey.

The Ulster operation was more audacious still as between 10 and 12 companies of foot and four troops of horse were quartered there.[2] However, they were stationed in towns, castles and forts in almost every corner of the province in a classical holding pattern for an army of occupation whose main function was putting down small pockets of unrest and bringing bands of brigands to justice. It was not the ideal arrangement for responding to a simultaneous surprise attack by a determined enemy on all the units in a discrete area. The nearest assistance would be coming from units at all points of the compass around the perimeter separated from one another by miles of possibly hostile countryside making it nigh impossible for them to combine forces before mounting a counterattack.

The original plan had been to attack Derry and Carrickfergus, but they were the two hardest nuts to crack given the strength of their fortifications and it was rejected as too ambitious. The focus then shifted to the six companies of foot and two troops of horse stationed in south and central Ulster. If they were overwhelmed, it would give the insurgents control of part of the province where much of the Earl of Tyrone's estates had been situated which would have advantages later in terms of recruitment as men remembered their ancestral loyalties. Possibly appeals of that nature had already borne fruit as the individual attacks such as that at Fort Mountjoy were carried out by local people using a variety of subterfuges, but the tactics involved there and elsewhere suggest a professional input at the planning stage.[3]

---

1   Lord Maguire's Relation written whilst in prison in England early in 1642: J. Nalson, *An Impartial Collection of the Great Affairs of State*, 2 vols (London 1683) ii, pp.543–55. This tells the complicated narrative of the planning from early 1641 onwards. For the disparaging remark about the wardens see J. Gilbert, *A Contemporary History of Affairs in Ireland 1641–1652*, 3 vols (Dublin: Irish Archaeological and Celtic Society', 1879–80) i, p.359.
2   The troops of Lord Grandison, Lord Conway, Sir Arthur Chichester and Sir John Borlace senior, and the companies of Lord Blayney, Sir Robert Stewart, Sir William Stewart, Sir Henry Tichborne, Sir Arthur Tyringham, Sir John Vaughan, Robert Bayley, John Barry, and George Blount, and possibly Sir Robert Farrer and William Billingsley stationed at Portrush and Strangford in 1642, but Farrer's was almost certainly in the Dublin area at the end of 1641 and Billingsley's in Leinster, not Ulster, soon afterwards. Chichester Fortescue's was at Dundalk: HMC, Ormonde Mss o.s. i, pp.124, 128, 141, 142.
3   Lenihan, *Consolidating Conquest*, pp.96–97.

Success in the second operation was essential for the first as the small body of men who had captured Dublin Castle could not be expected to hold onto it for long without reinforcements, as there were units of the standing army in Leinster only a day's march away. However, the big bonus of the Ulster operation was that it would immediately yield sufficient arms and ammunition to equip an army large enough to sweep aside whatever troops the Dublin government managed to assemble at short notice barring the way to the capital. After that the game would be won for the moment at least. What was left of the standing army would be tied down by planned and unplanned uprisings in Munster and Connaught or shut up and under siege in their surviving strongholds in Ulster and Leinster; Catholics all over Ireland would be coming off the fence in droves as they saw English hegemony collapsing before their eyes; and the insurgents' leaders would have time to organise a national defence against the inevitable response from across the Irish Sea. Also, by that time they expected the kings of France and Spain to have begun providing them with all manner of additional military supplies, and also given leave of absence to Irish officers serving in their armies whose presence in Ireland would enormously strengthen their army's command structure.[4]

In the event it was the Dublin operation that failed due to a lapse in security on the night of the 22nd the exact nature and circumstances of which will always be a matter of debate on account of the gaps and inconsistencies in the evidence provided by contemporaries or near contemporaries: the accounts provided by the informant Owen O'Connally, a Protestant convert; by two of the insurgents interviewed after the event; by the lord justices and their council in letters to the Earl of Leicester; and by Sir John Temple, Master of the Rolls in Ireland and a member of the lord justices' council ,who weaved the various accounts and some information of his own into what reads not just as a tale of derring-do but also a prime example of the working of God's providence whilst at the same time providing a lighter element in a book that otherwise made for very dire reading.

O'Connally and the lord justices skewed their narratives so not to draw attention to something they were desperate to hide, the informant because he had been more directly involved in the plot than it was safe to reveal, the lord justices because they had been too negligent in providing Dublin's defence and had ignored the warning of a plot received 10 or so days earlier. Temple, who was almost certainly not in Dublin on the night of the intended coup but arrived before the 25th, seems to be the exception, but he had every reason as a senior member of the New English government to toe the party line. As a bright and successful lawyer he had the rhetorical skills to do so including implying that he was impartial by being mildly critical of the lord justices for the way they had deployed the standing army before the uprising. It is therefore

---

4   Nalson, *Impartial Collection* ii, pp.543–45, 548, 551.

unlikely that he invented details of O'Connally's second escape which only appear in his account, as they added nothing to the strength of the case against the conspirators.[5]

The most authoritative narrative of the night's event is in the account of O'Connally's life written by Dr. Andrew Robinson for the Dictionary of Irish Biography.[6] This is lightly yet firmly in the Catholic tradition of portraying him as the arch betrayer and I would not dispute such a judgement. The account that follows is very similar to Dr. Robinson's as I have used the same primary sources, but it differs from it in number of respects, most particularly in regard to the factor which tipped O'Connally over into betraying the plot to the Dublin government.

The informant was told of a plot to overthrow the New English hegemony by his foster brother Hugh Og MacMahon, a former field officer in the Spanish army. This was some six months before the attempt to seize Dublin Castle, but it seems to have been similar to a scheme the Earl of Antrim claimed to have been trying to sell to the plotters in August and September 1641 which would have involved a relatively peaceful coup confined to the capital and managed by the Irish and Old English aristocracy.[7] O'Connally claimed that he tried to persuade MacMahon to break with the plotters, but probably agreed to give the Dublin operation his active support because of its narrow focus on the government. In the meantime he covered his back by informing several magistrates in his part of Ulster of rumours about conspiracies which were deliberately vague and for that reason ignored. He may also have convinced Mac Mahon that his Protestantism was only skin deep. Otherwise it is difficult to understand why his foster brother trusted him.

When O'Connally heard in mid October that Mac Mahon wanted him to leave home and join him, he knew what was in the offing and duly made his way to Dublin taking his sword with him. However, during a briefing session on the evening of the 22nd with the rest of Mac Mahon's desperados he discovered that the plot had widened into a nationwide conspiracy involving an uprising in Ulster that would coincide with the assault on the castle with hundreds if not thousands of Protestants being killed. When he asked permission to leave early the next day to warn his wife, who was English and a firm Protestant, he was told that it would be a waste of time with the implication being that he would soon find a new wife who was both Irish and a Catholic.

The revelation was traumatic, but O'Connally kept his wits about him sufficiently to peel off from the rest of the gang as it made its way across the city from one safe house to another, but by the time he arrived at Lord Justice Parsons' residence to spill the beans he was in a terrible state and unable to express himself coherently. This was

---

5   Temple, *Irish Rebellion*, pp.17–19, 27; Firth and Davis, *Regimental History of Cromwell's Army* ii, p.652.
6   This dictionary, which is an indispensable source for students of Irish history, is being produced and updated by the Royal Irish Academy. Robinson's biographical essay was published in 2013. It is easily readable online under O'Connally's name.
7   Cox, *Hibernia Anglicana* ii, p.208.

attributed to his excessive consumption of alcohol rather than shock, and he was sent away charged with finding out more information, but as a precaution Parsons put the city watch on alert to scour the streets looking for strangers. Mac Mahon and his men viewed O'Connally's return with suspicion but accepted his excuse that he had needed to relieve himself and had then lost his way. He was nevertheless threatened with death if he tried to leave the house and forced to surrender his sword. Although at their mercy O'Connally asked to relieve himself a second time as the tales of what was to come became more and more lurid, and when his escort to the toilet's attention wandered he leapt over a fence and ran off into the street where to his great good fortune he ran straight into some of the city watch before Mac Mahon's men could catch up with him. He was being marched off to prison when one of Lord Justice Parsons' servants encountered the patrol, having been sent to find him some time having elapsed since his departure. The servant vouched for the drunk and brought him safely to Lord Justice Borlace's house where members of the Council known to be in the city had been ordered to assemble it being as a safer place to meet than Parsons' as it was outside the city walls.

After being allowed some time to recover from the copious additional quantities of alcohol he had consumed during his second meeting with Mac Mahon and his gang, O'Connally was able to tell a coherent tale, which was recorded by a scribe and signed as a true record by the two lord justices and the three other members of the council who were present. At this point, or possibly after O'Connally's first escape, the order was given for the castle gates to be shut and the gates to be guarded, and for the wardens to be on the outlook for strangers. There was also a vague reference to armed support being sent to the castle, but this could well have been on the following day. As there was no mention of the halberdiers, it can be assumed that they were no more than a ceremonial guard not one that had a military function.[8]

The council had done all they could with the limited resources at their disposal, but at daybreak they would be in no better position than they had been on O'Connally's return.[9] The insurgents would be getting ready to pounce, and none of the standing army units were quartered close enough to the city to arrive before the afternoon. However, salvation arrived soon afterwards in the person of Sir Francis Willoughby.

---

8   Gilbert, *Contemporary History* i, pp.358–59; Temple, *Irish Rebellion*, pp.17–19, 26, 29; JHL iv, pp.415–16.
9   The next two paragraphs are based largely on Willoughby's own account in the archives of Trinity College, Dublin, which I have not been able to read because of the current restrictions placed on travel. Instead, I have used the passages in Carte *Life of Ormond* i, pp.339–41, and in Bagwell, *History of Ireland under the Stuarts* i, pp.321–22 that draw on it. Although not adverse to self-promotion, there is no reason for thinking that Willoughby's account is likely to be an accurate narrative of events as he himself had nothing to hide, but his correspondence over the years does how that he was not averse to blowing his own trumpet. For additional materials see CSPD 1641–43, pp.106, 120–25; CSPI 1633–47, p.787; HMC, Ormonde Mss o.s. i, pp.125–42 *passim*.

He had reached the city late on the evening of the 22nd having travelled from Galway to attend the next session of the Irish parliament that was only days away and, suspecting nothing, had gone to bed. As he made his way to Borlace's house early the following day for a council meeting he was intrigued by the castle gates being shut, and when he read O'Connolly's testimony he saw that danger of a coup had not passed and offered to take charge of the city's defences. He immediately secured the castle by closing the drawbridge, which remained in place for the next seven days, and putting a guard on a back entrance after ordering the staircase to be destroyed. He then persuaded the council members to move into the castle for their own safety and emphasised the seriousness of the situation by sleeping the night on the council table a practice he followed for the next week until he was sure than all danger had passed.

However well-conceived Willoughby's directions were, he would have been powerless to put them into effect without the help of trained soldiers to carry out his orders, and therein lay the lord justices' second piece of luck. Present in the city, and presumably unknown to the Council, were several hundred members of Sir Francis's former regiment who had returned to Ireland from Carlisle having been cashiered following the peace treaty with Scotland. The English parliament had made provision for them to be paid their arrears in full and according to Carte recommended that they should be reincorporated into the standing army because of their excellent conduct. On the night of 22/23 October they were seemingly spending their back pay or the prospect of it in the fleshpots of Dublin but they responded immediately to a command from their former colonel to rendezvous at the castle. There they received swords and firearms from the arsenal, and thus armed they assisted the civil authorities in searching for the members of the raiding party who by that time had called off the coup and gone to ground. Task accomplished they were put on the army payroll. Some were incorporated into the castle garrison under Willoughby's direct command as governor, whilst others joined the company that Philip Wenham, a former captain at Carlisle, was raising for a new regiment of volunteers under the command of Sir Henry Tichborne, who had been lieutenant colonel in the Carlisle garrison.[10]

The way in which the veterans of the standing army had rallied to the cause at the word of their former colonel was commendable, but the performance of standing army units in South Ulster was a different matter altogether. Under cover of darkness bands of insurgents under the overall command of Sir Phelim O'Neill successfully surprised and destroyed four of the targeted companies – John Barry's at Charlemont, George Blount's at Mountjoy, Sir Arthur Tyringham's at Newry and Lord Blayney's at Monaghan – whilst severely mauling two more – Sir Henry Tichborne's at Augher and Robert Bayley's at Cavan – and also lord Grandison's and Sir John Borlace senior's troops of horse. An additional bonus was the surrender of the company defending the town of Dundalk, which was carried at a rush after the capture of Newry and gave

---

10   HMC, Ormonde Mss n.s. ii, p.92; CSPI 1667–70, p.397.

the patriots control over the road between Dublin to Carrickfergus.[11] The night's work effectively reduced the 2,000 standing army foot soldiers theoretically available to the lord justices by at least 250 officers and men.[12]

A discussion of the causes of the disaster in Ulster is best left to the next chapter where the fate of the standing army as a whole will be discussed, but the beneficial impact on the patriot cause was not long in coming. For the moment the biggest gain was the military hardware and associated materials which were essential for waging war in the mid seventeenth century. In the various coups the patriots obtained many modern weapons including muskets purchased by Wentworth in the Netherlands, but the most important acquisition was at Newry, where in addition to muskets the patriots found 70 barrels of gunpowder, a small fraction of those lodged in Dublin Castle but sufficient to be able to fight against units of the standing army in a conventional engagement. Thus armed it is not surprising that Captain Fortescue's troops at Dundalk surrendered without a fight.

What the gunpowder was doing at Newry is far from clear. The only clue is an aside to the effect that that it had been placed there since 'the peace', which can only mean that between England and Scotland signed in August.[13] The 70 barrels were thus unlikely to have belonged previously to the New Army as its powder had been put under lock and key by Master of the Ordnance Borlace three months earlier, though contemporary correspondence does allow for not all of it being laid up in the arsenal at Dublin Castle. It is just possible that gunpowder had been sent back to Ireland from Carlisle through an informal undertaking during the peace negotiations between England and Scotland for the Scottish settlers in Ulster to be supplied with arms and ammunition for their personal defence to replace those which Wentworth had confiscated in 1639.[14] It must be acknowledged, however, that nothing pointing

---

11   HMC, Ormonde Mss, o.s. i, p.142. The fullest description of the whole operation is to be found in Carte, *Life of Ormond* i, pp.346–50, but some of the detail is incorrect. To take two examples the Lord Caulfield captured at Charlemont and then murdered was not the old man he described but his son who had inherited the barony in 1641, and Captain Blunt, not Captain Blayney, was in command at Fort Mountjoy. The two companies that were not totally destroyed were those of Sir Henry Tichborne and Robert Bayley. For this see below Chapter 16 and Appendix VI.
12   HMC, Ormonde Mss n.s. i, pp.5–6. Two thousand was the lord justices' calculation – six officers and 46 men per company multiplied by 40. Most contemporary or near-contemporary writers, however, follow Sir John Temple who claimed the lord justices had 2,297 foot. Temple gave the number as 41 after double-counting a company whose captain had changed in 1641, and then probably added the 240 commissioned and non-commissioned officers twice: *Irish Rebellion*, p.26.
13   HMC, Ormonde Mss n.s. ii, p.3.
14   CSPI 1633–47, p.295; Borlace, *History of the Execrable Rebellion*, p.12. The order for the Carlisle magazine to be removed should have taken effect by 10 October, but it was clearly still there on 4 November: JHL iv, pp.421, 427. See above Chapter 10 for the seizure of the Scottish settlers' weapons by Wentworth.

in that direction appears in the copious correspondence that survives for the last week of October 1641.[15]

The most likely reason for gunpowder being in store at Newry was that it was a reserve established at some time in the past following a directive for supplies to be available in all the provinces for use in emergencies, and that the store at Newry had been topped up from the Dublin magazine a few weeks before the uprising. There is a hint of this practice in a document relating to a survey of magazines throughout Ireland undertaken on Sir John Borlace's orders which is undated but attributed by the editor of the Calendar of State Papers Ireland 1633–47 to the year 1642. It must, however, have predated the uprising. After that it would have served no useful purpose. From the start the Master of the Ordnance would have been highly irresponsible to considering transport gunpowder overland even under armed escort given that it was precisely the commodity for waging war that the patriots lacked. Moreover, he needed all he had for the defence of Dublin and its environs.[16] I would therefore suggest given the reference to the peace mentioned above that the survey probably dates from September or early October 1641.

In the days immediately following the night of 22/23 October the reaction of the military leaders responsible for the defence of the English hegemony varied in line with the distance they were from the Ulster uprising. At one extreme was that of Lord Chichester, governor at Carrickfergus, namely resignation followed by panic. This is not surprising. The patriots were only a few miles away and his garrison consisted of no more than his son's troop of horse the company commanded by his cousin Chichester Fortescue having been moved to Dundalk a few weeks before where it was destroyed by patriot forces on the 23rd. In the middle were the lord justices rejoicing at God's providence in saving them from disaster and possible death at the hands of the men intent on capturing the seat of government but combined with growing concern about the flood of refugees poured into the capital from County Cavan and County Monaghan. The early letters of Sir William St. Leger, Lord President of Munster, at the other extreme were tinged with amusement at the idea of the Dublin government being alarmed by a band of 'naked rogues'.[17] However, as the days passed, it became increasingly clear that the lord justices were facing something more serious than a botched attack on the capital and an embarrassing uprising in part of Ulster. By early November, trouble was brewing in the other three provinces and by the end of the month the whole country was in an uproar. It is not therefore surprising that requests

---

15 A cover-up may also help to explain the gaping hole in the Dublin government's records for the six weeks preceding the uprising: CSPI 1633–47, pp.340–41.
16 CSPI 1633–47, p.358.
17 CSPI 1633–47, pp.341–42, 344; HMC, Ormonde Mss n.s. ii, pp.2–5; *ibid.*, Egmont Mss i, p.144.

for immediate military assistance from England and Scotland began on 23 October and became increasingly urgent and substantial as the days passed.[18]

Given that the time of the year meant that it might take six months for substantial assistance to arrive, it would have been totally misguided and possibly fatal for the Dublin government to sit on its hands and hope for the best, but unlike in 1608 an immediate counterattack was not practicable. The uprising was too widespread; the enemy too entrenched in south Ulster; and the Dublin government's remaining companies and troops too widely scattered; but at least it had a defensive strategy to fall back devised by Lord Wilmot. This was for the units of horse and foot in the interior of Ireland to converge on the principal ports, which were to be defended at all costs so that the Dublin government retained control over places through which reinforcements from England and military supplies could be fed into the fighting. But that was easier said than done. Would not the standing army units be ambushed as they marched across country in ones and twos?[19] Would it not be best to leave them where they were and thus win time by tying the enemy forces down into lengthy and hopefully costly sieges? To compensate for standing army units being otherwise engaged a mobile field army consisting of new units of horse and foot could be raised made up of Protestants and Catholic loyalist volunteers as there were plenty of weapons to arm them in the Dublin Castle, but would not the Catholics amongst them desert when they came face-to-face with patriot forces?[20] This would not be surprising as the desperate need for Catholic solidarity in the face of rampant English and Scottish Protestantism played a much greater role in the arguments the patriots used to win over fellow Catholics in 1641 than it had in the Nine Years' War. In the words of Padraig Lenihan it was the time 'to conquer or be conquered'.[21]

In the event the lord justices steered a middle path. Once it became apparent that the insurrection was too widespread and well organised to be put down by horse alone they ordered most of the standing army cavalry units to head for Dublin leaving a single troop in Munster and Connaught. They were followed soon afterwards by some of the companies stationed in Munster, Connaught and Leinster. The object was to establish a garrison that was strong enough deter the patriots from attempting to storm the walls and capture the capital by sheer force of numbers before English reinforcements arrived, but the surviving companies and troops stationed in Ulster were to remain where they were.[22] Second, they largely rejected the Earl of Ormond's proposal and the House of Commons' command that all the standing army companies should be doubled in size to the level achieved at the time of the Duke of Buckingham's wars.

---

18   HMC, Ormonde Mss n.s. ii, pp.4, 5, 9, 14, 21, 30, 33–34, 39, 49–52.
19   HMC, Ormonde Mss n.s. ii, pp.5–6, 17.
20   HMC, Ormonde Mss n.s. ii, pp.9, 23.
21   *Consolidating Conquest*, p.110.
22   CSPI 1633–47, pp.341, 344; HMC, Ormonde Mss n.s. ii, p.4; *ibid.*, o.s. i, pp.125–27. For the Lord President of Munster's comments about this see HMC, Egmont Mss i, p.145; Carte, *Life of Ormond* v, p.260.

Instead they commissioned well over 50 officers to raise companies from scratch – at first from volunteers and then via impressment.[23] Third, the lord justices lifted the ban on the four colonels leaving for Spain with their troops, though those who wanted to do so were hampered by lack of shipping, and it is doubtful if more than a few hundred left Ireland. Major Luke Taaffe, however, managed to set sail to Spain from Galway with his company in November 1641.[24] Fourth, they were happy for the new Lord Lieutenant to have appointed the Earl of Ormond as general commanding the armed forces until he arrived to take up his post.[25] The Earl of Leicester, however, never left England, but he did send two of his younger sons to take command of companies in the standing army, and soon afterwards his heir Lord Lisle arrived in Ireland at the head of a regiment of English cavalry.[26]

In addition the lord justices had made two important decisions. First, within days of the start of the uprising they showed that rather than tamely allowing the patriots to set siege to Dublin they would be pro-active in its defence. Learning from the examination of prisoners captured on 23 October that the patriots would soon be making a second attempt on the capital in order to complete their game plan, they ordered four Old Army units and a full regiment of volunteers led by experienced standing army officers to establish a garrison at Drogheda 30 miles to the north where the road between Ulster and the capital crossed the river Boyne.[27] This was sound delaying tactics. The patriots dare not advance on Dublin leaving such a large a garrison in their rear threatening their line of communications with the part of Ulster they controlled, but it would be difficult for them to capture the town quickly as they had no heavy artillery pieces with which to blow a large enough hole in its defences to facilitate a storm. All they could hope to do was to starve Drogheda into surrender or gain entrance to the town by subterfuge. The first would be a lengthy process whilst the second was tried on several occasions but came to nothing due to the governor Sir Henry Tichborne's vigilance. To the lord justices' relief the stratagem worked. The town held out for some months thus tying down thousands of hostile troops until it was relieved by sea in mid February and the besiegers left the area in early March.

---

23   Carte, *Life of Ormond* ii, p.4; JHC ii, p.313; HMC, Ormonde Mss o.s i, pp.124–25, 139–42; *ibid.*, ii, 75. Some were captains in the standing army who happened to be in Dublin when the crisis broke rather than with their companies in distant garrisons. As experienced officers their services were required immediately. In consequence Sir Francis Willoughby, Phillip Wenham, Robert Byron and Sir Henry Tichborne were commanders of one 'old' and one 'new' company by early 1642: HMC, Ormond Mss o.s. i, pp.130, 134, 140, 142; CSPI 1633–47, pp.787–88. For the number of expanded companies see Chapter 16.
24   This is implicit in HMC, Ormonde Mss n.s. ii, p.27; Carte, *Life of Ormond* ii, p.46. For the varied fortunes of Taaffe and Captain Shaugnasee see *Memoirs and Letters of Ulick, Marquis of Clanricarde* (London: J. Hughs for J. Dolding, 1757), pp.17, 28.
25   HMC, Ormond Mss n.s. ii, p.16.
26   JHL v, pp.123, 129; HMC, Ormonde Mss o.s. i, pp.124, 125, 142.
27   Temple, *Irish Rebellion*, pp.174–75; HMC, Ormonde Mss n.s. ii, pp.8–9, 23.

In the meantime several thousand English troops had landed at Dublin making the capital secure against any form of patriot attack.[28]

The lord justices also began issuing firearms and gunpowder from the castle magazine to Old English landed families living in the counties surrounding Dublin on the grounds that their ancestors had been loyal to Queen Elizabeth in the Nine Years' War, and that they themselves had sworn an oath of loyalty.[29] Within a few weeks, however, the government changed its mind. It was becoming increasingly clear that the Old English were wavering under a barrage of patriot pronouncements and personal appeals concentrating on the threat to their religion and Ireland's freedoms.[30] The only option available to the Dublin government was to demand the return of everything they had handed out, but at best they only got back about half of what had been distributed. The rest fell into enemy hands when in early December many Old English landowners broke with the Dublin government on the grounds that the patriots were better able to protect their estates and their tenants from the violence that was rapidly spreading from Ulster into other provinces.[31] Needless to say the lord justices and the council apologised profusely their naïve generosity having supplied the patriots with gunpowder and weapons that they most conspicuously lacked.

If the arming of Catholic landowners had been a disaster, calling units of horse and foot from the provinces for the defence of Dublin can be described as a small but undoubted success. None was ambushed en route; and none of the units left behind defending the remaining forts was forced to surrender until the summer of 1642 by which time the complexion of the war had changed. The only significant loss in the first few weeks of the emergency was the new citadel at Waterford, which fell like a ripe plum into patriot hands in early December its garrison having been withdrawn to defend Dublin. Sir Henry Tichborne feared that its artillery pieces would be sent by sea to the patriots besieging Drogheda, but this did not happen, and Waterford's loss did nothing initially to affect the military balance in Ireland. Military supplies from Catholic Europe took months to arrive and ships carrying them were wary of sailing past the modern fort at Duncannon, which guarded the mouth of the estuary that gave Waterford access to the sea, and which was garrisoned by a standing army company until the summer of 1645.[32]

---

28   Temple, *Irish Rebellion*, 178–82; HMC, Ormonde Mss n.s. ii, p.56. Tichborne's seemingly self-serving account printed in Temple is largely confirmed by Nicholas Bernard in *The Whole Passage of the Siege of Drogheda* (London: anon. for William Bladen, 1642).
29   HMC, Ormonde Mss n.s. ii, pp.5–6, 9, 33, 36–38.
30   See, for example, the letters sent to the Earl of Clanrickard and the gentry of Galway to persuade them to cease supporting the Dublin government: Gilbert, *Confederation* i, pp.245–46, 255–56.
31   HMC, Ormonde Mss n.s. ii, pp.33, 36–38.
32   CSPI 1615–25, pp.11, 548, 569; *ibid*. 1625–32, p.341; *ibid*., 1633–47, p.324; HMC, Ormonde Mss o.s. i, p.142. Earlier it had been argued that incoming ships would be out of range, but the value Parliamentarian forces during the war for independence vested in first

At the beginning of 1642 the lord justices' forces defending the capital comprised three raw regiments raised from scratch locally, a regiment from England commanded by Sir Simon Harcourt, and some troops and companies belonging to the standing army, but were they sufficiently numerous and well-trained to take the offensive? Carte was adamant that they were and used this as a stick to beat the lord justices who, he claimed, were committed to a cautious approach for personal reasons, namely cowardice, greed and treachery. They were worried about their own personal safety. They were also keen for the emergency to last for many months so that more and more Catholics would be drawn into supporting the patriot cause. Then when the rebellion was finally suppressed and the patriots' estates confiscated, the lord justices and their New English friends would make a killing and become very wealthy men. Lastly they were following instructions from the junto in London who were anxious for the crisis in Ireland to be prolonged until such time as they had deprived the King of all his remaining executive powers.[33]

To support the allegation that a major offensive was feasible Carte cooked the books. He claimed that by late December there were 26 or 27 companies of foot and nine troops of horse of the standing army in the Dublin area in good condition and ready for action. However, muster rolls, pay warrants and army lists show that the correct figure was no more than 13 companies and seven troops.[34] Moreover, the infantry were not the men who had been serving in Strafford's standing army in 1639 and who were admired for their discipline and expertise in the use of arms. At most Ormond would have had 5,000 foot under his command well over half of whom would have received little or no military training.

In such circumstances it would have been dangerous to begin a campaign to reconquer Ireland. The patriot forces, although not as well armed as Ormond's men, had the capacity to outnumber them.[35] They would also be very knowledgeable about the topography of Leinster where the first campaign would necessarily have been fought, and thus fully capable of picking off individual infantry units in ambushes and surprise attacks whilst avoiding a full-scale battle. This ability they had shown at Julianstown on 29 November when they beat up a newly raised regiment marching from the capital to strengthen Tichborne's garrison at Drogheda of whom only 200 or so reached their destination.[36] The odds of Ormond's army returning from a major incursion into patriot held territory so weakened as to be unable to defend Dublin's

---

retaining and then recapturing it suggest otherwise: CSPI 1633–47, pp.420, 465; Kenyon and Ohlmeyer *The Civil Wars*, p.224; M. Bennett, *Cromwell at War* (2017), p.180.
33 Carte, *Life of Ormond* ii, pp.6–7.
34 Carte, *Life of Ormond* ii, pp.4–7; HMC, Ormonde Mss o.s. i, pp.124–137; Gilbert, *Confederation*, pp.229–31; CSPI 1633–47, pp.765–88. For the calculation of the strength of the standing army in the Dublin area in December 14 see Chapter 16.
35 CSPI 1625–47, p.354.
36 HMC, Ormonde Mss n.s. ii, pp.31–32; Gilbert, *Confederation* i, pp.231–34; CSPI 1633–47, p.352.

walls, and therefore retain control of its port facilities, were very high. Even if he had sufficient soldiers left to defend the castle and to work its artillery pieces, the patriots would have sufficient men on the ground at the quayside to prevent English troops and supplies of gunpowder being landed.

16

The Dismemberment of the Standing Army

In the late spring of 1642 when on paper 20,000 or so officers and men were facing the patriot forces in Ireland or preparing to do so, the days of the Early Stuarts' standing army were numbered, but the process was long drawn out insofar as the individual troops and companies were concerned. In consequence a tiny number survived until the end of the 1640s, and one may have served in the Commonwealth army of occupation and that of the post-Restoration monarchy thanks to the political surefootedness of its commander Sir Charles Coote the younger, later 1st Earl of Mountrath.[1]

The corporate identity of the standing army was a different matter altogether as its passport to oblivion was stamped and sealed by the middle of 1642. The standing army made up of the small number of units that survived the successive disbandings of 1601 to 1605-06 did not have a regimental structure, and they were stationed in garrisons in all parts of Ireland separated from one another by miles of difficult country. There they remained often for years at a time with no provision for training to fight in larger bodies and with the few military operations they were required to perform taking place at the level of the troop or the company.

The coming together of the troops and companies scattered throughout Ireland into a body that could function as an army was in the mind of Viscount Falkland in 1625 faced with the prospect of a Spanish invasion. It changed from aspiration into reality during Viscount Wentworth's watch when his annual training sessions at Dublin designed to improve the drill and discipline of individual units developed into exercises involving larger formations in what would have been described in

---

1   If it was the case that Chidley Coote made it over to his brother Sir Charles when he left for England in 1643, and that it then became the colonel's company of his regiment, it can be traced in successive armies until 1662. Sir George St. George also had a company in Sir Charles Coote's regiment in 1647, but it was not his standing army one. I accept this as it is fully referenced in the BCW project's database of regiments. For the history of the colonel's company in Coote's regiment of foot from 1649 onwards see M. Wanklyn, *Reconstructing the New Model Army*, 2 vols (Solihull: Helion and Co., 2015–16) ii, pp.185, 209, 233, 249, 269.

twentieth-century parlance as field days.² It is not known for certain how the horse and foot were combined into larger units, but this would have enhanced their corporate identity as would the socialising that followed the day's activities referred to by Sir Arthur Blundell.

A further step towards corporate identity for the troops of horse came in 1640 when they were incorporated into the New Army and organised into regiments.³ When it was disbanded the cavalry were de-regimented and returned to the standing army as individual troops with their colonels and majors reverting to the rank of captain, but unlike Humpty Dumpty it would have been a relatively easy matter four months later to have put them back into regiments had the will been there.

With the foot it was a different matter. Although nearly all the captains in the standing armies were allotted companies in the New Army regiments, they did not take their men with them.⁴ Even so they would have gained experience of serving in regiments or battalions and in the process acquired knowledge of the tactics required when commanding formations larger than a company. In other respects, however, the years 1639 to 1641 marked a retreat in terms of the skills and disciplines soldiers needed for fighting at the company level and in larger formations acquired during Wentworth's training sessions. It began with the top-slicing of the entire standing army infantry to form Willoughby's regiment with the best soldiers being seconded and replaced by 500 impressed men with little or no military experience. There then followed a double disruption caused by the transfer of so many captains, lieutenants and ensigns into the New Army with many sergeants and more junior non-commissioned officers taking their place on temporary commissions who were demoted when the New Army was disbanded a year later.

The time for the units of the standing army to acquire a new purpose came in early December 1641. The Dublin area was militarily secure and suitable for serving as an army base from which New English hegemony could be reimposed on the entire kingdom; the Ulster patriots were fully occupied in the siege of Drogheda; units of standing army horse and foot were under orders to proceed to the capital from distant parts of the country; refugees from the provinces had fled to Dublin thus forming a body of potential Protestant recruits which had not previously existed which were already being recruited into new units; and the first reinforcements from across the Irish Sea were expected to arrive within days.

There were various ways in which the lord justices and their general could have organised the various formations under their control into a field army, but their room to manoeuvre was restricted by instructions from the English parliament as to how

2   See above Chapters 6 and 9.
3   See Appendix V.
4   See Chapter 15.

they were to proceed. In the belief that the uprising was still confined to Ulster it considered that they already had sufficient standing army cavalry, whereas 6,000 foot was all that was needed to stamp it out. Two infantry regiments 1,000 strong would be sent from England with the Lord Lieutenant and Sir Simon Harcourt as colonels. The standing army would then contribute the remainder with its 40 companies being increased from 50 to 100 officers and men each as at the time of the Duke of Buckingham's wars. However, on this occasion the recruits were to be raised in Ireland and not as previously by impressment supervised by lord lieutenants in the English counties.[5]

The initial planning was quickly overtaken by events. The four companies in the Dublin area were brought up to their wartime strength of 100 officers and men, but nothing more could be done until the other companies arrived. The lord justices, however, needed far more men immediately to defend the city's walls and to create a large enough force to garrison Drogheda once the decision had been taken to use it to try and delay the patriots' advance on the capital. All the town had by way of a garrison in late October were two half-strength companies supported by a single troop of horse belonging to the standing army, and a raw regiment of foot raised locally by Lord Moore. Moreover, Sir Faithful Fortescue the governor had just resigned declaring the town indefensible.[6]

To deal with its immediate problems the Dublin government raised several thousand men in three weeks primarily it claimed from refugees arriving in the capital from areas taken over by the patriots. They also had a regiment of 1,000 volunteers under Colonel Lawrence Crawford who appear to have been mainly Scottish by descent and 500 or so more men raised locally by Lord Lambart.[7] By early December the new formations would have surpassed the standing army in numbers even if all 36 of the companies not already in the capital had been ordered to come to Dublin, and if they had done so it seems highly improbable that there would have been sufficient men between the ages of 16 and 60 available to bring them up to full strength given the lord justices' recruiting operation during October and November, More than 2,000 able-bodied men would have been required as the seven companies attacked in Ulster on 22/23 October would have to have been raised almost if not entirely from scratch. However, this turned out not to be a problem as the companies that did arrive from the provinces were far fewer in number than the English parliament had planned, namely eight (though in fact net seven) as shown by the pay warrants issued by the lord justices between December 1641 and March 1642. The rest they had wisely decided

5   JHC ii, pp.312–13; JHL iv, p.437
6   Gilbert, *Confederation* i, pp.230–32; Temple, *Irish Rebellion*, pp.41–42, 174–75, 198; N. Bernard, *The Whole Proceedings of the Siege of Drogheda* (London, 1642), pp.1–3.
7   HMC, Ormonde Mss o.s. i, pp.123–140; *ibid.*, n.s. ii, p.40; CSPI 1633–47, pp.763–88. Sir William St. Leger's company had returned to Munster before Robert Byron's arrived.

should remain in the provinces defending the major ports and a small number of inland garrisons in Leinster and Connaught.[8]

Over the next six months the Lord Lieutenant, the lord justices and their advisers toyed with several ways of configuring the forces under their direct control, as opposed to those defending those parts of Munster, Connaught and Ulster not controlled by the patriots. These included standing army units, formations raised in Ireland from late October onwards, and others arriving at Dublin from England in ones and twos as the months passed. The diversity is bewildering, but there was one constant. Although the newly raised foot and the ones arriving by boat were organised in regiments, the standing army companies which could have been easily combined to form one if not two even if not brought up to full strength were not deployed in that manner. Instead they were scattered through the regiments raised in Ireland since the uprising but in such a casual manner that it cannot have been the result of a doctrinal decision aimed at improving the drill and discipline of new and inexperienced rank and file. Some regiments had as many as six companies, others none at all. Moreover, although nearly all the other companies in the newly raised regiments were 100 strong or close to it, the number of officers and men in the standing army companies that had arrived in Dublin from elsewhere in Ireland in December remained in the high forties. As will be shown, the lord justices had become suspicious of the standing army foot by the time regimentation would have been a possibility, but this was seemingly not shared by some of the captains in the Old Army promoted to colonel. Lord Lambart, for example, had more standing army companies in his regiment in March 1642 than any of the other lists compiled later in the year show a slimmed-down regiment with the Old Army companies mainly transferring to the Earl of Ormond's, where many of them remained until it was disbanded in the summer of 1647.[9]

Wariness on the part of the lord justices has one obvious explanation, namely the poor performance of the standing army in the first weeks of the uprising. In Munster, Connaught and those parts of Leinster at a distance from the capital, the foot avoided disasters, but they had had advance warning. Sensibly their officers kept them in a defensive role. Risking anything outside the perimeter of their garrisons' walls could well have resulted in the loss of the footholds in both provinces the Dublin government having weakened them in order to provide a large enough garrison for the capital. In Munster the lord president's spirited defence as described in his letters to the Earl of Ormond and to Lord Justice Parsons was based entirely on forays by his own troop of cavalry and the mounted escort of the William Peisley, the province's provost marshal, aided by two newly raised troops commanded by the sons of Lord Cork, but in time they were forced into a life of inactivity in the Cork garrison as the

---

8   HMC, Ormonde Mss n.s. ii, p.40; Temple, *Irish Rebellion*, p.27. The companies that were mustered were those of Lord President St. Leger, Lord Docwra, Sir John Sherlock, Sir George Hamilton, Sir Lorenzo Cary, and Captains John Ogle and Thomas Gates.

9   HMC, Ormonde Mss o.s. i, pp.123–41.

number of patriot troops in the field against them increased until infantry regiments arrived from England by sea.[10]

In Ulster the seven companies that had been attacked were taken completely by surprise by an imaginative range of subterfuges helped by the fact all bar one had taken place under the cover of darkness. That on the company at Dundalk was in full light of day but this was the only case where a military explanation was offered. The lieutenant in charge had had no gunpowder but was facing patriots who had recently raided the magazine at Newry. To make matters worse at Charlemont, Mountjoy and Augher the captains had been away from home, and at Monaghan, Newry and Dundalk they failed to organise any resistance before beating a solitary retreat to safety presumably on the only available horse. But that was not the end of the story. The first battle of Lisnagarvey fought five days later which saved Belfast and Carrickfergus from capture was won not by standing army units but by volunteer infantry aided by standing army cavalry.[11] The Derry area remained in government hands because it was not the focus of planned attacks, but although the praise was heaped on Sir William Stewart's regiment raised in late October and early November by royal commission in fighting against Sir Phelim O'Neill and the Ulster patriots, the contribution of his own company, which had been incorporated into it, cannot be judged one way or the other as none of the surviving evidence mentions it.[12]

The military reputation of the standing army infantry units in Ulster thus rests to a large extent on the two companies and the two troops that managed to survive to fight another day despite being targeted in surprise attacks. Half of Sir Henry Tichborne's company successfully held on after several assaults on Augher Castle in which uniquely the patriot forces were equipped with an artillery piece which was able to make holes in the walls. It was then relieved by troops from Derry who removed the survivors to the safety of another of Tichborne's houses at Lifford which served as one of the city's out-garrison. The other half had been quartered at Blessingbourne nearby and were presumably cut down before they could reach the safety of the castle.[13]

Better documented is the experience of Robert Bayley's company stationed in the town of Cavan. When trouble began, he lost some, possibly many, of his men through desertion but the rest managed to hole up in the County Cavan gaol which the insurgents could not storm because they had neither ordnance nor gunpowder. The defenders were nevertheless in great danger as they were heavily outnumbered and had no prospect of being relieved, but after a few days' stand-off Bayley negotiated an agreement by which hostilities ceased but his soldiers were required to disarm.

---

10 Carte, *Life or Ormond* v, pp.272, 295; HMC, Egmont Mss i, p.153.
11 CSPI 1647–60, pp.60–61; HMC, Ormonde Mss n.s. ii, p.8.
12 HMC, Cowper Mss ii, pp.298–300; *ibid.*, Ormonde Mss n.s. ii, pp.161,185; Audley Mervyn, *An Exact Relation* (1642).
13 Hickson, *Ireland in the Seventeenth Century* 2 vols (London: Longmans, 1884) i, p.225; HMC, Ormonde Mss o.s. i, p.142; Carte, *Life of Ormond* i, p.378; Lord Ernest Hamilton, *The Irish Rebellion of 1641* (London: John Murray, 1920), pp.190, 192.

These they concealed in Bayley's house some distance outside town but seem to have recovered them before making their escape a few days later under cover of darkness.[14]

Given the bad news that was pouring into the capital in the days following the losses in Ulster, Bayley's arrival did his military career a great deal of good. However, one account claimed that he only brought a handful of soldiers with him when he returned from Cavan, and there is little doubt that the company he was commanding as field officer in Colonel Crawford's regiment and then as full colonel was not the one he had commanded at Cavan even though the survivors may have been incorporated in it. In successive musters it was considerably larger than the 50 officers and men of a standing army company, and it was described as full of Scottish soldiers at its first mention in mid 1642.[15]

Although none of the four troops of horse stationed in Ulster was destroyed on the night of 22/23 October, their performance in the first few weeks of the insurgency was patchy. The attack on Sir John Borlace's troop stationed at Belturbet in County Cavan did not prevent the survivors rallying the following day and heading for the nearest government-controlled area where they made preparations to resist attack before obeying the lord justices' summons to join the rendezvous of army units at Dublin.[16] Lord Grandison's at Tandragee lost its trumpeter and quite a number of men but was able to take part in the battle at Lisnagarvey on 28 October commanded by Lieutenant St. John, its senior officer present on the day. Lord Conway's troop performed prodigies of valour in the same battle, but this only compensated for what had been widely regarded as cowardice in the botched relief of Captain Matthews and his wardens defending Dromore Castle a few days earlier. Captain Chichester's troop was less open to criticism on that occasion, but it gained little credit for its performance at Lisnagarvey as it did not arrive there until darkness was falling.[17]

In central Leinster the thwarting of the plot to seize Dublin owed nothing whatsoever to the units of standing army infantry stationed in the province as the castle had not been garrisoned, and Willoughby's former soldiers cannot be included as they were not put on the armed forces' payroll until after the emergency was over. There was also no way in which the successful defence of Drogheda could be attributed to the standing army's infantry. By far the largest component of the garrison were volunteers. Of the two regular companies present Rockley's seems to have done its duty, but the loyalty of Sir John Netterville, one of the captains, was highly suspect. Sir Henry Tichborne, the new governor, had the services of two troops of standing army cavalry, Lord Moore's and one sent to Drogheda just prior to the patriot forces arriving at the gates. Both played an important role in the town's defence, and they

---

14 Gilbert, *Contemporary History* i, pp.479, 486, 788; HMC, Ormonde Mss, n.s. ii, pp.23–24.
15 Gilbert, *Contemporary History* i, pp.478–79; HMC, Ormonde Mss o.s. i, pp.142, 156, 190, 197; *ibid.*, ii, pp.23–24, 61, 70, 85; Journal of the Irish House of Commons i, p.36.
16 Gilbert, *Contemporary History* i, pp.479–80.
17 CSPI 1647–60, pp.360–61; HMC, Egmont Mss i, pp.145–46.

were eventually joined by part of the Earl of Ormond's troop following the disaster that befell a regiment of raw recruits marching there from Dublin as reinforcements at the end of November which it was escorting. The party was ambushed at Julianstown just short of Drogheda and all but 200 of the foot were lost, though Ormond's lieutenant escaped with most of his men. It was a matter of dispute as to whether the horse had deserted the foot or the foot the horse, but whatever the reason the engagement was seen by the Dublin government and the patriots alike as convincing Catholics in other parts of Ireland to come off the fence and turn what had been as a provincial uprising into a truly national one.[18]

Carte gives an impressive picture of the units companies assembled at the capital in early December following the lord justices' orders, but it not a view shared by the Dublin government.[19] Admittedly the rendezvous was a standing army success story as it made it possible for a quarter of the infantry to be combined into a single regiment in a garrison capable of successfully defending the capital against patriot attack, but the seven companies which made it to Dublin sealed the standing army's fate as a corporate entity more effectively than the loss of so many men on the night of 22/23 October, which the Dublin government seem to have regarded initially as an unfortunate accident.

What is interesting about the first reaction of the lord justices and the council to what had happened in Ulster is that they did not try and blame it on the captains or the soldiers they commanded. In correspondence with England only the barest detail is given about the circumstances -a trick at Mountjoy, a breach of hospitality at Charlemont, and mobs of townspeople at Newry and Cavan. Lack of information may have been the reason in some cases, but they would have had witness statements from Monaghan within hours of the event and Newry soon after the company commanders having managed to escape with only what had happened at Dundalk requiring some explanation. Otherwise it is difficult to explain why the lord justices described Lord Blayney as worthy of promotion to colonel with his personal losses at the hands of the patriots, his house plundered and his family prisoners, eclipsing his failure to put up a fight at Monaghan.[20]

The Dublin government also doubled the size of the four standing army companies in the vicinity of the capital as the English parliament had instructed, but there was a seismic shift in an update on the progress of the uprising, which it sent to the Lord Lieutenant on 14 December, based on highly disturbing information about the confessional and ethnic composition of the standing army horse and foot it had received

---

18　Bernard, *Siege of Drogheda*, pp.1–3, 6, 16–17; Carte, *Life of Ormond* v, pp.266, 268; HMC, Ormonde Mss n.s. ii, p.31; Gilbert, *Contemporary History* i, p.15.
19　Carte, *Life of Ormond* ii, p.5; HMC, Ormonde Mss n.s. ii, p.40; Temple, *Irish Rebellion*, p.157.
20　HMC, Ormonde Mss n.s. ii, pp.3, 4, 7, 8, 11, 23; Borlace, *Execrable Irish Rebellion*, p.27.

the previous day from the muster master Sir John Veale, even though, possibly through embarrassment, it was tucked away in the corner of what was a very long letter.[21] The muster had been carried out between 4 and 13 December. It was incomplete especially insofar as the horse were concerned though it is not surprising that he only provided a total rather than a unit by unit breakdown given the size of the problem, but it does provide detailed information about the 11 standing army companies and the newly raised regiments of foot that were not at Drogheda or stationed in lesser garrisons in central Leinster.

Veale discovered few self-acknowledged Catholics – 8 percent of the 705 men in the standing army foot and 2.5 percent of the 2,000 in the new regiments. In the latter the largest number in any company of 100 officers and men was 15 and many had none at all, but in the standing army Sir George Hamilton's and Sir Lorenzo Cary's companies both contained 14 out of 46 private soldiers who self-identified as papists. This is not surprising. Hamilton was one of the four Catholic captains, and Cary's company had been stationed in Connaught where there were few Protestants capable of filling gaps in the ranks when they occurred.[22]

A positive view of the Catholic presence in the standing army emerges if the companies of Cary and Hamilton are excluded. In such circumstances the number per company in the rest would be insufficient for them to have acted as bad apples and undermined the commitment of their colleagues. On the other hand, a single Catholic would be able to provide the patriots with intelligence useful in preparing for a surprise attack. This may indeed have happened at Charlemont where they had advance knowledge of standing orders for weapons to be left outside the mess whilst the soldiers were taking their evening meal, presumably on the grounds that a minor quarrel might otherwise lead to bloodshed. However, the source could well have been the new captain who was a Catholic.[23]

But there was worse to come. An important driver of anti-Catholic hysteria in all the British kingdoms was that the papist threat came from people who concealed the fact rather than from those who were open about their faith. In consequence the total native population of Ireland were suspects including Protestant converts, and of the 705 men in the standing army companies 179 were described as Irish, which was about 25 percent of the total as opposed to 15 percent in the new regiments. And the muster master's comments showed that he was not convinced that all those who claimed not to be Catholics were bona fide Protestants. Against one company he wrote of the captain 'he alleges they all offer to take the oath of allegiance' and against a group of five companies including two from the standing army the words

---

21 HMC, Ormonde Mss n.s .ii, pp.11, 23, 40; Gilbert, *Confederation* i, pp.230–32.
22 Gilbert, *Confederation* i, pp.230–32; CSPI 1625–33, p.227; HMC, Ormonde Mss n.s. ii, pp.72–73, 146; Carte, *Life of Ormond* v, p.283.
23 Carte, *Life of Ormond* i, p.346.

'papist confessed' appear, which implies that he suspected that some of the others were papists unconfessed.[24]

In their correspondence once the results of the musters were known the lord justices did not mince their words. They confessed in their letter to the Lord Lieutenant that they had managed to assemble a force of 3,000 men, but many of the new recruits were unskilled in the use of arms and 'many others are of the Irish especially in the old foot companies … and about 200 horse of the Old Army whereof many are Irish'.[25] This was infiltration on a major scale, and it would not have taken much for Leicester to conclude that here at the very least there was a factor that would help to explain the chain of disasters in the northern garrisons.

The Dublin government did not, however, suggest any reasons how the fundamental change in the composition of the standing army had taken place, but insofar as the cavalry were concerned the increase in the number of mounted troops from 400 to 1,000 between 1634 and 1638 is the most likely explanation as there was no input of recruits from England in those years.[26] Insofar as the infantry were concerned the moving of men in and out of the standing army which started with the formation of the Carlisle regiment in 1639 created gaps in all 40 companies. Twice as much disruption would have been caused in the following year if I am wrong and Carte was right about the transfer of rank and file from the standing army to the New Army. There was also the perennial problem of filling gaps in the ranks with Protestants described elsewhere as there was had been no provision for impressed men to be shipped from England to Ireland since 1625. Captains would be very keen to keep their companies at full strength as their ability to make money on the side depended on the number of men under their command. They might also in Wentworth's day with the new emphasis on training and performance on the parade ground have been tempted to welcome men with military experience into their companies without questioning them too closely about where it had been acquired whilst at the same time turning a blind eye to their religious affiliation. A few months after the Ulster uprising an army commander dropped a heavy hint about what had been going on for years. Fellow officers were still taking on men 'who strive to creep in by promising to go to church which in their case causes us fear that it is but a delusion of the crafty Irish'.[27]

---

24   Gilbert, *Confederation* i, pp.230–32. The comment on Catholics in the horse may explain why Veale had merely given the numbers of men in the various troops as it was information his masters might not want to know, but the impression given by the lord justices is not surprising as troopers were not men impressed in England and none appear to have been sent to Ireland since the end of the Nine Years' War other than possibly in 1625. For this see Chapter 5.
25   Carte, *Life of Ormond* ii, p.5; HMC, Ormonde Mss n.s. ii, p.40; Gilbert, *Confederation*, pp.231–32.
26   HMC, Ormonde Mss n.s. ii, p.40. See Chapter 8 for the increase in the cavalry from 400 to 1,000 officers and men during Strafford's reform of the standing army.
27   HMC, Ormonde Mss n.s. ii, p.133. For Irish in the standing army in the period due to the difficulties in recruiting Protestants as soldiers died, deserted or were transferred see *ibid*.

But alarm bells should have been ringing well before 13 December. At the time of the uprising four of the captains of foot were practicing Catholics with the Earl of Clanricarde's company stationed in Connaught already well known in Wentworth's day to be full of papists, and within days of the uprising it was clear that two were patriot sympathisers if not worse. John Barry, whose company had been overrun at Charlemont, had gone into hiding for fear of being arrested as complicit in the plot to capture Dublin Castle, whilst Sir John Netterville, whose company formed part of the force defending Drogheda, not only questioned the wisdom of resisting the patriots but was also allegedly expelling Protestants from his company and replacing them with Catholics. Moreover, his father and brother had been amongst the leaders of the Old English landowners in Leinster who after some wavering had sided with the patriots. Denounced to Ormond by Tichborne, he was quickly removed.[28] But eliminating the senior officers was the easy part. More worrying was the prospect of mass desertions which had occurred twice already in the case of the company at Cavan and another whose name is not known which had been stationed in County Wicklow, but it was probably these rather than normal military practice which caused the lord justices to order an muster to take place before the arrival of the company marching from Kinsale.[29]

Deeds then followed words. All bar one of the companies that had arrived in Dublin in December remained there the only exception being the Lord President of Munster's which contained no Catholics and returned to Cork once the regiments from England began arriving, but those that entered the Earl of Ormond's army were never brought up to their full strength of 100 officers and men. This was a deliberate act not something caused by the pool of recruits drying up. When Sir Henry Tichborne asked the lord justices for permission to increase the size of the two standing army companies in the Drogheda garrison the request was refused, and Sir John Borlace junior had the same experience when his company arrived to take up garrison duty at Coleraine early in 1642: the risk of his recruiting potential traitors and turncoats was too great.[30]

The length of time the standing army companies remained under suspicion is uncertain. Time should have acted as a cleanser as most Catholics who had responded positively to the case for an uprising ought to have deserted in the first few weeks

---

pp.33, 36, 40, 49; Borlace, *Execrable Irish Rebellion*, p.29; Carte, *Life of Ormond* v, p.268; Temple, *Irish Rebellion*, p.103.
28   HMC, Ormonde Mss o.s. i, pp.124, 141; *ibid.*, o.s. ii, pp.46–7; Bernard, *Siege of Drogheda*, p.6; Knowler, *Strafforde's Letters* i, pp.308–09; Temple, *Irish Rebellion*, p.41; Cox, *Hibernia Anglicana*, pp.78, 88. For the two loyalist captains Clanricarde and Hamilton, see Appendix VI.
29   HMC, Ormonde Mss, n.s. ii, pp.23–24; Gilbert, *Confederation*, pp.230–32.
30   McKenny, *Laggan Army*, p.44; HMC, Ormonde Mss n.s. i, p.47.

following the uprising becoming countrywide. Lists of units in the Dublin area in the Ormond collection give the impression that the answer was never, as former standing army companies were kept on garrison duty in Dublin where they could be carefully watched by other units and by their commanding officers, until the Marquis surrendered the city to the Parliamentarian commander Michael Jones in July 1647 and left for exile on the Continent.[31] However, the lists that provide the detail date from 1644 and later and need to be put into context. In September 1643 on the King's orders Ormond, who had replaced Leicester as lord lieutenant, negotiated a truce with the patriot forces which remained in force for nearly three years during which time the army he commanded remained in its quarters. In contrast the year after the truce came to an end was a time of acute danger with little support from England forthcoming despite the end of the First Civil War. All the Marquis (as he then was) and his council could do was order the troops to do nothing to provoke the enemy. If they did so they were likely to be overwhelmed by sheer force of numbers and what little of Ireland they controlled lost in no time at all.[32]

In fact the companies of the standing army had had a good chance to redeem themselves in the spring of 1642 probably through the influence of Ormond and Lord Lambart who were clearly less worried about the loyalty of the standing army companies than the lord justices as they had willingly accepted them into their regiments. When the Earl set out on his first major expedition into patriot held territory in April 1642, he commanded a polyglot army of English and newly raise Irish regiments as well an unknown number of standing army companies. Having recaptured several important towns in Leinster, he returned slowly towards Dublin laden down with plunder including 300 dairy cattle whereupon the patriot militia tried to block his path and a battle ensued at Kilrush. In Wenceslas Hollar's depiction of the Ormond's deployment, the cavalry as usual were stationed on the wings with the standing army's horse on the left and the English on the right. The infantry in the centre were drawn up in eight battalions in three lines with a standing army battalion commanded by Lambart's lieutenant colonel Sir John Sherlock on the far left of the front line.[33] The troops on the right made very good progress against the patriot regiments facing them but those on the left which had not initially been attacked stood their ground, whereupon the Old Army cavalry aided by several hundred musketeers from Sherlock's battalion chased them from the battlefield and then played an effective role in the pursuit, but this minor triumph had no effect on the standing army's corporate future as more profound issues intervened.[34]

---

31 HMC, Ormonde Mss o.s. i, pp.148–97.
32 J.S. Wheeler, *The Irish and British Wars 1637–1654* (London: Routledge, 2002), pp.122, 150–54, 160–61; HMC, Ormonde Mss o.s. i, pp.148–98; Carte, *Life of Ormond* v, pp.524–25.
33 HMC, Ormonde Mss o.s. i, p.138; CSPI 1633–47, p.306; Gilbert, *Confederation* i, p.232.
34 Carte, *Life of Ormond* ii, pp.250–52, which uses Captain Yarner's report to the House of Commons read on 2 May. Hollar's depiction of the battle can be found in several places

What killed any hopes that the insurgency would be suppressed quickly after Kilrush, Ormond's army disbanded, and the standing army companies returned to their home garrisons ended in June when the First English Civil War burst into life and military resources for Ireland were not only stopped but were snatched back. Within weeks what the future held in store was confirmed by the decision of the English parliament, which by then was controlled by the junto and its supporters, to draft three out of four new regiments of foot and at least two troops of horse raised for service in Ireland into their field army commanded by the Earl of Essex. It should not therefore be a matter of surprise that when the forces of king and parliament fought their first major battle at Edgehill three months later two of the three regiments left the field before coming to grips with the enemy whilst one of the troops, famously commanded by Sir Faithful Fortescue, changed sides as the fighting began.[35]

on the internet.
35   There was a fifth regiment recruiting in the Bristol area commanded by Colonel Bamfield according to a nineteenth-century source. It was not at Edgehill and Peter Young places it with considerable reservations at Northampton, but it may have been shipped to Ireland with the Earl of Kelly's regiment under a different colonel: Young, *Edgehill 1642* (Kineton: Roundway Press, 1967), pp.240, 245; C. Scott, A. Turton and E. Von Arni, *The Battle of Edgehill: A Reinterpretation* (Barnsley: Pen and Sword, 2004), pp.58, 117.

17

Death and Rebirth

The King had been executed in January 1649 and a republic proclaimed. In response a handful of former standing army captains joined Ormond, now a marquis, who headed up a rainbow coalition of Irish, Old English, a few New English and Scots, and some English royalist officers in exile, bound together by nothing stronger than loyalty to the Stuart monarchy, but they were probably commanding new formations. Others including such stalwarts as Sir Francis Willoughby had been arrested during the summer by Colonel Michael Jones, the Commonwealth's commander at Dublin, and sent as prisoners to England as Ormond's forces advanced on the Irish capital.[1] However, a few officers were still on the army payroll. Sir John Borlace the younger for example led a brigade when Jones routed Ormond at Rathmines just outside the walls of Dublin on 2 August 1649 which included what was left of the standing army foot and the regiments raised in both Ireland and England that had fought against the patriots between 1641 and 1646.[2]

Within days Oliver Cromwell arrived in Ireland at the head of a corps of the New Model Army. One of his first acts was to disband Borlace's brigade and use it as a recruit presumably for regiments sent to Ireland from England in the interval between the First and Second English Civil Wars, and when Ormond's forces in Munster changed sides a few months later they suffered the same fate. Most of what was left of Old Horse serving in Ulster were probably lost in the fighting there in the last months of 1649 culminating in the second Battle of Lisnagarvey on 6 December. Thereafter apart from Sir Charles Coote's company mentioned earlier the only unit of

---

1 HMC, Duke of Portland Mss i, p.486.
2 After his regiment was disbanded Cromwell recommended Borlace for further employment, the reducing of his regiment was not in the least a reflection on him' but a cost-saving exercise: Sir Charles Firth and G. Davies, *The Regimental History of Cromwell's Army*, 2 vols (Oxford: University Press, 1940) ii, p.632. For Michael Jones's utter conviction in the summer of 1649 that God would severely punish soldiers who did not take vengeance on the patriots for the atrocities they had committed eight years before, see HMC, Portland Mss i, p.486.

the standing army that may still have been on the Commonwealth army payroll was Sir John Sherlock's. He had apparently transferred in 1647 from a regiment containing standing army units to one recently sent to Ireland from Lancashire commanded by Colonel John Moore. Whether Sherlock took his company with him cannot be ascertained, but if he did the line of the descent from the army of the 1630s came to an abrupt halt when Moore's regiment was disbanded a few months before Sherlock's death in 1652.[3]

Throughout the 1650s the New Model Army defenders of the English hegemony in Ireland were stationed there in a much larger numbers than the army of the first Stuart kings. Although reduced in size as guerrilla warfare conducted by the so-called Tories flickered and then died, there were still 11 regiments of foot and seven of horse there in 1659 most of whom were English Protestants with a small number of New English who had avoided the blandishments of the rainbow coalition.[4] Moreover, the English hegemony had become more burdensome and intrusive than ever. The pay arrears of Cromwell's troops were settled by donation of the donation of land confiscated from those seen as the regime's enemies both Catholic and Protestant. There was also a concerted move to expel the Irish from the other three provinces and resettle them in Connaught, and Roman Catholic worship was forbidden in private and in public.

With the restoration of the monarchy in 1660 the Commonwealth standing army was purged and all its officers apart from a handful who had chosen the optimum moment to change sides whilst the British republic was in its death throes. However, the New Model Army units, though de-regimented, were not disbanded as there was still the need to keep Protestant rule in place by force in England's first colony, but the connection with the first Stuart monarchs' standing army was tenuous in the extreme. That it existed at all was only because a few of the former captains were given captaincies when the Commonwealth army was reorganised: Ormond, of course, who by then was a duke; Sir Henry Tichborne, Sir Robert Byron, Sir Robert Stewart, Sir Thomas Wharton, and Sir Francis Butler amongst the company commanders; and a solitary troop commander Captain Arthur Chichester, by then 1st Earl of Donegal. However, as a group they were lost amongst the 200 or so captains in the army lists for 1661–2 whose military careers ranged across the spectrum from the unforgettably named Seafowl Gibson, who had first served as a company commander at Drogheda in the winter of 1641–2, to Ralph Wilson who had risen steadily through the ranks of the New Model to become governor of Limerick in 1660. There were the sons of former standing army officers and men who had served in regiments sent from England to Ireland from between 1641 and Cromwell's invasion and in the rainbow coalition army of 1649–50, but also several who had never served in Ireland but had supported

---

3   Firth and Davies, *Regimental History* ii, pp.650–51; Wanklyn, *Reconstructing the New Model Army* ii, pp.189–90, 212.
4   Wanklyn, *Reconstructing the New Model Army* ii, pp.247–50.

General George Monck through thick and thin in the lead-up to the Restoration despite the odds being firmly against him.[5]

It is doubtful if many of the survivors of King Charles I's standing army regarded their new command as anything other than a mark of honour with the prospect of some financial return if the government in Ireland could find the money. Not surprisingly given their age nearly all died in the early 1660s or were quietly retired when Ormond returned as lord lieutenant and purged the army of officers considered too physically or mentally unfit to play a meaningful part in preserving Ireland's security, the opportunity having been provided by a plot by ex-Cromwellian officers to seize Dublin Castle, which as in 1641 was only discovered at the last moment.[6] Ormond and his successors as lord lieutenant kept as assiduous a control over the new standing army as Strafford had of the old, but there was a significant difference. Larger than it had been in his time, and therefore potentially a big piece on the board in the game of politics in Later Stuart Britain. It was also an army composed of people living in Ireland and not an English army operating overseas, though as has been shown the standing army of the early Stuarts in its last few years had been moving fast in that direction.

---

5   Wanklyn, *Reconstructing the New Model Army* ii, pp.247–50, 259–72.
6   Carte, *Life of Ormond* iv, pp.123–25.

Appendix I

The Strength of the Standing Army 1601–1641

Date	Companies of Foot	Total	Troops of Horse[1]	Total
November 1601	c. 150	18,550	27	1,299
January 1603[2]	Not given	12,370	Not given	1,000
October 1603	67	8,050	17 + 4	950
January 1605[3]	30	3,000	8+ 2	374
March 1606	22	1,150	8 + 2	374
April 1606	18	880	5 + 3	234
October 1606[4]	18	900	5 + 3	234
November 1608	27 + 1	2,680	6+ 5	316
September 1610	27	2,100	6 + 5	316
January 1611	27	2,100	6 + 5	304
1613[5]	27	1,400	6 + 5	194
February 1622	27	1,350	6 + 5	212
July 1624	27	1,350	6 + 4	170
1625	36	3,600	Not given	400
1629[6]	50	2,700?[7]	8 + 1	400

1. The additions are smaller bodies of horse such as provost marshals' escorts, which were not included in the establishment from 1625 onwards, and the marshal of the army's retinue.
2. CSPI 1601–03, pp.200–01, 550.
3. CSPI 1603–06, pp.90–92, 252–53.
4. CSPI 1603–06, pp.433–36, 441; ibid. 16060–8, pp.1–2.
5. CSPI 1608–10, pp.32–33, 96–97, 509–10; *ibid.*, 1611–14, pp.7–9; Fynes Moryson, *Itinerary*, iii, pp.355–57.
6. CSPI 1615–25, pp.343, 517; *ibid.* 1625–32, p.41; *ibi*d. 1633–47, p.534.
7. The 1629 list is headed 50 per company, but this only refers to the 34 in the first paragraph, namely 25 of the 27 in the standing army in 1624 and the nine raised in England for service in Ireland in the following year. The second paragraph contains the names of 16 companies 10 of which belonged to Sir Piers Crosby's regiment, which was some 700 strong, with the rest made up of two from the standing army and four from the survivors of the Cadiz expedition that were not shipped to England in August 1627 for

1/1632	40	2,000	8 + 1	400[8]
1636	40	2,000	9 + 1	600
10/1639	40	2,000	13 + 1	1,000
1641[9]	41	2,000[10]	14	1,000

the first attempt to relieve La Rochelle. The strength of the Cadiz companies when they were disbanded in 1626 or 1627 and the rank and file reallocated to the four new captains is not known, but their strength on paper is likely to have been 50 at most.

8   In his instructions to Lord Wentworth the King mentioned six troops of horse amounting to 300 men, but all eight troops in the 1629 listing were in the army throughout the 1630s.

9   CSPI 1625–32, pp.649–50; Knowler, *Strafforde's Letters* ii, p.64; TNA, SP63/257, ff.50–51.

10 HMC, Ormonde Mss n.s. ii, pp.5–6. For the incorrect figure given in Temple, *Irish Rebellion*, p.26 see Chapter 15.

Appendix II

Standing Army Units 1606 to 1608

V Veteran of the Nine Years' War
M Military experience but mainly obtained in other theatres of war.

Cavalry

Captains Commanding Troops of Horse

1	Sir Arthur Chichester V	Lord Deputy of Ireland
2	Sir Henry Brouncker V	Lord President of Munster d. 1607
	Baron Danvers M	Lord President of Munster 1608
3	Sir Richard Wingfield V	Marshal of the Army[1]
4	Sir Henry Docwra V	Treasurer at War

New Troops Created in 1608

5	Sir Oliver Lambart V	
6	Sir Garret Moore[2] V	

Escorts

	Sir Edmund Waynham V	Provost Marshall of Munster

---

1. The Marshal only commanded an escort in 1608, which he presumably raised from scratch. The Earl of Clanricarde replaced him as a troop commander.
2. Chichester suggested that Moore and Lambart should each have a new half troop of horse immediately after the flight of the earls: CSPI 1606–08, p.265.

Others Commanding Small Bodies of Horse

	Sir Henry Folliott V	
	Sir Edward Herbert V	
	Edward, 3rd Baron Cromwell M	

Infantry

Captains Commanding Companies of Foot

1	Sir Arthur Chichester V	
2	Richard, 4th Earl of Clanricarde V	Lord President of Connaught
3	Sir Henry Brouncker V	d. 1607. Succeeded by Lord Danvers
4	Sir Henry Docwra V George Paulet, John Vaughan V	r. 1606. k. 1607[3]
5	Sir Richard Wingfield V	
6	Sir Henry Power V	
7	Sir Richard Moryson V	
8	Sir Francis Rush V	
9	Sir Fulk Conway V	
10	Sir Henry Folliott V	
11	Sir Edward Blayney V	
12	Sir Toby Caulfield V	
13	Sir Thomas Rotheram V	
14	Sir Thomas Roper V	
15	Sir Francis Roe V	
16	Sir Richard Hansard V	
17	3rd Baron Cromwell M 4th Baron Cromwell	d. 1607. Eldest son

---

3   See Chapter 2 for the details of the 1606 sale, Paulet's death, and Vaughan's appointment.

Old Companies Disbanded Before 1615

	Sir Charles Wilmot V William Newce[4] V	r. 1607

Every officer of horse and foot listed above was a veteran of the Nine Years' War apart from Lord Cromwell, who had had a distinguished military career but not in Ireland

New Companies in Continuous Service from 1608

18	Donogh, 4th Earl of Thomond V	
19	Sir Oliver St. John V	Master of the Ordnance*
20	Sir Thomas Ridgway	Treasurer at War[5] *
21	Hercules Francis Cooke[6]	
22	Sir Thomas Phillips[7] V	
23	Sir James Perrott[8]	
24	William Stewart[9] M	
25	Patrick Crawford M	
26	Christopher St. Lawrence V	Later 10th Baron Howth
(27)	Not recruited. Funds saved used to complete the fortifications of Carrickfergus	

---

4   He had commanded a company in Spanish service after being cashiered at the end of the Nine Years' War: CSPD 1603–10, p.324.
5   An out-and-out civilian who ruffled the feathers of the veteran officers by choosing to join his company in suppressing O'Doherty's rebellion. For this see Chapter 2.
6   The son of Sir Anthony Cooke, a captain in the Nine Years' War and nephew of Sir Richard Cooke, Lord Chancellor of Ireland. Sir Anthony was still alive, but his company had been disbanded in 1603: CSPI 1603–06, p.110; *ibid.* 1606–08, p.80; ibid. 1608–10, p.10.
7   Phillips's name does not appear in the lists in the Carew Manuscripts pp.235–44, but he was a servitor with confiscated lands: T. Moody, 'Sir Thomas Phillips servitor', *Irish Historical* Studies 1 (1939), p.251.
8   Brother-in-law of Sir Arthur Chichester, he had a company quartered at Newry for two years and then apparently sold it to Captain Bassett in order to attend the English parliament: <www.historyofparliamentonline.org> 1604–1629, Members' Biographies; CSPI 1608–10, p.367.
9   Stewart's and Crawford's companies were raised in Scotland at the time of O'Doherty's rebellion and placed on the Irish establishment soon afterwards: CSPI 1608–10, p.10.

New Companies Disbanded Post 1608

| | Sir Ralph Bingley[10] | |

---

10 See Appendix III.

Appendix III

Standing Army Units 1608 to 1623

---

* In command of the unit

Numbers in parentheses indicate a degree of uncertainty about the succession.

The documentation presently available for the period 1615 to 1623 does not always make it possible to be completely certain of the succession in the case of a small number of companies. The rationale behind allocating numbers 15, 16 and 22 is as follows:

Number 16. The links between Sir Richard Hansard and Henry Tichborne is the castle of Lifford, also known as the Liffey. In 1621, a few years after Hansard's death James I gave the Lifford estate to Tichborne as well as a company in the standing army. Half of Tichborne's company was quartered at Lifford in County Donegal in 1642.[1]

Number 22 Windsor's terror campaign in 1627–28 was in the north-east of Ulster for which Toome would have been the ideal base from which to operate. It had also been Sir Thomas Phillips's fort, and he disappeared from the army lists between 1624 and 1629. Sir Claude Hamilton, who replaced Phillips as custodian of Toome, did not hold a command in the standing army.

Number 15. There is therefore a high degree of probability that it was Blundell who acquired Sir Francis Roe's company.

---

1 HMC, Ormonde Mss o.s. i, p.142; Belmore, *Fermanagh and Tyrone*, pp.164–66.

Captains Commanding Troops of Horse

	1608	1611	1615	1623
1	Sir Arthur Chichester[2] V	*	* ennobled	*
2	Baron Danvers, Lord President of Munster V	*	* retired 1615	
3	4th Earl of Clanricarde Ditto of Connaught V	*	* retired 1616	
4	Sir Henry Docwra[3] V			
5	Sir Oliver Lambart[4] V		* died	
6	Sir Garret Moore V	*	* ennobled	*

New Troop Commanders Post 1608

2	Earl of Thomond[5] Lord President of Munster V			*
3	Sir Charles Wilmot Ditto of Connaught[6] V			*ennobled
4	John Kingsmill[7]	*	* knighted	*
5	Sir Oliver St. John[8] Lord Deputy 1615 V			* ennobled

2 He ceased to be lord deputy in 1616 but retained command of his troop and his company.
3 He had certainly resigned his troop by September 1610 but did not regain it when appointed as treasurer at war in 1616. See below for his company of foot: CSPI 1608–10, p.509.
4 He was ennobled in 1618 as Baron Lambart but died in the same year: CSPI 1615–25, pp.184, 207, 257.
5 He succeeded Danvers as lord president of Munster in 1615.
6 CSPI 1615–25, p.28.
7 A large landowner in Ulster as a result of the confiscations following the flight of Tyrone and Tyrconnell, he purchased the troop from Sir Henry Docwra in about 1609: CSPI 1608–10, pp.19, 509. He does not seem to have fought in the Nine Years' War, but other Kingsmills did.
8 He was ennobled as Viscount Grandison.

Commanders of Smaller Units

Escorts

	Sir Richard Wingfield as marshal[9] V	*	*	* ennobled
	Charles Coote as muster master of Connaught V	*	*	* knighted
	Arthur Bassett as muster master of Munster Richard Aldworth ditto[10] V	promoted *	* *	*knighted
Casuals	Sir Henry Folliott V	*	*	* ennobled. died 1622[11]
	Sir Edward Herbert V	*	*	*[12]

Infantry

Captains commanding companies of foot 1608–1624

	1608	1611	1615 and after	1622
1	Sir Arthur Chichester V	*	* ennobled	*
2	Earl of Clanricarde V	*	*	*
3	Baron Danvers V	*	* resigned	
4	John Vaughan V	*	*	*
5	Sir Richard Wingfield V	*	* ennobled	*
6	Sir Henry Power V	*	* ennobled[13]	*
7	Sir Richard Moryson Vice Pres. of Munster V	*	*	*
8	Sir Francis Rush V	*	* died 1623	
9	Sir Fulk Conway V	*	*	*
10	Sir Henry Folliott V	*	* died 1622	
11	Sir Edward Blayney V	*	* ennobled	*
12	Sir Toby Caulfield V	*	* ennobled	*

9   Marshal of the Army in Ireland since 1600: CSPI 1599–1600, p.447. His new title was Lord Powerscourt.
10 He was lieutenant in Captain George Blundell's company which was disbanded in 1603. The ensign was Arthur Blundell: CSPI 1603–06, p.110.
11 A personal retinue, it lapsed on his death in 1622.
12 For the termination of this mini troop in 1629 or thereabouts see Appendix IV.
13 As Lord Valentia.

13	Sir Thomas Rotheram V	*	*	*
14	Sir Thomas Roper V	*	*	*
(15)	Sir Francis Roe[14] V	*	* resigned	
(16)	Sir Richard Hansard[15] V	*	* died 1619	
17	4th Lord Cromwell	*	*	*
18	Earl of Thomond V	*	*	*
19	Sir Oliver St. John V	*	*	*
20	Sir Thomas Ridgeway[16]	*	* resigned 1616	
21	Hercules Francis Cooke	*	* knighted	*
(22)	Sir Thomas Phillips V	*	* resigned[17]	
23	Sir James Perrott			
24	William Stewart [18] M	*	* knighted	*
25	Patrick Crawford[19] M	*	* died 1615	
26	Lord Howth[20] V	*		
27	As 26	*		

14   A deed transferring Fort Mountjoy to Lord Ochiltree shows that Roe was alive when he gave up his command, but he was dead by the end of 1620: CSPI 1615–25, pp.285; CSPI 1647–60, p.351; Belmore, *Fermanagh and Tyrone*, pp.138–42.

15   CSPI 1633–47, p.197. In 1620 the company at Lifford was commanded by a Captain Garnold: *ibid.* 1615–25, p.285. This was almost certainly the Captain Roger Gosnold, who had resigned from the standing army before May 1622 to fight in defence of the Palatinate: APC 38, p.205.

16   Recently appointed financial expert from England.

17   There is no mention of Phillips's resignation in any of his subsequent copious writings criticising the plantation of West Ulster by the guilds of London, but it is most unlikely that he was dismissed. A self-made man his expertise in matters affecting fortifications and logistics was very well respected, and the English government employed him as an inspector in that capacity until his death in the early 1630s: APC 40, pp.157–60; CSPI 1625–32, pp.400, 643 and elsewhere; *ibid.* 1633–47, p.285 (c. 1627, not 1641 as claimed by the editor).

18   CSPI 1608–10, p.10.

19   Crawford's company was involved in 1615/16 in the capture of Islay from the Clan MacDonnell where he was killed: CSPI 1615–25, p.7.

20   This troublesome lord was threatened with losing his company in 1611. The initial intention was to reduce it by half from 100 to 50 officers and men, but it was disbanded the following year apparently as part of a bargain by which no action would be taken against him provided that he lived quietly on his estate near Dublin. The funds saved were used to fortify Carrickfergus: CSPI 1611–14, pp.48, 60, 61, 84, 160, 283; *ibid.* 1615–25, p 176.

Companies Disbanded After 1611 But Before 1615

	Lord Lambart ex-Sir Ralph Bingley[21] V			
	William Newce[22] V			

New Company Commanders 1608–1624

		Reason for the appointment	1611	1615	1624
3	Earl of Thomond V	Lord President of Munster 1615			*
8	1st Viscount Falkland	Lord Deputy 1622–1629[23]			*
10	Sir Lawrence Esmond V	A respected officer holding military commands in Ireland for the past 20 years[24]			*
15	Arthur Blundell V	Patronage but relevant military experience[25]			*knighted

21 Bingley's was only one of two companies 50 strong in 1608. He does not appear in the 1610 army list but Lambart's does and so he is most likely to have been Bingley's successor. By October 1611, however, Lambart's company of 50 had been disbanded: CSPI 1608–10, pp.33, 510; ibid. 1611–14, p.160. Though the word disband is missing, the first paragraph of the 1611 list clearly enumerates the units affected whilst the following one lists those being retained.
22 Newce's company suffered the same fate as Lambart's: CSPI 1608–10, p.510; *ibid.* 1611–14, p.160.
23 Falkland was supposed to have a company recruited by head slicing the existing companies, but a comparison of the army lists of 1622 and 1623 shows that he took over Sir Francis Rush's company. He had accompanied the 2nd Earl of Essex to Ireland in 1599 but does not seem to have commanded a company: Shaw, *The Knights of England* ii, p.96.
24 Esmond was a captain in the standing army from 1598 to 1606 and thereafter commander of Duncannon fort defending Waterford harbour: CSPI 1598–99, p.100; *ibid.* 1603–06, p.256; *ibid.* 1606–08, p.558. He was given a company between February 1622 and April 1623 in lieu of his pension: CSPI 1615–25, pp.343, 517, 543. He can only have succeeded Lord Folliott who died in 1622 and whose heir was a minor.
25 Ensign in George Blundell's company in 1603: CSPI 1603–6, pp.110, 256. They were the brothers of Sir Francis Blundell, who held the position of the King's remembrancer for matters affecting Ireland and was a client of the Duke of Buckingham. Arthur married a wife from Antwerp, suggesting that he served in the Spanish army in the Netherlands after losing his place in the army in Ireland: <www.historyofparliamentonline.org> 1604–29, House of Commons, Members' Biographies, Sir Francis Blundell; Harleian Society xix (1884), p.161.

16	Roger Gosnold	Company commander at Lifford 1620–21			*knighted
	Henry Tichborne M	Younger son of a leading Hampshire landed family[26]			
18	Sir Barnaby O'Brian[27]	Younger son of Earl Thomond			*
20	Sir Henry Docwra V	Appointed as Treasurer at war 1616			*ennobled
22	Sir William Windsor V	Captain in the Nine Years' War but a chequered career thereafter[28]			*
23	Arthur Bassett	Ex-provost marshal. Cousin of Sir Arthur Chichester[29]	*	*	*
25	Roger Hope M	A Scottish settler in Ulster[30]			* knighted
26	Sir Arthur Savage V	New company made possible by saving on the fortification of Carrickfergus in 1615[31]		*	*
27	Sir Charles Wilmot[32] V	Ditto			*

26 He had pursued a military career in Ireland and the Low Countries: Belmore, *Fermanagh and Tyrone*, pp.164–66.
27 Barnaby was too young to have fought in the Nine Years' War but old enough to sit in the Irish parliament of 1613–15. He appears to have been given his father's company in 1615 when Thomond took over Lord Danvers's or soon afterwards. He was certainly a company commander in 1619: APC 36 p.372.
28 Windsor's company was disbanded in 1603 and he then took service in the Spanish army in Netherlands. Soon afterwards he came under suspicion for involvement in the Gunpowder Plot and was imprisoned on a visit to England either for this or for murder. He then apparently fled overseas but was knighted in Ireland in 1618: CSPI 1603–06, p.204; *ibid.* 1606–08, p.538; *ibid.* 1615–25,p.233; HMC, Salisbury Mss 17, pp.32, 64, 72, 153, 200; *ibid.*, HMC Salisbury Mss 19, p.486.
29 CSPI 1608–10, p.97.
30 He was known as Captain Hope well before receiving his commission and his name was associated with Stewart and Crawford. Possibly he was serving as a lieutenant in one or other company: CSPI 1608–10, p.428.
31 CSPI 1608–10, p.379; *ibid.* 1611–14, pp.179, 406, 489. Sir Arthur was a distinguished veteran of the Nine Years' War returning to live in Ireland.
32 Wilmot had just been appointed Lord President of Connaught. The other half of the resources devoted to the fortification of Carrickfergus was set aside in March 1615 for providing him with a company his predecessor as lord president having decided to retain

Appendix IV

Standing Army Units 1624–1641

Changes in the commanders of units in the standing army were much more frequent in the second half of the period covered by this book than the first but identifying who succeeded whom and when was easy between 1624 and 1629 because of the numerous army lists, but no such lists survive for the 10 years between October 1629 and October 1639 whilst references to changes in the State Papers tail off in the 1630s. In the case of the cavalry it has been possible to attach names to units with a high degree of confidence but this is not so with the infantry. It helps that in all but two cases it has been possible to discover within a year or so when a captain's career in the standing army came to an end, but vacancies came so thick and fast during Wentworth's watch and this, combined with his failure to mention nearly all of them in his correspondence, means that I have been forced to resort to something not far short of guesswork when naming the successors. As in Appendix III I have indicated where this occurs by putting the number in parentheses.

1629–1633

	Previous Captain	New Captain
(12)	Arthur Chichester	William Billingsley
(21)	Sir Francis Cooke	George Blount
(37)	George Herbert	William Peisley

1634–1636

(2)	4th Earl of Clanricarde	Sir Arthur Loftus
(5)	Lord Powerscourt	Robert Farrer
(13)	Sir Thomas Rotheram	John Sherlock
(23)	Sir Arthur Bassett	John Giffard

his. The change was not recorded in the 1615 army list because it would not have come into force until the 1616 establishment took effect in October: CSPI 1615–25, p.25.

1637–1639

(10)	Lord Esmond	Sir Robert Loftus
(17)	Viscount Lecale	Sir Thomas Wharton
(32)	Evan Lloyd	Robert Bayley

Cavalry

The Troops in the Standing Army Raised Before 1624

	1624	1629	1639	1641
1	Lord Chichester died 1625 V			
2	Earl of Thomond died late 1624 V			
3	1st Viscount Wilmot V	*	*	*
4	Sir John Kingsmill sold troop to the Earl of Ormond	*		
5	1st Viscount Grandison died 1630 V	*		
6	1st Viscount Moore died 1627 V			

Retinues

	Lord Powerscourt Viscount Valentia sold position of marshal 1639 to the 2nd Viscount Conway[1] M	* died 1634		
	Sir Richard Aldworth V William Peisley junior[2]	* died 1629	*	*
	Sir Charles Coote V	*	*	*

---

1 Viscount Conway's commission issued in January 1640 gave him the right to an escort of 30 troopers and a trumpeter, but the unit does not appear in the army lists in the Ormond papers following the Earl's appointment as commander of the standing army in November 1641: CSPI 1633–47, p.240; HMC, Ormonde Mss o.s. i, *passim*.

2 The two provost masters' escorts were removed from the army establishment in 1629 and do not appear in the army list for 1641. They are, however, named in the 1639 list together with their colleagues for Leinster and Ulster. In the first weeks after the patriotic uprising began in Munster, Peisley was using his retinue as a small troop of horse: A. Clarke, *Prelude to the Restoration in Ireland* (Cambridge: the University Press, 1999), p.203; TNA, SP63/257, f.50; Temple, *Irish* Rebellion, pp.25–6; HMC, Ormonde Mss o.s. i, p.126.

Casuals

	Sir Edward Herbert George Herbert	Made unit over to his son[3] V Last mentioned in 1626, but George claimed it continued to exist[4]		

New commanders of existing units 1624–1641

	Name	Context	1629	1639	1641
1	Viscount Valentia 1st Viscount Chichester Arthur Chichester	Resigned captaincy 1627. Nephew of Arthur, Baron Chichester. Resigned 1638 Eldest son of Viscount Chichester	*	*[5]	*
3	Sir Edward Villiers Sir William St. Leger	Lord President of Munster. Duke of Buckingham's brother. Died 1626. Lord President of Munster M	*	*	*
4	12th Earl of Ormond Sir George Wentworth	Old English Protestant landowner. Captain of a new troop of cuirassiers 1638. Brother of the Lord Deputy.		*	*
5	2nd Viscount Grandison	Nephew and heir of the 1st Viscount		*	*
6	2nd Viscount Moore	Eldest son of the 1st Viscount	*	*	*

---

3 CSPI 1647–60, pp.80, 273, 325.
4 CSPI 1660–63, pp.136, 147.
5 The fact that Sir Faithful Fortescue does not mention this as a case of father being allowed to transfer his captaincy to a son when he was asking for permission to do this in 1639 suggests very strongly that the transfer occurred early in the 1630s: Thomas, Baron Clermont, *History of the Fortescue Family*, pp.180–81.

New Troops Created During the War with Spain and Retained in 1629[6]

	Name	Context	1629	1639	1641
7	Sir Robert McLellan Viscount Lecale M	Scottish landowner. Resigned 1638. Compromise candidate.[7]	*	*	*
8	Sir James Blount V Sir Thomas Dutton[8] M Viscount Wentworth 2nd Earl of Strafford	Drowned at sea 1628[9] Scoutmaster of the army. Died 1634. Lord Deputy. Executed 1641 Eldest son of Wentworth.	*	*	*

Additional troops created between 1634 and 1641

	Name	Context	1639	1641
9	Robert, Lord Dillon	Senior member of Council raised 1634	*	*
10	Earl of Ormond	Lieutenant general of horse raised 1638	*	*
11	Sir John Borlace M	Master of the Artillery ditto	*	*
12	2nd Viscount Conway M	Incoming marshal of the army[10] ditto	*	*
13	Sir Adam Loftus	The new treasurer at war[11] ditto	*	*
14	Earl of Leicester M	The new lord lieutenant raised 1641		*

6   Sir Thomas Stafford raised a troop of 25 horse in England in 1625, but it does not seem to have been in existence in early 1629: CSPI 1625–32, p.411; *ibid.* 1647–60, p.136.

7   McLellan, raised to the Scottish peerage in 1633 as Lord Kirkcudbright, wished his nephew and lieutenant Robert Maxwell to succeed him. Wentworth was in fundamental disagreement. For the subsequent spat between Maxwell, the Lord Deputy and Queen Henrietta Maria, see Chapter 9.

8   He was serving as a captain in the Netherlands by 1610: HMC, De Lisle and Dudley Mss iv, p.199.

9   Blount had a command in Ireland in the Nine Years' War. Afterwards like Sir William Windsor he joined the Spanish forces in the Netherlands and was suspected of knowing about the Gunpowder Plot. He does not seem to have raised the troop as he wanted to take over an existing unit, and so it was probably Stafford's. Blount is first mentioned as having been drowned in December 1628: HMC, Salisbury Mss 17, pp.10, 32; CSPI 1625–32, p.411; *ibid.* 1647–60, p.136.

10   The final terms were not agreed until late 1639: CSPI 1633–47, pp.232, 234.

11   CSPI 1633–47, p.122; CSPD 1641–43, p.448.

Infantry

The Companies in the Standing Army Raised Before 1624

	1624	1629	1639	1641
1	Lord Chichester died 1625 V			
2	Earl of Clanrickard V	* died 1636		
3	Earl of Thomond died 1624 V			
4	Sir John Vaughan V	*	*	*
5	Lord Powerscourt V	* died 1634		
6	Lord Valentia resigned 1628 V			
7	Sir Richard Moryson died 1625 V			
8	Viscount Falkland.[12] forced to resign 1628			
9	Sir Fulk Conway died 1624 V			
10	Baron Esmond V	* removed[13]		*
11	Baron Blayney resigned c. 1628[14] V			
12	Baron Caulfield died 1627 V			
13	Sir Thomas Rotherham V	*resigned[15]		
14	Lord Baltinglass V	* resigned 1634		
(15)	Sir Arthur Blundell V	*	*	
16	Sir Henry Tichborne M	*	*	*
17	Baron Cromwell. Viscount Lecale 1628 M	* resigned 1638[16]		
18	Sir Barnaby O'Brian	* resigned 1635		
19	Viscount Grandison V	* died 1630		
20	Baron Docwra resigned 1628 V			

12 For the row that followed see Chapter 6..
13 Esmond was deprived of his company c. 1637 for passing on the rumour that Lord Wentworth was guilty of causing a sick prisoner's death by striking him with a cane in a fit of temper: CSPI 1633–47, p.324.
14 CSPI 1625–32, p.272.
15 The resignation probably coincided with his retirement in 1635 from his post as inspector of fortifications in Ireland. He was still physically fit as he raised a new company after the outbreak of trouble in Ireland in late 1641: CSPI 1633–47, p.47; HMC, Ormonde Mss o.s. i., p.129.
16 Lecale probably gave up his company when he succeeded Lord Kirkcudbright as troop commander in 1638. Wentworth was not keen on captains having two commands.

21	Sir Francis Cooke	* resigned[17]		
(22)	Sir William Windsor died 1628 V			
23	Sir Arthur Bassett	* resigned[18]		
24	Sir William Stewart M	*	*	*
25	Sir Roger Hope died 1628 M			
26	Sir Arthur Savage V	* died 1632		
27	Viscount Wilmot V	*	*	

Commanders of New Companies Raised in 1625

	Name	Context	1629	1639	1641
28	The Earl of Desmond	Favourite of James I. Died 1628.			
29	Sir William St. Leger M	Lord President of Munster			
30	Lord Dunkellin	Son and heir of 4th Earl of Clanricarde	*	*	*
31	Sir Arthur Tyringham	Courtier changing career[19]	*	*	*
32	Sir Robert Yaxley M	Professional soldier. Died soon after resigning 1629.[20]			
33	Sir Faithful Fortescue	Nephew of Lord Chichester. Resigned c. 1638.[21]	*		

17 This was probably very soon after the King gave his consent to the October 1629 army list. In the summer he was petitioning for his arrears to be paid, which was commonly a sign that an officer wished to give up his command. The lord justices agreed, but the sum involved was so large that Wentworth tried to claw the money back, though without success: CSPI 1625–33, p.476; *ibid.* 1647–60, p.76; Knowler, *Strafforde's* Letters i, p.76.
18 Sir Arthur probably left for England permanently after sitting as an MP in the Irish parliament which met in 1634. He inherited the Devonshire estates of his elder brother in 1635 and went on to serve the King in the First Civil War as a colonel of foot: <www.historyofparliamentonline.org> 1660–1685, House of Commons, Members' Biographies.
19 <www.historyofparliamentonline.org>, House of Commons 1604–1629, Members' Biographies.
20 <www.historyofparliamentonline.org>, House of Common 1604–1629, Members' Biographies.
21 This was in favour of his eldest son Chichester: Clermont, *Fortescue Family*, p.180.

34	Sir John Ogle M	Professional soldier in Holland.[22] Resigned 1638.	*		
35	Edward Thynne M	Professional soldier. Died 1628.			
36	Charles Price M	Welsh MP. Some army experience.[23]	*	*	*

The Four Companies Recruited from Cadiz Expedition Units in 1626

37	Richard Vaughan M	Killed at La Rochelle 1627[24]			
38	Sir Richard Aldworth V	Provost Marshal Munster. Died 1629			
39	Sir George Flower V	Governor of Waterford[25]	*	*	
40	Sir Charles Coote V	Provost Marshal Connaught	*	*	*

New Company Commanders 1624–1641

1624–1629

	Name	Background	1629	1639	1641
1	Sir Frederick Hamilton	Rich landowner in Ulster post 1608[26]	*	*	*
3	Sir Edward Villiers Sir William St. Leger M	Died 1626	*	*	*

---

22 He was colonel of an English regiment by 1610: HMC, De Lisle and Dudley Mss iv, p.199.
23 <www.historyofparliamentonline.org> 1604–1629, House of Commons, Members' Biographies.
24 Captain in Lord Valentia's regiment in 1625 in the Cadiz expedition. His company was stationed in Ireland 1625–27. He was senior captain at Cork in 1626 the second captain being Sir Francis Willoughby: Spring, *First Bri*tish Army, pp.230, 232; CSPI 1625–32, p.194.
25 CSPI 1615–25, p.566.
26 Hamilton's experience as an officer in the Swedish army post-dated his commission in the standing army.

6	2nd Lord Lambart	Claimed he was promised a captaincy as son of a deceased senior officer[27]	*	*	*
7	Sir Henry Moryson M	Son of Sir Richard Died early 1630[28]	*		
8	Sir John Borlace[29] M	Distinguished professional soldier who fought in Europe. Resigned c. 1638	*		
9	Lucius Cary Sir Francis Willoughby[30] V	Elder son of Lord Falkland.[31] Distinguished professional soldier.	*	*	*
11	Sir Henry Blayney	Son and heir of 1st Lord Blayney	*	*	*
12	Arthur Chichester	Eldest son of Viscount Chichester[32]	*		
20	Sir Theodore Docwra	Eldest son of 1st Lord Docwra	*	*	*
(22)	1st Viscount Conway[33] M	Secretary of State. Died January 1631.	*		

27 For his complaint about being passed over despite his father's distinguished record in the army in Ireland see CSPI 1647–60, p.348. Lambart was paid as captain of foot from 1/9/28: APC 44, p.409.
28 He died in early 1630 possibly after having resigned a few months earlier: CSPI 1625–32, pp.480, 544, 573, 595.
29 HMC, Cowper Mss i, p.424. He had exchanged his company for a newly raised troop of cavalry in early 1639.
30 Willoughby had been major general in the first La Rochelle expedition having left his company in Dutch service: CSPD 1627–28, pp.181, 352. The King ordered him to have a company in the army in Ireland and he seems to have been initially allotted one recruited from soldiers who had fought in the Cadiz expedition. For this see CSPI 1625–32, p.401. He had, however, been granted Lucius Cary's company by the winter of 1629–30: *ibid.*, p.503.
31 Appointed in 1624 he was deprived of his company on his father's dismissal as lord deputy. He tried unsuccessfully to arrange a duel with his successor. For this Chapter 5
32 CSPI 1625–32, pp.24, 221, 263, 329. He resigned before 1639 when he was commanding a troop of horse.
33 An elderly man, he had commanded troops in the United Provinces in peace and in war. In June 1627 the King decreed that he should have the first troop or company to fall vacant, and that was Sir William Windsor's: CSPI 1625–32, pp.242, 353, 356.

25	Sir George Hamilton	Recommended by the King[34]	*	*	*
28	Sir Thomas Wenham[35]	Heir to an English landed family. No recent connections with Ireland. Resigned by 1639.	*		
29	Sir Roger Jones V?[36]	Privy Councillor. Ennobled as Lord Ranelagh 1629. Joint Lord President of Connaught 1630	*	*	*
32	Evan Lloyd	Welsh landowner. Died 1637.[37]	*		
35	Lord Mountnorris[38]	Civilian administrator. Cashiered 1635.	*		
37	George Herbert	No record after the 1629 army list. Must have resigned as he lived till the 1660s[39]	*		
38	Sir John Netterville[40]	Heir to his father, an Old English Catholic peer	*	*	*

34 CSPI 1625–32, pp.203, 275. This was in recognition of his large estate in Ireland and his distinguished Scottish ancestry. A younger son of the Earl of Abercorn he can only have been about 20 years of age when commissioned.
35 The King ordered Falkland to award him the first vacant company. This was just before the death of Richard, Earl of Desmond: CSPI 1625–32, p.312. Wenham was appointed a privy councillor in Ireland in 1634 but thereafter seems to have lost interest in the country. He had resigned his captaincy before 10/1639: *ibid*. 1633–47, p.75. He became 2nd Viscount Wenham in 1640. The 3rd Viscount was his brother Captain Phillip, who succeeded to his captaincy: G.E.C., Complete Peerage, xii pt ii.
36 Jones was constable of Sligo Castle in 1611, but this did not necessarily mean that he had served in the armed forces: C. Carew Mss vi, p.183.
37 *A Dictionary of Welsh Biographies*: Lloyd family of Bodidris, co. Denbigh.
38 When merely Francis Annersley in the middle years of King James's reign, he was almost invariably given a civilian title not a military one. However, in one document dating from 1610 he was included amongst former captains. For the circumstances in which he was stripped of his command by Wentworth in 1636 see above Chapter 8.
39 CSPI 1647–60, pp.80, 273, 325; *ibid*. 1660–63, pp.136, 147.
40 Sir Richard Aldworth, who was provost marshal for Munster and before that a captain in Queen Elizabeth's army in Ireland, was in command of a company of veterans of the Cadiz expedition at Limerick in late 1626 even though he had taken no part in it. He died, or possibly resigned, in early 1629, and was replaced by John Netterville: CSPI 1625–32, pp.194, 541; *ibid.*, 1647–60, p.180.

1630-1638

	Name	Context		
(2)	Sir Arthur Loftus	Son of Sir Adam, the treasurer at war	*	*
(5)	Sir Robert Farrer M	Professional soldier and protege of Wentworth. In Ireland by 10/1633 and a captain in the army by 11/1634.[41]	*	*
7	Lord Conway, later the 2nd Viscount M Robert Stewart M	Senior officer in Buckingham's wars. In post late 1629–1638.[42] Extensive service in Swedish army.[43]	*	*	*
8	John Borlace M?	Succeeded his father.[44] Previous military experience highly likely.	*	*
(10)	Sir Robert Loftus	Political ally of Wentworth.[45] Died late 1640	*	
(12)	William Billingsley	Allegedly a former page to Strafford[46]	*	*

---

41 Spring, *First British Army*, pp.23, 26–27, 231, 237, 252; Knowler, *Strafforde's Letters* i, pp.132, 355.
42 CSPI 1625–32, p.480. The 2nd Viscount's father did not die until 1631, but he was summoned to sit in the House of Lords in 1629 by virtue of his father's subsidiary title of Baron Conway.
43 Knowler, *Strafforde's Letters* ii, pp.79, 203.
44 Clermont, *Fortescue Family*, p.180. He may subsequently have made the company over to his father. It is described in Sir John Temple's list of October 1641 as commanded by Sir John Borlace, but Sir John Borlace junior was not knighted until November 1641: Shaw, *Book of Knights* ii, p.211. This may have been a mistake on Temple's part, but two lists compiled in early 1642 state that Lord Justice Borlace commanded an old company and Sir John Borlace junior a newly raised one. Both were in garrison at Dublin by 1644: HMC, Ormond Mss o.s. i, pp.125, 129, 148, 161–62.
45 Wedgwood, *The King's Peace*, p.209; CSPI 1633–47, p.221; Clermont, *Fortescue Family*, p.181.
46 This man's brothers included Edward and John who served under him in the New Army and were subsequently commissioned as captains in Ormond's army. Billingsley was probably the fourth son of Francis Billingsley esquire of Astley Abbots, Shropshire, who

(13)	Sir John Giffard⁴⁷ M			*	*
14	2nd Lord Baltinglass	Succeeded his father in 1634⁴⁸		*	*
(17)	Sir Thomas Wharton	Brother of the English peer Lord Wharton⁴⁹		*	*
18	Robert Byron	Younger brother of the courtier and soldier Sir John Byron		*	*
19	Sir George St. George V	Lieutenant to the 1st Lord Grandison		*	*
(21)	George Blount V	Blood relative of Lord Mountjoy. Captain in the Nine Years' War. Reactivated by 10/33. MP for Coleraine 1634⁵⁰		*	*
22	Lord Falkland Sir Lorenzo Cary	Reinstated in 1/1631 Died in 9/1633⁵¹ Younger son of Lord Falkland. Succeeded his father.		*	*

also had brothers named Edward and John: CSPI 1633–47, pp.63, 65; Heraldic Visitation of Shropshire 1623, *Harleian Society* 28 (1889): HMC, Ormonde Mss o.s. i, *passim*. However, the captain in the standing army was almost certainly the man who tried to free Strafford from the Tower of London in early May 1641 to save him from execution: Adamson, *The Noble Revolt*, pp.281, 640.

47 His father had been a captain in the army in Ireland and died defending his property in 1598, whilst he himself had served the King in the Netherlands. The most likely occasion for the award of a captaincy was when Giffard's stepsister married Wentworth's brother in 1636. In that year he was knighted by the Lord Deputy, and two years later Wentworth used him to discredit Lord Chancellor Loftus: APC 45, p.79; CSPI 1598–99, pp.353, 355; *ibid*. 1633–47, pp.121, 180; *ibid*. 1660–62, pp.173, 177.

48 In a petition to King Charles II he claimed to have succeeded his father in 1634 by royal command and as Captain Thomas Roper he took part in Lord Mountnorris's court martial in the following year: CSPI 1666–70, p.408; Knowler, *Strafforde's Letters* i, p.498.

49 A young man with no known military experience, he was negotiating for the purchase of a company in 1636 but without success: Knowler, *Strafforde's Letters* ii, p.15.

50 CSPI 1601–03, p.349; *ibid*. 1633–47, p.65; *ibid*., 1669–70, p.684; Knowler, *Strafforde's Letters* ii, p.13.

51 HMC, Cowper Mss i, p.424.

(23)	John Sherlock M	Served in operations against La Rochelle. Recommended for a command in Ireland in 1630.[52] Knighted 1636.		*	*
26	Lord Wentworth	Lord Deputy from 1632		*	
28	Philip Wenham M?	Succeeded his brother[53]		*	*
(32)	Robert Bayley M?	Probably a professional soldier and a Scot. First mentioned in the 1639 army list.		*	*
33	Chichester Fortescue	Succeeded his father c. 1638[54]		*	*
34	John Ogle M	Succeeded his father after 1633 but before 1639[55]		*	*
35	2nd Lord Caulfield[56]	Brother and heir of the 1st Lord Caulfield. No known military experience. Died 1640.		*	
(37)	William Peisley senior	Sergeant at arms to lord deputies since 1625. MP for Augher in 1640. Presumably dead by 5/41 when a by-election was held to choose his successor.[57]		*	

52 CSPI 1625–32, p.626.
53 See above for Sir Thomas Wenman. Philip was possibly the Captain Waynman who had served in the Palatinate: CSPI 1647–60, p.47.
54 Clermont, *Fortescue Family*, pp.180–81
55 In 1638 Sir John petitioned the King for payment of arrears for service in Ireland whilst the first mention of Captain John is in the 1639 army list. Ogle junior was probably the Ensign Ogle serving in Lord Valentia's regiment in the Cadiz expedition: Spring, *First British Army*, p.230.
56 He had succeeded his brother as master of artillery but was removed by Wentworth for his lack of experience, his frequent absences from Dublin, and what may have been something affecting his mobility. His appointment as a company commander in 1/1636 looks like a consolation prize: Knowler, *Strafford's Letters* i, pp.197, 512.
57 He was the son of Bartholomew Peisley, Comptroller of the Household to Falkland and Wentworth, who died in 1638: Belmore, *Fermanagh and Tyrone*, pp.225–27; Clarke, *Prelude to the Restoration*, p.203.

1639–1641

10	Baron Esmond V	Pardoned and given back his old company in 7/1641[58]			*
(15)	3rd Baron Castlestewart	Protestant Irish landowner. Succeeded his father-in-law Sir Arthur Blundell in 6/1641.[59]			*
26	Earl of Leicester M	Lord Lieutenant of Ireland June 1641			*
(27)	Francis Butler[60]				*
35	John Barry M	Professional soldier[61]			*
(37)	Thomas Rockley	First mentioned in Temple's list but he or one of his brothers was chosen to command a company in the New Army in 4/1640[62]			*
(39)	Thomas Games[63] M	A professional soldier			*

58 CSPI 1647–60, p.324. There was a six months' gap at the least between Esmond's reappointment and Sir Robert Loftus's death, which seems a long time for a vacancy to be unfilled. Possibly Thomas Rockley was first appointed to command this company but reallocated to Peisley's company when Esmond's appeal was upheld.
59 CSPI 1633–47, pp.280, 283, 310.
60 Knowler, *Strafforde's Letter*s ii, p.364. His uncle George Butler was a long-standing client of Viscount Wentworth's: <www.historyofparliamentonline.org>, House of Commons 1604–29, Members' Biographies. The fact that Francis was only a captain lieutenant in the New Army suggests that his commission as full captain was issued later than April 1640 and possibly after the New Army was disbanded in the spring of 1641. As he was quartered at Athlone at the start of the patriotic uprising, he almost certainly took over Lord Wilmot's company.
61 HMC, Egmont Mss i, p.126.
62 Born in 1618 he was the Earl of Strafford's godson: Anon., *Stainborough and Rockley: the historical associations and rural attraction*s (1853), p.72.
63 This man is identified in the index of CSPI 1633–47 as Captain Thomas James, a naval commander in Irish waters, who Charles I wished to have Sir George Flower's company when he relinquished it, but James was ill in November 1634 and may well have been dead by the time of Flower's death in *c*.1640: CSPI 1633–47, pp.1, 82–83, 767, 771. Thomas Games is more likely to have been the Lieutenant Games who served under Captain Rawlings in Sir Francis Willoughby's regiment in the second La Rochelle expedition, and who Lady Spry, widow of a colonel killed in the first La Rochelle expedition, subsequently recommended for a post in the standing army: Spring, *First British Army*, p.248; CSPD 1629–31, p.461.

Appendix V

Regiments in the New Army

---

* indicates Old Army captains
Bolding is used to identify men who subsequently served as captains and above in the Protestant forces in Ireland following the patriotic uprising, but who had not held the rank of captain in the standing army before 23 October 1641.
Names italicised are those of officers who are known to have served in regiments belonging to the patriot armies between 1641 and the 1643 truce.

First Regiment: Leinster – Facings: Red and White

	Co. Commanders	**Lieutenants**	**Ensigns**
Colonel	Earl of Strafford*	Francis Butler*	**John Maurice**
Lt. Colonel	Sir Robert Farrer*	**Thomas Mason**	Patrick Byrne
Major	Sir George St. George*	**John Wentworth**	William St. George
Captains	Viscount Baltinglass*	Richard Byrne	Edward Croston
	Baron Blayney*	**Lewis Owen**	Oliver Perse
	Baron Lambart *	Francis Spence	Nicholas Lowe
	Sir Robert Loftus*	**Fulk Martin**	George Martin
	Sir Robert Stewart*	Richard Dennis	Edward Kennedie
	Sir Francis Butler	Edward Flower	Michael Butler
	Sir William St. Leger*	Gerald Grace	**William Stephens**

Second Regiment: Munster – Facings: Watchet (Blue/Green) and White

Colonel	Sir William St. Leger*	Thomas Pigot	
Lt. Colonel	Phillip Mainwaring	**Agmon. Muschamp**	
Major	XXX Pigot	**William Pigot**	
Captains	**Sir John Browne**	Richard Cosby	

	Edward Matthews	Thomas Salvyn	Henry Butler[64]
	Henry Thropps	Allan Poviee	XXX Poyntz
	Bartholomew Peisley[65]	**Henry Peisley**	John Jones
	Robert Newcomen	XXX Newcomen	Thomas Dutton
	Edward Fenell		
	Warham St. Leger	Pyne Rochford	

Third Regiment: Leinster – Facings: Yellow and Red

Colonel	Robert, Lord Dillon*	Robert Scott	
Lt. Colonel	Sir John Giffard*		
Major	**Thomas Searle**	George Bettridge	James Mounday
Captains	(William) Billingsley*	**Edward Billingsley**	**John Billingsley**
	Sir James Dillon[66]		
	Richard Netterville		
	James Rochford	Richard Stafford	William Rochford
	Walter Slingsby		
	John Digby	John Craven	Francis Skinner
	John Fortescue		

Fourth Regiment: Connaught – Facings: Orange Tawney and Green

Colonel	Sir Charles Coote*		William Gilbert
Lt. Colonel	*Theobald Taaffe*[67]		
Major	William Peisley*	**George Saville**	George Stockdale
Captains	Chichester Fortescue*	George Ogilby	
	Sir James Dillon sen[68]		

64 Captain before May 1641: Bodleian, Carte Mss i, f..365. Associated with Captain Thropps.
65 Dead by April 1641: Bodleian, Carte Mss i, f.356.
66 The eldest son of Lord Dillon, who became 3rd Earl of Roscommon in August 1642. A Protestant convert and brother-in-law of Viscount Wentworth.
67 Later the 2nd Viscount Taaffe.
68 Younger son of the Earl of Roscommon and brother of Robert Lord Dillon.

	Luke Taaffe[69]		
	Taaffe junior		
	Chidley Coote		
	George Peisley	John Waldron	
	XXX Garnier	John Flemyng	Carbery Regan
	Not named		

Fifth Regiment: Connaught – Facings: White and Green

Colonel	Sir Henry Bruce		
Lt. Colonel	*John Read*		
Major	XXX Bayley*	**John Cambell**	
Captains	Sir John Netterville*		
	Sir George Hamilton*		Henry Smith
	Sir John Sherlock *	Henry Neville	
	Seafowl Gibson		Arthur Daykins
	Miles Bourke		
	Alexander Innis		
	Bryan McDonough	Ames Barton	
Additional	Michael [*sic*] Bourke	Ill. Coote suggested that Capt. John Moore should succeed him[70]	

Sixth Regiment: Munster – Facings: Green and White

Colonel	Sir Francis Willoughby*		
Lt. Colonel	Sir Arthur. Blundell*		
Major	Lorenzo Cary *	John Banastre	
Captains	2nd Lord Docwra *	**Edward Loftus**	John Docwra
	Toby Caulfield[71]	**John Martyn**	George Arundell

69 Younger brother of the 2nd Viscount. He took troops to Spain in November 1641: Clanricarde, *Memoirs* and *Letters*, pp.17, 28.
70 Bodleian, Carte Mss i, f.243.
71 Succeeded his father as the 3rd Baron Caulfield in 12/40. Killed by a patriot soldier when he was a prisoner following the Ulster uprising on 22/23 October 1641.

	William Willoughby		
	Edward? Warner[72]	**Hannibal Bagnall**	
	Francis Willoughby	William Butcher	
	XXX Ketleby		
	William Shaghensee	John Lester	Dermot Dallye

Seventh Regiment: England – Facings: Olive and Blue

Colonel	Sir Arthur Tyringham*		
Lt. Colonel	Charles Price*	Peirce Lacey	John Bromfield
Major	XXX Blunt*	Arthur Smith	
Captains	**Christopher Roper**		
	James Bridgman		
	John Jackson		
	Robert Smith		
	Thomas Phillips		
	Not named		
	Not named		

Eighth Regiment: Ulster – Facings: White, Ash and Red

Colonel	Sir Henry Tichburne*		
Lt. Colonel	Robert Byron*	John Duck	**Hercules Withers**
Major	Sir Arthur Loftus*	**Ralph Allen**	Ratchford
Captains	**Walter Loftus**	William Ballard	Walter Roch
	XXX Hearle?[73]		
	Jacob Lovell	Walter Cotton	Jonathan Wray
	XXX Colville		Humphrey Roberts
	John Savage		John Weldon
	Audley Mervyn	Luke Marriott	Erasmus Dillon
	XXX Gascoyne?	Henry Lee	

72 A Captain Edward Warner was in post in early 1641: Bodleian, Carte Mss i, f.355
73 If Nicholas, he was a captain in the Lord Deputy's forces in December 1641: CSPI 1632–45, pp.770–82.

Ninth Regiment: England – Facings: Greedaline and Green

Colonel	Sir Thomas Wharton*	**Edward Mainwaring**	Thomas Richardson
Lt. Colonel	Sir John Borlace jun.*	Dalton Tinsley	
Major	John Ogle *		
Captains	**Patrick Trevor**		
	Francis King[1]	XXX Little	
	XXX Rockley *?[2]		
	XXX Hutchinson		
	XXX Brereton		
	Not named		
	Not named		

Tenth Regiment: Leister/Munster – Facings: Purple and Yellow

Colonel	John Butler		
Lt. Colonel	William Wintour		
Major	William Butler		
Captains	Sir Frederick Hamilton*		
	Rory McGuire		
	Dermot Bryan	Tig McNamara	Daniel Bryan
	Pierce Butler	William Gognagone	John Butler
	Cornelius Cronin		
	Not named		
	Not named		

Cavalry

Wentworth described the cavalry as already raised, and this was largely correct. With the exception of Major Barry's and the two Lucas's troops, they were units belonging to the standing army. All had the same captains in October 1641 (apart

---

1   Captain in a regiment raised in England to put down the patriotic uprising: HMC, Ormonde Mss o.s. i, p.124.
2   There is no evidence as yet that Thomas Rockley held a commission in the standing army in 1640. This man could therefore be one of his brothers who also had military careers: Anon., *Stain*borough and *Rockley*, pp.70–73.

from Strafford's, which passed to his eldest son after his execution) and at least half had the same junior officers. This is apparent from army and garrison listings in the Ormond manuscripts and from muster rolls there and elsewhere cited in chapters 16 and Appendix VI. The three troops that were not part of the standing army were raised in England by August 1640.

1st Regiment

	Troop Commander	**Lieutenant**	**Cornet**
Colonel	Earl of Strafford *	Sir Faithful Fortescue	**William Billingsley**
Major	Sir George Wentworth *	**Thomas Harman**	
Captains	Viscount Lecale *	**James Vaughan**	
	Lord Dillon *	**Robert King**	
	Sir John Borlace *	**Richard Ryves**	
	Sir Adam Loftus *	William Hamden	
	Arthur Chichester *	Edward Leventhorpe	

2nd Regiment

Colonel	Earl of Ormond *	**Patrick Weymss**	
Major	XXX Barry	**Joseph St. John**	
Captains	Viscount Moore *	**Francis Moore**	
	Viscount Conway *	Thomas Fisher	
	Viscount Wilmot *	**Sir Edward Povey**	
	Sir William St. Leger *	Simon Bridge	

3rd Regiment (the Commissary General's)

Colonel	Sir Thomas Lucas		
Major	Sir Charles Lucas		
Captains	Viscount Grandison*		
	Not named		
	Not named		
	Not named		

Appendix VI

The Fate of Old Army Units Post October 1641

Almost all the material used to compile Appendix VI comes from Historical Manuscripts Commission, Ormonde Manuscripts old series volume one, pages 123–200. There is an excellent index in volume three of the old series, and so I have only given a citation if the information comes from elsewhere.

Cavalry

		1642	1645	1647[3]	Later
1	Arthur Chichester	*	*	*	
2	Sir William St. Leger Sir Fulk Huncks[4]	* d. 1642	*		
3	1st Viscount Wilmot 2nd Viscount Wilmot Sir Edward Povey	* d. 1643	*	*5	
4	Sir George Wentworth	*	*	*	
5	2nd Viscount Grandison 3rd Viscount Grandison	* k.1643	*	*	*6
6	2nd Viscount Moore 3rd Viscount Moore	* k.1643	*7	*	*8

3   A list of the Old Army cavalry troops compiled in June 1647 is to be found in HMC, Ormonde Mss o.s. ii, p.62.
4   Colonel in the expeditionary force in England fighting for King Charles I 1643–5.
5   Lieutenant and effective commander of the troop from 1640 onwards.
6   He was commanding a small troop in Ormond's army in 9/49: HMC, Ormonde Mss o.s. i, p.207.
7   Placed in command of his father's troop in 10/43: CSPI 1633–47 p.387.
8   Moore commanded a huge troop in Ormond's royalist coalition army established in Ireland in 1649 following King Charles I's execution. This suggests it had been recently raised, though it could have included *inter alia* his old troop: HMC, Ormonde Mss o.s i, p.206.

7	Viscount Lecale James Clotworthy	*	*9	*	*10
8	2nd Earl of Strafford	*	*	*	
9	2nd Earl of Roscommon[11] 3rd Earl of Roscommon	* d. 1642	*	*	*?12
10	Earl of Ormond	*	*	*	
11	Sir John Borlace senior	*	*	*	
12	2nd Viscount Conway Edward Conway[13]	* r. 1645	*	*	*
13	Sir Adam Loftus	*	*	*	
14	2nd Earl of Leicester Abraham Yarner[14]	*	*	*	

Infantry

	Company commander	Notes
1	Sir Frederick Hamilton	Old army company still in existence in 1646 in Connaught[15]

9 Clotworthy replaced Lord Lecale on Parliament's orders in 10/45: CSPI 1633–47, p.417.
10 Clotworthy's former troop was still in existence in 1/49: Gilbert, *Confe*deration ii, p.464.
11 This was Robert Lord Dillon, the eldest son of the first earl, who had commanded a troop in the standing army. He succeeded his father in 1641 but died very soon afterwards.
12 In 1649 he was in command of 20 or so troopers in the royalist army in Ireland. Unlike Moore's very large troop it does not sound like a body of newly raised men: HMC, Ormonde Mss o.s. i, p.207.
13 In 3/45 Conway was commissioned by the Committee of Both Kingdoms as captain of his father's troop: CSPD 1644–45, p.375. He was appointed governor of Coleraine by Parliament in 10/48 and thus may still have commanded it: CSPI 1647–60, p.33.
14 He was lieutenant of the Lord Lieutenant's troop in early 1642 and presumably became captain when the King dismissed Leicester in 1643: CSPI 1633–47, p.778.
15 CSPI 1633–47, p.434. As a confirmed Presbyterian he did not accept the truce negotiated by Ormond in 1643 and returned to Scotland where he died in 1647. One of his sons, either Frederick or James, may have succeeded him.

(2)	Sir Arthur Loftus	In the Dublin garrison in 1644, but Loftus will have been deprived of his command soon after as he had taken Parliament's side against the Ormond truce. Hs successor is not known.[16]
3	Sir William St. Leger	Moved to Dublin in 11/41 but returned to Munster in the spring and was presumably incorporated into St. Leger's newly commissioned regiment. He died in 6/41.[17] His successor as company commander is not known.
4	Sir John Vaughan	Absorbed into the Derry garrison regiment raised from the English civilian population of the city and its environs before Vaughan's death in 1643. Successor not known but numbered amongst the regiment's six company commanders beginning with Samuel Pitt given in McKenny.[18]
(5)	Sir Robert Farrer	Dublin garrison 1641. Buried there in 1643. Successor not known.
6	Lord Lambart	Incorporated into Lambart's regiment which garrisoned Dublin. The regiment was disbanded by Michael Jones in 6/47.[19]
7	Sir Robert Stewart	Incorporated into the Derry garrison in 1642. Nothing further known.[20]
8	Sir John Borlace junior	In garrison at Coleraine in 1642. Presumably shipped back to Dublin when the Scottish army took over the garrison. In the Dublin garrison in 1/47 it probably survived like Borlace's regiment until 8/49.[21]

16 He had ingratiated himself with Parliament by December 1644 and was raising troops to garrison Duncannon fort soon afterwards: CSPD 1644, p.368; CSPD 1644–45, pp.48, 183, 190.
17 HMC, Ormonde Mss o.s. I, pp.125, 135; *ibid.* n.s. ii, p.167.
18 JHC ii, p.563; MacKenny, *Laggan* Army, p.44.
19 Cox, *Hibernia Anglicana* ii, pp.194–95.
20 MacKenny, *Laggan* Army, p.44.
21 Sir John fought as colonel of foot at the battle of Rathmines in August 1649: Firth and Davies, *Regimental History* ii, pp.631–32.

9	Sir Francis Willoughby	It defended the fort at Galway where it was stationed in 1641 but surrendered on terms in 6/43 whereupon it was shipped to Dublin. Sent to England in 3/44 but captured at sea and the Irish on board drowned.[22]
10	Lord Esmond	He sided with Parliament after the Ormond truce and he and the company remained at Duncannon until it was captured by patriot troops in 1645.
11	Lord Blayney	Destroyed at Monaghan 10/41. New company 1642.
(12)	William Billingsley	In garrison at Strangford 4/42. In Sir Henry Tichborne's regiment 12/42.[23] Nothing further known.
(13)	Sir John Giffard	His company was part of the regiment under his command quartered in Dublin and at his residence, Castle Jordan in Leinster, 1644–47. Regiment disbanded by Michael Jones in 1647 but Giffard was given command of a troop of horse as a consolation.[24]
14	Lord Baltinglass	In garrison at Yougal and increased to 100 men in 1642. It was then incorporated into some formation in Lord Inchiquin's army. Disbanded by Oliver Cromwell after the surrender of Inchiquin's Protestant officers in 1650.[25]
(15)	Lord Castlestewart	In the Trim garrison 7/48. Later in the year he commanded a regiment in Ormond's coalition army, and so it may have transferred.[26]
(16)	Sir Henry Tichborne	Half destroyed in Ulster 10/41. The rest were at Lifford in 1642. Probably absorbed into the Laggan army. Tichborne had a newly raised company at Drogheda 11/41.[27]

22 J. Hardiman, *The History of Galway* (Dublin Falds and Son, 1820), p.121.
23 HMC, Ormonde Mss o.s. ii, p.12.
24 HMC, Ormonde Mss o.s.ii, pp.17, 45; ibid., Egmont Mss ii, pp.421–24.
25 CSPI 1666–70, p.408.
26 HMC, Ormonde Mss o.s. ii, pp.76, 83.
27 Gilbert, *Contemporary History* i, pp.468–69; J.S. Reid, *History of the Presbyterian Church in Ireland* 2 vols (London: Whittaker and Co, 1837) i, pp.333–34.

(17)	Sir Thomas Wharton	In the Dublin garrison in 1644 with Wharton described as absent. He was opposed to the Ormond truce and from then onwards worked with Parliament as an adviser on Irish affairs. Successor as company commander not known.
18	Robert Byron	At Cork 10/41. Marched to Dublin 11/41. Old and new company in the Dublin area 1642. Probably sent to England in 11/43 under Byron as colonel.
19	Sir George St. George	Still in existence in 1646 in Connaught.[28]
20	Lord Docwra	Moved to Dublin in 11/41. Dublin garrison until 1647.
(21)	George Blount	His company was destroyed at Fort Mountjoy in 10/41. It was not recruited.[29]
(22)	Lorenzo Cary	Marched from Galway to Dublin 11/1641. Cary was killed in battle in 1/1642 probably by one of his own men.
	Algernon Sidney	Son of the Lord Lieutenant. Left for England in the summer of 1643 presumably in disapproval of Ormond's negotiations with the patriots. Arrested as a Royalist but proved his innocence and fought in the Earl of Manchester's regiment in 1644–5.[30]
(23)	Sir John Sherlock	Dublin garrison 1647[31]
24	Sir William Stewart	Incorporated into Stewart's regiment in the Laggan army raised in late 1641. Sir William died in 1647.[32] Successor not known.

---

28 CSPI 1633–47, p.434.
29 Gilbert, *Contemporary* History i, p.548.
30 Wanklyn, *Reconstructing the New Mod*el Army i, pp.52–62.
31 His army service in Ireland did not end until 1651 at the earliest, but he was probably not commanding the same company as in 1642: Wanklyn, *Reconstructing the New Model* Army ii, pp.189–90, 212.
32 HMC, Portland Mss i, p.430.

25	Sir George Hamilton 2nd Lord Folliott	Roman Catholic. Resigned *c.* 12/41. Dublin garrison from 12/41 to 1/47. Governor of Derry for Parliament 1646–48 but he did not take his company with him. It was probably disbanded by Michael Jones in 6/47 but Folliott continued in military service till 10/48.[33]
(26)	Earl of Leicester	Forced by the King to resign as lord lieutenant in 11/43. Replaced by Ormond. Successor as company commander not known.
(27)	Francis Butler	Defending Athlone 1641–43. Probably went to England with Sir Robert Byron's regiment of which Butler was lieutenant colonel.[34]
28	Philip Wenman	Company at Cork 1642. Nothing known thereafter but possibly incorporated into a regiment in Inchiquin's army. Newly raised company at Drogheda 11/41.
29	Lord Ranelagh	Athlone garrison 1641–43. Ranelagh and his regiment left Athlone for Dublin in 6/43 with most of his troops describing the place as no longer defensible. Condemned by the lords justices, he left for Oxford to appeal to the King and died there later in the year. Nothing further is known about the company.[35]
30	Earl of Clanricarde	In County Galway in 1642. Presumably remained in service for some years afterwards as Clanricarde's military career developed.[36]
31	Sir Arthur Tyringham	Destroyed at Newry in 10/41. Tyringham died early in 1642.
	Robert Sidney	Son of the Lord Lieutenant. Probably did not recruit the company, but he commanded a company at Dublin in 1643 as Captain Sidney junior. Gave up his commission in the summer of 1643 and returned to England.

---

33 CSPI 1647–60, p.30.
34 <www.historyofparliamentonline.org>, Members' Biographies.
35 Carte, *Life of Ormond* ii, pp.387–91; G.E.C., *Complete Peerage*, vol. X.
36 Dictionary of Irish Biography.

(32)	Robert Bayley	Company badly handled at Cavan 10/41. Major in former Colonel Crawford's regiment in 1644. Possibly took over Robert Sterling's company who like Crawford was fighting for Parliament in England in 1644.[1]
33	Chichester Fortescue	Destroyed at Dundalk in 10/41. Not recruited. Newly raised company at Drogheda 11/41.
34	John Ogle	Moved to Dublin 11/41. In the garrison until early 1647. Nothing further known.
35	John Barry	Destroyed at Claremont 10/41. Not recruited.
36	Charles Price	His company defended the castle at Limerick till it surrendered under Captain George Courtney's command in 6/42.[2] Price had returned to England by then and was a fervent supporter of the King but was killed in a duel in 1645.[3] Nothing further is known about his company.
37	Thomas Rockley	Died soon after 9/42.[4] Successor not known.
38	Sir John Netterville Earl of Ormond	Roman Catholic. Dismissed 1/42. Dublin garrison to 1647.
(39)	Thomas Games	Moved to Dublin from Waterford 11/41. Dublin garrison until late 1643. Company may have been shipped to England in 11/43.[5]
40	Sir Charles Coote Chidley Coote	Handed company over to his younger son by early 1642. Fighting in Sir William Brereton' regiment in Cheshire 1644–46 having presumably resigned his Irish command.[6]

1 Gilbert, *Contemporary History* i, pp.479–80. In June 1642 Bayley's soldiers were described as a company of Scotsmen, Crawford's regiment was largely Scottish in composition, and many Scottish surnames appear in a muster of the company for 1644: CSPI 1633–47, p.788; HMC, Ormonde Mss, o.s.i, p.160. Bayley's company in the pre-1641 army cannot have been Scottish, though he himself may have been.
2 J. Ferrar, *The History of Limerick* (Limerick: Watson and Co., 1787), p.36.
3 <www.historyofparliamentonline.org>, House of Commons 1604–29, Members' Biographies.
4 HMC, Ormonde Mss o.s. ii, p.9.
5 Games was allegedly killed during the siege of Nantwich in January 1644, but reference is not supplied: <http://www.bcw-project.org/ >
6 R.N. Dore, The Letter Books of Sir William Brereton, *Lancs. And Cheshire Record Society*, 2 vols, 1984, 1990, i, pp.27, 28; *ibid*. ii, appendix xi. See Chapter 16 for possible survival of this company to 1660.

Bibliography

Archives
Bodleian Library, Oxford   Carte Mss i, ii
The National Archives, Kew   SP63/257

Printed Primary Sources, Edited Primary Sources and Calendars
Acts of the Privy Council 1600–04, 1613–1631, R. Dasend, E. Anderson, J. Lyle, R. Monger, P. Penfold (eds.) (London: HMSO, 1906–1964)
Baillie, Robert, *Letters and Journals 1637–1662*, vols 72, 73, 77 (Edinburgh: Bannatyne Club, 1841)
Bernard, Nicholas, *The Whole Proceedings of the Siege of Drogheda in Ireland* (London: William Bladen, 1642)
Memoirs and Letters of Ulick, First Marquis of Clanricarde, John, 11th Earl of Clanricarde, ed. (London: J. Hughes for J. Dudley, 1757)
Calendar of the Carew Manuscripts, J. Brewer and W. Bullen (eds), 6 vols (London: Longmans, 1869–73)
Calendar of State Papers Domestic: James I 1603–25, M. Green (ed.) (London: Longman, 1857–72); Charles I 1625–49 J. Bruce and W. Hamilton (eds) (London: 1873–93)
Calendar of State Papers Ireland: Elizabeth I 1588–1603, H. Hamilton, E. Atkinson, and R. Mahaffy (eds) (London: HMSO, 1885–1910); James I 1603–1625, C. Russell and R. Prendergast (eds) (London: HMSO, 1872–80); Charles I and Commonwealth 1625–1660, R. Mahaffy (ed.) (London: HMSO, 1900–03); Charles II 1660–1670, R. Mahaffy (ed.) (London: HMSO, 1905–10)
Calendar of State Papers Venetian 1637–42, A. Hinds (ed.) (London; HMSO 1923–4)
Carte, Thomas, *A Collection of Original Letters and Papers concerning the Affairs of England 1641–1660*, 2 vols (London: J. Betterham, 1739)
Carew, George, Earl of Totnes and Sir Thomas Stafford, *Pacata Hibernia*, 3 vols (London: R. Milbourne, 1633 reprinted in Dublin 1810)
Desiderata Curiosa Hibernica, J. Lodge (ed.), 2 vols (Dublin: J. Hay, 1772)
C.H. Firth (ed.), *Papers relating to Thomas Wentworth, First Earl of Strafford* (London: Camden Society, 2nd series liii, 1895)

Gardiner, Samuel R. (ed.), *Constitutional Documents of the Puritan Revolution 1625–1660* (Oxford: University Press, 1951 reprint)

Gardiner, Samuel R. (ed.), *The Hamilton Papers being selections from original letters in the possession of the Duke of Hamilton and Brandon relating to the period 1638–1651* (London: Camden Society 2nd series xxvii, 1880)

Gilbert, Sir John, *The Irish Confederation and War in Ireland 1641–1652*, 7 vols (Dublin: Irish Archaeological and Celtic Society, 1882)

Gilbert, Sir John (ed.), *A Contemporary History of Affairs in Ireland from AD 1641–1652*, 4 vols (Dublin: Irish Archaeological and Celtic Society, 1879)

Hardwicke, Philip Earl of, *Miscellaneous State Papers from 1501 to 1726*, 2 vols (London: W. Strahan and T. Cadell 1778)

Hickson, Mary, *Ireland in the Seventeenth Century*, 2 vols (London: Longmans, 1884)

Historical Manuscript Commission, the Appendix to the 3rd Report, the Manuscripts of the Duke of Portland, the Marquis of Ormonde, the Marquis of Salisbury, the Marquis of Abergavenny, Earl Cowper, the Earl of Egmont

Hyde, Edward, Earl of Clarendon, *The History of the Rebellion and Civil Wars in England*, W. Macray (ed.), 6 vols (Oxford: University Press, 1888)

Journal of the English House of Commons, vol. ii 1640–43 (London: HMSO, 1802)

Journal of the English House of Lords, vol. iv 1629–42 (London: HMSO, after 1767)

Journal of the Irish House of Commons, vol. 8, annotated index

Knowler, William, *The Earl of Strafforde's Letters and Dispatches*, 2 vols (London: W. Bowyer, 1739)

Maclean J. (ed.), *Letters of Sir Robert Cecil to Sir William Carew* (London: Camden Society 88, 1864)

Moryson, Fynes, *Itinerary of his Ten Years' Travel*, 3 vols (London: John Beale, 1617)

Nalson, John, *An Impartial Collection of the Great Affairs of State 1639–1649*, 2 vols (London: S. Mearne et al., 1682)

O'Donovan (ed.), *Annals of the Kingdom of Ireland by the Four Masters*, 7 vols (Dublin: Hodges and Smith, 1854)

Rushworth, John, *Historical Collections of Private Passages of State*, 8 vols (London: D. Browne, 1721 reprint)

Shaw, William A., *The Knights of England*, 2 vols (London: Sherratt and Hughes, 1906)

State Papers collected by Edward Hyde, Earl of Clarendon from the Year 1621, Richard Scrope and Thomas Monkhouse (eds), 3 vols (Oxford: University Press, 1767–86)

Temple, Sir John, *The Irish Rebellion* (London: S. Gillibrand, 1646)

Williams, Sir Roger, *A Briefe Discourse of Warre* (London: Thomas Orwin, 1590)

Whitaker, Thomas, *The Life and Original Correspondence of Sir George Radcliffe* (London: Longmans etc., 1810)

Secondary Sources
Adamson, John, *The Noble Revolt* (London: Weidenfeld and Nicolson, 2007)
Anon., *Stainborough and Rockley: the historical associations and rural attractions* (1853)
Bagwell, Richard, *Ireland under the Tudors*, 3 vols (London: Longmans 1888)
Bagwell, Richard, *Ireland under the Stuarts*, 2 vols (London: Longmans, 1909)
Bennett, Martyn, *Cromwell at War* (London: I.B. Taurus, 2017)
Blakemore, David, *Destructive and Formidable: British Infantry Firepower 1642–1765* (Frontline Books, London: 2014)
Borlace, Edmund, *A History of the Execrable Irish Rebellion* (London: Brome, Clavel and Chipwell, 1680)
Braddick, Michael, *The Fire and the Fury* (London: Allen Lane, 2008)
Carte, Thomas, *The Life of James Butler, Duke of Ormond*, 6 vols (Oxford: University Press, 1851 reprint)
Clarke, A., *Prelude to Restoration in England* (Cambridge: University Press, 1999)
Cliffe, J.T., *The Yorkshire Gentry from Reformation to Civil War* (London: Athlone, 1969)
Cox, Sir Richard, *Hibernia Anglicana*, 2 vols (London: Joseph Watts, 1687)
Cust, Richard, *Charles I: a Political Biography* (London: Pearson, Longmans, 2005)
Donald, Peter, *An Uncounselled King* (Cambridge: University Press, 1990)
Doran, Susan, *Elizabeth I and her Circle* (Oxford: University Press, 2015)
Edwards, Peter, *Dealing in Death: The Arms Trade and the British Civil Wars* (Stroud: Sutton Publications, 2000)
Ferrar, J., *The History of Limerick* (Limerick: A. Watson and Co, 1787)
Firth, Sir Charles, *Cromwell's Army*, 4th edn (London: Methuen, 1962)
Firth, Sir Charles and Davies, Godfrey, *The Regimental History of Cromwell's Armies*, 2 vols (Oxford: University Press, 1940)
Fissel, Mark, *The Bishops' Wars* (Cambridge: University Press, 1994)
Fletcher, Anthony, *The Outbreak of the English Civil War* (London: Arnold, 1981)
Gardiner, Samuel R., *A History of England from the Accession of James I to the Outbreak of the Civil War*, 10 vols (London: Longmans, 1888)
Gentles, Ian, *The English Revolution and the Wars in Three Kingdoms 1637–1652* (Harlow: Pearson, Longmans, 2007)
Hamilton, Lord Ernest, *The Irish Rebellion with a history of the events leading up to and succeeding it* (London: John Murray, 1922)
Hardiman, J., *The History of Galway* (Dublin: W. Falds and Sons, 1820),
Kenyon, John and Ohlmeyer, Jane, *The Civil Wars* (Oxford: University Press, 1998)
Lenihan, Padraig, *Consolidating Conquest: Ireland 1603–1727* (Harlow: Pearson, Longmans, 2008)
MacKenny, Keith, *The Laggan Army in Ireland 1640–1685* (Dublin: Four Courts Press, 2005)
Reid, J., *History of the Presbyterian Church in Ireland*, 2 vols (London: Whittaker and Co, 1837)
Roberts, Keith, *Cromwell's War Machine*, (Barnsley: Pen and Sword, 2005)
Russell, Conrad, *The Causes of the English Civil War* (Oxford: University Press, 1990)

Scott, Christopher, Turton, Alan and Eric Von Arni, *Edgehill: The Battle Reinterpreted* (Barnsley: Pen and Sword, 2004)
Smith, David, *A History of the Modern British Isles* (Oxford: University Press, 1990)
Spring, Laurence, *The First British Army 1624–1628* (Solihull: Helion and Co., 2016)
Stevenson, David, *Highland Warrior: Alasdair McColla and the Civil Wars*, 2nd ed. (Edinburgh: Saltire Society, 1994)
Stevenson, David, *Scottish Covenanters and Irish Confederates* (Belfast: Ulster Historical Foundation, 1981)
Stoyle, Mark, *Soldiers and Strangers: An Ethnic History of the English Civil War* (London: Yale University Press, 2005)
Terry, Charles, *The Life and Campaigns of Alexander Leslie, Earl of Leven* (London: Longmans, Green, 1899)
Wanklyn, Malcolm, *Reconstructing the New Model Army*, 2 vols (Solihull: Helion and Co., 2015–16)
Wedgwood, C.V., *The King's Peace* (London: Collins, 1955)
Wernham, Richard B., *The Return of the Armadas* (Cambridge: University Press, 1994)
Wheeler, James Scott, *The Irish and British Wars 1637–1654* (London: Routledge, 2002)
Woolrych, Austin, *Britain in Revolution* (Oxford: University Press, 2002)
Young, Peter, *Edgehill 1642* (Kineton: Roundwood Press, 1967)

Articles
P. Hardacre, 'Patronage and purchase in the Irish standing army under Thomas Wentworth, Earl of Strafford 1632–1640', *J. Society of Army Historical Research* 67 (1988)
M. Wanklyn, 'Cromwell's Generalship and the Conquest of Scotland 1650–51', *Cromwelliana*, series 3, no. 4 (2015)

Dictionaries
The Oxford Dictionary of National Biography, Colin Matthews, Brian Harrison, Lawrence Goodman and Sir David Cannadine (eds), 69 vols (Oxford: University Press, 2004–2022)
Dictionary of Irish Biography (Cambridge: University Press 2009; Royal Irish Academy, 2009–2022)
Dictionary of Welsh Biography to 1940, R.T. Jenkins and J.E. Lloyd (eds) (London: Hon. Society of Cymmrodorion, 1959)

Databases Online
The British Civil War Project <http://bcw-project.org>
The History of Parliament: The House of Commons 1604–1629, alphabetical listing of members' biographies <https://www.historyofparliamentonline.org/research/members>

Index

Index of People

Aguila, Dom Juan del   13-16
Albert, the Archduke   20, 30, 68
Aldworth, Sir Richard   74, 229
Alleyne, George   32
Andrews, Eusebius   165
Annersley, Sir Francis, later Viscount Mountnorris   85, 95, 97, 113, 136, 229
Antrim, Randal MacDonnell, 1st Earl of   32
Antrim, Randal MacDonnell, 2nd Earl of   121, 122-23, 125, 128-30, 132, 133, 140, 143, 149, 156, 164, 179, 184
Argyll, Archibald Campbell, 7th Earl of   55
Argyll, Archibald Campbell, 8th Earl of   121, 124, 128, 131, 133, 140, 149, 150
Armagh, the Archbishop of   73
Armstrong, Sir Thomas   147
Arundel, Thomas Howard, Earl of   147

Baltinglass, Thomas Roper, 2nd Viscount   231
Barriffe, William   117
Barry, Garrett   170, 175
Barry, John   165, 182, 186, 170, 175, 203
Barrymore, David Barry, 1st Earl of   134
Bassett, Sir Arthur   226
Bayley, Robert   182, 186, 187, 198-99, 245
Belling, Christopher   170
Bertie, Sir Peregrine   74
Billingsley, William   182, 230-31
Bingley, Sir Ralph   72, 74
Bingley, Sir Richard   31
Birchenshaw, Ralph   45-47
Blayney, Henry, 2nd Baron Blayney   182, 186, 187, 200

Blount, Captain George   103, 126, 182, 186, 187, 224
Blount, Sir James   36, 224
Blundell, Sir Arthur   126, 195, 219
Bodley, Sir John   42
Borlace, Sir John I   81, 107, 112, 114, 138, 146, 147, 161, 162, 166, 167, 182, 185, 186, 187-88, 190-92, 199, 200, 230
Borlace, Sir John II   203, 206, 230
Brabazon, Edward, 1st Baron Brabazon   48
Brouncker, Sir Henry   23, 24, 80
Bruce, Edward   13
Bruce, Sir Henry   133, 147, 148, 150
Buckingham, George Villiers, Duke of   40, 50, 57-58, 62-64, 72, 75, 80, 81, 92, 117, 139, 149
Butler, Francis   207, 233
Butler, Lieutenant Colonel John   74, 77, 190
Button, Sir Thomas   88
Byron, Sir Nicholas   144, 148
Byron, Robert   190, 196, 207

Carew, Sir George, later Lord Carew and Earl of Totnes   32-35, 42-43, 46, 49, 58, 64, 95
Carte, Thomas   vi, 53, 139, 142, 145-46, 149-50, 151, 156, 161, 168, 178, 186, 192, 200, 202
Cary, Henry, 1st Viscount Falkland *See* Falkland
Cary, Lucius, 2nd Viscount Falkland   62, 79
Cary, Lorenzo   104, 105, 170, 197, 201
Castle Stewart, Andrew Stewart, 3rd Baron   76
Caulfield, Toby, 1st Baron Caulfield   107
Caulfield, William, 2nd Baron Caulfield   107, 187

Caulfield, Toby, 3rd Baron Caulfield   187
Cecil, Sir Robert, later Earl of Salisbury
   17-18, 23, 24, 32
Chamberlain, Captain Thomas   69
Charles, Prince of Wales, subsequently King Charles I   49, 52, 54-142, 144, 148-49, 153-56, 159-61, 163-67, 170, 173-75, 178-79, 206, 208
Chichester, Sir Arthur later Baron Chichester   23, 25-27, 31, 33-3, 57, 58, 62-63, 66, 71-73, 79, 83, 87, 91, 92, 94-102, 104, 106, 111, 116, 119-32, 19, 40, 41, 42-43, 46, 49, 51, 52, 58, 60, 62, 64, 78, 80, 92, 95, 104, 113
Chichester, Captain Arthur   182, 199, 207
Chichester, Edward, 1st Viscount Chichester   188
Christian IV, King of Denmark   72, 77
Clanricarde, Richard Bourke, 4th Earl of   19, 70, 80, 97, 108, 191, 211
Clanricarde, Ulick Bourke, Lord Dunkellin, later 5th Earl of   62, 64, 97, 108, 150, 191, 203
Clarendon, Edward Hyde, earl of   178
Clotworthy, Sir John   178
Coke, Sir John   86, 95, 99-100, 103, 104, 111, 116, 122, 123, 126, 127, 130, 147
Conway, Edward, 1st Viscount Conway   62, 64
Conway, Edward, 2nd Viscount Conway   143, 154, 155, 161, 182, 199, 222
Conway, Sir Fulk   62
Conyers, Sir John   154, 155
Cooke, Sir Francis   213, 226
Cooke, Sir Richard   38
Coote, Sir Charles I   80, 96, 147, 148, 150
Coote, Sir Charles II   194, 206
Coote, Chidley   194
Cork, Richard Boyle, 1st Earl of   79, 83, 84-85, 86, 88, 93, 99, 115, 134, 138, 197
Cottington, Francis, 1st Baron Cottington   87, 96, 104, 124
Cranfield, Lionel, later 1st Earl of Middlesex   40-41, 50, 58, 62, 67, 81
Crawford, Colonel Lawrence   196, 199
Crawford, Captain Patrick   27, 37
Crispe, Captain   74
Cromwell, Oliver   31, 143, 206, 225
Cromwell, Thomas, 4th Baron Cromwell   61, 64, 65, 114, 117
Crosby, Sir Piers   74-77, 81, 83, 84, 99, 136, 141, 209

Danvers, Henry, Baron Danvers later Earl of Danby   95
Derby, William Stanley, 6th Earl of   59, 65
Desmond, Richard Preston, Earl of   64
Desmond, George Fielding, Earl of   116
Devlin, Richard Nugent, Baron, later 1st Earl of West Meath   27
D'Ewes, Sir Simons   176
Dillon, Sir James   170
Dillon, Sir Lucas   76
Dillon, Sir Robert alias Lord Kilkenny West   76, 109, 133, 138, 150, 151, 161
Docwra, Sir Henry, later 1st Baron Docwra   14, 27, 44, 47, 52, 67
Docwra Theodore, 2nd Baron Docwra   197
Dorchester, Dudley Carlton, Viscount   83
Dutton, Sir Thomas   48, 108

Elector Palatine and King of Bohemia, Frederick   39, 50, 54, 57, 72
Elector Palatine, Karl Ludwig   124, 173
Elizabeth I, Queen of England and Ireland   13, 17-18, 24, 35, 44, 45, 57, 64, 98, 126, 191
Elizabeth, Princess, Queen of Bohemia   50, 72, 159
Elphinstone, Captain William   74
Esmond, Laurence, 1st Baron Esmond   97, 113, 136, 219
Esmond, Thomas   75
Essex, Robert Devereux, 2nd Earl of   13, 21, 70, 219
Essex, Robert Devereux, 3rd Earl of   173, 205

Fairfax, Sir Thomas   110
Falkland, Henry Cary, 1st Viscount   43, 51-52, 55, 56, 61, 62-64, 65-78, 81-82, 84, 93, 95-96, 104, 115, 194, 219
Farrer, Sir Robert   103, 114, 137, 141, 149, 182
Flower, Sir George   74, 150
Flower, William   171, 233
Forbes, Captain Arthur   76
Fortescue, Chichester   182, 187-88, 205
Fortescue, Sir Faithful   62, 64, 104, 196

Games, Captain Thomas   197, 233
Giffard, Sir John   231

Gosnold alias Garnold, Captain Roger   218
Graham, Lieutenant   107
Grandison, William Villiers, 2nd Viscount   182, 186, 199
Gustavus Adolphus, King of Sweden   83

Hadsor, Richard   86
Hamilton, Sir George   197, 201, 203
Hamilton, James Hamilton, Marquis of   105, 124, 125, 126, 128
Hampden, John   173
Hansard, Sir Richard   28, 215
Harcourt, Sir Simon   192, 196
Harte, Captain   28
Henrietta Maria, Queen of England   116
Herbert, Sir Edward   82
Herbert, George   82
Holland, Henry Rich, 1st Earl of   80, 133, 134, 137, 147
Hollar, Wenceslas   204
Hooke, Captain Francis   88
Hopton, Sir Arthur   140

Isabella, the Archduchess   20-21, 25, 30, 68, 88

James I, King of England and Scotland   18-21, 23-24, 28, 29, 30, 32-35, 38-39, 40, 42, 46-50, 52, 53, 54, 55-58, 61, 62, 63, 64, 66, 80, 120, 121, 132
Jones, Colonel Michael   204, 206

Kilkenny West, Lord. *See* Sir Robert Dillon
Killeen, Luke Plunkett, 9th Baron, later 1st Earl of Fingall   76
King, Sir John   45-47
King, Sir Robert   46, 103
Kingsmill, Sir John   106, 216

Lambart alias Lambert, Sir Oliver, later 1st Baron Lambart   37, 211, 218
Lambart alias Lambert, Charles, 2nd Baron Lambart   196, 197, 204, 228
Lane, Sir Richard   46
Laud, William Archbishop of Canterbury   94, 121, 122
Leicester, Robert Sidney, 2nd Earl of   167, 183, 191, 196, 202, 204
Leveson, Sir Richard   13-14
Lilburne, John   165
Lisle, Philip Sidney, Lord   191

Loftus, Sir Adam I, Lord Chancellor of Ireland   55, 79, 84, 86, 88, 93, 99, 115, 121, 138
Loftus, Sir Adam II (of Rathfarnham)   76
Loftus, Sir Arthur   162
Lorne, Archibald Campbell, Lord   *See* Argyll, 8th Earl of
Louis XIII, King   166
Lucas, Sir Thomas   147, 151-52, 167, 168

McLellan, Sir Robert, later Baron Kirkcudbright   68, 116
Mac Mahon, Hugh og   184-85
Maguire, Captain John   55-56
Mary I, Queen of Scotland   132
Matthews, Captain   199
Maxwell, Lieutenant Robert   116
Montgomery, Hugh, 1st Viscount Montgomery   175
Moore, Garret Moore, 1st Viscount Moore   211
Moore, Charles Moore, 2nd Viscount Moore   196, 199
Moore, Henry Moore, 3rd Viscount Moore   240
Moore, Colonel John   207
Moore, Lieutenant Thomas   74
Moryson, Fynes   16
Moryson, Sir Richard   38, 50
Mountjoy, Charles Blount, 6th Baron, later earl of Devonshire   13-21, 22, 32, 38, 40, 46, 137
Mountnorris, 1st Viscount. *See* Francis Annersley

Netterville, Sir John   82, 203
Newburgh, Edward Barrett, Lord   104
Newce, Captain William   21
Northumberland, Algernon Percy, 10th Earl of   104, 121, 124, 135, 146, 148, 154, 155, 156

O'Connally, Owen   183-86
O'Doherty, Sir Cahir   27-29, 30, 33, 42
O'Neill, Captain Charles   55
O'Neill, Sir Phelim   186, 198
Ogle, Sir John   64, 232
Ogle, John   197, 232
Ormond, James Butler, 12th Earl of and later 1st Duke   53, 139, 145-47, 149, 151, 152, 156, 157, 167, 179, 189, 191, 192, 197,

200, 203, 204-05, 206-08
Ormond, Thomas Butler, 10th Earl of   39, 139
Ormond, Walter Butler, 11th Earl of   139

Parsons, Sir William   161, 162, 166, 176, 82, 184-85, 190-92, 197, 200
Paulet, Sir George   27-29
Peisley, William senior   232
Peisley, William junior   222
Pelham, Captain   74
Percy, Henry   104
Perrott, Sir James   69, 213
Philip III, King of Spain   13, 18, 20-21, 24, 25
Philip IV, King of Spain   55, 56, 57, 58, 65, 68, 71, 83, 85, 92, 140, 165, 166, 170, 173, 175
Phillips, Sir Thomas   213, 215, 218
Plunkett, Richard   171, 174, 175
Porter, George   171, 174
Portland, Richard Weston, 1st Earl of   95, 98, 104
Power, Henry, later 1st Viscount Valentia   15
Preston, Richard, Earl of Desmond   64
Price, Captain Charles   62, 63, 64
Pym, John   163, 173

Radcliffe, Sir George   93, 147, 149, 150, 160
Rawdon, George   114, 161
Ranelagh, Roger Jones, 1st Viscount   96, 150
Ridgway, Sir Thomas   44
Rockley, Captain Thomas   199
Rotherham, Sir Thomas   225

St. George, Sir George   194
St. John, Oliver, later 1st Viscount Grandison   32, 36, 40, 41, 43-52, 58, 78, 95, 104
St. John, Lieutenant   199
St. Lawrence, Captain Christopher, later Lord Howth   21, 218
St. Leger, Sir William   64, 88-89, 138, 146, 148, 150, 152, 188, 189, 196, 197, 203
Savage, Lieutenant John   151
Searle, Major Thomas   171
Shaugnasee, Captain   191
Sherlock, Sir John   197, 204, 207
Sidney, Captain Algernon   191

Sidney, Captain Robert   191
Slanning, Sir Nicholas   147
Somerset, Robert Carr, Earl of   80
Spottiswood, Sir Henry   131
Stafford, Sir Thomas   64, 224
Stewart, Andrew   76
Stewart, Sir Robert I   30
Stewart, Sir Robert II   182, 207
Stewart, Sir William   27, 182, 198
Stewart, Captain William   74

Taaffe, Major Luke   191
Taaffe, Theodore   170
Temple, Sir John   168, 176, 183, 187, 191
Thomond, Donogh O'Brian, 4th Earl of   41, 43, 67
Thynne, Captain Edward   62, 64
Tichborne, Sir Henry   126, 150, 151, 182, 186, 187, 190, 191, 192, 198, 199, 203, 207, 215
Tyrconnell, Hugh Roe O'Donnell, king of Tyrconnell   13-16
Tyrconnell, Rory O'Donnell, Earl of   24-26, 28, 30, 140
Tyringham, Sir Arthur   62, 64, 182, 186
Tyrone, Hugh O'Neill, Earl of   13-21, 24-26, 28, 30, 55-56, 84, 123, 140, 182

Vane, Sir Henry   130, 147, 161-62, 176
Vaughan, Sir John   53, 150, 182
Vaughan, Captain Richard   74, 227
Vaux, Henry, 5th Baron Vaux   55
Veale, Sir John   201-02
Villiers, Sir Edward   63

Wandesford, Sir Christopher   93, 133, 138, 146, 150, 161-62
Warwick, Robert Rich, Earl of   173
Wenham, Philip   126, 186, 190
Wenham, Sir Thomas   126, 229
Wentworth, Sir George   115
Wentworth, Thomas Viscount, later 1st Earl of Strafford   53, 64, 83, 86, 87, 89, 91-102, 103-18, 121-32, 133-44, 145-49, 153-57, 159-61, 163, 165, 167, 187, 194-95, 202, 203, 208
Westmeath, Richard Nugent, 1st Earl of (see Lord Devlin)   76
Wharton, Sir Thomas   207, 231
Williams, Captain Lewis   74
Williams, Captain Michael   74

Willoughby, Sir Francis 74, 78, 82, 126-28, 131, 141, 144, 147-49, 150, 185, 186, 190, 191, 195, 199, 206, 228
Willoughby, Lieutenant William 151
Wilmot, Charles. 1st Viscount Wilmot 52, 69, 79-82, 84, 85, 86-88, 96-97, 108, 148, 189
Wimbledon, Edward Cecil, Baron 93, 110, 117
Windebank, Sir Francis 111, 124, 129, 138, 148, 153, 154, 156
Windsor, Sir William 21, 220
Wingfield, Sir Richard, later 1st Viscount Powerscourt 55, 80, 211, 217
Winwood, Sir Richard 38
Wintour, Sir John 170
Wintour, William 170

Yarner, Captain Abraham 205
Yaxley, Sir Robert 64

Index of Places

Aberdeen 125
Africa, North 30, 88
Anglesey 65
Antrim, County 26
Atlantic 68, 71, 148
Athlone 81, 96-97
Ayr 125, 142, 143

Baltimore 13, 88-89
Barnstaple 18, 25, 59, 65
Belturbet 199
Berehaven 88
Berwick 125, 128, 129, 134, 135, 136, 137, 154, 155
Biscay, Bay of 70, 84
Blessingbourne 198
Bohemia 54, 58
Boyne, the River 190
Brazil 83
Bristol 18, 25, 32, 65

Cadiz 52, 59, 67, 69, 70, 72, 74, 75, 81, 93, 209
Caernarvonshire 36
Carlingford 30
Carlisle 125-28, 133, 134, 135, 137, 140, 144, 147-48, 151, 152, 155, 186, 187
Carrickfergus 20, 36, 41, 65, 127, 131, 142, 146, 150, 152, 153, 156, 157, 159, 161, 182, 187, 188, 198
Castle Haven 13, 15
Castle Park Fort, Kinsale 20, 34
Catalonia 170
Cavan, County and Town 100, 186, 188, 198, 199, 200, 203
Charlemont Fort 20, 186, 198, 200, 203
Chester 25, 36, 65, 88, 145
Clyde, the River 125, 142
Coldstream 134, 155
Coleraine 20, 26, 33, 36, 121, 123, 203
Connaught 14, 40, 44, 47-48, 70, 74, 80, 97, 104, 122, 131, 141, 150, 163, 183, 189, 197, 201, 207
Cork 14, 19-20, 23, 25, 42-43, 66, 71, 79, 197, 203
Cornwall 25, 59, 80
Culmore Fort, 28
Cumberland 59, 126, 144, 155, 156

Denmark 77
Derry alias Londonderry 26-29, 33, 36, 53, 67, 68, 182, 198
Devonshire 26
Donegal, County 27, 131
Drogheda 190, 191, 192, 195-96, 199, 200, 203
Dublin 14, 27, 51, 56, 59, 67, 68, 81, 85, 87, 88, 96, 100, 103, 113-14, 118, 142, 145, 146, 150, 152, 154, 162, 175, 183, 186, 188, 189, 190, 191, 192, 195-97, 199, 204, 206
Dumfries 134
Dumbarton 142
Duncannon Fort 20, 42-43, 66, 191
Dundalk 182, 186, 188, 198, 200
Dunkirk 68, 83, 187
Durham, County 152, 155, 159

Edinburgh 120, 132, 135, 179
English Channel 68, 80,
Enniskillen 33
Europe, Catholic 24, 25, 57, 58
Europe, Protestant 25, 57, 58
Essex 77

Fermanagh, County 100
Forth, the Firth of 143
France 25, 40, 46, 61, 74, 77, 81, 92, 119, 163, 168, 170, 171

Galway 20, 42, 97,108, 170, 186, 190, 191
Germany 57, 60, 84, 124, 170, 172, 173, 178
Glasgow 130

Haulbowline Fort 20, 34, 42-43, 6
Holland *See* United Provinces
Holy Island 125-26

Inner Hebrides 26, 37, 121, 128, 130, 149
Irish Sea 13, 41, 48, 59
Islay 26, 37
Italy 173

Julianstown 192

Kelso 134
Kerry, County 18, 79, 80
Kilbeggan House 65
Killybegs Bay 20, 70, 114
King John's fort 66
Kinsale 13-16, 34, 42, 66, 88, 107
Kintyre, Mull of 26, 128, 143

Lancashire 25
La Rochelle 52, 72-78, 80, 81, 141
Leinster 14, 19, 74, 103, 131, 141, 150, 183, 189, 192, 197, 199, 201, 203
Leith 135
Leix, County 51
Lifford alias The Liffey 198, 215
Limerick 19-20, 34, 42
Liverpool 59, 65
Loch Foyle 14, 28
London 24, 27, 33, 40,45. 59, 60, 66, 68, 80, 85, 88, 112, 121, 124, 142, 143, 145, 154, 159, 160, 165, 192
Lough Foyle 14, 28
Lough Neagh 20
Low Countries *See* Netherlands unspecified

Madrid 58, 83, 85
Man, Isle of 31, 88
Milford Haven 65
Monaghan , county and town 186, 188, 198, 200
Mountjoy Fort 20, 186, 198, 200
Munster 19, 23, 26, 38, 41, 43, 50, 80, 95, 103, 122, 131, 134, 139, 141, 150, 175, 183, 189, 197, 206

Netherlands, the Independent and their inhabitants the Dutch *See* the United Provinces
Netherlands, Spanish 25, 30, 66, 87
Netherlands unspecified 48, 108, 109, 112, 114, 115, 121, 152, 153, 187
Newcastle 31, 96, 143, 154, 155, 159
Newry 186, 187, 188, 198, 200
New World, the 58, 68, 70
North Sea 68
Northumberland 68, 152, 155, 159

Omagh 33

Palatinate, The 39, 61, 70, 169, 173, 179
Pale, The 52
Plymouth 13, 80
Portsmouth 77
Portugal 83, 88, 170

Ratisbon 170, 173
Rome 25

Scotland vii, 20, 24, 26, 31, 55, 68, 119-26, 128-32, 135, 142, 145, 156-57
Scotland, West Coast 128-30, 133, 141-44, 155-57
Scottish Highlands 128, 129, 130, 149
Skye, Isle of 131
Sligo 20
Somerset 26
Spain 13-17, 21, 24, 25, 30, 32, 36, 57, 61, 66, 77, 81, 84, 85, 107,86, 88, 92, 140, 163,168, 170, 172, 173, 176, 190
Sweden 31, 109

Tandragee 199
Tees, the River 159
Thames, the 153
Trent, the River 91
Tory Island 28

Ulster 13-15, 20, 26, 27, 30, 32-36, 37, 41, 44, 47-48, 54, 66, 67, 74, 83, 103, 107, 120-22, 128, 131, 135, 141, 150, 157, 161, 162, 163, 175, 178, 181, 182, 183, 184, 187, 188, 190, 191, 196, 197, 198, 200
United Provinces 13, 17, 24, 30, 58-59, 63, 65, 68, 72, 83, 107, 109, 112, 131, 140, 173

Waterford   19-20, 25, 42-43, 66, 70, 85, 191
Westmoreland   155
Whitehaven   126, 127, 142
Wicklow, County   77, 99-100, 203
Wirrall, The   142
Workington   25, 126, 134, 142

York   129, 144, 154, 157
Yorkshire   65, 93, 149, 160

Index of Miscellaneous Terms

Associations, Communities, Clans and Septs
Major
Irish   19-20, 23, 37, 41, 51, 54, 73, 75, 93, 94, 98, 100, 103, 161, 174, 184
New English   19, 23, 38, 41, 71, 73, 75, 76, 93, 94, 101, 103, 123, 141, 161, 174, 178, 182, 183, 195, 207
Old English   19, 23, 37, 41, 51, 57, 71, 76, 84, 93, 94, 95, 98, 100-03, 121, 161, 174, 184, 191
Scottish Covenanters   121-58, 160, 170-74
Ulster Scottish   31, 32, 122, 127, 128, 135, 141

Minor, Formal and Informal
Byrne Sept, The   77
Campbell, The Clan   26, 121, 128, 133, 163
McDonald, The Clan   26, 37
Irish Patriots   75, 151, 152, 168, 174-94, 197-98, 200, 204
MacDonnell Sept, The   128 *See* also earls of Antrim
Moore Sept, The   51
O'Doherty Sept, The   28
Pirates and Privateers   68, 83, 88-89
Swordsmen   20, 30-31, 51, 73, 168
Trained Bands   52, 85-86, 92, 100, 127, 136-37, 150

Battles and Smaller Engagements
Edgehill 1642   205
Julianstown 1641   192, 199-200
Kilrush 1642   40, 204
Kinsale 1601   15-16, 40, 70
Lisnagarvey 1641   198, 199
Lisnagarvey 1649   206
Newburn 1640   155
Newbury 1643   78
Rathmines 1649   206
Yellow Ford 1598   13

Castles, Citadels and Garrisons
Augher   186, 198
Birt   28
Carlisle   126
Cork   25, 42-43, 66
Culmore   28
Dromore   199
Dublin   20, 32, 96, 138, 179-81, 183, 184, 187, 188, 189, 193, 203, 208
Dumbarton   125, 129, 137, 142, 157
Dunyveg   37
Dunluce   32
Edinburgh   125, 137
Galway   20
Kilkenny   14, 146, 149, 157
Limerick   20, 148
London, Tower of   31, 67, 107, 109, 111
Toome   215
Wardens   2, 23, 39, 43, 44, 48, 182, 185, 199
Waterford   25, 42-43, 66, 191

Military Kit
Artillery   14, 41, 70, 112, 152, 156, 193
Gunpowder   31-32, 66, 85, 100, 112, 181, 187-88, 191, 198
Weapons and Equipment for the Horse   69, 76, 105-06, 107-08, 109-11, 140
Weapons and Equipment for the Foot 76, 107-08, 111-12, 118, 140, 152-53, 182, 187, 189

The Standing Army
Increases in   25, 27, 59-66, 71, 76, 108-09, 123, 196-97
Officers, appointment of   27-29, 60-64, 94, 104-05, 114-17
Pay and arrears   23, 43, 48-53, 67, 71-73, 75-77, 97-101, 161-62, 164, 166
Recruitment   25, 27, 33, 35-36, 59-65, 76, 108-09, 141, 151-52, 201-03
Reductions in   17, 21-24, 33-35, 72-73, 76, 79-86
Training   53, 65, 112-14, 127, 152

Treaties and Truces
Berwick, 1639   132, 137, 140, 142

Ormond's Truce 1643   204
London, 1604   21, 22
Madrid 1629   83, 85
Ripon 1640   160, 163

Wars
Armada War, the   58, 68
Bishops' Wars, the   128, 134, 160
Duke of Buckingham's Wars, the   77, 107, 123, 189, 196
Dutch War of Independence *See* the United Provinces
English Civil Wars, the   153, 174, 205, 206
Nine Years' War, the   13, 17, 19, 41, 67, 71, 79, 81, 115, 138, 168, 176, 189, 213

Other titles in the Century of the Soldier series

No 1 *'Famous by my Sword'*: The Army of Montrose and the Military Revolution

No 2 *Marlborough's Other Army:* The British Army and the Campaigns of the First Peninsular War, 1702–1712

No 3 *Cavalier Capital:* Oxford in the English Civil War 1642–1646

No 4 *Reconstructing the New Model Army: Vol 1:* Regimental Lists April 1645 to May 1649

No 5 *To Settle the Crown:* Waging Civil War in Shropshire, 1642-1648

No 6 *The First British Army, 1624–1628:* The Army of the Duke of Buckingham

No 7 *Better Begging Than Fighting:* The Royalist Army in Exile in the War against Cromwell 1656-1660

No 8 *Reconstructing the New Model Army: Vol 2:* Regimental Lists April 1649 to May 1663

No 9 *The Battle of Montgomery 1644:* The English Civil War in the Welsh Borderlands

No 10 *The Arte Militaire:* The Application of 17th Century Military Manuals to Conflict Archaeology

No 11 *No Armour But Courage:* Colonel Sir George Lisle, 1615-1648

No 12 *Cromwell's Buffoon:* The Life and Career of the Regicide, Thomas Pride

No 14 *Hey for Old Robin!* The Campaigns and Armies of the Earl of Essex During the First Civil War, 1642-44

No 15 *The Bavarian Army during the Thirty Years War*

No 16 *The Army of James II, 1685-1688:* The Birth of the British Army

No 17 *Civil War London:* A Military History of London under Charles I and Oliver Cromwell

No 18 *The Other Norfolk Admirals:* Myngs, Narbrough and Shovell

No 19 *A New Way of Fighting:* Professionalism in the English Civil War

No 20 *Crucible of the Jacobite '15:* The Battle of Sheriffmuir 1715

No 21 *'A Rabble of Gentility':* The Royalist Northern Horse, 1644-45

No 22 *Peter the Great Humbled:* The Russo-Ottoman War of 1711

No 23 *The Russian Army In The Great Northern War 1700-21:* Organisation, Matériel, Training, Combat Experience and Uniforms

No 24 *The Last Army:* The Battle of Stow-on-the-Wold and the End of the Civil War in the Welsh Marches, 1646

No 25 *The Battle of the White Mountain 1620 and the Bohemian Revolt, 1618-22*

No 26 *The Swedish Army in the Great Northern War 1700-21:* Organisation, Equipment, Campaigns and Uniforms

No 27 *St. Ruth's Fatal Gamble:* The Battle of Aughrim 1691 and the Fall Of Jacobite Ireland

No 28 *Muscovy's Soldiers:* The Emergence of the Russian Army 1462-1689

No 29 *Home and Away:* The British Experience of War 1618–1721

No 30 *From Solebay to the Texel:* The Third Anglo-Dutch War, 1672-1674

No 31 *The Battle of Killiecrankie:* The First Jacobite Campaign, 1689-1691

No 32 *The Most Heavy Stroke:* The Battle of Roundway Down 1643

No 33 *The Cretan War (1645-1671):* The Venetian-Ottoman Struggle in the Mediterranean

No 34 *Peter the Great's Revenge:* The Russian Siege of Narva in 1704

No 35 *The Battle Of Glenshiel:* The Jacobite Rising in 1719

No 36 *Armies And Enemies Of Louis XIV:* Volume 1 - Western Europe 1688-1714: France, Britain, Holland

No 37 *William III's Italian Ally:* Piedmont and the War of the League of Augsburg 1683-1697

No 38 *Wars and Soldiers in the Early Reign of Louis XIV:* Volume 1 - The Army of the United Provinces of the Netherlands, 1660-1687

No 39 *In The Emperor's Service:* Wallenstein's Army, 1625-1634

No 40 *Charles XI's War:* The Scanian War Between Sweden and Denmark, 1675-1679

No 41 *The Armies and Wars of The Sun King 1643-1715:* Volume 1: The Guard of Louis XIV

No 42 *The Armies Of Philip IV Of Spain 1621-1665:* The Fight For European Supremacy

No 43 *Marlborough's Other Army:* The British Army and the Campaigns of the First Peninsular War, 1702–1712

No 44 *The Last Spanish Armada:* Britain And The War Of The Quadruple Alliance, 1718-1720

No 45 *Essential Agony:* The Battle of Dunbar 1650

No 46 *The Campaigns of Sir William Waller*

No 47 *Wars and Soldiers in the Early Reign of Louis XIV:* Volume 2 - The Imperial Army, 1660-1689

No 48 *The Saxon Mars and His Force:* The Saxon Army During The Reign Of John George III 1680–1691

No 49 ***The King's Irish:*** *The Royalist Anglo-Irish Foot of the English Civil War*

No 50 ***The Armies and Wars of the Sun King 1643-1715:*** *Volume 2: The Infantry of Louis XIV*

No 51 ***More Like Lions Than Men:*** *Sir William Brereton and the Cheshire Army of Parliament, 1642-46*

No 52 ***I Am Minded to Rise:*** *The Clothing, Weapons and Accoutrements of the Jacobites from 1689 to 1719*

No 53 ***The Perfection of Military Discipline:*** *The Plug Bayonet and the English Army 1660-1705*

No 54 ***The Lion From the North:*** *The Swedish Army During the Thirty Years War: Volume 1, 1618-1632*

No 55 ***Wars and Soldiers in the Early Reign of Louis XIV:*** *Volume 3 - The Armies of the Ottoman Empire 1645-1718*

No 56 ***St. Ruth's Fatal Gamble:*** *The Battle of Aughrim 1691 and the Fall Of Jacobite Ireland*

No 57 ***Fighting for Liberty:*** *Argyll & Monmouth's Military Campaigns against the Government of King James, 1685*

No 58 ***The Armies and Wars of the Sun King 1643-1715:*** *Volume 3: The Cavalry of Louis XIV*

No 59 ***The Lion From the North:*** *The Swedish Army During the Thirty Years War: Volume 2, 1632-1648*

No 60 ***By Defeating My Enemies:*** *Charles XII of Sweden and the Great Northern War 1682-1721*

No 61 ***Despite Destruction, Misery and Privations..:*** *The Polish Army in Prussia during the war against Sweden 1626-1629*

No 62 ***The Armies of Sir Ralph Hopton:*** *The Royalist Armies of the West 1642-46*

No 63 ***Italy, Piedmont, and the War of the Spanish Succession 1701-1712***

No 64 ***'Cannon played from the great fort':*** *Sieges in the Severn Valley during the English Civil War 1642-1646*

No 65 ***Carl Gustav Armfelt*** *and the Struggle for Finland During the Great Northern War*

No 66 ***In the Midst of the Kingdom:*** *The Royalist War Effort in the North Midlands 1642-1646*

No 67 ***The Anglo-Spanish War 1655-1660:*** *Volume 1: The War in the West Indies*

No 68 ***For a Parliament Freely Chosen:*** *The Rebellion of Sir George Booth, 1659*

No 69 ***The Bavarian Army During the Thirty Years War 1618-1648:*** *The Backbone of the Catholic League (revised second edition)*

No 70 ***The Armies and Wars of the Sun King 1643-1715:*** *Volume 4: The War of the Spanish Succession, Artillery, Engineers and Militias*

No 71 ***No Armour But Courage:*** *Colonel Sir George Lisle, 1615-1648 (Paperback reprint)*

No 72 ***The New Knights:*** *The Development of Cavalry in Western Europe, 1562-1700*

No 73 ***Cavalier Capital:*** *Oxford in the English Civil War 1642–1646 (Paperback reprint)*

No 74 ***The Anglo-Spanish War 1655-1660:*** *Volume 2: War in Jamaica*

No 75 ***The Perfect Militia:*** *The Stuart Trained Bands of England and Wales 1603-1642*

No 76 ***Wars and Soldiers in the Early Reign of Louis XIV:*** *Volume 4 - The Armies of Spain 1659-1688*

No 77 ***The Battle of Nördlingen 1634:*** *The Bloody Fight Between Tercios and Brigades*

No 78 ***Wars and Soldiers in the Early Reign of Louis XIV:*** *Volume 5 - The Portuguese Army 1659-1690*

No 79 ***We Came, We Saw, God Conquered:*** *The Polish-Lithuanian Commonwealth's military effort in the relief of Vienna, 1683*

No 80 ***Charles X's Wars:*** *Volume 1 - Armies of the Swedish Deluge, 1655-1660*

No 81 ***Cromwell's Buffoon:*** *The Life and Career of the Regicide, Thomas Pride (Paperback reprint)*

No 82 ***The Colonial Ironsides:*** *English Expeditions under the Commonwealth and Protectorate, 1650–1660*

No 83 ***The English Garrison of Tangier:*** *Charles II's Colonial Venture in the Mediterranean, 1661–1684*

No 84 ***The Second Battle of Preston, 1715:*** *The Last Battle on English Soil*

No 85 ***To Settle the Crown:*** *Waging Civil War in Shropshire, 1642-1648 (Paperback reprint)*

No 86 ***A Very Gallant Gentleman:*** *Colonel Francis Thornhagh (1617–1648) and the Nottinghamshire Horse*

No 87 ***Charles X's Wars:*** *Volume 2 - The Wars in the East, 1655–1657*

No 88 ***The Shōgun's Soldiers:*** *The Daily Life of Samurai and Soldiers in Edo Period Japan, 1603–1721 Volume 1*

No 89 ***Campaigns of the Eastern Association:*** *The Rise of Oliver Cromwell, 1642–1645*

No 90 ***The Army of Occupation in Ireland 1603–42:*** *Defending the Protestant Hegemony*

SERIES SPECIALS:

No 1 ***Charles XII's Karoliners:*** *Volume 1: The Swedish Infantry & Artillery of the Great Northern War 1700–1721*